CIVILIZATION

DURING THE MIDDLE AGES

CIVILIZATION

DURING THE MIDDLE AGES

ESPECIALLY IN
RELATION TO MODERN CIVILIZATION

BY

GEORGE BURTON ADAMS

PROFESSOR OF HISTORY IN YALE COLLEGE

REVISED EDITION

BARNES & NOBLE, Inc.
NEW YORK
PUBLISHERS & BOOKSELLERS SINCE 1873

Printed in the United States of America

FROM THE PREFACE TO THE FIRST EDITION

THE object of this book is to show how the foundations of our civilization were laid in the past and how its chief elements were introduced, and to depict its progressive development until it had assumed its most characteristic modern features. Its purpose is to show the movement and direction of historic forces, and the relation of the facts of history one to another. In other words, it is to present as clear a view as possible of what is the most important thing for all introductory study at least, and for the permanent intellectual furniture of most—the orderly and organic growth of our civilization. If anywhere the details have been allowed to obscure the general movement, there I have failed to realize my intention.

This being the object of the book, the notes have been confined as closely as possible to references to the best of easily accessible books where fuller accounts may be found, or which contain translations of the original sources, and to the statement of points which seemed important in themselves, but which did not find a natural place in the text. In a few cases where a single authority has been closely followed, a reference has been added. Otherwise reference has not been made to the authorities used. Those who are familiar with the literature of the subjects treated will be able to recognize them, and they will be able also, I believe, to find some evidence of original knowledge and of independent judgment.

This book is an outgrowth of the author's *Primer of Mediæval Civilization* in the "History Primer Series," and that book may perhaps be used with advantage as a more full summary than the one given in the last chapter of this volume.

NEW HAVEN, *December* 21, 1893.

PREFACE TO THE REVISED EDITION

IN the present edition numerous revisions have been made and some pages rewritten or added. I can hardly hope that I or my friends have detected all statements needing to be modified, but the attempt has been made to do so. I am indebted for suggestions in this direction to many who have used the book, and particularly to Professors George L. Burr, of Cornell, Dana C. Munro, of Wisconsin, and Henry B. Wright, of Yale, Universities.

Since bibliographical helps are now much more readily accessible to the student than twenty years ago, it has not seemed necessary to retain notes of a general bibliographical character, and they have been dropped. The number of special bibliographical references has been somewhat increased.

NEW HAVEN, *June* 3, 1914.

CONTENTS

MEDIEVAL CIVILIZATION

CHAPTER I

INTRODUCTION

HISTORY is commonly divided, for convenience' sake, into three great periods—ancient, medieval, and modern. Such a division is, to this extent, a natural one that each of these periods in a large view of it is distinguished by certain peculiarities from the others. Ancient history began in an unknown antiquity, and is characterized by a very considerable progress of civilization along three or four separate lines. Each of these was the work of a distinct people, the results of whose labors were not combined into a common whole until near the close of this period, though the process of combination in some particulars had been long under way. As the period approached its end the vitality of the ancient races appears to have declined and the progress of civilization ceased, except, perhaps, along a single line.

Medieval history opens with the introduction of a new and youthful race upon the stage—a race destined to take up the work of the ancient world and to carry it on. But the men of this race were at the beginning upon a far lower stage of civilization than antiquity had reached. In order to comprehend its work and continue it, they must be brought up to that level. This was necessarily a long and slow process, accompanied with much apparent loss of civilization, much ignorance and anarchy, and

3

many merely temporary makeshifts in ideas and institutions. But gradually improvement began, the new society came to comprehend more and more clearly the work it had to do and the results gained by its predecessors, it began to add new achievements to the old ones, and the period closed when at last the new nations, in fairly complete possession of the work of the ancient world in literature, science, philosophy, and religion, opened with the greatest energy and vigor a new age of progress. This is medieval history, the first part of it—the "dark ages," if it is right to call them by that name—when ancient civilization fell a prey to savage violence and superstition; the last part of it, the recovery of most of that civilization, with some important additions, by the now transformed barbarians—the period which we call, when it has fully opened, the age of the Renaissance.

Modern history, again, is characterized by the most rapid and successful advance along a great variety of lines, not now, so much as in the ancient world, the distinctive work of separate peoples, but all parts of a common world civilization which all nations alike possess.

While, however, we can point out in this way distinguishing features of these larger periods, we must carefully bear in mind the elementary fact of all history, that there are no clearly marked boundary lines between its subdivisions. One age passes into another by a gradual transformation which is entirely unnoticed by the actors of the time, and which can be far more clearly pointed out by the historian as an accomplished fact than by anything in the process.

The traditional date for the close of ancient history is the year 476 A. D., but recent historians differ widely in the specific date they choose. The great fact which marks the close of that age and the beginning of a new one is the conquest of the Western Roman Empire by the German tribes, a process which occupied the whole of the fifth century and more. But if we are to select any special date to mark the change, the year 476 is probably the best for the purpose. The conquest was then well under way, and in that year the title of Emperor of Rome was given up in the West, where it had been for a long time a mere shadow; an embassy was sent to Constantinople to say that the West would be satisfied with the one emperor in the East, and to request him to commit the government of Italy to Odoaker. At the moment all the other provinces of the West were occupied, or just about to be occupied, by new German kingdoms, some faintly acknowledging the supremacy of the empire, others not at all.

When we turn to the close of medieval history we find even less general agreement as to the specific date which shall be selected to stand for that fact. For one author it is 1453, the fall of the Eastern Roman Empire through the capture of Constantinople by the Turks; for another, 1492, the discovery of America; for another, 1520, the full opening of the Reformation. This variety of date is in itself very significant. It unconsciously marks the extremely important fact that the middle ages come to an end at different dates in the different lines of advance —manifestly earlier in politics and economics than upon the intellectual side—a fact which must receive more detailed attention in the proper place. Each author is under strong temptation to select for the close of the general period the date of its close in that particular field in which he is especially interested. For the purpose of the present sketch the date 1520 must be chosen, because, although upon the political side the whole Reformation period is clearly in the full current of modern international politics, still, in other directions, it just as plainly marks the transition from medieval to modern times, and so fixes the completion for the whole round of civilization of the period which we are especially to study.

This period is one, then, of something more than a thousand years, lying roughly between the dates 476 and 1520. It is an exceedingly important period to study for the purpose of gaining a conception of the greater movements of history as a whole, because, coming as an age of transition between two ages of greater apparent advance, its opening conditions cannot be understood without considerable knowledge of the results of ancient history, and its closing age carries us so far into the current of modern history that we necessarily gain some idea of the forces which determine the new directions, and thus the whole course of history is, to a considerable extent, covered by any careful study of its middle period. In order to obtain such a view as this it will be a necessary part of our plan to look somewhat in detail at the situation of things in the last age of ancient history, and also in the opening age of modern history, though somewhat less fully, because its character and conditions are more familiar to us.

The period so defined is also a long one in the life of the race—somewhere near a third of its recorded history. It must be in itself important, and in order to understand it thoroughly we must first of all obtain as clear a conception as possible of its place in the general history of the world.

We have already very briefly indicated what its character is. It is a transition age. Lying, as it does, between two ages, in each of which there is an especially rapid advance of civilization, it is not itself primarily an age of progress. As compared with either ancient or modern history, the additions which were made during the middle ages to the common stock of civilization are few and unimportant. Absolutely, perhaps, they are not so. We shall be able by the time our work is finished to make a considerable catalogue of things which have been gained during these centuries in the way of institutions, and of ideas, and of positive knowledge. But the most important of them fall within the last part of the period, and they are really indications that the age is drawing to a close, and a new and different one coming on. Progress, however much there may have been, is not its distinctive characteristic.

There is a popular recognition of this fact in the general opinion that the medieval is a very barren and uninteresting period of history—the "dark ages"—so confused and without evident plan that its facts are a mere disorganized jumble, impossible to reduce to system or to hold in mind. This must be emphatically true for every one, unless there can be found running through all its confusion some single line of evolution which will give it meaning and organization. If we can discover what was the larger general work which had to be done during this period for the civilization of the world, then we shall find the smaller details—the individual steps in the doing of that work—falling into place, becoming systematic, and orderly, and easy to remember. And most certainly there must be some such general meaning of the age. The orderly and regular progress of history makes it impossible that it should be otherwise. Whether that meaning can be correctly stated or not is much more uncertain. It is the difficulty of doing this which makes medieval history seem so comparatively barren a period.

The most evident general meaning of the age is that which has been hinted at above. It is assimilation. The greatest work which had to be done was to bring the German barbarian, who had taken possession of the ancient world and become everywhere the ruling race, up to such a level of attainment and understanding that he would be able to take up the work of civilization where antiquity had been forced to suspend it and go on with it from that point.

Progress had ceased in the ancient world. Having

brought civilization up to a certain point, the classical peoples seem to have been able to carry it no farther. Even in those fields where the most remarkable results had been attained, as, for example, in that of the Roman law, nothing farther seemed to be possible, except to work over the old results into new forms. Only in a single line, and that more or less in opposition to the general society of which it formed a part—only in the Christian church—was there any evidence of energy and hopeful life. The creative power of antiquity seems to have been exhausted.

But in this statement the word *seems* must be made emphatic. We have no 'ight whatever to assert dogmatically that it was so. The analogy between the life of a man and the life of a race—childhood, middle life, old age, death—is an attractive one, but it is necessary to remember that it is the merest analogy, without any support in facts. History gives us no clear case of any nation perishing from old age. It is altogether probable that if the Roman world had been left to itself—had not been conquered and taken possession of by a foreign race —it would in time have recovered its productive power and begun a new age of advance. Some early instances of revived strength, as under Constantine and Theodosius, show the possibility of this. The Eastern Roman Empire, under far less favorable conditions than would have existed in the Western, did do this later to a limited extent. The West would certainly have accomplished much more.

But the opportunity was not to be granted it. Ever since the days of Marius and the first Cæsar the Germans had been waiting an opportunity to force their way to the west and south. Watching for any unguarded point, attacking from the middle of the second century with constantly increasing boldness and frequency, as the power of resistance declined, they finally found the empire too weak to repel them any longer, and, breaking through the outer shell, had everything their own way. They took possession of the whole Western Empire. Province after province passed into their hands. Everywhere they overthrew the existing government and set up kingdoms of their own, some of them short-lived and crude, others full of promise and of longer continuance, but everywhere they became the ruling race—the Roman was the subject.

But if they were physically the stronger race, and gifted with some legal and political notions worthy to join with those of the Romans in equal partnership, they were in other regards rude and barbarous—children in knowledge and understanding—in the actual point of civilization which they had reached by themselves, scarcely, if indeed at all, above the level of the best tribes of North American Indians. In capacity for civilization, in their ability to meet a corrupt civilization of a higher grade than their own and not be permanently injured by it— though certainly some of the best of them, the Franks, for instance, seem to have had quite as great a capacity for absorbing the bad as the good—in the rapidity with which they responded to the stimulus of new ideas and experiences they were apparently superior even to the Cherokee.[1] Yet in very many ways—in ideas, in dress, in habits and ways of living, in methods of warfare and diplomacy—the parallel is very close and interesting,[2] and if we can imagine a civilized land taken possession of by bands of warriors not materially above the best of our Indians in actual attainment, though superior to them

[1] It is, perhaps, hardly fair to the Cherokee to demand that he should have made as much progress in one hundred years as the Franks did in three hundred, and when one examines the facts impartially it is by no means so clear that he is not equalling the German rate of advance, and greatly surpassing it, as indeed he ought.

[2] For a description of some of these particulars, see the imaginary capture of a Roman frontier town by a German band, in Dahn's novelette, *Felicitas*. For some others, see the account of the Saxon wars of Charlemagne, in Emerton's *Introduction to the Middle Ages*, chap. XIII.

in spirit and in moral tone, the picture will not be far wrong.

They were filled with wonder at the evidences of skill and art which they saw on all sides, but they did not understand them and they could not use them. The story of the German warrior who, astonished at seeing ducks apparently swimming on the floor of the ante-chamber in which he was waiting, dashed his battle-axe at the beautiful mosaic to see if they were living is thoroughly typical of the whole age. Much they destroyed through ignorance and much in merely childish or savage moods. Much more was forgotten and disappeared because no one any longer cared for it or demanded its use. Art, which had long been slowly dying, at last perished. Science, no longer of interest to any one, disappeared. The knowledge of the Greek language was forgotten; the Latin in popular use was greatly corrupted. Skill of handicraft was lost. Roads and bridges fell out of repair. Intercommunication became difficult; commerce declined. Few common ideas and interests were left to bind the different parts of the empire, or even of a province, together. The new governments were rarely able to enforce obedience everywhere and often hardly cared to try. Crimes of violence became common. Force reigned where law and order had been supreme, and life and property were far less secure than they had been.[1]

It is not strange that these things happened or that the ages which followed them should seem to be dark ages.

[1] A very interesting comparison could be made of the successive changes of condition in Gaul by reading together passages from Cæsar, like I, 17, 18, VI, 11–15, and others, to show the state of the province as he found it; the letters of Sidonius Apollinaris, just on the eve of the conquest—translated in Hodgkin, *Italy and Her Invaders*, vol. II, pp. 321–352—to show what must have been its condition in the best days of Roman occupation; and the story of Sicharius, in Gregory of Tours, VII, 47, and IX, 19—condensed in Emerton's *Introduction to the Middle Ages*, pp. 85–87—or the passage translated from Gregory at p. 147 of this book, to show its condition under the Franks.

How could it possibly be otherwise? Upon a society in which the productive force was already declining—a decaying and weakening civilization—came a mighty deluge of ignorance, an army of barbarians, to take control of everything, thinking of nothing beyond the physical life of the moment, knowing nothing of art or science or skill, and caring nothing for them. How could these things be preserved under such conditions as a part of the conscious possession of men? The decline, which had begun before the Germans came, must now go on still more rapidly until everything seemed to be forgotten. The whole Western world fell back into a more primitive stage of civilization, which it had once passed by, and became more material, ignorant, and superstitious than it had been. It would have required a greater miracle than is anywhere recorded to have kept alive in the general population of the West the civilization of Greece and Rome during such times, for it would have required the reconstruction of human nature and the modification of all historical laws.

The larger part of all that the ancient world had gained seemed to be lost. But it was so in appearance only. Almost, if not quite, every achievement of the Greeks and the Romans in thought, in science, in law, in the practical arts is now a part of our civilization, either among the tools of our daily life or in the long-forgotten or perhaps disowned foundation-stones which have disappeared from sight because we have built some more complete structure upon them, a structure which could never have been built, however, had not these foundations first been laid by some one. All of real value which had been gained was to be preserved in the world's permanent civilization. For the moment it seemed lost, but it was only for the moment, and in the end the recovery was to be complete. By a long process of education, by its own natural growth, under the influence of the remains of the ancient civilization, by no means small or unimportant, which worked effectively from the very first, by widening experience and outside stimulus, the barbarian society which resulted from the conquest was at last brought up to a level from which it could comprehend the classic civilization, at least to a point where it could see that it had very much still to learn from the ancients. Then, with an enthusiasm which the race has rarely felt, it made itself master, in a generation or two, of all that it had not known of the classic work—of its thought and art and science— and, from the beginning thus secured, advanced to the still more marvellous achievements of modern times.

This age of final recovery—the age of the Renaissance— marks thus the completion of that process of education —the absorption of the German in the civilization which he had conquered, so completely that he was able to take it up at the point at which the Greek and the Roman had been obliged to drop it and to carry it on to still higher results. And so the Renaissance age is the last age of medieval history, and medieval history is the history of that education and absorption, of the process by which the German was brought into the classical world, and by which out of the two—the Roman civilization and the German energy and vigor and productive power, and new ideas and institutions—a new organic unity was formed —modern society. This was the problem: To make out of the barbarized sixth century, stagnant and fragmentary, with little common life, without ideals or enthusiasms, the fifteenth century in full possession again of a common world civilization, keen, pushing, and enthusiastic. This was what the middle ages had to do, and this was what they did.

It was a slow process. It occupied nearly the whole of a thousand years. And it was necessarily slow. Rome had civilized the Celts of Gaul and made thorough Romans out of them in a hundred years; but in the case of

the Germans there were at least two very good reasons
why no such speedy work could be done. In the first
place, they were the conquering race, not the conquered,
a fact which made enormous difference. It was their
governments, their laws and institutions, their ideas, their
idioms even, which were imposed upon the Romans, not
the Roman upon them; and, although the higher civilization of their subjects began its work upon them at once,
it was only such parts of it as especially impressed them,
not the whole round of it—with much of it, indeed, they
never came in contact. In the second place, the Rome
of the fifth century was no longer the Rome of the first.
Her digestive and assimilating power was gone; indeed, in
the interval the process had even been reversed and she
had herself already become barbarized, and Germanized
also, unable to resist any longer the influence of the constantly increasing number of barbarians introduced into
the empire through her armies and her slave pens. If
Rome in the fifth century, characterized as she then was,
had conquered Germany, she could hardly have Romanized it in much less time than was actually required.

But this work, however slow, began at once. From
the moment when the German came into close contact
with the Roman, whether as subject or as master, he recognized the fact that there was something in the Roman
civilization superior to his own, and he did not consider
it beneath him to borrow and to learn, in the majority
of cases, no doubt, without any conscious purpose, sometimes, certainly, of deliberate intention.[1] If we compare

[1] Through the whole course of history the Teutonic race has been characterized, above most other races, by its ability to adapt itself to a changed
environment and to become in a short time completely in harmony with
new conditions. It is this, more than anything else, which has given it its
enormous influence over modern history. Whether it be the Teuton in the
Roman Empire, or the Northman in France or Sicily, or the Dane, or Prus-
sian, or Hollander in America, in every case, in a surprisingly short time,
the immigrant has become as thoroughly at home in the new land as if he

with modern times the amount of advance made in the five centuries following the fifth, it certainly seems very like "a cycle of Cathay"; but if we judge it according to the conditions of the time the gain was really large and the amount of the Roman civilization preserved was greater than we could have expected theoretically. We shall see, almost before the political system gets into any settled shape, decided improvement in knowledge and interest in science, the beginning of a steady progress which never ceases.

Here, then, is the work of the middle ages. To the results of ancient history were to be added the ideas and institutions of the Germans; to the enfeebled Roman race was to be added the youthful energy and vigor of the German. Under the conditions which existed this union could not be made—a harmonious and homogeneous Christendom could not be formed except through centuries of time, through anarchy, and ignorance, and superstition. In other words, the work of the middle ages was not primarily progress, it was to form the organically united and homogeneous modern world out of the heterogeneous and often hostile elements which the ancient world supplied, and so to furnish the essential condition for an advance beyond any point possible to the ancients. That this work was thoroughly done the twentieth century abundantly testifies. It will be our task to follow its accomplishment, step by step, from the day when the barbarian warrior supplanted the Greek philosopher and the Roman statesman until we reach the full tide of modern progress.

had occupied it for centuries, indistinguishable, indeed, from the native. The modern German of the Fatherland may be disposed to lament that language and special race features disappear so quickly, but the student of history can easily see that in no other way could the race have been, as it has been, the great creative power of modern civilization.

CHAPTER II

WHAT THE MIDDLE AGES STARTED WITH

It follows from what has been said in the introduction that our twentieth-century civilization has not merely that complexity of character of which we are so conscious, but also that it is complex in origin. Its distinct elements are the work of generations widely separated from one another in time and space. It has been brought together into a common whole from a thousand different sources. This fact is very familiar as regards the work of historic times. We recall at once from what different ages and peoples the printing-press, the theory of evolution, the representative system, the Divine Comedy entered our civilization and how they enriched it. It is less easy to realize the presence there, in almost unchanged form, of the work of primitive generations who lived before the possibility of record. And yet, for example, we have only just ceased to kindle a fire and to raise wheat after methods practically identical with those of the primitive man —the modification is still not essential—and the discovery of either of these two arts was, no doubt, as great a step in advance at the time when it was made as any the world has since taken. The same thing may be said, in a slightly modified form, of what is in some of our States the unit of our political system—the town-meeting.

Of the sources from which the different parts of our civilization have been brought together in historic times there are four which greatly exceed in importance all the others. They are Greece, Rome, Christianity, and the Germans. Many separate elements have come from other sources, some of them modifying very essentially our ideas or institutions—the alphabet from the eastern end of the Mediterranean Sea, philosophical notions from the Tigris valley, mathematical methods from Hindostan. But so far as we yet know, leaving one side what the further investigation of the monuments of early peoples may have to teach us, except the four mentioned, no great body of civilization, the entire work of no people, has been taken up into our civilization as one of its great constituent parts. Should we attempt to make a fifth co-ordinate with these four, we should need to group together the separate contributions of the various oriental nations made at widely separated times during the whole course of history and having no connection with one another. But the work of the Greeks as an organic whole lies at the foundation of all later progress.

Of these four, three had been brought together before the close of ancient history. By its conquest of the classical world Rome had added the Greek civilization to its own and prepared the way for the introduction of the ideas and influences which came from Christianity, and from these three sources, in the main, had been formed that practically uniform civilization which the Germans found throughout the Roman Empire when they took possession of it. To ascertain, then, what the middle ages had to start with, and the contribution of the ancient world to the twentieth century, it is necessary to examine, though as briefly as possible, the results of Greek and of Roman work and the elements introduced by Christianity.

The contribution of Greece comes naturally first in order. This was made, we may say, exclusively in the departments of literature and art, philosophy and science. Other work of hers which may have had a permanent influence is comparatively insignificant. The work of the Greeks in literature and art is too well known to need

more than a mention.   It is hardly too strong to say that
it still remains the richest contribution to this side of our
civilization made by any people in the course of history;
and it is very easy to believe that, with the adoption of
more appreciative methods of study in our schools, it
might have an even greater influence in the future than
it has ever had in the past, for it works always upon the
spirit of the individual man.   It was this part of Greek
work more than any other which made the conquest of
the Roman world, so that even those parts of Latin literature which must be considered something more than
mere copies of the Greek are still deeply tinged with the
Greek influence.

But the Greek mind was as active and as creative in
the fields of philosophy and of science as in those of literature and art.   Greek thought lies at the foundation of
all modern speculation, and Aristotle and Plato are still
"the masters of those who know."   All the great problems of philosophy were directly or indirectly attacked by
the Greeks, and their varying solutions were formed, before the close of their active intellectual life, into finely
wrought systems.   These Greek systems of thought furnished the Romans with their philosophical beliefs and
deeply affected the speculative theology of the Christian
church, and a few brief sentences from one of them furnished the starting-point for the endless speculations and
the barren civil wars of the Realists and Nominalists in
the later middle ages.

Among the Greeks philosophy and science were very
closely related to one another.   The philosopher was apt
to be the student of natural and physical science as well,
and it was thought that the arrangement of the universe
and the component elements of all bodies might be determined by speculation.   This was especially true of the
early periods of Greek thinking.   It is characteristic of
all early thinking that it turns with every problem to

speculation rather than to investigation, and characteristic of advancing knowledge that it is constantly enlarging the number of those subjects which, it is clearly seen, are to be carried to a real solution only by experiment and observation.

This last stage of knowledge was reached by the Greeks more or less completely in regard to a great variety of subjects, and the amount and character of their scientific work is astonishing considering its early date. Their favorite lines of work were mathematics and the physical sciences, physics and astronomy, and they made greater advances in these than in the natural-history sciences like zoology and botany. This scientific work hardly affected the Romans, and it was entirely forgotten by the Christian nations of the West during the middle ages; but when modern science opened in the Renaissance age it began clearly and consciously on the foundations laid down by the Greeks. In every line the first step was to find out what the ancients had known and then to begin a new progress from the point which they had reached. The first medical lectures were comments on the Greek text, almost as much philological as scientific, and Copernicus's first step, in preparation of the scientific revolution which he wrought, was to search the classics for a theory of the solar system different from the Ptolemaic. This is true of all the sciences—of those in which the Greek work has finally been thrown aside as worthless as of those in which it still forms a part. The science of the Greeks was, no doubt, in many cases entirely mistaken; but these mistakes represent, in all probability, stages of inquiry through which the mind had necessarily to pass in reaching the truth, and the work of the Greeks, though mistaken, was a positive gain.

So brief and general a statement can give no idea of the marvellous character of Greek work, miraculous almost considering its early date, the smallness of the land,

and the few generations which performed it.   But a correct appreciation of that work is now so general that it may suffice for the present purpose.[1]

It would hardly seem necessary, but for a popular misconception, to add to this account of the work of the Greeks, which permanently influenced history, the negative statement that none of this work was political.   The history of the Greek republics is interesting reading, and it seems as if the restless activity of their political life ought to have resulted in something of value for all time; but, as a matter of fact, it did not—unless it be an example of warning.   The Greeks had a very keen interest in politics—they tried all sorts of political experiments, and they show us an immense variety of political forms. But all this interest was intellectual rather than practical.   It was the keenness of the competition, the excitement of the game, which had the greatest charm for them, and they went into the assembly to decide a political question in very much the same spirit in which they went into the theatre to see a new play.   Scarcely a state can be found among them which makes a real success of any government, and in the histories of most of them, revolutions are as frequent and as meaningless as anywhere in Latin America.   They were not practically a creative political people, and not a single political expedient of theirs was a permanent contribution to the in-

---

[1] This appreciation of Greek work is even coming, in some cases, to express itself in extravagant forms.   Says Renan, in the Preface of his *History of Israel*, vol. I: "The framework of human culture created by Greece is susceptible of indefinite enlargement, but it is complete in its several parts. Progress will consist constantly in developing what Greece has conceived, in executing the designs which she has, so to speak, traced out for us," p. i. "I will even add that, in my opinion, the greatest miracle on record is Greece herself," p. x.   Symonds quotes, with apparent approval, as follows: "A writer no less sober in his philosophy than eloquent in his language has lately asserted that, 'except the blind forces of nature, nothing moves in this world which is not Greek in its origin.'"—(*Revival of Learning*, p. 112.) The passage quoted is better evidence, certainly, of the writer's eloquence than of his sobriety.

stitutional life of the race, as was the imperial government of the Romans or the representative system of the
English.[1] The world did not later borrow from them or
build on their foundations. In the science of politics, as
in other sciences, the Greeks did extraordinary work, and
in this way may have had some influence, untraceable for
the most part, on the minds of statesmen of later ages.
The *Politics* of Aristotle has been called as modern a book
as Euclid, and it is a modern book for precisely the reason
that Euclid is, because it is a thoroughly inductive study
based upon a very wide investigation of political facts.
His collection of constitutions for study numbered one
hundred and fifty-eight. But the science of politics and
the creation of workable political institutions are two different things.[2]

When we turn to the work of Rome we are struck with
the contrast which it presents to that of Greece. It
would seem as if each people of the ancient world had
had its special line of work to accomplish, and, doing
this, had not been able to do anything beyond. At all
events, Rome was strong where Greece was weak, and
weak where Greece was strong. Her work was political
and legal, scarcely at all artistic or intellectual. We

[1] Even federal government cannot be considered an exception to this
statement. As a part of the world's future political machinery federal
government is unquestionably a creation of the United States, and wherever
else in history the federal principle may have been in use, its growth into a
national institution, to be employed on a vastly larger scale than ever before, is too plainly a natural development out of the peculiar conditions and
circumstances of our colonial governments ever to be attributed to any
foreign influence.

[2] The scholar who compares carefully the Greek constitutions with the
Roman will undoubtedly consider the former to be finer and more finished
specimens of political work. The imperfect and incomplete character
which the Roman constitution presents, at almost any point of its history,
the number of institutions it exhibits which appear to be temporary expedients merely, are necessary results of its method of growth to meet demands as they rose from time to time; they are evidences, indeed, of its
highly practical character.

could not well afford to be without the Latin literature. In some departments—lyric poetry, satire, and history, for instance—it is of a distinctly high order. It presents us fine specimens of elegance and polish, and there will probably always be those who will consider these the most important literary qualities, as there will always be those who rank Pope among the greatest of poets. But, compared with the Greek, Latin literature lacks originality, depth, and power. The ancients themselves were not without a more or less conscious feeling of this contrast, and while Latin literature is saturated with the influences of Greek thought, scarcely a single, if indeed any instance can be found until the very last days of Greek literature, in which a Greek author appears conscious of the existence of a Latin literature.

The same things could be said even more strongly of Roman art and science, but perhaps Roman philosophy exhibits better than anything else the contrast between the two peoples. There was no original Roman philosophy. The Roman simply thought over into other forms the results which the Greeks had reached. A good example of this is that sort of eclectic philosophizing so familiar to us in the works of Cicero—a rhetorical popularizing of what seemed to him the best in Greek thinking without any original speculation of his own, at its best nothing more than a sympathetic comment or paraphrase. This difference between the two races is seen still more clearly in that form of Greek philosophy which the Romans cultivated with especial fondness, and in which they produced two such famous names as Seneca and Marcus Aurelius. It was the intensely ethical character of Stoicism which attracted them, with its ideal of strong manhood and its principles so naturally applicable to the circumstances in which a cultivated Roman found himself under the early empire. And it was on this purely practical side that the Roman cultivated Stoicism. He praised virtue in earnest phrases, he exhorted himself and other people to right living, he tried to make it a missionary philosophy and to bring its guidance and support to the help of men in general, he turned its abstract formulas into specific precepts of law, but he did not develop it as a science or a philosophy. The whole Roman mind was practical and not at all æsthetic or speculative.

And it was on this practical side that the Roman mind found its mission. The great work of Rome for the world was political and legal. Whatever rank we give to Greece for its literature, we must give an equally high rank to Rome for the results of its genius for government. If it may be true, as is sometimes said, that in the course of history there is no literature which rivals the Greek except the English, it is perhaps even more true that the Anglo-Saxon is the only race which can be placed beside the Roman in creative power in law and politics. A somewhat detailed examination of the work which Rome did in this direction is demanded because the foundation fact of all modern civilization is the Roman Empire, or more accurately, perhaps, it is the external framework of all later history.

The opportunity to exert such an important political influence came to Rome, of course, as a result of her military successes and her wide conquests; but these are themselves not the least of the evidences of her ruling genius. It was an opportunity which none but a great political people could have created or could have used to any good purpose when it came to them. Rome's conquests were not mere military occupations. After a generation or two the peoples which had most stubbornly resisted her advance had become Roman, those of them at least who were not already in possession of a civilization as high as her own. From the very beginning of her career, in the absorption of the little rival city states around her in Italy, she treated her subjects as friends

and not as conquered enemies. She allowed the utmost
local independence and freedom of self-government possible under her strong control of all general affairs. She did
not interfere with local prejudices or superstitions where
they were not harmful to the common good. She knew
how to make her subjects understand that her interests
were identical with theirs and that their best good was
to be found in strengthening her power, as Hannibal discovered to his cost. She opened the line of promotion
and success beyond the narrow limits of their own locality to ambitious spirits throughout the provinces. Balbus, a Spaniard, was consul in Rome forty years before
the Christian era. She made no conscious attempt anywhere to Romanize the provincials, nor any use of violent
methods to mould them into a common race; but she
thoroughly convinced them by reasonable evidence, by its
constant presence and its beneficial results, of the superiority of her civilization to theirs. She won them completely by the peace and good order which she everywhere
kept, by the decided advantages of a common language,
a common law, common commercial arrangements, a uniform coinage, vastly improved means of intercommunication, and by no means least of all, by common treatment for the men of every race. The literature and the
inscriptions give us abundant evidence of the affection-
ate regard in which this Roman rule was held in every
quarter. That such good government was without exceptions is certainly not maintained, and it gradually
changed into a bad government as time went on and as
the task of absorbing an unceasing stream of new barbarians proved too great for the exhausted empire. But
even where Rome's rule was least favorable to the subject, it was, until the last age, much better than the conditions which had anywhere preceded it, and the work of
Romanization was completed before it became anywhere a
serious evil.

The result of such a policy was speedily apparent. It was a process of absorption into a common Roman race willingly undergone by the provincial. If there was any conscious effort to bring about such a result it was on the part of the provincial, not on that of the government, and he certainly made no conscious effort to prevent it. And this was a genuine absorption, not a mere contented and quiet living under a foreign government. The local dress, religion, manners, family names, language, and literature, political and legal institutions, and race pride almost or entirely disappeared, did disappear for all except the lowest classes, and everything became Roman—became really Roman, so that neither they nor the Romans of blood ever felt in any way the difference of descent, as we never do in the case of the thoroughly Americanized German, whose family name alone betrays his origin. Gaul, Spain, and Africa have all been called more Roman than Rome itself. Some of the provinces possessed schools of rhetoric, that is, training in the use of the Latin tongue, so famous that they were sought by pupils from all parts of the empire. Gaul furnished some of the most celebrated grammarians of the Latin language, and that distinguished Spanish family must not be forgotten which gave the two Senecas and Lucan to Latin literature, and the proconsul Gallio to Christian history, in the incident recorded in the Acts, which illustrates so strikingly the attitude of the cultured Roman toward the earliest Christianity. In political life the case of Balbus has been mentioned. Before the first century closed another Spaniard—Nerva—had become emperor, and as time went on, the emperors were, more and more frequently, drawn from the provincials. In the days when the empire was falling to pieces and local commanders were taking advantage of their military strength to make themselves independent rulers, nowhere was there any return to an earlier national autonomy, but everywhere the commander became a Roman emperor, and reproduced, as perfectly as circumstances would admit, the Roman arrangements, court forms, officials, senate, and even coinage, and, more surprising still, in the very last days of the empire some of its most earnest and devoted defenders against their own race were Germans or of German descent.

It would be easy to multiply evidences of the completeness of this Romanization, but perhaps language forms the best example of all, because it is one of the things which a race trying to maintain a separate existence would most consciously strive to retain, as witness the Welsh of to-day, and because the evidence remains clear to our own time, in the speech of modern Europe, that the national languages passed out of use and Latin became the universal language from the mouth of the Douro to the mouth of the Danube. Not that this happened for every man. In the remoter country districts and among the lowest classes the national language long remained as a local dialect. In some of the most inaccessible parts the national speech permanently survived, as among the Basques and in Brittany. But Latin became the universal language of all the well-to-do classes. Nor was this change brought about because any one consciously dropped the use of his native language and adopted Latin in its place. It simply became a very great convenience for all the ordinary purposes of life for everybody to know the Latin in addition to his native tongue. He learned it with no expectation of giving up his own, and doubtless for a generation or two the two languages would go on side by side as generally spoken languages, and the local speech would only gradually become unfashionable and disappear. Indeed, in some cases, as for example in the Punic of North Africa, we know that a very considerable literary activity continued in the local language after Latin had become universally spoken.[1]

[1] Schiller, *Kaiserzeit*, vol. I, p. 887.

In one part of the empire there is an apparent exception to this absorption of the native races into the Roman. In the eastern half of the ancient world another language had become universal and another civilization almost as prevalent as the Roman in the West. The historical reason for this is familiar. At the time when the political life of Greece proper was reaching its lowest decline came the Grecized Macedonian, and with the military superiority of the Greek soldier constructed a great oriental empire, and, although this empire was scarcely at all Greek in its political or institutional life—was, indeed, in many ways the exact opposite of anything which the genuine Greek political life could have produced—yet the great superiority of the Greek intellectual civilization and the fact that Greek was the language of the government and of the ruling class made the Greek language and Greek ideas universal.[1] These were thoroughly established throughout the East at the time of the Roman conquest, so that Rome came in contact there with a universal civilization as high as her own. Naturally it retained its place. Except politically Rome had nothing to offer the East, and there was not that need of a unifying and assimilating work there which Rome had performed in the West. But politically Rome had much to offer, and her political influence became as decided and as permanent in the East as in the West. Law and governmental institutions and forms became entirely Roman. Latin became the language of government and law and remained so until the end of the sixth century. In Greek compendiums and translations the legislation of Justinian remained the basis of the law of the later Eastern Empire. Even when so distant a portion of the Roman

[1] The New Testament is a familiar proof of this in the matter of language. Such passages as Acts 14 : 11 and 22 : 2 are cited as indicating, in a very interesting way, how the native language continued as a dialect alongside the universal language.

dominion as Palmyra attempted, in the third century, to found a new oriental state, it did it under political forms that were Roman,[1] and the subjects of the modern Turkish Empire have had no reason to rejoice in what their rulers learned of the Romans in the matter of taxation. The exception presented by the East to the universal Romanization of the ancient world is more apparent than real.

In this power of assimilation the Roman presented, as has already been suggested, a marked contrast to the Greek. To Athens had been offered, in the Confederacy of Delos, the same opportunity which came to Rome. Sparta had it again after the Peloponnesian War. The difficulties in the way were but little greater than those which confronted Rome in Italy; but neither Greek state was able to take any step towards a real consolidation of Greece, and the empires of both fell to pieces at the first opportunity. This difference and even the reasons for it were so obvious that they did not escape the notice of the observers of those times. The remarkable speech which Tacitus, in the twenty-fourth chapter of the Eleventh Book of the *Annals*, puts into the mouth of the Emperor Claudius illustrates so many of the points which have just been discussed, as well as this, that I venture to insert a portion of it. The question having arisen as to the admission of Gauls into the senate, and various arguments being advanced against it, Claudius said: "My own ancestors, the most remote of whom, Clausus, though of Sabine origin, was adopted into the number of the Roman citizens, and also of the patricians, exhort me to follow the same plan in managing the state, and transfer to ourselves whatever there may be anywhere that is good. For I remember that we had the Julii from Alba, . . . and, not to mention every ancient case, from Etruria and Lucania and all Italy men were received into

[1] Schiller, *Kaiserzeit*, vol. I, p. 887.

the senate, and finally even from as far as the Alps, and
this, too, was not done for single men alone, but lands
and races became one with us and our state grew strong
and flourished. . . . Are we sorry that the Balbi came
to us from Spain, or men not less distinguished from
Gallia Narbonensis? Their posterity are still with us,
nor do they yield to us in love for this fatherland. Was
anything else the ruin of the Lacedæmonians and Athenians, though they were strong in arms, than that they
held off from them as aliens those whom they had conquered? But Romulus, the founder of our city, was so
wise that upon the same day he treated many people
first as enemies and then as citizens. Foreigners have
ruled over us, and to intrust the magistracies to the sons
of freedmen is not, as many think, a recent thing, but was
frequently done in former times." [1]

This subject deserves even fuller statement and illustration because it was by means of this thorough Romanization of the world that the work of Rome obtained its
decided and permanent influence on all later history.
Without this it must have perished. It was the completeness of this assimilation which fixed the Roman ideas
so firmly in the minds of all her subjects that the later
flood of German barbarism, which swept over the empire,

---

[1] Still earlier, a Greek, Dionysius of Halicarnassus, in his *Roman Antiq-
uities*, book II, chaps. XVI and XVII, after describing the treatment of their
subjects by the Romans, which had "not a little contributed to raise them
to the empire they have acquired," says: "When I compare the customs
of the Greeks with these, I can find no reason to extol either those of the
Lacedæmonians, or of the Thebans, or even of the Athenians, who value
themselves the most for their wisdom; all who, jealous of their nobility
and communicating to none or to very few the privileges of their cities . . .
were so far from receiving any advantage from this haughtiness that they
became the greatest sufferers by it."—(Translation of Edward Spellman,
London, 1758.)

A recent writer asserts that the constitution of Athens, as described by
Aristotle, rendered a great Athenian empire impossible because it did not
allow sufficient rights to subjects and allies. (*Preussische Jahrbücher*, Bd.
68, pp. 119–120.)

was not able to obliterate them, but must even, in the end, yield itself to their influence.

But this is by no means the only important result which followed from the unity which Rome established in the ancient world. Most obviously, Rome gave to all the West a higher civilization than it had had. She placed the provinces, within a generation or two, in a position which it would have taken them centuries of unaided development to reach. This is very clear, for instance, in the matter of government and order, to any reader of Cæsar's Gallic War. And so it was upon every side of civilization.

This empire also held back the German conquest for three centuries or more. That process of armed migration which the Cimbri and Teutones foreshadowed at the end of the second century B. C., and which Ariovistus had certainly begun in Cæsar's time, Rome stopped; and it could only be begun again by Alaric and Clovis. During all the intervening time the Germans were surging against the Roman barriers; from the time of Marcus Aurelius the struggle against them was a desperate one, and it became finally a hopeless one. But these four centuries which Rome had gained were enough. During them the provinces were thoroughly Romanized, Christianity spread itself throughout the empire and took on that compact and strong organization which was so vitally necessary in the confusion of the following time,[1] and the Roman law received its scientific development and its precise statement.

The historical importance of the mere fact that it was an organic unity which Rome established, and not sim-

[1] "It may almost seem as if the continuance of the Roman Empire in the fourth and fifth centuries had only the purpose of preparing the way for Christianity. For as soon as this had penetrated into all the provinces and become strong enough to maintain its own existence against rebellion and heresy, the empire became a prey to the Barbarians."—(Wilhelm Arnold, *Deutsche Geschichte, Fränkische Zeit*, I, p. 164.)

ply a collection of fragments artificially held together by military force, that the civilized world was made, as it were, one nation, cannot be overstated. Indeed, it is quite impossible to state it so that its full significance can be seen in the words. The historic sense, the scientific imagination of the reader, must come to his aid. That this was the character of the union which Rome established has already been illustrated. It was a union not in externals merely but in every department of thought and action; and it was so thorough, the Gaul became so completely a Roman, that when the Roman government disappeared he had no idea of being anything else than a Roman. The immediate result of this was that the Romanized provincial began at once the process of Romanizing his German conquerors, and succeeded everywhere where he had a fair chance; and it was because of this that, despite the fall of Rome, Roman institutions were perpetuated.[1]

The more remote result of it was that strong influence which this idea of unity, of a single world-embracing empire, exercised over the minds of men through all the early middle ages. It was this, together with the influence of that more real union—the great united church whose existence had been made possible only by this Roman unity—which kept Europe from falling into isolated fragments in the days of feudalism. More remotely still, that modern federation of nations which we call Christendom, based upon so large a stock of common

---

[1] Just as in our own case, it is probable that the larger part of those who appear in our census reports as of foreign parentage are foreign in no proper sense. They are an important part of our Americanizing force. As we know by daily observation, the Americanized foreigner is a powerful aid to us in assimilating the recent foreigner, and the Scandinavians of our Northwest, or, with most marvellous certainty, when we consider the conditions, the negro of the South could be trusted to perpetuate our political ideas and institutions, if our republic fell, as surely as the Gaul did his adopted institutions. Witness the Republic of Liberia, notwithstanding all its limited success, one of the most remarkable political facts of history.

ideas and traditions, is the outgrowth of Roman unity. It would very likely have been created in time by something else if not by this, but as history actually is, it was done by Rome.

Finally, this Roman unity made possible the spread of Christianity. With the religious ideas which prevailed in the ancient world before the advent of Rome, the moment a Christian missionary had attempted to proclaim his religion outside the bounds of Judea, he would have been arrested and executed as attempting a revolution in the state. It needed the toleration throughout the empire of each national religion alongside every other, and the melting of all local national governments whose life and prosperity had been thought to be bound up in the prosperity of the national religion, into a great all-containing government which could afford to tolerate all forms of religion which had been proved by the logic of war to be inferior to its own, it needed these results of the conquests of Rome before Christianity could become universal. As says Renan: "It is not easy to imagine how in the face of an Asia Minor, a Greece, an Italy, split up into a hundred small republics; of a Gaul, a Spain, an Africa, an Egypt, in possession of their old national institutions, the apostles could have succeeded, or even how their project could have been started. The unity of the empire was the condition precedent of all religious proselytism on a grand scale if it was to place itself above the nationalities." [1]

In these ways the conquest of the world by Rome and the use which it had known how to make of it decisively influenced the whole course of history. But, in addition to this, some of the specific features of Rome's political work have had very important results. That one of these which has had the longest continued direct influence

[1] Report of Hibbert Lecture, in London *Times* of April 7, 1880, p. 11; Renan, *English Conferences*, translation of C. E. Clement, p. 21.

is the Roman law; indeed, it is a fact of great interest
in this connection that the direct influence of the Roman
law is even yet extending.

The very considerable body of law which had grown
up in the days of the republic, somewhat narrow and
harsh from the circumstances of its tribal origin, passed
in the empire under conditions which favored both important modifications of its character and very rapid and
wide extension. No longer the law of a little state, or of
a single fairly homogeneous people, but of a great empire
and of numerous totally distinct races, the circumstances
of the case, together with the native Roman genius, would
have led, without any foreign influence, to a very decided
softening of the ruder features of the law and its development in the direction of general justice. But just at this
time came Stoicism with its ethical teaching, so deeply
interesting to the Roman mind, and with many of its
precepts shaped as if deliberately intended for application in some system of law. These are the sources of
that very decided amelioration and ethical and scientific
reorganization of the Roman law which, beginning soon
after the opening of the second century, went on so long as
it was a living system. It must be recognized as clearly
established that in this process of humanizing the law
Christianity had no share which can be traced until we
reach the time of the Christian empire in the fourth century. Then, although the humanizing work goes on
upon the lines already laid down, some influence of genuine Christian ideas may be traced, as well as of theological and ecclesiastical notions.

Growing in the two ways in which all great systems of
law grow—by statute enactment and by the establishment of precedents and the decision of cases, containing
both written and unwritten law—the body of this law
had come to be by the fourth Christian century enormous and very difficult to use. Scattered in innumer-

able treatises, full of repetitions and superfluous matter, not without contradictions, and entirely without the help of printing and indexes, which do so much to aid us in our struggle with a similar mass of law, the necessity of codification forced itself upon the Roman mind as it may, perhaps, in time upon the Anglo-Saxon. We have, first, attempts at codification by private individuals—the Gregorian and Hermogenian codes, probably of the fourth century, and containing only imperial constitutions, that is, statute law. Then we have the Theodosian code, of the Emperor Theodosius II, published in A. D. 438, containing also only statute law, though it seems likely that the emperor intended to include, before the close of the work, the whole body of the law. This code, formed just at the time of the occupation of the Western Empire by the Germans, was of very decided influence on all the early middle ages. Then came the final codification in the formation of the *Corpus Juris Civilis* by the Emperor Justinian between the years 528 and 534.

This comprised:

I. The Code proper, containing the imperial constitutions or statute law then in force, reduced to its lowest terms by cutting away all unnecessary matter, repetitions, and contradictions, and covering chiefly, though not exclusively, public and ecclesiastical law.

II. The Digest, or Pandects, containing in the same reduced form the common or case law, comprised mainly in the *responsa* of the jurisconsults, similar in character to the decisions of our judges, and covering chiefly private law, and especially the law of property.[1]

III. The Institutes, a brief statement of the principles

---

[1] This is what we should call in our system "unwritten law," though the Romans themselves reckoned the *responsa* in the written law (*Institutes*, I, ii, 3), and they had under the empire in a certain limited way the force of statute law. Until towards the close of republican times, a classification which makes public law synonymous with statute, and private with common law, is accurate enough, but it is not so for the days of the empire.

of the law intended as a text-book for law students and
perhaps even for more general use as an introduction to
a knowledge of the law.

IV. The Novellæ, or Novels, imperial constitutions,
covering various subjects, issued by Justinian himself
after the completion of the Code. These are usually
spoken of as if formed into a definite collection as a part
of the *Corpus Juris*. This, however, was not done by
Justinian, nor apparently ever in any authoritative way,
and the collections of the Novels which have come down
to us differ somewhat from one another in their contents.

The most important effect of this codification from our
point of view was this: By it the enormous and scattered mass of the law, which would in that form undoubtedly have perished—as a historical fact the books
from which it was made did mostly perish—was boiled
down into clear and concise statement and into a few
volumes which could easily be preserved. By means of
the definite form thus given it, being put into a book
which can be studied to-day just as it existed in the
sixth century, there was secured a direct and immediate
contact of the principles of the Roman law with every
future generation.

The specific influence of this law is not difficult to
trace. Soon after the revival of its study in the law
schools of Italy, in the twelfth century, the political conditions of Europe offered an unusual opportunity to the
class of thoroughly trained lawyers which was thus formed.
Under their influence this clear and scientific body of law
was substituted in many of the continental states for the
native law, which, owing to the peculiar circumstances of
the feudal age, was even more confused and unscientific
than customary law usually is; or, if in some cases not
actually substituted for it, became the law for cases not
already covered by the customary law. This substitution
was greatly aided by the fact that in these feudal states

absolute monarchies were forming which found a natural ally and assistant in the spirit of the Roman law. As a result, this law is still a part of the living and actual law of many modern nations. Owing to the French and Spanish colonial occupation, it became the law of a part of the territory now within the United States and forms the actual law of Louisiana in the Code of 1824, which is English in language but Roman in law and technical expressions. Even the general Anglo-Saxon law, which retained its native character and its power of natural self-development, has been profoundly influenced in particular doctrines—like that of inheritance, for example—by the Roman law. Still more remarkable is the fact that, in consequence of its permanence in the Eastern Empire, this law was taken up by the Mohammedan states and became the most important source of their law, contributing, it is asserted, far more than the Koran to the legal system which now rules throughout the Mohammedan world.

Apart from the direct influence of the system as a whole, many of the concise maxims of the Roman law, from their almost proverbial character, came to have an influence on later ideas and facts. The most familiar instance of this is the absolutist maxim, *Quod principi placuit legis habet vigorem*,[1] which exerted a considerable influence in favor of the usurpation of legislative rights by the monarchs at the close of the middle ages, and, together with the marked centralizing tendency of the system as a whole, became one of the most effective causes of the formation of absolute monarchies in the continental states.[2]

[1] *Institutes*, I, ii, 6.

[2] An example of the influence of such maxims, of especial interest to Americans, is to be found in the phrase "All men are created equal," and like phrases, which are of so frequent occurrence in the political documents and the writings of the time of our Revolution. These are maxims which passed into the Roman law from Stoicism. They came into new and very

In another great field the influence of the Roman law was equally creative—in the law and theology of the church. The great system of canon law which grew up in the government and administration of the church during medieval times is based almost exclusively on the Roman law, and in its practical interpretation in the church courts the principle was admitted that whatever was ambiguous or obscure in it was to be explained by reference to the Roman law. In the theology of the Western church the influence of the Roman law was less direct but hardly less important. "In following down the stream of Latin theology, from Augustine to the latest of the schoolmen, we might trace in the handling of such topics as sin, the atonement, penance, indulgences, absolution, the silent influence of the conceptions which Roman jurisprudence had made current."[1] The same strong influence may be traced in the terminology and the ideas of many other sciences, and in such ethico-political notions as the divine right of kings, the duty of passive obedience, and the social contract theory of government.[2] Indeed, it is not too much to say that no other product of the human mind, not even the Greek philosophy, has had so far-reaching, nor, in its immediate original form, so permanent an influence as the Roman law.

Another specific product of the Roman political system

frequent use, after the revival of the Roman law, in the charters of emancipation which are so numerous at the close of the middle ages as a statement of the reason which led to the granting of the charter. Brought again into notice in this way, their very concise statement of what seemed to be a great truth, and one especially attractive to theorists in states enjoying little actual liberty, kept them from being forgotten, and they passed into the writings of the speculative philosophers of the seventeenth and eighteenth centuries, and from this source into the political documents of the close of the eighteenth. Especially interesting is their operation as actual law, in at least one case, in a way which would have astonished the old Roman jurists. Inserted in the constitution of Massachusetts, they gave rise to a decision of her supreme court, in 1780, declaring slavery no longer legal in that State.

[1] Professor George P. Fisher, *Discussions in History and Theology*, p. 48.
[2] See Maine, *Ancient Law*, pp. 329 ff.

has had as long a life and almost as wide an influence—
the imperial government. Formed out of a democratic
republic where the name of king was intensely hated, by
the necessities which arose from the government of a vast
empire, a real despotism but of a new type, under new
forms and a new name, while to all external appearance
the old republic continued as before, it is itself one of the
best examples of the institution-making power of the
Romans.[1] Its strong centralization delayed for generations the fall of Rome; its real majesty and august ceremonial profoundly impressed the German conquerors; it
became one of the most powerful causes which created
the papacy and furnished it a model in almost every department of its activity; the absolutisms of modern Europe were largely shaped by it; and the modern forms of
the word Cæsar, Kaiser and Czar, in governments of a
similar type, however different in detail, are a proof of
the power and permanence of its influence in regions where
Rome never had any direct control. We shall need to
devote some space at a later point to the powerful preservative action of two ideas which came to be associated
with this government—that it was divinely intended to
embrace the whole world and to last as long as the world
should last.

These cases may suffice for illustration, but they are
by no means the only specific instances of the abiding
character of Rome's political work which could be mentioned. Modern political vocabularies testify to its permanence as clearly as our scientific vocabularies do to the
influence of the Arabs, and many evidences of it will
occur to us as our work proceeds.

We have, then, these contributions to civilization from
the ancient world. From Greece an unequalled litera-

[1] As the exactly opposite process, turning a monarchy into a republic
while retaining monarchical forms, is of the institution-making power of
the Anglo-Saxons.

ture and art and the foundations of philosophy and science. From Rome a highly perfected system of law, a model of most effective absolutism, and the union of the ancient world in an organic whole—the foundation of all later history.

We must remember, however, in closing this chapter, that we have omitted even from this general sketch one large side of civilization to which we can give no adequate treatment here or elsewhere. It is what may be called the economic and mechanical side. There passed over to the middle ages from the ancients large gains of this sort. Knowledge of the mechanical arts, acquired skill and inventions; methods of agriculture and navigation; organized trade and commerce not all of which disappeared; accumulations of capital; cleared and improved land, houses, roads, and bridges, many of which continued in use across the whole of medieval times; administrative methods both in general and local government; in a word, all sorts of practical knowledge and training and many mechanical appliances. The economic influence of the Roman Empire affected in many ways indeed the larger movements of history. The comparative free trade which the empire established, the constitution of the Roman villa or farm, the beginning of the process which transformed the slave into the serf, the forced dependence of the small landholder upon the large one, are important instances. These things constitute together, in some respects, the most primary and fundamental department of civilization, and must not be forgotten, though, with the exception of a few instances which we shall notice, they demand, like the greater part of political history, special and specific treatment.

CHAPTER III

THE ADDITION OF CHRISTIANITY

INTO this Roman Empire there came the Christian religion, adding its own contribution of great ideas to those of the Greeks and Romans, and in the end acting as the first of the great influences transforming the ancient into the modern world. It appeared just after the empire had received its organization as a monarchy; it grew very slowly by count of numbers during the next suceeding generations, while the empire was still strong and perfecting its organization; as the Roman power decayed it began to spread with greater rapidity, till, by the middle of the fourth century, on the eve of the German conquest, it was the prevailing religion—not perhaps in actual numbers, but certainly in influence and energy and in the real control of society.

During its early career, at least, the progress of this new faith was rendered slow by certain facts which were characteristic of it. Its adherents were few. They were from the lowest ranks of society, workmen and slaves —more largely also women than men—so that it attracted very little attention from persons of position and influence. Its missionaries also were Jews, a turbulent race, not to be assimilated, and as much despised and hated by the pagan Roman as by the medieval Christian. Wherever it attracted any notice, therefore, it seems to have been regarded as some rebel faction of the Jews, gone mad upon some obscure point of the national superstition—an outcast sect of an outcast race.

Again, it is a permanent characteristic of Christianity that many, at least, of its external features in any particular age—the points of conduct upon which it insists with the greatest emphasis—are determined, we may almost say are selected, by the character of the great evils which, for the time being, it has especially to fight. In the first age the greatest enemy to be overcome was paganism. Christianity had other truths of importance to teach, and other evils to overcome, but the one deadly foe whose complete possession of society must be first of all destroyed was the worship of many gods. This complete contrast between the new religion and the dominant heathenism led necessarily to a strictness in the teaching and practice of the monotheistic doctrine which the pagan society found it hard to understand, and which placed Christianity at a disadvantage in competition with the numerous other oriental religions which were at this time spreading over the Roman Empire, for Christianity would seem to the observant Roman nothing more than one of this general class.

These other religions said to the Roman: Continue to worship your own gods, worship as many gods as you please, only take this one in addition; they are good, but we bring you something better on some particular point, some more perfect statement of the common truth, accept this also. Christianity said: No. All these teachings are false, all idol worship is a deadly sin. You must abandon all these beliefs and accept this alone as the only true and exclusive faith. And this teaching the Christians carried out in their daily living even, in frequent cases concerning such minutiæ as food to be eaten and occupations to be pursued. This was a demand entirely new and incomprehensible to the ordinary heathen mind, trained in the idea of an unlimited pantheon, though a tendency towards monotheism may be found in the more advanced religious thought of the time. It is not strange that the determination of the Christian to die rather than to perform the simplest rite of pagan worship seemed to the Roman the most obstinate and insane stupidity. In other words, the native attitude of the ancient mind towards questions of religion needed to be completely revolutionized before the new faith could be victorious—a task of immense difficulty and not completely performed in that age, as we shall see when we come to consider the transformation of Christian ideas which resulted from the struggle.

And yet, notwithstanding these obstacles, and the apparently slight chance of success which it had, Christianity made extremely rapid progress in relative increase. Starting from an insignificant province, from a despised race, proclaimed by a mere handful of ignorant workmen, demanding self-control and renunciation before unheard of, certain to arouse in time powerful enemies in the highly cultivated and critical society which it attacked, the odds against it were tremendous. But within a single generation it had been successfully taught in all the central provinces of the Roman Empire and far beyond its boundaries. In the second century its progress among all classes was very rapid. In less than three hundred years from the crucifixion it had become the recognized religion of the imperial court and had been placed on a footing of legal equality with paganism throughout the empire, and before that century closed it was the only legal religion. Its progress seems miraculous, and Freeman has not overstated the case in the following sentence: "The miracle of miracles, greater than dried-up seas and cloven rocks, greater than the dead rising again to life, was when the Augustus on his throne, Pontiff of the gods of Rome, himself a god to the subjects of Rome, bent himself to become the worshipper of a crucified provincial of his empire."[1] It must have possessed certain great com-

[1] Freeman, *Periods of European History*, p. 67.

pensating advantages to give it so speedy a victory in the face of such difficulties.

By far the most important of these advantages was the definiteness and confidence of its teaching on the questions of the immortality of the soul and the expiation of sin. Whatever cause may be assigned for it, the fact is clear that the society of the empire was intensely interested in these two questions. At the end of the republic, the faith of the Romans in their national mythology may have grown weak, but their interest in the deeper problems of religion had only quickened. In the early days of the empire the first mentioned was the more absorbing question—Does the soul live after death? Can we know anything of the future life? and various forms of religion, chiefly from the East, like the worship of Isis, gained numerous adherents for a time, because they seemed to offer some more complete revelation upon this point. As the dark days came on and evils crowded upon the empire, the other question demanded more attention, and the practice of various expiatory rites—of oriental origin again and horribly bloody and revolting in character—became frequent in the West. Of these the most prominent was Mithraism, which at one time seemed to be a serious rival to Christianity.[1] But for the earnest man who is seeking after help in some spiritual need which is clearly realized, the practice of rites and ceremonies is never permanently satisfactory, and Christianity possessed an enormous advantage over its rivals in the character of its teaching upon these points, and in the confidence of its faith. The Christian teacher did not say: I believe. He said: I know. On the question of immortality he appealed to an actual case of resurrection, supported, as he said, by the testimony of many witnesses

---

[1] See a brief description of these rites in Hodgkin, *Italy and Her Invaders*, vol. I, p. 562, note (second edition), and especially Franz Cumont, *The Mysteries of Mithra*, translation of T. J. McCormack, 1903.

—the founder of his faith, not raised from the dead by some miracle-worker calling him forth by incantations, but rising, himself, by the power of an inner and higher life which was beyond the reach of death, the first-fruits of them that slept. On the question of the forgiveness of sin he appealed to the cases of innumerable individuals —even of communities and tribes—transformed by the power of his gospel from lives of sin and degradation to orderly and righteous living.[1]

The one thing which was the essential peculiarity of this teaching, as compared with other religions, was, no doubt, also the thing which was the source of the Christian's extreme confidence and of his permanent faith. This was the belief of the Christian that an intimate personal tie had been established between himself and God by the Saviour. The tender fatherhood of God, willing to forgive the sinful man, and to create in him anew the forces of a pure life, was, to the disciple, the central truth of the gospel. The love of God replaced the fear of God as a controlling principle and became a far greater force than that had ever been. The Christian apostle did not demand belief in any system of intellectual truth. The primitive Christianity had apparently no required theology.[2] He did not demand that certain rites and ceremonies should be performed. The rites of the primitive Christianity were of the simplest sort and not regarded as causes. What he demanded was personal love for a personal Saviour. His was the proclamation—in the one way to make it a practical force in daily civilization, not a mere theory in the text-books of scholars—of the fundamental truth which all philosophy had sought, the unity of God and man, the harmony of the finite and

---

[1] Almost all the early Christian literature can now be read in English.

[2] "It is the glory of the earliest church that it had for its people no demanded creed of abstract doctrine whatsoever."—(Phillips Brooks, in the *Princeton Review*, March, 1879, p. 306.) Compare Fisher, *Beginnings of Christianity*, p. 566.

the infinite. And it did become a great force, and remained so in proportion as it was not obscured by later misconceptions. There can be no question but that this personal faith in a personal Saviour, this belief in the love of God and the reality of heaven brought to thousands of the poor and ignorant, and in as high a degree, the comfort and confidence and fearlessness of fate, the calmness and consolations which philosophy brought to the highly cultured few.[1]

This peculiar personal character of its faith, was undoubtedly, as was just remarked, the source of that overbearing confidence of belief in its answer to the two great religious demands of the age which gave Christianity a decided advantage over every other religion. The completeness with which it satisfied the deepest religious needs of the time, the fulness of consolation which it brought to the wretched and sorrowing, these were the most effective causes of its rapid spread and of the permanence of its hold upon its followers.

While these are the most important, some few of the subsidiary causes of its rapid advance deserve mention. The study of the Greek philosophy, and especially that of Plato, led some to Christianity after it began to attract the attention of the educated classes. But here, again, it was the greater definiteness and confidence of its answer to the questions which the Greek philosophy raised which formed the decisive reason for its acceptance. The persecutions had their usual effect. They attracted the attention of many to the new faith who would otherwise have passed it by unnoticed, and they forced men to ask if there must not be something more in it than appeared on the surface to account for the calmness and joy of the Christian in the face of death.

---

[1] It should be understood here and elsewhere that these matters are stated not as religious truths but as facts which have their part in the history of the time and which the historian is bound not to overlook.

The earnestness and enthusiasm of all early converts to a new form of faith were especially characteristic of the Christians and seemed especially contagious. The effect of Christianity on the lives of those who embraced it was constantly appealed to by the early Christians as evidence of the character of their religion, and it must have been an extremely forcible argument. It would be very interesting, if space allowed us to do so, to examine in detail the ethical influence of early Christianity so far as the evidence permits. There can be no question but that, so long as it remained a pure and simple religion, its influence worked a moral revolution in those who came under it. It is only necessary to recall the ethical exhortations in the New Testament, or the lists of sins, the doers of which cannot enter the kingdom of heaven, and to remember such facts as the regulations against taking part in, or even attending, the gladiatorial games—the most intensely exciting amusement of the ancient world, or the proscribing of certain occupations—metal workers, actors, sometimes even soldiers or officers of the state—to realize how complete a control over conduct it attempted and how squarely it attacked the characteristic sins of the age, and although Christianity did not succeed in destroying sin in the world, nor even within its own membership, the cases seem to have been numerous in which the process went far enough to furnish a strong argument in making other converts.

Like all great movements of the kind, the spread of Christianity is not to be explained by the action of a single cause, and others, perhaps as important as these, contributed to the rapidity of its advance. However the fact may be accounted for, the number of its adherents soon became great enough to attract to itself the attention of the state. Whatever may be true of the first century, whether or not the Roman government was conscious in that age of any distinction between Christians and Jews, or whether it had any clear idea of what it was doing in the persecutions under such tyrants as Nero and Domitian, it is certain that, early in the second century, it came to have an understanding of Christianity and its attitude towards the state religion—an attitude which the conscientious Roman ruler could hardly pass unnoticed.

The action of the Roman government in respect to many of the new religions which were making their way towards the West was inconsistent. It was an alternation of careless indifference, or even apparent favor, with spasmodic attempts at repression which really accomplished nothing. But there was in Christianity an element of hostility towards the state which none of the other new religions contained. While they might lead to a neglect of the state religion by the greater interest excited in the new faith, Christianity insisted upon the entire abandonment of the national worship, not as an inferior religion but as an actual and particularly heinous sin. According to all the ideas of the Romans, such a demand could be nothing but rebellion and treason. The safety of the state depended upon the fidelity of the citizens to the national worship. If the gods were duly honored and the sacrifices carefully performed, the state flourished; if they were neglected or carelessly worshipped, misfortunes followed. Undoubtedly this belief on its practical, if not on its theoretical side had greatly weakened during the prosperous times of Rome's history. But it had not been abandoned, and when public misfortunes became frequent and the power of the state seemed declining, it was natural that the earnest reformer should believe the neglect of the gods to be the source of the evil and seek a restoration of prosperity by means of a restoration of the national religion; or, if not himself fully confident of this, it was natural that he should believe that the "reflex influence" of an earnest national worship would check the causes of decline.

It follows from this that the time of systematic and deliberate persecution comes when the real statesmen of the empire have become conscious of the deadly nature of her disease. It seems evident that we must say that, during the first century, the government had no distinct consciousness of the existence of Christianity. The second century is a time of local and temporary enforcement of the laws against the Christians. With the third century we reach an age of fearfully rapid decline and of most earnest attempts, at intervals, by clear-sighted emperors, to turn back the tide, and this is the age of planned and thoroughgoing imperial persecution. There was really no alternative for men like Decius and Valerian and Diocletian. Christianity was a vast, organized defiance of the law. It vehemently denounced the national religion as a deadly sin. It earnestly denied any paramount duty of loyalty to the state, and appealed to a higher loyalty to another fatherland. No restoration of earlier Roman conditions, such as the reformers hoped for, could be possible unless it was overcome.[1]

But it was too late. Christianity was now too strong. These systematic persecutions of the third century failed, and the last, Diocletian's, ended in a virtual confession of defeat. Not that the Christians were now in the

---

[1] The whole subject of the teaching of early Christianity upon the relation of the individual to the state, and its effect in the Roman Empire, is a very interesting one. It has been repeatedly asserted that the extreme vividness with which it conceived of the higher interest of the life to come in comparison with this life, and of citizenship in the kingdom of Christ as wider and more obligatory than any earthly citizenship, was one of the serious causes of the dissolution of the Roman state. The proof of this assertion seems to me entirely inadequate. The most that can be maintained with certainty is that the attitude of the Christians was a very serious obstacle to the efforts at restoration and revival in the middle empire, so serious an obstacle, indeed, that it goes far, when looked at from the point of view of the Roman statesman, to justify the attempts of the reforming emperors to put down Christianity by force even, since there was no possible means of bringing its adherents back to their duty to the state. That the teaching of Christianity was a positive cause of dissolution I do not think can be shown.

majority. They were far from it, and did not become so until long afterwards. No exact figures are possible, but it seems certain that at the beginning of the fourth century they were not more than one-tenth of the total population in the eastern half of the empire, nor more than one-fifteenth in the western. But they had an importance altogether disproportionate to their numbers. A gloomy and hopeless fear of the future was settling over the pagan world. It seemed to be coming to realize that its best days were past and that its highest creations were falling into decay, and to be losing its earlier self-confident spirit and energy. But the Christians had been inspired with a new hope for the future which was wholly independent of the fate of the empire. The convulsions and revolutions of the present could only be prefatory to a better era, and the Christian community was full of enthusiasm and energy and the vigor of a new life, in marked contrast to the pagan. Again, the Christian was a distinctly city population; that is, their numbers, however small they may have been as compared with the whole, were massed in the especial points of influence, occupied the strategic positions throughout the empire. Still further, their organization, though less close than it was soon to be, gave them means of speedy communication and common action. Undoubtedly, their power was greater than their relative numbers and probably greater than they themselves knew. But it was not long before the man came who suspected the fact, and, in turning it to his personal advantage, secured the triumph of Christianity over paganism.

That Constantine declared himself a supporter of Christianity from a conviction of its truth or from religious motives cannot be maintained. Indeed, there is no evidence to show that he ever became in heart a real Christian. His motive is not hard to guess. As he started out from his small frontier province with his little army to conquer the empire, the odds against him were tremendous. But there have not been many men in history of clearer political insight than his. It is not rash to suppose that he reasoned with himself that if he proclaimed himself the protector of this hitherto illegal and persecuted sect they would rally to his support with all their enthusiasm, and that he would secure the aid of the most vigorous faction in the state. The great weakness of heathenism, in contrast with Christianity, must have been apparent to so keen an observer. Without union among its scattered forces, without leadership, believing in itself with no devoted confidence, without faith in the future, with no mission in the present to awaken energy and life, it was not the party which an ambitious and clear-headed young man would choose to lead to victory. The motive which induced him to support Christianity was purely political, and the result certainly proved his judgment correct.

But in another sense the act of Constantine has a further significance and is a part of a wider movement.

The transformation of the Roman Empire from the ancient to the medieval was made in the half century which followed the accession of Diocletian. The changes introduced by him in forms and constitution, as modified and carried farther by Constantine, marked an entire revolution, a complete change of front. The empire cut itself loose from its past. It no longer pretended to be what it had been at first. It frankly recognized the situation as it was and no longer attempted to restore the old. It had faced the future. This change logically carried with it the recognition of Christianity. It is by no means certain that Diocletian was not vaguely conscious of this. Constantine realized it clearly enough for action, though he might not have been able to put it in this form of statement.

For Christianity, as for the empire, this was an age of

transition, an age of transformation in character and in constitution, the results of which will occupy us elsewhere.

It remains for us to point out, so far as it is possible, the contributions of Christianity to our civilization, as one of the four great sources from which that civilization was originally derived. What are the new elements which were brought into human life and progress by the Christian religion?

In making an attempt to do this it is necessary at the outset to notice briefly, by way of caution, two or three elementary facts which will be stated more fully in a later chapter. In the first place, we are to examine the effect of Christianity as an historical force, not as a divine religion. Whether its claim to an especial divine character be true or false makes no difference in this inquiry. Here we are to seek the influences which certainly follow from it as historical facts, whichever hypothesis may be adopted.

In the second place, we are concerned here neither with the results which were accomplished by the Christian theology, nor with those which followed from the church as a government or an ecclesiastical institution. In both these directions the Christian religion furnished the foundation for great historical constructions which had extremely important results. But in neither case is Christianity as a religion the really creative power, and the results which followed from the dogmatic system, or from the church, can be credited to the religion only in so far as it furnished an occasion for the action of the forces which really called them into existence. It is with the religious that we are concerned at this point, and not with the theological or the ecclesiastical, though these affect our history elsewhere.

Again, it should be noticed that influences of a religious nature, like those of pure ideas of any sort, are difficult to trace with absolute exactness. Their action is much less likely to be made a matter of record than is that of other causes which may have contributed to the common result. There can be no question, for example, but that the teachings of the gospel were decisive influences, in thousands of individual cases in the United States, in creating a public opinion against slavery before the Civil War; but it would be far more difficult to write the history of their action than to write the history of the political influences which combined with them. We are often confined to inference in such cases in the absence of positive proof, but the inference may be so obvious as to be equivalent to proof.

Taking up, then, the work of Christianity for civilization, we must first consider its influence upon the world's religious ideas in the strict sense of the word, and it will be in this direction that its most important influence will be found. Religion forms one great side of civilization, and whatever raises the world's religious conceptions to a higher level must be, it need hardly be said, among the great civilizing forces of history.[1]

As a contribution to the religious side of civilization the general work of Christianity is not difficult to state. The work of this new religion, which stands first in logical order, was to free the monotheistic idea which the Jews had attained from the narrow tribal conditions which had made the general acceptance of it impossible and to make it the ruling idea of God in the Christian world, from which it passed later to the Mohammedan. God was to be henceforth one God.

It introduced with this idea of the one only true God a wholly different conception of his character and of his

---

[1] In considering in the first part of this chapter those ideas of the early Christianity which aided in its rapid extension throughout the ancient world, some of its teachings and results which were new have already been indicated. They will be repeated in this connection for completeness' sake.

relation to man from any that had prevailed before, emphasizing the fatherhood of God and his love for man. This idea of the fatherhood of God, typified and proclaimed in an extremely effective form in the sonship of Christ, man's elder brother, brought man near to God and gave him a new point of view for all the future. Love became the great religious force of the new age. In the practical working of Christianity this idea did not remain a mere idea. It was transformed into a positive force in history through the keen conception which the individual Christian had of the immediate personal relationship between himself and God, by virtue of which the power of the Almighty would come to his aid in his endeavor to make himself like God. In other words, Christianity not merely taught that this relationship was an ideal possibility, but it made men believe it as a fact, so that they actually lived with a sense of the divine power in them.

This was in reality, to repeat what was said in another connection, the proclamation of the unity of God and man, of the finite and the infinite, not as a philosophical idea merely, or speculative theory, but as something actually to be realized by common men. The "way of return" in which the world of the time was so deeply interested was opened to all. A sense of reconciliation and harmony with God might become, Christianity said, a conscious fact of daily life for every individual. The convert was required to bring himself into a psychological condition of submission to the will of God of which the inevitable result was a sense of actual reconciliation.

Christianity also taught, as a necessary result of the Christian conception of the relation between God and man, that religion has a direct practical mission as an ethical teacher and help. This was a new and most important step in advance. The ancient national religions had made no ethical demand of the worshipper. The character attributed to the gods could not be helpful to any man. The pagan priest had never looked upon himself as a teacher of morals, or conceived of any reformatory mission for his religion. The Greek or Roman in need of ethical aid and comfort sought the philosopher and not the priest. This whole condition of things Christianity revolutionized. The pure ideal of character which it held aloft in its conception of God, its clear assertion of the necessity and the possibility of such a character for every man which it made in the gospel narrative, created an intimate bond between religion and ethics unknown before.[1] The religious life which Christianity aimed to create in the individual must of necessity express itself in right conduct. This was its true fruit, its external test, and to perfect this the energy of the new religion was especially directed.

It is no doubt true that these religious conceptions did not immediately and completely gain the victory over the older and cruder. The struggle between the old and the new was often obstinate and long continued, and the higher conception long obscured by persistence of the

[1] The Old Testament in this, as in some other of the points mentioned, foreshadows the clearer teaching of the New. St. Augustine perceived this difference between Christianity and the Roman religion, and in the *City of God* challenged the pagans to produce instances of moral teaching in their religion. See especially bk. II, chap. 6. The fact that the Greek and Roman religions, which are the pagan religions of the ancient world in the direct line of our civilization, remained to the end strongly political or æsthetic in character, probably prevented them from reaching the idea of a connection between the national religion and private morals, and left the recognition of this truth to the poets and philosophers, who certainly came near to it. See, for example, Cicero, *De Natura Deorum*, I, i, 3 and 4. The case of Socrates is very much to the point. He saw as clearly, probably, as ever any pagan, the connection between man's character and God, and, in what is a very remarkable way, also, with that conscious submission of the will to God which is a necessary condition of spiritual knowledge. But Socrates was put to death because his teaching was thought to be dangerous to the state. In some of the other pagan religions, like the Egyptian, this connection was more clearly seen, and, though not contributing directly to our civilization, such cases are, in themselves, instructive.

lower. But in so far as these ideas are now the possession of men, it must be reckoned to the credit of Christianity, and whoever, even if he deny to Christianity a
peculiarly divine character or any finality as a religion,
may yet hope that a still more perfect understanding and
realization of religious truth will be gained in the future,
must recognize in Christianity the foundations on which
it will be built.

So much, at least, may be said with confidence upon
the contribution which Christianity made to the strictly
religious side of our civilization. If what has just been
asserted of the connection which the Christian teaching
established between religion and ethics be true, it follows
that a further influence of this religion is to be traced in
the direction of practical ethics.

Here is to be noticed, first of all, the lofty ideal of a
pure and sinless life which Christianity held before all
men in its story of the life of Christ, as a model which
they were to follow, as the divinely given pattern according to which they were to shape their own lives. For
Christianity did not conceive of Christ's life as the life
of a God impossible for man, but as a divinely aided
human life, as the life of a divine being who had been
willing to become really a man and to put himself into
those conditions and limitations in the midst of which
man must live in order that he might be taught to realize
the possibilities of his own life. Or, as it has been finely
said, this life of Christ "revealed to man both the human
side of God and the divine side of man." The Christian
ideal was not like the Stoic, a mere ideal which had never
been attained. In this respect Christianity made a most
decided advance upon Stoicism in the fact that it pointed
to an actual life which had realized its ideal, as well as
in its further teaching that man had not to depend solely
upon the power of his own will in his endeavor to attain it.

In the second place, Christianity taught, most espe-

cially, that the duty of conformity to this ideal and of
fidelity to the higher moral law was the supreme law of
conduct, whatever the power might be which demanded
anything to the contrary. Christianity clearly asserted
that the supreme moral law was distinct from the law of
the state and of a higher validity. It was not exactly a
new idea that there existed a moral law separate from
the law of the state to which man ought to conform.
Stoicism at least perceived the fact. But that this law
demanded a rightful obedience of the individual when
the positive requirement of the state conflicted with it
was an advance, though certainly the pagan ethics could
not have been far from this truth. But Christianity did
not stop with this. It furnished a direct practical ex-
hibition of the principle in a constant succession of the
most public and most dramatic examples in every period
of persecution. Within its own membership, also, it proceeded to the positive enforcement of this supreme moral
law in the system of church penances, very early developed at least in some directions. The church began to
hold its membership directly responsible for acts of which
the state took no account. Whatever may be said of
the system of penances of any later date, there can be
no question but that it was in primitive times a most
effective moral teacher.

In the third place, Christianity taught that the con
scious relationship established between the individual and
God in this life would determine his destiny in the life to
come, and that, consequently, a right moral character,
as the necessary product of that relationship, as the indispensable fruit and test of the harmony of the human
will with the divine will, was of infinite importance.
Wrong living and immoral life would destroy that harmony between God and man upon which an eternity of
happiness depended. I doubt if the early Christianity
anywhere formulated this teaching in exactly this shape,

but if the statement was more concrete in form the ethical meaning and influence were precisely as stated.[1]

It followed necessarily from this belief that many actions of which the ancient law had taken no account, and which the ancient society had regarded as unimportant, or even as indifferent, morally, might have a tremendous significance as elements of permanent character, determining the attitude of the individual towards God. It is, without doubt, chiefly through the influence of this teaching, through the introduction of the idea of sin as a controlling idea in ethics, that the work of Christianity has been done in raising the general moral standard and in clarifying specific ethical judgments, as in the change, to specify one of the most striking cases, which has been brought about in the character of the judgment passed upon sexual wrong-doing.

Another conclusion from this teaching in regard to character was that the determining factor in all ethical judgment of the individual must be the inner character and not the external act; that the external act is of importance only as a sign of what the inner character is. This also was not exactly a new idea, but Christianity put it in a far more vivid and striking form than ever before when it recorded, in the book which was read and reread as the special religious guide and manual of all believers, the impressive words of its founder in which he proclaimed, in regard to some of the most easily besetting sins of every age, that the passion cherished in the heart carries with it the guilt of the act itself.

[1] But see St. Augustine, *City of God*, XXI, 25 (Dods's translation, vol. II, p. 459): "And therefore neither ought such persons as lead an abandoned and damnable life to be confident of salvation, though they persevere to the end in the communion of the church Catholic, and comfort themselves with the words, 'He that endureth to the end shall be saved.' By the iniquity of their life they abandon that very righteousness of life which Christ is to them, whether it be . . . by doing any one of those things of which [the apostle] says, 'They who do such things shall not inherit the kingdom of God.'" (Gal. 5 : 21). Compare, also, the opening sentences of XIX, 4.

In the fourth place, among the contributions of Christianity to ethics—and in some respects this was its most decisive ethical influence—Christianity taught a doctrine of hope to the morally depraved and debased in character. It taught that if the inner character was not right, it might be transformed by the grace of God, if the individual would accept for himself the culminating truth of its religious teaching, forgiveness of sin through faith in the work of Christ, that it might be transformed all at once, by a single supreme choice, a conscious submission of the will to God, so that the man would come to love what he had hated and hate what he had loved. And it also taught that the power which had so transformed the life would continue a constant divine aid in the moral endeavors and struggles of the new life. The essential thing to be regarded here, entirely independent of any religious significance which it may have, is the historical fact that Christianity did create in the minds of men a firm and confiding belief in such a transformation.[1]

It begot in the debased and despairing outcast a firm assurance that he had escaped wholly from his past life; that its associations and temptations would no longer have any power over him, but that he was as free to begin a new life as if he had been born again. In this belief which it created, Christianity was introducing an entirely new factor into history. The greatest problem of prac-

---

[1] Origen quotes Celsus as saying: "And yet, indeed, it is manifest to every one that no one by chastisement, much less by merciful treatment, could effect a complete change in those who are sinners both by nature and custom, for to change nature is an exceedingly difficult thing." After calling attention to the fact that philosophy had sometimes worked such a change of character, Origen says: "But when we consider that those discourses, which Celsus terms 'vulgar,' are filled with power, as if they were spells, and see that they at once convert multitudes from a life of licentiousness to one of extreme regularity, and from a life of wickedness to a better, . . . why should we not justly admire the power which they contain."—(Translation of Origen, in *Ante-Nicene Library*, vol. II, pp. 145-147.)

tical ethics has always been, not to get men to recognize the truth intellectually, but to get them to be true in conduct to their ethical convictions. It is a fact, no doubt, that Stoicism taught a very high system of moral truth; it even attempted, as a sort of missionary philosophy, to persuade men to live according to the laws of right; but it recognized its powerlessness to make Stoics of the masses. In the work which it did in this direction is to be found one of the greatest contributions of Christianity to the ethical regeneration of the world. In the directly personal character of its central truth, Christ the Saviour of each individual man, in the firm confidence which it created that the power of God had transformed the life and would constantly aid in the struggle to keep it right, and in the creative power of love, rising in the heart of man to meet the love of God, Christianity set a new ethically regenerating force at work in the world. And it is through the emphasizing of these ideas that the transforming power of Christianity has been exercised. In proportion as Christianity has kept these truths at the front in its teaching and realized them in its prevailing life, it has been a great force in leading men to a higher ethical level. As it has put something else in their place as the main thing to be emphasized, whether external forms or doctrinal beliefs, it has failed of its mission and limited its own power, and this has been undoubtedly the case through long periods of time. It has been said that the church never sullied the purity of its moral teaching; but it must be confessed that there are ages of Christian history when the theoretical teaching seems to be almost the only thing that did remain pure, and when this had but little real influence upon the general life of the time. Genuine Christianity, in such an age, was certainly almost lost to sight, living on in those unpretending lives which attracted no attention at the time, but of which we find the traces even in the darkest days. One of the most hopeful signs of our own time is the recovery of influence and emphasis in the active Christianity of to-day which these ethical ideas have made.

It is hardly possible to overstate the importance of the new power thus brought into the moral life of the world. Science forbids us to believe it possible to add any new force of importance to the sum total of physical forces already at work in the universe. But it would seem as if we certainly came upon the fact here that with Christianity there was added to the sum total of energies in action in human history a new increment of ethical force. Something which had not existed in the world before actually made it easier for men to escape from the bondage of evil habits and to realize their ideals of a moral life. It may be difficult to follow through their details the results which have been thus secured, because they are realized in character and in individuals in spheres of life where record is unusual, and by forces that are silent and unobserved in action. But publicans and sinners transformed into saints of Christian history are by no means confined to the gospel days.[1]

There remain to be considered certain results which Christianity has accomplished, either by itself or in combination with influences from other sources, which do not

---

[1] Very little has been said in the above passage of the influence of Christianity upon specific ethical doctrines, and for these reasons: Upon certain points, the brotherhood of man, for example, it does not seem to me that the things ordinarily said are true. Upon some others I am very much in doubt what ought to be said, as upon the duty of self-sacrifice for others, an idea of conduct which appears to be undergoing transformation at the present time. But in the main, for this reason: It was no part of the peculiar mission of Christianity to make known specific ethical principles. It needs no revelation to make them known to men. The laws of conduct are as much a part of the constituent laws of man's being as are the laws of logic, and the growing experience of man teaches him what these laws are in the one case as it does in the other, and enlarges and clarifies and ennobles his ethical ideas precisely as it does his mathematical. The peculiar mission of Christianity is in the religious sphere, and its relation to ethics is, as indicated above, in the vital necessity which it places upon the

naturally fall under either its religious or its directly ethical work.

Another chapter will treat, under the elements of civilization which the Germans introduced, of the origin of the modern idea of the worth of the individual man as compared with the classic idea of the greater importance of the state. One source out of which the modern idea has grown is, without doubt, the supreme value placed upon the individual man in the Christian teaching of the vastly greater importance of the life to come than of this life or any of its interests, of the infinite destinies before each man, all depending upon his individual choice and character. The attitude of the early church in this matter, towards the state under which it existed, the Roman Empire, was probably more extreme than its attitude towards any later government, and yet there have been some ages in which the contrast between the higher interests of the individual and those of the state has been drawn almost as sharply, and the teaching of Christianity on the point has certainly been clear and unmistakable. That this teaching led to the adoption of positive institutions in any free government cannot be affirmed. Its influence is to be found rather in the line of the ideas by which we defend our right to individual liberty.

Christianity taught also the equality of all men in the sight of God. It taught this not merely as an abstract idea. Stoicism had done that. But in the early Christianity, at least, it put the idea into practice so far as it was possible to do so. The master was held to treat his slave as a brother. They both stood on the same foot-

individual, of living better, as the life which is in the vine makes it, of necessity, bear fruit.

I quote the following passage from a distinguished living divine as an example of the careless writing which is often done on the specific ethical influence of Christianity: "It is not without significance that the first hospitals, the first schools, the first free states have been Christian. Monasteries were the first hospitals; monks were the first teachers."

ing within the church, and its offices and dignities were open to both alike. If the early story that, in the third century, a slave became bishop of Rome is doubtful, the fact that such a story came to be believed at all is significant; and certainly in feudal days, when the church fell largely under the feudal influence, instances are not uncommon of men from the lowest classes rising to positions in the church of the highest rank. The teaching of the church always kept before men the idea of the equality in moral rights and in final destiny of all men. That it was the chiefly effective force in establishing practical equality, so far as it has been established, can hardly be asserted.[1]

Again, Christianity demanded the complete separation of church and state and asserted that each must be recognized as having its own distinct and independent mission to perform. In the ancient world the two had been

[1] Under this point something may be said upon the discussions, which have been frequent in the past, on the specific influence of Christianity in the abolition of slavery and in the advancement of woman to a position of equality with man. It is clear to the careful student of history that both these reforms have been brought about by a combination of economic, social, and moral causes, of which the Christian teaching forms only a single element. The attempt on the part of some to claim for Christianity more of a share in these results than can be fairly claimed grows apparently out of a misapprehension of the nature and field of Christian influence. Ethical exhortation, and denunciation of vice, and the example of noble lives are most powerful forces in the moral advancement of the race, and it is absurd to deny them, as some seem desirous to do, their proper share in the result. But where, as often happens, an institution which involves a moral evil is bound up with the economic and social conditions of a given stage of civilization, it requires more than a moral conviction, more even than a general moral conviction that it is wrong, to secure its overthrow, however important such a moral conviction may be as one of the necessary causes of its destruction. In such a case, also, the process of creating a general moral condemnation of the evil is always a long and slow one, and not infrequently the professed teachers of morals are to be found upon the wrong side. So long as economic and social conditions, real or supposed, favor the continuance of an institution or a practice, plausible moral arguments in its support are not difficult to find; when influences from various sources begin to combine against the evil, then the true principles of ethics come to their aid and hasten the common result.

intimately associated, and the religious organization had been looked upon as very largely a branch of the political. This view of the relationship contained a great danger for the growing church—the danger of being absorbed in the state, of losing all independence of development, and of being diverted from its own proper work to serve political ends. It was undoubtedly this danger which forced the early church to develop so clearly the doctrine of independence of state control which is involved in Christianity and to insist upon it so strongly against Roman emperors and German kings.

That the modern complete separation of church and state, as we have it in the United States, has grown out of a protest again the position of the church itself on this question, is not a proof that the separation of church and state is not an outgrowth of Christian teaching, but furnishes us only a further instance of the fact that the later church, as a whole, did not remain true to the fundamental principles of Christianity, and that these had to be recovered by a reformation of some kind. When the church had secured its independence of the state, and perfected its organization, and grown strong, it went a step further and asserted the right of the church to control the state. That this principle in practical operation is as dangerous as the other, which absorbs the church in the state, it needs no argument to prove; but it also needs none to prove that both are equally foreign to the teachings of Christianity.

The gain to civilization from the complete separation of church and state is easily seen. It is an essential condition of free thought and free discussion that the totally distinct spheres of the two institutions should be recognized, and without it intellectual progress, except in the realm of theory and barren speculation, would be, if not impossible, beset with almost insurmountable difficulties.

Finally, Christianity had awakened in a part of the ancient society a new hopefulness and energy and productive power even before the Germans had brought in the reinforcement of their vigorous life. How much this might have amounted to had the Germans not come, and had the conditions of the following age been favorable, cannot be said; but it is a result deserving of notice both as showing the tendency of Christianity and as indicating undoubtedly one of the sources of a reviving civilization soon to come.

The example of this influence of Christianity, to which attention has been most frequently called, is the contrast between the contemporary pagan and Christian literatures from the third century on. The pagan is more refined and polished, but it is empty and barren, spiritless imitation of classic models. The Christian literature of the same generations is cruder and less elegant, but it is full of spirit and vigor and energetic life. There is something to be said and some purpose in saying it.

In closing this account one cannot avoid recurring to what was implied at the outset. It is impossible not to feel the incompleteness of any statement of the influence of Christianity upon civilization. Some of the more obvious and apparent results can be mentioned, but its full work cannot be traced. This is mainly for the reason stated: its operation lies in the realm of the silent and unobserved forces which act upon the individual character and the springs of action, but which can, in the nature of the case, leave no record of themselves for later time.

CHAPTER IV

WITH the introduction of one more, the four chief sources of our civilization were brought together. The Germans had waited long. That restless movement of their tribes in search of new lands which overwhelmed the empire in the fifth century had begun five hundred years earlier. The invasion of the Cimbri and Teutones at the end of the second century B. C. had held Rome in terror for a decade, and Julius Cæsar, fifty years later, had found his opportunity to begin the conquest of Gaul in expelling the already successful army of the German Ariovistus from its occupation of Gallic territory. If it had not been for the Romans the German occupation of western Europe would have followed at once, more slowly perhaps than when it actually occurred, but without a check. But now they had been forced to wait for centuries, learning always more and more of the wonders and riches of the desired lands, growing constantly more and more eager to possess them, striving, many generations of them, to find some weak spot through which they might force their way, but always held back. At last their time came.

The Germans were by nature restless and fond of adventure. There was overpopulation at home, and the lack of land to support their people, with their primitive methods of agriculture, was seriously felt. It was this necessity to find more land for their growing numbers which was, beyond question, the impelling force in their earlier attacks and later conquest of the Roman

Empire. But the first successful invasion, the first permanent occupation of Roman territory was not brought about by either of these causes.

Upon the great Germanic kingdom of the Goths, which had been formed by the genius of Ermanaric just after the middle of the fourth century and which occupied a considerable part of European Russia, stretching from the Don to the Danube, fell an invasion of the Huns. They were a Mongolian or Tartar race, frightful to the sight, skilled in their peculiar tactics, swift to attack, vanishing before the return blow, and they were too strong for the more civilized Goths. Of the two tribal divisions of the Gothic race the greater part of the Ostrogoths, or East Goths, submitted to the Huns, were incorporated in their empire, and remained subject to it and tributary to its army until that empire fell to pieces a century later. The Visigoths, however, fell back before the advance of the Huns, and appeared on the Danube frontier as suppliants for the Roman protection. It was granted them and they were transported to the southern bank. It was a dangerous experiment, but all went well at first, and all might have continued to go well even with so great a risk. But the smallest risk is too great for a state rotten with political corruption. The opportunity for plunder was too great to be resisted by the officers in charge, and they forced the Goths to buy the food which should have been given them, and sold them back their hostages, and sold them back their arms. The treason which is latent in every form of the spoils doctrine could hardly go farther than this. The patience of a German race with arms in its hands under brutal mistreatment was soon exhausted, and they burst into a flame of revolt, swept everything before them, and at last, far within the bounds of the empire, a hostile German tribe destroyed a Roman army and slew the Emperor Valens.

This crossing of the Danube frontier, in 376 A. D., and this battle of Hadrianople, in 378, are the events which mark the beginning of the permanent occupation of the Roman Empire by the German tribes.

It was the beginning of the age of conquest, but the empire was already largely German. Julius Cæsar had begun the practice of enlisting German auxiliaries in the Roman armies, and, although the practice had grown very slowly at first, in the later years it had assumed enormous proportions, until whole armies were German, and entire German tribes, under the command of their native chiefs, and preserving all their tribal organization, entered the Roman service. Such tribes had been settled in lands along the frontier on condition of keeping out all others. If possible, even larger numbers had been introduced as slaves. From the days of Marius on, in larger and smaller bodies, the influx had been constant until they were present everywhere—in the towns as house slaves, in the country as *coloni* bound to the soil. In the conquest these Germans already within the empire were no doubt a more important element than the records indicate. The indifference of the inhabitants to the German occupation, which is everywhere manifest, was very likely due in some part to the large number of Germans already around them, and, in some cases, as in the last invasion of Alaric, we can get a glimpse of the positive aid they rendered; in a larger number, unquestionably, of the cases which were recorded, we find them the bravest and most effective of Rome's defenders.

The great Emperor Theodosius was able to restore order in the East and to hold the Visigoths in check as nominal Roman subjects—indeed as faithful allies of his, but they retained as their own the lands which they had occupied in the Danube valley. On his death, in 395, they began to move again, incited perhaps by some change in the policy of the government towards them which they regarded as a slight, impelled, more likely, by the race restlessness or by the ambition of the young Alaric, now just coming to the leadership. They ravaged Thrace, threatened Constantinople, turned south into Greece, past Athens, which was spared, and into the Peloponnesus. Here Alaric was checked by the skill of Stilicho, the Vandal, guardian of the Western emperor, and, though not actually subdued, accepted bribes and titles and returned to the Danube valley. In a few years he was on the march again, this time towards the west. Once more Stilicho forced him back (402), but this time he took a position near the head of the Adriatic, from which it would be easy to turn in either direction as circumstances might invite.

In the meantime the storm was descending from every quarter. The fatal weakness of the empire in this final period, the want of an army, had made it necessary to call in a part of the frontier garrisons to meet the attack of Alaric. The frontiers could no longer be defended. One great horde of men, whose exact tribal relationships are not known, under command of Radagaisus, poured down from western Germany into the neighborhood of Florence (405). Here what seems to have been the main body was outgeneralled and annihilated by Stilicho, and inflicted no injury upon the empire, beyond the increased exhaustion which, in its weakened condition, followed every such strain.

But far worse things than this were happening elsewhere in this opening decade of the fifth century—the most awful moment of the barbarian deluge. Britain, Gaul, and Spain, abandoned by their rightful defenders, harried by invading tribes and by revolted troops and the ephemeral emperors of their creation, fell out of the empire never to be recovered again except in name. An army of related tribes—Burgundians, Vandals, Suevi, Alani—broke through the Rhine frontier at the end of

the year 406, and after a few years of aimless plundering
found permanent homes within the empire—the Burgundians in eastern Gaul, in lands which have retained their
name, and as nominal subjects of the emperor, whose
sanction they received, but in reality as an independent state.   The other tribes passed through the Pyrenees
into Spain, which they carved into kingdoms for themselves, lasting with varying degrees of permanence.   In
the following year, 407, the last Roman troops abandoned Britain to its fate and, following a new Constantine, whom they had proclaimed emperor, crossed over
into Gaul to add to the confusion there.

In Italy the tragedy of the empire drew rapidly to a
climax.   Stilicho, justly or unjustly, excited the suspi-
cion of the Emperor Honorius and was put to death in
408.   Alaric's opportunity had come.   Without a moment's delay he swept into Italy, took possession of all
the open country, and finally, in 410, stormed the city
itself, now for almost a thousand years untouched by an
enemy.   What Alaric would have done with the peninsula, now virtually his conquest, no one can say.   As he
was on the point of crossing over into Africa to compel that province to forward the usual food supplies
to Rome, he died suddenly, and the Visigoths elected
Athaulf, his brother-in-law, to be their king.   He seems
to have thought it hopeless to try to found a permanent
kingdom in Italy and led his people into Gaul.   There,
without any formal alliance with the Romans, he married
his prisoner, Placidia, the sister of Honorius, and aided
to put down the usurping tyrants.   After his death his
successor, Wallia, formed a compact with the emperor,
and recovered for the empire a part of the territory which
had been occupied by the Germans in Spain, and finally,
in 419, by a new treaty, the Visigoths received a permanent grant of land in southwestern Gaul, as nominal
Roman subjects.   This formed the beginning of the Visi-

gothic kingdom, which lasted until the invasion of the Saracens in the eighth century. From this beginning it gradually spread towards the north until it reached the Loire, and towards the south until it embraced the whole Spanish peninsula. As they had been the first to break the Roman frontier, so they were the first to found a permanent and recognized kingdom within the empire— the recognized kingdom of the Burgundians being a year or two later.

Nearly all the Germans who had settled in Spain were gradually conquered and absorbed in the Visigothic state. But the Vandals, in 429, abandoned their Spanish lands and crossed over into Africa. According to a doubtful story they were invited by a disaffected Roman governor; more likely they dreaded the approach of the Visigoths, who had, in their first invasion of Spain, destroyed a part of the Vandal race. In Africa they met with some vigorous resistance, but in a few years had gained possession of it all, and rapidly developed a naval power which became the terror of the Mediterranean, even as far as Constantinople. In 455 they seized the city of Rome and held it for a few days, sacking it more savagely than Alaric had done.

Just at this time a danger far more serious than came from any German invasion threatened the dying empire —more serious because it would mean the triumph of a more hopeless Asiatic and Mongolian barbarism. The invasion of the Huns, which had set the Germans in motion, had resulted in the formation of a Hunnic empire north of the Danube, to which most of Germany was subject. Now a great king had come to the throne, Attila, the Scourge of God. Seemingly afire with that purposeless, senseless rage of conquest which has led more than one devastating Mongolian host, he fell, with his great army, in which many German nations were serving, on Gaul. But the Mongolians have never yet been able

to do in the West what they have so often done in the
East, in the way of almost unlimited conquest, and in
Gaul his invasion was speedily stopped. Aetius, himself
of barbarian descent, had succeeded in adding to the
Roman army which he had brought together, the forces
of the German states in Gaul, Visigoths, Burgundians,
and Franks, persuaded that their own best interests were
identical with Rome's. In the great battle of the nations which followed, in 451, in the Catalaunian plain,
near Troyes, German and Roman stood together for European and Aryan civilization against Asiatic and Mongolian, and saved the day. In the next year Attila in-
vaded Italy, but almost at the beginning of his march
turned back and retired to his own lands. Why we do
not know, perhaps impressed by the solemn embassy of
Pope Leo I, more probably hindered by some more material difficulty. Hardly had he reached home when he
suddenly died, his empire fell to pieces, and the Germans,
who had been subject to it, again became independent.

In the years of Attila's invasions the Saxons were gaining their first permanent hold upon Britain. As early
as the end of the third century their piratical attacks had
begun. Exactly after the style of their relatives, the
vikings of a later time, they had sailed along the coast
and plundered any unguarded spot. The Romans had
been obliged to organize a special coast-guard, under the
count of the Saxon Shore, to protect the province from
their raids. When the Roman troops left Britain to its
fate, in 407, the Saxons soon found out their opportunity. The attacks of another enemy, the barbarian Celts
of the north and west, upon the Romanized inhabitants,
only made it easier for this more dangerous foe to gain
a permanent foothold, even with the consent of the provincials. But once landed they could not be kept within
bounds. More and more came; many little kingdoms
were founded, till almost the whole eastern and southern

shores were occupied. The resistance of the Celts to the advance of the Saxons seems to have been, however, much the most obstinate and stubborn which any German invasion encountered. The result of this was that the German newcomers did not settle themselves down here, as elsewhere, in the midst of a Roman population, which they treated to all intents and purposes as on an equality with themselves, and which far outnumbered them. If the provincials were not actually exterminated or driven back, which seems improbable, they were reduced to a decidedly inferior position, very likely to slavery, so that they were able to exercise no such influence upon their conquerors as other provincials did.[1]

In the meantime Italy itself was lost to the empire, except for a brief recovery in the next century. The death of Valentinian III, in 455, whose capital indeed had not been at Rome but at Ravenna, had brought the house of Theodosius to an end. A rapid succession of powerless emperors followed, nearly all of them appointed and deposed by the leaders of the German troops, who were now the only protectors of Italy. Finally, the last of them, or the one who has been traditionally considered the last, Romulus nicknamed Augustulus, was deposed in 476, and the leader of the Germans, Odovacar, determined to appoint no successor. An embassy was sent to Constantinople to recognize Zeno as emperor of the reunited empire and to ask him to appoint Odovacar as his representative in Italy. This is the so-called Fall of the Western Empire; but it was not recognized as such by either the Eastern or the Western Romans, or by the Germans themselves, even though Odovacar's request had not been granted by Zeno. Odovacar ruled

[1] That the Anglo-Saxons, however, continued some of the Roman arrangements, especially in the matter of the villa or farm organization, seems probable, and further investigation is likely to increase our knowledge of their indebtedness.

the Germans who were in Italy as their king, and he was
at the head of a practically independent kingdom, but he
did not understand that fact as clearly as we do, and,
in the theory of the time, he was still commanding a
Roman army and guarding a Roman province under the
emperor.   All the provinces of the Western Empire were
now occupied by German kingdoms, except a fragment
here and there; but all those on the continent still regarded themselves as in the empire and acknowledged
at least a nominal subjection to the emperor.

Odovacar's reign was not long.   On the breaking up of
Attila's kingdom the Ostrogoths had been received into
the empire and given lands south of the Danube.   Here,
more recently, they had become very troublesome under
their young king Theodoric, and when he finally proposed
to Zeno to recover Italy from Odovacar, the offer was
readily accepted.   The conquest was not altogether easy
and occupied some years; but it was at last completed,
and Odovacar was slain by the hand of Theodoric.   The
Ostrogothic kingdom thus established was the most remarkable of all the early German states.   Theodoric had
spent his early life as a hostage in Constantinople, and
if he did not learn to read and write there, he learned
many other things.   If we may judge by the tendency of
his reign, rather than by any specific acts which prove
his policy beyond dispute, he seems to have recognized
more consciously than any other barbarian king the fact
that any permanent state must be based on a union of
the two populations and the two civilizations in a new
common nation.   If it is impossible to show that he deliberately sought such a union, it is certain that his policy,
if it could have been continued for a generation or two
longer, would have produced such a result.   He continued
in operation the Roman laws, judicial tribunals, administrative system, and taxes.   He divided lands among the
Goths without exciting the hatred of the Romans, and

Romans and Goths served together in tribunals for the hearing of cases in which the parties were of the two peoples. Agriculture and commerce revived, means of communication were improved, and art and literature seemed to feel new life. Order was maintained, property was secure, and toleration enforced. But more than a single generation is needed to bring about a real union between two such widely differing races as these. Progress under Theodoric was too rapid for endurance; indeed, in many cases, it seemed to be more real than it actually was, and after his death discord and discontent, held down by the power of his will, revealed themselves rapidly. In another generation the Ostrogothic kingdom and the Ostrogothic race were things of the past.

There had been a great recovery of strength in the empire in the East. The army had been improved and the finances set in order. And now the great Emperor Justinian had come to the throne with the ambition to restore the old control over the West, and to bring back as many of the provinces as possible to actual obedience. He had not merely an army and resources, but he had the no less necessary condition of success, one of the great generals of history, Belisarius. A quarrel in the Vandal royal family, the deposing of a king descended on the mother's side from the imperial house of Theodosius, gave him an opportunity to make his first attack on Africa, and in a brief campaign that province was restored to the empire. Then came the turn of Italy, and although the Goths made a most heroic resistance and were able to prolong the struggle for twenty years, the odds against them were too great. Their kingdom fell, and one of the most attractive of the early German nations disappeared from history, the few survivors joining the Visigoths in Spain.

A very important result of this brief recovery of Italy by the Roman power was the introduction there, into use and into the schools, of the Justinian Code. The Ostrogoths had made use of the Theodosian Code for such Roman law as they had need of, and the other German states continued to do this. But now the more complete Justinian Code was brought to Italy and survived there to be made the foundation, after some centuries, of a renewed and most influential study of the Roman law, through all the West.

The southern part of Italy was destined to remain under the government of the emperor at Constantinople for five hundred years, but the northern part was speedily lost. It was occupied, after fifteen years, by the Lombards, coming from the same region as the Ostrogoths, the last of the invasions of this period, and the last kingdom to be established on Roman soil. Their occupation of the north, however, was never complete. Venice remained independent, nominally under the emperor, and Ravenna and a strip along the eastern coast and across to the western, including Rome, remained under the Roman governor, the exarch of Ravenna. Rome was gradually cut off from these other lands by the slow Lombard advance, and the opportunity was presented to the bishops of Rome, which they were not slow to utilize, to become virtually independent and to found a little principality as temporal rulers. This forms an intimate part, however, of a wider current of events in the West which we must soon take up.

One fact of very great importance for all this long period of conquest, but one easy to be overlooked in the history of more stirring events, is that the life of the provincial, on the country lands and in the towns, went on much the same as before. He was subjected to a rapid change of masters; he was deprived now and again of a part of his lands; he had to submit to occasional plundering; life and property were not secure. But he lived on and produced enough to keep the world alive.

He took himself no part in the wars. He had apparently little interest in the result; indeed, the coming in of the German was often an improvement of condition for him. He had not been altogether prosperous or secure before. At any rate, he kept at work, and he held to his language, and to his legal and economic customs, and to his religion, and he became thus a most important but disregarded factor of the future.

Such is, in brief, and with a single exception, reserved for separate treatment, the history of the introduction of the German peoples into the classic world. As we pass in outline the history of this conquest we cannot avoid the question why this Roman power, which so short a time beforehand made the conquest of the world, was able to offer no more effectual resistance to these invaders. If we examine carefully the series of events, the immediate reason is not difficult to see. The Roman power was exhausted when the final attack came. There is no evidence that the German onset was in any decisive way more violent now than two centuries earlier, but at the middle of the second century the Romans were still able to repel the attack with success, if not easily. It would perhaps be more accurate to say that Marcus Aurelius, in his struggle with the Quadi and Marcomanni was the first to feel the growing exhaustion of the state, and the first to resort to the doubtful expedients so common later to maintain the strength of the army. But the state still appeared strong and was, in reality, strong enough for two centuries to come to keep off its enemies in some way. But at the end of the fourth century, even that appearance of strength was gone. The frontiers could no longer be guarded, the provinces were empty, the capital itself hardly defended. The Roman strength was exhausted. But in saying this we only remove the question one step farther back. What are the reasons why this Roman race, the strongest of the world up to this time, had declined so rapidly and now fell easily a prey to enemies it had once overcome?

It is impossible to give in a few paragraphs any complete and accurate conception of the causes which led to the fall of Rome. Those causes were so numerous and so involved with one another in their action, they were at work through so long a time, the full understanding of their operation requires so extensive a knowledge of the laws which govern the economic and political action of men, that volumes would be required for a clear presentation of the subject. A brief account of the matter is made still further difficult from the fact that the fall of Rome has been very often made the subject of partial and incomplete treatment in order to prove some particular point, perhaps to make vivid the contrast between the Christian church and the heathen society which it came to regenerate, perhaps to make manifest the political dangers which arise from the moral corruption of a people. Undoubtedly, the Christian church had a mission of regeneration of great importance for the ancient society, as well as for the individual, but no progress is made towards proving this fact by picturing the dark side of that society only, to the exclusion of all its virtues. Undoubtedly, also, moral corruption is a most fruitful source of political ruin, but hardly in the way in which the professional moralists would sometimes have us think. What can be attempted here is barely more than an enumeration, as complete as possible within these limits, of the various causes which worked together to undermine the strength of the Roman state.

In general, it may be said, that these causes are the same as those which led to the overthrow of the republic and the establishment of the empire. Coming plainly into view by the close of the second Punic War, they continue in operation through the whole later history unchecked, or barely checked for the moment here and there, and bringing with them naturally other related causes and increasingly disastrous results. The establishment of the empire at the beginning of the Christian era was undoubtedly, in the condition of things at the time, a political necessity, but that is not the same thing as saying that the causes which led to the fall of the republic were beneficial causes; and no one would probably seriously maintain, though some have seemed to imply as much, that the Romans would have found it impossible to adapt the government of the republic to the wider demands of the empire, had they preserved their earlier characteristics. The monarchy became a political necessity, not because the Romans were unable to govern the empire, but because they were no longer able to govern themselves, and the causes which had brought them to this pass continuing to act as before, in the end exhausted the power of the empire. That the republic fell under the influence of these causes in a much shorter time than the empire is an instance of the abundantly supported historical principle that political corruption and decline are far more dangerous to a democratic government than to a monarchy.

The causes of the fall of Rome may be roughly divided into two great groups—first, the moral causes; second, the economic. It must be acknowledged, however, that this division is not a strictly scientific one. The two classes are not co-ordinate. The economic causes are more immediate in their action, those which are strictly moral causes are more indirect and remote. They are the causes of causes. The influence of personal immorality and corruption upon the state has often been made the subject of careless writing and sometimes of wild speculation and is a matter which needs more real investigation than it has yet received. It seems to be altogether likely, however, that such an investigation will

show that private vice becomes dangerous to the state
only where it is translated into political corruption or
economic disease, and that individual immorality may go
very far—that it has gone in some actual cases, indeed,
almost if not quite as far as among the Romans—without
involving the destruction of the state, if it does not affect the public life or the economic resources of the nation. It is because certain forms of personal vice translate themselves so quickly and easily into public causes
that the morals of its citizens are of importance to the
state, as a matter of self-protection.

The vices which were especially prevalent among the
Romans were precisely of this sort. These were, in the
first place, the physical vices—drunkenness, gluttony, and
licentiousness. It is entirely impossible to give any detailed account of the condition of a large portion of the
Roman society in these respects. Fortunately, it is not
necessary. The description has been so often attempted
for one purpose or another and has been made so frank
and unreserved, that a popular impression has been undoubtedly created that these vices were far more universal
and extreme throughout the Roman world than they
really were. No doubt they did affect certain classes of
the population—the country people, the middle classes
where these still existed—to a greater extent than a corresponding condition would in modern times, because, for
one reason, of the existence of slavery, and yet it is certain that the extreme cases and the most injurious results are to be found in the large cities and among the
wealthy class, while the provinces and the middle classes
were comparatively uncontaminated. It seems probable,
however, though by no means certain, that the influence
of these vices did extend far enough to affect the national
life. Their influence upon the race, where it is felt, is
precisely the same as that upon the individual. Energy,
will-power, self-reliance in the face of danger are lost,

and the recuperative and reproductive power declines or disappears. These are exactly the results which appeared, from some cause, throughout the Roman Empire in its last age. It is a remarkable fact, to which attention has been called, that, though many of the Roman towns were still strongly walled, and though the Germans were very unskilled in the art of siege, yet, while numbers of the towns maintain themselves for a time, there are few instances during the whole period of the conquest of heroic resistance to the invaders by the population of the provinces. It is almost always a barbarian general and a barbarian army which undertakes the defence; or, where we find a case of a different sort, as in the defence of Orleans against the Huns, there is manifestly present a new element of energy and self-reliance not supplied by the Roman society proper, but by the Christian portion of it. Such a decline of the national will-power it would hardly be correct to trace to the operation of this one physical influence alone, and it is altogether likely that no such effect would have followed had not this cause been combined with others which are to be noticed later. Yet it must be kept in mind that this influence when present is usually a decisive one and may have contributed as much, or more, than any other single force to the common result. So the other results which followed from this group of moral causes—decline of population, inability to recover losses from plagues and famines, destruction of capital, indifference to public affairs—are perhaps best looked at among the economic causes, where they naturally appear. It is into economic causes, properly speaking, that the physical vices translate themselves when they affect the public life.

To this group of causes we must add the operation of the intense and desperate struggle for wealth which began under the republic and continued under the empire—a less conspicuous feature, perhaps of the later period, but not less fatal in its effects. Some later times have probably seen as inordinate a passion for wealth as the Roman, and as crafty scheming to get it without earning it, and this condition of things, as in the case of the physical vices, seems to become a serious danger to the state only when it is translated, when it leads to the misuse of official position or legislative power. The peculiar circumstances of the last age of the republic made this translation into a political cause extremely easy, almost unavoidable. The government of lately conquered provinces, to be exploited for the benefit of the state, offered a secure opportunity for extortion and peculation which the official, trained in the spirit of the time, could hardly resist. Decided reformation in this regard was certainly made under the empire, but the spirit and the practice never disappeared. It was a source of great weakness to the empire in the days of decline and a fatal obstacle to thorough reformation that so large a proportion of the official class looked upon their offices as a source of gain or advancement and were ready on any occasion to sacrifice the interests of the state to their own private interests.[1]

When we turn to the economic causes which aided in the fall of Rome we stand appalled at their number and variety. It would seem as if, when the empire had once started on the downward path, all things worked together against it and all the springs of national prosperity were poisoned. It is possible here to point out only the most important of these causes, and, in such a brief account, we shall find our way to a clear understanding only if we remember that the immediate cause of the fall of Rome was exhaustion—exhaustion of resources and exhaustion of population. There are to be grouped together, then, the most decisive causes which show how the accumulated capital of the empire—in property and in men—

[1] See above, p. 65, the extremely important instance at the crossing of the Danube by the Visigoths.

came to be destroyed, and why no more was produced to take its place.

Slavery is naturally the first among these causes to occur to mind, and, whatever may have been the moral dangers of the Roman slave system, the economic evils which it worked were still more fatal to the state. In the first place, it was a system wasteful and unproductive of men. By it a large part of the natural population of the empire, for this was probably, even in the later times, the chief source of slaves, was placed in a condition not merely where it was used up and disappeared with fearful rapidity, but also where it tended to reproduce itself much less rapidly than it would have done as a body of free laborers. In this way there was probably always a considerable loss of population, certainly the slave system went far to prevent what should have been the normal increase and to make it impossible to recover sudden losses of population, such as occurred in times of pestilence. Slavery is also an expensive means of production. The returns on the capital invested, except in unusual conditions, are small, and the incentive to improvement in methods of production extremely slight. The history of our Southern States since the Civil War, as compared with their earlier history, shows this conclusively. And it destroys capital with great rapidity. Economically, the slave is merely a machine. The use of a machine tends to destroy it. But when a modern steam-engine is destroyed it is easily and quickly replaced and the total loss to the capital of the generation in material rendered useless is not great. Much of it may be used over again to make some new machine. But when the slave was used up not merely was so much capital destroyed but a part of the total productive force of the generation was permanently annihilated. It could not be replaced. The slave system invested a large proportion of the capital of the empire in a relatively unprofi-

table form and tended to use up rapidly its productive
force. Again, the slave system tended to extinguish the
class of free laborers both in city and country. In the
cities it did this by supplying the demand for labor of
all kinds and by making labor odious—never, perhaps,
to such an extent as in our Southern States, but still in a
marked degree. In the country it gave the capitalist
advantage over the small landowner in a variety of ways
and made it easy to drive him to the wall and to swallow
up his holding. As a result, although the class of small
cultivators never entirely disappeared, yet in some parts
of the empire very few were left, and vast estates cultivated by slave labor were formed everywhere, and the
middle class, the solid resource of every state, tended to
disappear between the very wealthy on one side and the
slave class and the city rabble on the other. It must
be remembered, however, that the positive evil effects of
slavery were felt more decisively in the earlier than in
the later period of the empire. As the empire drew to an
end, the economic conditions were forcing upon it, unconsciously but inevitably, the extinction of slavery—its
transformation into serfdom, and, although this transformation was not completed in Roman days,[1] it had gone
far enough to survive the German conquest, and far enough
to be a decided gain both to the state and to the slave.

Another economic cause of primary importance was the
public games and the free distribution of food, especially
the latter. The public games were a great drain upon
the resources of the state, but the food donatives were
a more serious evil. The distribution of wheat to the
poorer citizens at a price below the market price, which
was begun towards the end of the second century B. C.
as a demagogic measure, could not well be stopped.
One demagogue bid against another and the empire was

[1] Indeed, slavery did not entirely disappear from Europe during the
middle ages.

obliged to continue the practice. It resulted finally in
the regular distribution of baked loaves of bread, and
occasionally at least of oil, wine, meat, and clothes, and
it was extended gradually from the capital to the larger
provincial cities, and even to the smaller towns. The
worst effect of it was not that it maintained in the towns
an unemployed mob, hard to be used for any good purpose but easy to be excited by any demagogic appeal.
Two results followed, which were even more fatal. In
the first place, the government, at public expense, presented a constant temptation to the middle class to abandon the struggle for existence and to sink into the pro-
letariat. The hard-pressed poor farmer who saw all his
toil fail to improve his condition was easily persuaded
to escape from the grinding competition into the town
and into a class entirely unproductive, or which produced
only the least possible. But the decline of production
was not all. A continually increasing portion of the
wealth produced each year by the classes which remained
productive was destroyed without adding anything to the
permanent capital of the empire. The products of the
provinces were drained into the towns and sent nothing
back—the expense being met by a taxation which rested
chiefly on the land itself. In normal conditions the products of the farm go into the city. But while the artisan
is eating the wheat he is making cloth, which goes back
to the farm containing the total value of the wheat. But
in Rome the economic result was precisely the same as
if the government had collected the products of the farm
in a heap and burned them. That is to say, at the moment when the empire needed most of all to build up a
middle class and to encourage the accumulation of resources, the state was, by its own act, destroying the one
and making the other impossible.

Another one of those causes which is commonly considered of importance was the heavy and expensive taxa-

tion. It seems doubtful, however, whether the taxation of the empire was heavier or, indeed, as heavy as that of most modern states. If there had been general prosperity and the production and saving of wealth which ought to have existed, it is probable that a heavier burden of taxation could have been borne without serious inconvenience.[1] It was the disordered economic condition which rendered the taxation injurious, as it undoubtedly was. To this must be added the expensive method of collection. The indirect taxes were farmed out—a method which makes the collection a private speculation and extorts from the people much larger sums than the government receives. The land taxes were no longer farmed, but the responsibility for collecting them and turning them over to the government was placed upon the local community of larger landowners—a method which lent itself readily to injustice and oppression, and which made the prosperous and thrifty man pay the taxes of his unsuccessful neighbor.[2]

To these more striking causes may be added a considerable group of hardly less effective ones. A debased currency constantly fluctuating in value and growing more scanty. A constant drain of the precious metals —currency and capital—into the oriental states to pay for luxuries of dress and food, unproductive and soon destroyed. A declining fertility of soil, which with the increasing lack of capital could not be restored. A diminishing supply of laborers, felt severely in many places by the large landowners, and which led to the systematic introduction of barbarians by the government. A still

[1] The history of many American cities shows that a burden of taxation, probably higher than rested on the Romans under the empire, can be borne without serious results—shows, indeed, how high taxation, in some cases at least, is an unavoidable result and a sign of great prosperity and rapid growth.

[2] See in Taine's *Ancient Régime*, book V, chap. II, an interesting account of the methods and results of a similar system of tax collection in France in the eighteenth century.

more dangerous incorporation of barbarians into the army from a similar lack of men. Natural calamities, pestilences, and earthquakes, which certainly might fall upon any state, but which in the empire left permanent holes in the population, while an economically healthy state would have entirely recovered such losses in a generation or two. A declining police and military protection, seen in such facts as the often-told story of the Frankish prisoners of the Emperor Probus,[1] or in the occasional inroad of a German tribe which committed irreparable damage before it could be subdued.

Much of this means that the task which Rome had undertaken, or which had been in a way forced upon her, of bringing the world up to her level had proved in the end too great for her civilizing and absorbing power. She had too scanty resources in men to continue indefinitely lifting quickly above themselves the barbarians bordering on the empire or constantly streaming into it. For it is population which is the absorbing material. It has been said that if Rome could have conquered and civilized the Germans as she had the Gauls, the empire would never have fallen. That is true, but that is exactly what Rome could not do, and found she could not even in the first Christian century. At the Rhine and the Danube, Rome reached not merely the limits of her geographical empire but of the empire of her civilization. The Germans gained immensely from their contact with Rome, but with their advent the current began to flow backward. They rose in civilization far more quickly than they otherwise could have done, but in the process the civilizing force was reduced and greatly diluted, and the civilization of the world was lowered.

Enough has been said to show the direction in which

[1] Transported by the emperor to the region of the Black Sea, they seized upon some ships and made their way through the length of the Mediterranean, attacking cities, and apparently meeting little resistance; finally they passed out into the Atlantic and reached their home in the Rhine valley.

the causes of the fall of the Roman Empire are to be sought, and to show that long study and a full account are necessary to any adequate presentation of them. They lay deep, at the very foundation of society, as is evident from the fact that in periods of tranquillity and apparent strength, as under the good emperors in the second century, or in the fourth century from Constantine to the breaking of the Danube frontier, there was no recovery, no trustworthy return of strength, rather when, at the close of such a period, the real test came, the empire was found to be weaker than before.

I have used throughout the expression "fall of Rome" as a convenient phrase. But if the nature of the disease from which the empire suffered has been correctly indicated, the term is clearly an incorrect one. Rome did not fall. She was overthrown. Her strength was exhausted, but it was the attack which was fatal. But for that she could undoubtedly have recovered. The word overthrown, in turn, conveys too strong an impression. The empire was at the moment empty and the Germans entered in and took possession.

It is, indeed, a serious mistake to regard this revolution exclusively from the standpoint of a "fall," as if it were merely the destruction of the ancient civilization. It was something far more than that.[1] It was the neces-

[1] The continuance of the empire in the East through these early centuries of the middle ages, maintaining a degree of civilization superior to anything in the contemporary West, must not be forgotten. It acted for long generations as a barrier against invasions from the farther East, and upon certain individual features of civilization, especially upon art, it was a direct source of beneficent influence. Mr. Frederic Harrison, in the Rede lecture of Cambridge University for 1900, included in revised form in his *Among My Books* (1912), has stated the case for the "Empire of New Rome" as strongly as the facts will permit. The general impression which the lecture makes concerning the influence of Byzantine civilization upon the West, as distinguished from the statement of specific facts, is, indeed, something of an exaggeration. There are few cases in which the Eastern Empire can be shown to have done more than to preserve and transmit.

sary reorganization and rearrangement preparatory to a new and higher civilization. From this point of view the period of the fall of Rome was an age of progress. It was not merely an age of "fall," but also of conquest, and this fact, along with the establishment of Christianity, is the vitally important fact of these centuries. But it is so because it was something more than a mere conquest. The Germans brought with them race characteristics and ideas and institutions which, though they were those of a primitive people, were noble and well developed, able to enter into a competition with those of a higher civilization on something like equal terms. Add the fact that the Teutonic race became the ruling race of Christendom, and we can understand how it came to be one of the determining sources of our civilization and how the period of the "fall of Rome" is one of the great constructive ages of history.

CHAPTER V

WHAT THE GERMANS ADDED

IN passing to the special consideration of the additions which the Germans made to the ancient civilization, it is necessary to give the first place to what was probably their most valuable contribution, the Germans themselves. This implies not merely that the governments which they set up in the place of the Roman were, in very many cases, an improvement upon the practical anarchy which passed under the name of the empire, and a welcome relief to the provincials, as they were, but also that there was a more permanent influence introduced in the fact that they brought in a young, vigorous, and healthy race to form a considerable element in the population of every European state. It is possible that in some parts of the empire the number of new settlers was not large, and yet it has been said of each of the Latin-speaking countries that it contains districts where the German physical characteristics—light hair and blue eyes—still predominate among the inhabitants and indicate a large Teutonic immigration. The amount of German blood which went to form the modern nations must have been considerable, for we need to add to the invading forces the large numbers settled in the empire earlier as slaves and soldiers. The German was, to be sure, a savage, and it may be that his bringing in brought in also greater ignorance and decline and "darkness" than would otherwise have been; but in the existing conditions this was a necessity, and the results justify the cost. Possibly, as has been intimated, the Roman world might have recovered its strength and entered upon a new age of production without their aid. But had it done so, even more successfully than seems at all probable, the product would have lacked the qualities added by the Germans. The settlement of the Teutonic tribes was not merely the introduction of a new set of ideas and institutions to combine with the old, it was also the introduction of fresh blood and youthful mind, the muscle and the brains which were in the future to do the larger share of the world's work.

Besides the addition of themselves they brought with them, as a decided characteristic of the race, a very high idea of personal independence, of the value and importance of the individual man as compared with the state. This can be seen in the proud spirit of the individual warrior—a characteristic of many barbarian races. It can be seen still more clearly in another characteristic of barbarian races in those crude systems of criminal justice out of which these tribes were just emerging in the migration period. They exhibit the injured man apparently never thinking that the public authority is the proper power to punish the wrong-doer, but taking the punishment into his own hands as the only natural resort in such a case. It can be seen again in the fact that when the state does begin to assume the right to punish crime, it cannot venture to inflict personal chastisement, or to interfere with the liberty of the freeman. It must limit itself to imposing money fines, part of which goes to the injured party as indicative of his rights in the case, and it can be seen finally in the democratic cast of all their earliest governments. The unit of the whole public life is the individual man, not the state.

We have seen in the third chapter how the early Christianity taught a closely related idea; how it proclaimed certain rights and interests of the individual to be far

higher and more important than any duties he could owe
the state. How much the one set of these ideas reinforced
the other it is impossible to say. We can trace their continued influence only by way of inference. Somewhere
between the ancient days and the present the idea of the
relation of the individual to the state has been transformed. In the ancient time the state was an end in and
for itself far more than it has ever been in the modern.
To the Greek or the Roman the state was everything, the
individual comparatively nothing. His domestic and religious life, as well as his political, found their ultimate
object in the state. Now, the state is regarded as a
means rather than an end. Its object is thought to be
to secure for the individual the fullest and freest development possible in a community life, and the state which
secures this with the least governing and the least machinery is held to be the best state. Whether this view
of the state is to be a permanent one or not, even if, as
some vaguely expect, the modern state should be destined
to give way in the end to some more highly organized
form of common action than history has yet known, still
the change which put the modern in the place of the
ancient idea would remain one of the most important
changes in the history of civilization, and the question
of the reasons for it one of the most interesting questions. The natural influence of Christian teaching and
German spirit working together would seem to be to
lead to such a transformation. That they did actually
do so is far easier to assert than to prove. Probably the
most that can be said confidently is this: The idea of
the independence and supreme worth of the individual,
so strongly felt and expressed in the early medieval centuries passes almost wholly out of the consciousness of
the later middle ages except partially upon the political
side where a closely related idea—which grew, in part,
it seems likely, out of this earlier one—finds expression

in feudalism. But, in general, the individual ceases to be the primary element of society and is absorbed, not now in the state, but in the corporation, the guild, the commune, the order, the hierarchy. The revival of the older idea in modern times is to be traced with certainty only to two sources. One is that revolution of the whole intellectual standpoint of the middle ages which was wrought by the Renaissance and the Reformation, recovering Christian as well as classical ideas which had long been lost, emphasizing again the supreme worth of the individual and establishing the right of private judgment. The other is the gradual development of the primitive German institutions into modern free governments. These two together form most important sources of the renewal of the democratic spirit which is so characteristic of our age, and, with that, of the emphasis which we again lay on the individual man and his rights.[1]

Of the new elements introduced by the Germans, whose continued life and influence we can most clearly trace to our own time, the most important were political and institutional.

The Germans were passing at the time of their con-

[1] That this transformation was aided also by economic causes, such, for example, as the influence of the colonies upon the old world, is no doubt true, but it is not possible to do more at present than to point out the probability. Many of the demands of the workman of to-day are manifestly quite as much due to the spread of democratic ideas as to any direct economic cause.

The text refers, of course, to the rights of the individual as expressed in the practical and institutional life of the community rather than in theoretical and speculative treatises. The emphatic and repeated statement of the rights of the individual, as against the ruler, by the Jesuits of the sixteenth century, for instance, was of no value in the historical development of liberty. Undoubtedly the political contrivances by which we secure for the individual the greatest possible freedom under an efficient government are, in the main, the outgrowth of the German institutions which are considered in the following paragraphs. But the question is: What was the original source and whence the constant reinforcement of the spirit which defended and developed these primitive institutions?

tact with the Romans through a stage of political development through which the classical nations had passed
long before. The political arrangements of the primitive
Germans of Tacitus were in many ways very closely like
those of the primitive Greeks of Homer. But in the
case of the Germans the race possessed so solid and conservative a political character, and these primitive institutions had received such definiteness of form that they
were able to survive for centuries the danger of absorption and annihilation which faced them in the more
highly developed Roman institutions, and, through some
channels at least, permanently to influence the public life
of the world. And while the classical nations, starting
from the same beginning, failed to construct successful
and permanent free governments, but ended in a universal despotism in which such of the forms of free government as survived had lost all meaning, in the history
of the Teutonic nations, on the contrary, the experience
of absolute monarchy, through which the germs of liberty
were destined to pass, did not destroy their life or more
than temporarily check their growth.

It may be said in general that the Germans brought
in some of the more important of the elements out of
which the intervening centuries have developed modern
free constitutional governments. But these elements are
to be recognized as clearly democratic much more plainly
in the Germany of Tacitus than in the states which were
established on Roman soil. It is evident that the conquest exposed them to a double danger. In the first
place, in those countries where the Germans settled down
in the midst of a Roman population they were exposed
to the example of the Roman government and to the influence of the Roman state machinery, important parts of
which were often allowed to continue in operation at least
for a time, both these tending to impress on the barbarian
ruler the value of centralization and absolutism. The

importance of this influence has been disputed by some
scholars, but impartial investigation leaves no doubt that
due to the Roman example there was a strong tendency
to increase the power of the king at the expense of the
people. In the second place, the influence of the conquest itself was in the same direction. It exposed the
tribe to greater dangers than it had ever before experi-
enced, it planted it in the midst of a conquered population more numerous than itself, it demanded that the
whole power of the state should be wielded by a single
will and to a single purpose. The tendency of dangerous
crises in the life even of the freest nation is towards centralization. This result is seen everywhere in these new
states, with especial clearness in the case of the Anglo-
Saxons, where the first-mentioned cause—the Roman
example—had no opportunity to work. The fact must
therefore be distinctly recognized that the first development which these German institutions underwent was
away from liberty and towards absolutism.

Of these original institutions three are of especial importance and interest in their bearing upon later times,
and these are selected for specific notice.

First, the public assemblies. The early Germans had
assemblies of two grades. The highest in grade was the
assembly of all the freemen of the tribe, according to
Tacitus, which we may call the tribal or national assembly.
This possessed distinct legislative rights, like a market
democracy, at least so much as a right of decision for or
against important measures submitted to it by a smaller
council of elders or chiefs. In it were elected the kings,
when necessary, and the chiefs of the smaller districts,
and it also acted on occasion as a judicial tribunal for the
hearing and decision of such cases as might be brought
before it. It would seem as if this assembly would furnish a most promising beginning, which ought to grow
into a free and national system of legislation. As a matter

of fact it did not. The national assembly was one of the earliest victims of the centralizing tendency, and everywhere sank into a mere form or entirely disappeared. This was as true of England as of any continental state, and though it is probable that the smaller assembly of chiefs, the *concilium principum*, which accompanied the national assembly, remained through the successive changes of government and of its own composition until it grew into the House of Lords, even this is not perfectly certain. It is, however, for our present purpose, a matter of no importance whether it did or not, for, whatever its origin, the assembly of notables under the Norman and early Angevin kings was no longer in any sense a public assembly, nor did it have in any true sense a representative character or independent legislative power.

The origin of the modern representative system cannot be determined with any certainty, but for any possible early source we must turn to the assemblies of the second grade in the original German states. In these the freemen of the smaller locality—the hundred or canton —came together in a public meeting which possessed, no doubt, legislative power over matters purely local, but whose most important function seems to have been judicial—a local court, presided over by a chief, who announced the verdict, which, however, derived its validity from the decision of the assembly, or, in later times, of a number of their body appointed to act for the whole. These local courts, probably, as has been suggested,[1] because of the comparatively restricted character of the powers which they possessed, were destined to a long life. On the Continent they lasted until the very end of the middle ages, when they were generally overthrown by the introduction of the Roman law, too highly scientific for their simple methods. In England they lasted

[1] Stubbs, *Constitutional History of England*, vol. I, p. 92.

until they furnished the model, and possibly the suggestion, for a far more important institution—the House of Commons. How many grades of these local courts there were on the continent below the national assembly is a matter of dispute. In England there was in the later days of the Saxon state a series of three. The lowest was the township assembly, concerned only with matters of very slight importance and surviving still in the English vestry meeting and the New England town meeting.[1] Above this was the hundred's court into which entered, at least in early Norman times, a distinctly representative element, the assembly containing, together with other men, four representatives sent from certain townships. Then, third, the tribal assembly of the original little settlement, or the small kingdom of the early conquest, seems to have survived when this kingdom was swallowed up in a larger one, and to have originated a new grade in the hierarchy of assemblies, the county assembly or shire court. At any rate, whatever may have been its origin, and whatever may be the final decision of the vigorously disputed question, whether in the Frankish state there were any assemblies or courts for the counties distinct from the courts of the hundreds, it is certain that courts of this grade came into existence in England and were of the utmost importance there. In them, too, the representative principle was expressed, townships of the shire being represented, as in the hundred's court, by four chosen representatives. These courts, also, passed essentially unchanged through the English feudal and absolutist period, at least into the second half of the thirteenth century, maintaining local self-government and

---

[1] There may be a question as to how strongly this connection between the New England town meeting and the local assembly of the primitive Germans should be asserted, because of the lack of direct evidence for some of the intermediate links. But while this want of evidence, in exact documentary shape, must be admitted, it is certainly hypercriticism to refuse, in consequence, to admit the overwhelming probability of such a connection.

preserving more of the primitive freedom than survived elsewhere. It is possible at a later time that the representative principle originating in them was transferred to the national legislature, creating our modern national representative system—the most important single contribution to the machinery of government made in historic times, with the possible exception of federal government.

The first of the special political elements brought in by the Germans is, then, the public assembly, the original germ from which our modern free legislatures may have grown.

The second one of these special elements to be noticed is the elective monarchy. The freemen of all the early German tribes clearly possessed, or had at one time possessed, the right of electing their king. In all these tribes, however, the tendency was just as clearly towards the establishment of hereditary succession. It depended entirely upon the special circumstances of each case whether the forms of an election, preserved everywhere for a considerable time, sank into mere forms without meaning, and finally out of sight, or whether they retained life and meaning and became recognized as constitutional.

In Germany an accidental circumstance—the fact that no dynasty lasted for more than three or four generations—kept alive the principle of election until it resulted in a real elective monarchy; but, owing to another circumstance—the loss on the part of the royal power itself of all control over the state—this fact had no valuable results for liberty. In France an accidental circumstance again—the fact that for more than three hundred years after the election of the Capetian family to the throne, it never lacked a direct male heir, had the opposite result, and the principle of election passed entirely out of sight and the monarchy became strictly hereditary. In England the monarchy also became, in time, strictly hereditary, and the original right of election disappeared. But the principle did not pass entirely out of remembrance, and later, though with no apparent connection with the earlier principle, a series of doubtful successions and of depositions created a new elective right, or what is far more important, its corollary, the right of the people to depose an unsatisfactory king and put another in his place. An idea of this kind, but plainly feudal in origin, seems to have been recognized by some, at least in the contest for the crown between Stephen and Matilda, towards the middle of the twelfth century; less consciously in the deposition of Edward II in 1327; more clearly in the case of Richard II in 1399, and at the end of the Yorkist line in 1485, in both these cases the rightful heirs being set aside in favor of others. It came to the fullest consciousness and the clearest expression in the Revolution of 1688, and in the accession of the House of Hanover in 1715. These cases established definitely in the British Constitution the principle that the sovereign obtains his right to rule from the consent of the people, and this has been distinctly recognized by the princes of the House of Hanover. It will be seen at once that this is a vitally important principle if a monarchy is to be transformed into what is virtually a republican government. Without the clear recognition of this principle, explicitly or implicitly, by the reigning sovereign, it would be impossible to continue a historic line of kings at the head of a republic, the object which is sought, and more or less completely secured, by all modern constitutional monarchies.[1]

[1] That this principle has no immediate bearing on the Constitution of the United States is evident. But if we turn back to 1776 it may be clearly seen that it was regarded as one of the most important principles which justified the Revolution. The Declaration of Independence, after enumerating the acts of tyranny on the part of the king, says: "A Prince whose character is thus marked by every act which may define a Tyrant, is unfit to be the ruler of a free People." This sentence states explicitly the fact

The third element of free government originating with the Germans was an independent or self-developing system of law. The law systems of all the Germans at the time of the invasion were very crude, both in the law itself and in the method of its enforcement, but they were all characterized alike by this fact that the law was ascertained, defined, and declared by the courts, or, in other words, since the courts were public assemblies, by the people themselves. It follows necessarily from this that the courts, by establishing precedents, by declaring customs which had grown up in the community to have the force of law, and by applying the common judgment and sense of justice of the people to new cases, as they arose, were constantly enlarging the body of the law and building up by a natural process of growth a great body of customary or common law—unwritten law. The importance of this practice as an element of liberty does not consist in the law itself which is created in this way. That is apt to be unscientific and experimental. It consists in the fact that the law is not imposed upon the people by a power outside itself, and declared and enforced by a series of irresponsible agents, but that the people themselves make it and also interpret, modify, and enforce it. This practice continued in vigorous life

that a free people may have a king, and with equal clearness the principle that if he is unfit he may be set aside. It is worthy of notice that, in that part of the Declaration which is really Anglo-Saxon in origin and spirit, this is the only statement made of any principle which justifies the Revolution, the body of the Declaration consists of evidence to prove the unfitness asserted.

It will be noticed that this special Anglo-Saxon principle is only a form of the broader right of revolution. The historical line sketched above merely represents the channel through which the race has been brought to a practical consciousness of the broader principle. Its peculiar historical significance, however, does not lie in that fact, since the race must inevitably have become conscious, as all races have, of the right of revolution. It lies in the fact that it has led to the formation of a constitutional theory in monarchical states, which if cordially accepted by the sovereign, tends to do away with the necessity of revolution.

in the continental states much longer than any other of
the specific institutions mentioned, and, together with the
popular courts which gave it expression, preserved some
remains of freedom long after it had entirely disappeared
from every other part of the state. In the last part of
the middle ages the adoption of the Roman law, and the
system of scientific jurisprudence which that law fostered,
practically destroyed on the Continent these self-developing bodies of law.[1] When the control of the courts
passed into the hands of men trained to regard the Roman
law as their only model, and when the Roman-law maxim,
Quod principi placuit legis habet vigorem was adopted by
the newly formed nations, and became a native maxim,
as in the French, *Si veut le roi, si veut la loi*, then the
control of the people over the law had ceased, and all
law-making power had been centred in the sovereign.
In England this revolution never took place. The common law has continued to develop in the same natural
way, though by a somewhat different process, through
every generation of its history, and, however seriously
at any point the native principles may have been modified by the introduction of foreign ideas and doctrines of
law, such modification has never been of a character to
check for a moment the natural growth of the common
law, or to deprive it of its independence of the executive
and legislative branches of government, which are the

---

[1] The Roman law did not everywhere take the place of the customary
law as the sole law of the community. In many places the customary law
remained as the prevailing local law. But it ceased to grow. The principle was generally admitted that in new cases for which the customary
law did not provide, recourse should be had to the Roman law, and the
customary law itself was reduced to written and more scientific shape under
the influence of the lawyers. Nor should it be understood that the Germanic law made no permanent contributions to the details of the law in
those places where it was on the whole supplanted by the Roman law. A
specific history of law would show that these contributions were numerous
and important even in directions where the Roman law was very highly
developed.

vitally important points.[1] It is at this moment, in every
quarter of the Anglo-Saxon world, and in the midst of a
thousand new conditions of social and geographical environment, as vigorous and creative a part of the nation's
life as ever in the past, and one of the most important
processes of our free self-government.[2] In the United
States the existence of a written constitution, as fundamental law, setting bounds to the action of the national
legislature, has led to a most important and valuable
extension of this principle in the power which the courts
have assumed, without expressed sanction, to declare a
law regularly passed by the national legislature unconstitutional and therefore null and void. This practice
will also be adopted in some form, almost of necessity,
by British courts in dealing with acts passed by an Irish
Parliament if one should be established by an imperial
statute limiting its legislative powers.

These three institutions, though by no means covering
every detail which might be mentioned, are the most
important political elements brought into modern civi-

---

[1] That the common law has been radically revolutionized by statute on
some subjects in very recent times, as, for example, in real-estate law, is
not an evidence of the decline of this self-developing power. It is rather
due to the rapid and revolutionary change in society itself, which demands
equally rapid and revolutionary change in the law to accompany it. The
statutes themselves are subjected at once to the ordinary process of com-
mon-law development in the interpretation and application of them made
by the courts.

[2] It is the habit of German students of law to say hard things of the
English common law. They call it confused and unscientific and full of
repetitions and contradictory. And it must be acknowledged that these
things are to some extent true. But there is no doubt that precisely the
same things could have been said with equal justice of the Roman law during the ages of its growth, and it is well to remember that, as the Roman
law took on a more scientific form, and was reduced to an organized system,
its life and power of growth ceased. History does not show any necessary
connection between these two events; but certainly, if the formation of a
scientific system on the basis of the English common law is to mean that our
law and institution-making power is past, then every Anglo-Saxon may
most heartily pray that our law may long remain unscientific.

lization by the German race. The great system of free self-government which the Anglo-Saxons have built upon this foundation is making the conquest of the world. After much experimenting in other directions under the lead of the French, all the modern nations which have adopted constitutional government are returning to the Anglo-Saxon model as expressed either in England or in the United States, making such modifications of type as local necessities, or local prejudices not yet overcome, may require. That the political future of the world belongs to Anglo-Saxon institutions seems assured.[1]

One other specific institution of the early Germans deserves a passing notice in this chapter because of its later influence. That is the *comitatus*—the band of young warriors who were bound by an especially strong bond of fidelity to the service of a chief, were maintained by him, and followed him to war. It was formerly supposed that this institution gave rise to the feudal system. The German chief, it was thought, taking the lands which fell to him in the conquest, divided them among the members of his *comitatus*, and, because they remained under the same bond of fidelity to him, as their lord, after they had received their land, the feudal system was created at once. But great institutions like feudalism are never struck out at a single blow, and this theory of its origin was long ago abandoned by continental scholars though living on in English books. We shall find, later on, an important influ-

---

[1] That one not infrequently hears among the Germans to-day most vigorous denial of their great indebtedness to Anglo-Saxon institutions is one characteristic of the temporary phase of growth through which Germany is just now passing, and which affords a most interesting study to the student of comparative politics. It is a symptom of the same sort as the sneer at parliamentary government which may occasionally be heard from German university platforms, one among several traits, so keenly noted by Lieber in the France of the Second Empire, in his *Civil Liberty and Self-Government*, which may now be found with equal clearness in Germany.

ence which the *comitatus* exercised upon feudalism in some
points of detail, but it is not one of the sources from
which the larger institutional features of the feudal system arose.

Much has also been written upon the influence of certain special ideas held by the early Germans, such as their
theological and ethical ideas and their high regard for
woman, much more indeed than the facts will warrant.

That they had a high respect for woman as compared
with that of the classical world of their time is undoubted,
but it does not seem to have been higher than that of
Aryan races in general—the classical nations themselves
—when in the same stage of civilization, and in general
it is sufficient to refer to what has been said on the subject in the chapter on the influence of Christianity.

Of the influence of their ethical notions and of their
somewhat lofty conception of God, the most that can be
affirmed with any certainty is, that they had ideas which
would make the Christian teachings seem not altogether
foreign to them, and which very possibly made easy the
transition to Christianity.   Even such a statement as this
is, however, an inference from the apparent nature of the
case, rather than from the recorded facts, and that these
ideas led them to any more perfect understanding of
Christianity, or to any more sympathetic development
of it, than would have been the case without them, is a
theory without historical support.

The coming in of the Germans brought face to face
the four chief elements of our civilization: the Greek
with its art and science, much of it for the time forgotten;
the Roman with its political institutions and legal ideas,
and furnishing the empire as the common ground upon
which all stood; the Christian with its religious and moral
ideas;   and the German with other political and legal
ideas, and with a reinforcement of fresh blood and life.

By the end of the sixth century these all existed side by side in the nominal Roman Empire. It was the work of the remaining centuries of the middle ages to unite them into a single organic whole—the groundwork of modern civilization.

But the introduction of the last element, the Germans, was a conquest—a conquest rendered possible by the inability of the old civilization any longer to defend itself against their attack. It is one of the miracles of history that such a conquest should have occurred, the violent occupation of the empire by the invasion of an inferior race, with so little destruction of civilization, with so complete an absorption, in the end, of the conqueror by the conquered. That there was loss of civilization is not denied. The general average was greatly lowered. The centuries that follow were in some ways the "dark ages." But the strange thing is that, considering what happened, the darkness was not deeper and that the recovery was so complete. It must be possible to point out some reasons why the conquest of the ancient world by the Germans was so little what might be expected.

In a single word, the reason is to be found in the impression which the world they had conquered made upon the Germans. They conquered it, and they treated it as a conquered world. They destroyed and plundered what they pleased, and it was not a little. They took possession of the land and they set up their own tribal governments in place of the Roman. And yet they recognized, in a way, even the worst of them, their inferiority to the people they had overcome. They found upon every side of them evidences of a command over nature such as they had never acquired: cities, buildings, roads, bridges, and ships; wealth and art, skill in mechanics and skill in government, the like of which they had never known; ideas firmly held that the Roman system of things was divinely ordained and eternal; a church strongly organized and with an imposing ceremonial, officered by venerable and saintly men, and speaking with an overpowering positiveness and an awful authority that did not yield before the strongest barbarian king. The impression which these things made upon the mind of the German must have been profound. In no other way can the result be accounted for. Their conquest was a physical conquest, and as a physical conquest it was complete, but it scarcely went farther. In government and law there was little change for the Roman; in religion and language, none at all. Other things, schools and commercial arrangements for instance, the Germans would have been glad to maintain at the Roman level if they had known how. Half unconsciously they adopted the belief in the divinely founded and eternal empire, and in a vague way recognized its continuance after they had overthrown it. As time went on, and they identified themselves more closely still with the people, ideas, and institutions of the old civilization, their belief in the permanence of the empire became more clear, and furnished the foundation for the Roman Empire of Charlemagne, and for the Holy Roman Empire to which that led, a strong influence for unity in the most chaotic portion of medieval history.

If from one point of view, it seems strange that so much that was Roman remained, looked at from the side of the superiority of the ancient civilization and the evident impression which it made upon the Germans, it seems strange, in turn, that so much that was German survived. It is one of the most fundamental facts of the history of civilization that this was a union upon fairly equal terms of German and Roman to form a new whole and to begin a new progress.

Having now brought together all the chief elements of medieval history, we have next to take up the first great movement which properly belongs to that history itself in so far as the introduction of the Germans is not to be so described—the transformation of the primitive Christian organization into a monarchical church.

CHAPTER VI

THE FORMATION OF THE PAPACY

THE centuries whose outline we have been studying were dark and despairing centuries for the patriotic Roman. It seemed as if the world was falling to ruin around him. Calamity followed calamity in quick succession. Pestilence, famine, earthquake, rebellion, and invasion trod one upon the heels of the other without cessation. The world was coming to an end. He could not see as we can now see that the foundations were being laid for new states greater than his own, and that the life-giving elements of a new and higher civilization were being added to the old. He could see only what was manifestly true, that the greatest political power of history was passing away.

But not all the ancient society shared this feeling of despair. A considerable body of Roman citizens looked to the future with hope, and had no fear that all that men had gained would be lost, and they, as well as the Germans, were laying new foundations, broad and strong, for the future to build upon. We have examined the early history of the Christian church, its slight beginning, its conflict with paganism, and its final victory, and the new ideas which it introduced. But the history of the early church as a religion is only a small part of its history. Upon the foundation offered by the simple and scarcely organized society of the pentecostal days was gradually constructed, by the operation of causes far different from any contained in the four gospels, the most

permanent and most powerful organization of history—
the Roman church. During all the dark days of the
German settlement and of the confused political conditions which followed, it was the most effective preservative and assimilative force at work, and while all the
other great creations of the middle ages—the Holy
Roman Empire and the feudal system—have passed away
leaving only shadowy remains behind them, it has continued down into our own times, a world-embracing
power of great and living influence, notwithstanding the
loss of much to which it once laid claim. It is then a
matter of the utmost importance in the history of civilization to trace the steps by which the primitive church,
as the New Testament describes it, was transformed into
this vast and highly perfected "work of human policy,"
as Macaulay justly called it.

Into the question of the origin of the episcopate, belonging to the history of the primitive church, I shall
not go. Suffice it to say that, however simply and
loosely organized the primitive church may have been,
by the time of the conversion of Constantine the principal causes were already at work which transformed it
into a hierarchical organization, and their results were
already plainly manifest in the growing separation of
clergy from laity as a different body with distinct rights
and privileges, and divided within itself into various
grades of rank and power. It will be the work of this
chapter to trace the further operation of these and other
causes which transformed this organization of the early
fourth century, more aristocratic than monarchical in
character at that point, into the theocratic absolutism of
later times. The process was not complete in the period
which falls within the chapter, but it was so fully under
way that only some revolutionary change of direction in
the currents of history could have prevented its accomplishment.

As, according to the most probable view, one of the
clergy of a city had been able to create a power over the
others, and give rise to the office of bishop, in its later
meaning, so it was natural that the next step in logical
order should be taken, and the bishop of the most important or capital city of a province should extend his
power over the other bishops of the province and create
the office of archbishop. One more step, equally logical,
remained to be taken when the bishop of the greatest
city of a large region—Alexandria or Antioch—or of the
capital city of the empire, should create a power over
archbishops and bishops alike, and found an ecclesiastical
monarchy.

This indicates, however, only a general tendency. It
tells us nothing of the causes which enabled the forming
constitution actually to take the direction which this tendency indicated. Had not the circumstances of the time
favored growth along this line, these beginnings, however
promising and apparently natural, could have led to no
result. It is, then, to the favoring circumstances, all
seeming to conspire together to cherish this natural tendency, to the conditions in which this growing church
constitution was placed, that we must turn to ascertain
the real causes of the monarchical government which
resulted.

In beginning a study of these causes it is necessary,
before all else, to fix clearly in mind the fact that the
Christian religion was not one of them. There is no one
form of government or organization to which, as a religion, it directly leads.

It is, indeed, a thing most vitally important, here and
throughout the whole course of history, that the church
should be distinguished from Christianity. Connected
with the history of this religion there are three totally
distinct things, each finding its beginning, its opportu-

nity to grow, in the earliest Christianity, but each produced by a totally different set of causes and having an almost wholly independent life, a life at any rate in no way necessarily controlled by either of the others.

One of these is Christianity considered as a religion simply; that personal faith in, and love for, a divine Saviour and a divine Father by him revealed which brings the individual into conscious unity with God, and becomes for him an unequalled help in right living; that personal faith which exists apparently with equal perfection and equally complete results under every ecclesiastical system and in connection with every form of dogmatic belief. That such a power exists and that such results follow from these causes is manifest from an overwhelming abundance of evidence to any student of historical details, whatever bitter hatred or murderous cruelty may have grown out of theological differences, or whatever lying trickery out of ecclesiastical strife.

The second of these is the church as an organization, an ecclesiastical system, a governmental or political institution. Based upon a body of people who profess the Christian religion, it is nevertheless an outgrowth of their political, legal, organizing instincts, and not of anything whatever connected with the religion as a religion. It would seem as if this must be entirely clear to any one who remembers how perfectly the same religious life has shown itself, the same religious results have been achieved, under the most widely varying forms of organization possible to thought. Xavier and Wesley and Woolman, whatever faults of character or of temperament remained unsubdued, are all alike instances of the transforming and inspiring power of the same single force.

The third is the dogmatic system, the body of theological beliefs of a given age or people. Based again on the primary facts of the Christian religion, it is not created or rendered necessary in the least by anything connected

with that religion as religion merely, but is an outgrowth
wholly of the scientific instinct, of the natural and inevitable attempt of the mind to explain these primary facts,
and to construct the explanations made into a reasonable
and logical system. These explanatory theories differ
very widely from one another, as it is necessary that they
should, since they are formed under varying philosophical
preconceptions, and the varying conditions of different
ages and different races, but these differences of scientific
system do not in the slightest degree imply any difference
in the primary facts and experiences whose explanation
is attempted. It is an incontestable fact that many a
bloody civil war has been fought between Christian sects
who did not differ from one another upon any essential
religious truth whatever. In the weakness of their not
yet wholly civilized or Christianized human nature their
varying explanations seemed to them as vitally important
as the fundamental fact itself which they were attempting to explain, and so they burned and tortured to save
men's souls.

These dogmatic systems and these ecclesiastical systems both grow out of necessities of human nature. The
mind must seek some philosophical explanation for familiar facts, and a group of people influenced by the same
desires and motives must take upon themselves that form
of organization which seems to them the most natural.
But neither the dogmatic system, nor the ecclesiastical
system, of any given time or place, is Christianity. The
causes which have created the one are not those which
have created the other, and the one set of causes must
not be held responsible for results which have followed
from the other. So completely indispensable is this distinction that absolutely no trustworthy reasoning about
Christian history is possible if it is lost sight of; causes
and effects become inextricably confused, and wholly unnecessary blundering and bitter controversy have often
been the result.

These truths may be said to be commonplaces of the best religious thinking of to-day, but they have been so constantly disregarded in historical study and writing that they ought to be emphasized even at the expense of repetition.

Of the direct causes which did further the tendency already begun in the church towards a monarchical constitution, the most potent and effective may be brought under two heads—the change which took place in the popular understanding of Christianity itself, and the influence of Rome.

For the first two centuries Christianity had continued to be, comparatively speaking, the simple and spiritual religion of its primitive days. Two very serious attempts had been made to change its character, but without success. One of these had been an attempt to unite the old Jewish system with it, and if not to compel the Gentile Christian to become almost a Jew, at least to compel Christianity to adopt some of the characteristic forms and ideas of Judaism. We can discern evidences of this struggle between the new and the old in the New Testament. The other was an attempt to engraft upon Christianity certain speculations of oriental philosophy concerning the nature of the supernatural and the order of the universe. This gave rise to the heresy known as Gnosticism and to a long and severe contest, ending, as the earlier strife had done, in the preservation in all essential points of the primitive Christianity.

In the meantime there was developing, from the very slight beginnings of the early days, a theological system and a ritual. In both these directions these first two attempts to change the character of Christianity had great influence. Every heresy which was strong enough to offer battle had a decided effect upon the growth of theology by compelling greater definiteness of belief and clearness of statement.

Much the most powerful force, however, in transforming the slender theological stock of the primitive documents into a vast and complex dogmatic system was the Greek philosophy. The speculative instinct of the Greek would not allow him to rest in the few simple facts which Christianity taught. The questions which those facts raise in every thinking mind, he must attempt to solve, and in doing so it is his philosophizing genius and his already formed philosophy which he calls to his aid. By the time of the conversion of Constantine this theological system had assumed large proportions, and some of its most recondite problems were already under discussion.

But notwithstanding all these attacks upon it, and additions to it from outside sources, the Christian religion had remained until towards the middle of the third century essentially unchanged. Men came into it because it answered their religious needs, and at some cost to themselves of difficulty and danger, and its power over them was that of a spiritual faith.

But when the Christian church began to grow rapidly, and its social standing to improve, and when priests and bishops began to hold positions of influence and power and to manage considerable financial interests, then men began to come into it from other motives than conviction—because it was fashionable, or because its offices were attractive to the ambitious. When Christianity became the religion of the court and of the state this tendency was greatly increased. Masses of men passed in name over into Christianity with no understanding of what it was, bringing with them the crude religious conceptions and practices of paganism, unable to understand the spiritual truths of Christianity and with no share in the inner spiritual life of the Christian.

The result could easily be predicted. No system—religious, political, or philosophical—could survive the invasion of so much alien material not in harmony with its fundamental teachings without serious loss. It was unavoidable that Christianity should decline towards the pagan level. It is not easy under any circumstances to keep alive a keen perception of higher spiritual truths in the mass of mankind. In such circumstances as these it was entirely impossible, and though perhaps never lost sight of by the better spirits, these truths gradually passed out of the popular religious consciousness, and their place was taken by something easier to understand, and answering to a lower religious need.

The clearest illustration, probably, of this paganizing process is the introduction of the worship of saints. The pagan, trained in polytheistic notions, having a separate divinity for every interest of life, found the Christian monotheistic idea hard to understand. The one only God seemed to him far off and cold, hard to reach with the prayers of a mere man. He felt the necessity of putting in between himself and God the nearer and more human subordinate divinities who had been made familiar to him by his earlier religion, and who seemed to him easier of access. And so he created a Christian polythe ism, partly by putting some holy man of the past in the place of the pagan divinity, assigning to him the special guardianship of the same interest or locality, sometimes, as we can now see, actually translating the pagan divinity himself into a Christian saint.

This process was no doubt aided by the general barbarization of the Roman society which was going on at the same time, and which shows itself in language and art and military tactics, and in almost every direction; but it affected Christianity chiefly through the mass of really unchristianized material which entered the church. The resulting product had undoubtedly an immensely elevating and purifying effect on the paganism of the empire. The truths taught through it, and held in mind by means of it, were higher and better than anything in the old system. It furnished, very possibly, the only practicable road by which the mass of the people could pass to an understanding of the more perfect ideas which they needed to learn, and the Catholic church has not been without a plausible defence for very similar practices, adopted more consciously and at a later date, in the conversion of pagan nations. But notwithstanding all this, it denoted a very decided change to a lower level in the popular understanding of Christianity.

While, however, the introduction of the worship of saints is a striking illustration of this paganization of Christianity, another result of it was much more important in the development of the constitution of the church, that result which is called the "externalizing" of Christianity—its transformation from a religion of the spirit into a religion of externals.

In the place of the inner spiritual life, as the determining characteristic of the Christian, were placed, more and more as the spiritual side was lost sight of, forms and intellectual beliefs and membership in a visible church. If one accepted the theology of the church, and conformed to its regulations, and was in regular standing in some orthodox local church, he was a Christian. If he refused to accept some point of the theology and was cast out of the church, or if for any reason he was not to be found within its recognized visible membership, then he was not a Christian, no matter what profession he might make.[1] Such tests as these were much easier to understand and to apply than the older spiritual conceptions.

---

[1] "Do they who are met together outside the church of Christ think that Christ is with them when they have met? Even if such persons may have been put to death in confession of the Name, this stain is not washed away by their blood. . . . It is not possible for one to be a martyr who is not in the church. . . . They cannot abide with God who are unwilling to be in concord with the church."—St. Cyprian of Carthage, *De Cath. Eccl. Unitate*, chaps. 13 and 14.

It may be difficult to see, as some have suggested, how Christianity could have been preserved at all, during the ages which were to follow, without this compact organization, and without this great body of theology, esteemed so vitally important as to be maintained at all hazards, and, because it was purely intellectual, far more easily retained in times of general decline than the deeper spiritual truths of religion. But the whole effect was to transform Christianity in the world into a definite, visible body, sharply defined from non-Christians and from heretics, distinguished everywhere by the same external, easily recognized signs and marks, its members readily counted and measured.

When the idea of such a distinct unity came to prevail, and when it had begun to express itself in the use of common ceremonies and a common creed, made with great care to conform to the recognized standards, it was perfectly natural, inevitable indeed, that a further step should be taken, that the mere fact of the formation to such an extent of a universal community, should become itself a most powerful force in creating a community of law and administration; in forming, in other words, a common ecclesiastical government which should correspond to and guard and regulate the community of ceremonies and doctrines already formed. The constant appeal to an ideal unity tended strongly to create a real one.

The second of the two great causes which led to the formation of the monarchical church was Rome—the group of influences and ideas which grew out of the history and position of Rome and the Roman Empire. So decisive and controlling are these ideas and influences, when taken together, that we may say that without them the monarchical church would never have existed.

In the first place, Rome was the capital of the political world. What could be more natural than that it should be looked upon also as the religious capital of the world.

The fact that he was the bishop of the actual capital city was perhaps the most important cause which established the power of the patriarch of Constantinople over the East. But even after the establishment of Constantinople Rome continued to be looked upon as in some especial sense the central city and capital of the world, and the feeling which had helped the bishop of Constantinople was a much greater aid to the bishop of Rome, though he may himself have declined to admit the fact.

In the second place, the Roman imperialism was the only constitutional model which the early church had before it. As it began to grow into a common organization of widely separated provinces, it could hardly do otherwise than to take the shape of the only government of that sort which the world had known, and to copy not merely names, like diocese, but also offices and methods. It is an interesting fact, however, that this copying was by no means slavish, but along with it a free political genius was also at work, inventing new institutions for new needs, as is seen, at least in its more characteristic features, in the important evolution of the church council.

Again, in the third place, just as the ancient Greek philosophic spirit awoke to a new life and power in developing the theological system of the early church, so also the old Roman genius for political organization and rule found a new field for its activity, and a new empire to found in the creation of the papacy. There was no longer any opportunity for it in the political sphere. Its work was finished there, but in the history of the Western church there was a succession of great spirits, men of imperial ideas and genius, which recalls the line of statesmen of earlier Roman days, and accomplished a similar work. Julius, Innocent, Leo, and Gregory, each the first of his name, bishops of Rome, and Ambrose, bishop of Milan, are examples, only, of the men who, whether the opportunity which was offered them to advance the power of their office and to create definite constitutional precedents was large or small, saw in it its fullest possibilities and used it for the utmost gain. It was in the minds of these men, and in the atmosphere of Rome, where every influence was of empire and all the traditions imperial, that the idea first took shape that the one great church should find its head, its divinely ordained primate, in the bishop of Rome; vaguely at first, no doubt, and with slowly growing consciousness, but definitely enough to form a consistent working model, through all the varying circumstances of their different reigns.

Under this head also should be included the legal tendency of the Roman mind. To this more than to anything else is due the creation of a great body of theology suited in character to the Western mind—a system not so finely speculative as the Eastern, but practical and legal and clearly systematic. This gave to the West, as a defining and organizing core, a body of doctrines of its own, independent of the Eastern, and tended to give it, also, a secure position as a separate church organization. The genius, indeed, of its great constructive theologian, St. Augustine, one of the greatest names in the intellectual history of the world, surpasses even the genius of its great constructive pontiffs. It was his work to give to the Western church, just beginning to take on its separate existence, the crystallizing body of thought which it needed to put into definite and scientific statement the things for which it stood and which gave it distinctive existence. The church did not remain true to all the teachings of St. Augustine, but the influence of his theology in the formative age of the Roman church may easily be inferred from the strong constructive influence which it exerted in a later and more familiar age when ecclesiastical organizations were again taking shape—in the age of the Reformation.

Again, the idea of the divinely founded and eternal

empire of Rome was a most potent influence. In the
pagan mind this idea had been formed under the influence of the widely extended conquests of Rome, doubtless as a vague reaching after a reasonable explanation
of such wonderful successes and such an unparalleled
power. This idea the Christians also had taken up and
transformed into a still wider conception, adding to it
that idea which they held so strongly of the growing
kingdom of Christ which was to fill the whole world.
In doing so, they made it the foundation of what has
been called justly, at least so far as definiteness of conception goes, the first philosophy of history.[1] Rome was
for the Christian, as for the pagan, 'a divinely founded
empire and destined to be eternal. The one God, however, took the place of the pagan divinities as the divine
architect, and his final purpose was to be found, the
Christian believed, not in a great political empire but in the
one great spiritual and religious unity of the world which
that political empire had rendered possible. Rome prepared the way for and prefigured the kingdom of Christ.

The influence of this conception upon the idea of the
Christian church, as forming a world-embracing unity
organized into one united government, can hardly be
overstated. The fact that we may now be able to put
the thought into more definite language than even St.
Augustine in any single passage, is no evidence that its
influence was not profound, and there can be no doubt
but that this "idea of Rome" was one of the most powerful forces in creating that conception of a necessary

---

[1] St. Augustine's idea of the two cities, the two opposed commonwealths
continuing through history, the city of God or of righteousness, and the
city of Satan or of wickedness, is a clearly conceived philosophy of history,
and one which still retains its hold, even literally, in the form in which he
stated it, over many minds. It needs, indeed, but very little modification
of terms and definitions, but little variation in description of the eternal
conflict between good and evil, to be accepted, as a fairly correct description of what history is, by one who holds any of the modern theories.

church unity in belief and organization which is one of the corner-stones, the one essential foundation, indeed, of the Roman Catholic monarchy.

There ought to be mentioned, perhaps, in close connection with this idea of the divine purpose in history, though it cannot be clearly proved to be an outgrowth of it, the belief which grew up in the church, of the position assigned to the Apostle Peter. The more or less conscious belief in a necessary church unity must certainly have been wide-spread before any such idea could have been formed regarding him, but when it had once taken shape it became a most efficient influence in creating an actual unity and making Rome its centre. It is hard, in the absence of decisive historical evidence, to avoid the conclusion that the belief that Rome was destined by Providence to be the religious capital of the world, was the sole basis of the tradition that Peter was bishop of Rome.[1] The two lines of belief certainly ran together as may be indicated in this way: A literal interpretation of certain passages in the New Testament appears to indicate that Christ gave to Peter authority over the other apostles; therefore Peter's church would have authority over other churches. But the divine plan of history makes Rome the political capital of all the world; therefore it was the divine purpose, since the political exists for the sake of the religious, that Rome should be the world's religious capital. So Peter, the prince of the apostles, founds his church in Rome, the capital city, and by Christ's direct authority and by the evident divine plan of history the Roman church is supreme over all other churches.

This argument was undoubtedly first developed in a purely theoretical form against heretics and separatists, as in the treatise of Cyprian of Carthage already quoted.

[1] See, however, the strong argument in favor of the tradition in Ramsay's *The Church in the Roman Empire before A. D. 170.* London, 1893.

Christ gave to Peter an ideal supremacy over the other
apostles as a symbol of the great truth which he taught
in so many forms that the spiritual kingdom which he
founded should remain one and indivisible. But it was
impossible that the idea once formed should remain
merely theoretical. As the monarchical constitution
began to take shape, it must itself become an actual
ground of belief that such a constitution was divinely
ordained, and, with the change in the general conception
of Christianity which has been noticed from the spiritual
to the external, the appeal to the actual and visible organization as an evidence of the divine intention would
be an exceedingly strong argument.

In many directions the special situation of the Roman
church and its peculiar characteristics were of very great
value in extending its influence, and finally in establishing its supremacy.

It was situated in the only great city of the West.
There were in the West no cities like Alexandria and Antioch in the East, natural capitals of great geographical
divisions of the empire, whose bishops would be tempted
to cherish plans of independence and extended rule.
Carthage was early shut out from any such possible rivalry by the Arian Vandal conquest of Africa, which
forced the African church into closer dependence upon
Rome. The actual struggle of Milan and Arles for independence shows how great the danger from this source
might have been had stronger cities existed.

The Roman church was the only apostolic church in
the West. It was an apostolic church, even if not Peter's,
for Paul had labored there and had written it a very important epistle. As doubts and divisions began to arise
in the church on various theological points, such churches
were thought to preserve a more pure tradition of the
primitive teaching than others, and questions of difficulty began to be referred to them for advice and explana-

tion, and their doctrine began to be looked upon as a standard. Rome was the only church in the West to which such reference could be made.[1]

The Roman was the largest and strongest church in the West. It was also much the richest church and it had been very generous in its gifts to poorer and weaker churches, which looked to it for help.

It was also with remarkable uniformity an orthodox church. In the days of the forming theology and of the forming primacy there was great danger that the Roman church or the Roman bishop might, now and then, adopt a doctrine which the opinion of the majority would not finally sanction, a danger which became practically impossible when the primacy was once established. The fact that this actually happened in only one or two unimportant cases gained for the doctrinal opinion of the bishop of Rome a weight of authority which it could not otherwise have had. This general doctrinal orthodoxy is, perhaps, partly accounted for by the fact that theological differences were much less numerous and less extreme in the West than in the more subtly philosophical East. At any rate, this fact made the recognition of the doctrinal authority of the Roman church a relatively simple matter. But while the opinions which it represented gained the victory over all opposing views, the Roman church, nevertheless, was very tolerant of variations of belief which it did not consider essential, and it did not make the conditions hard for the return of the dissenter who had seen the error of his ways. The general tolerance and wisdom of its doctrinal oversight made the growth of a uniformity of belief under its headship comparatively easy.

[1] As an early instance, we have Theodosius the Great declaring his will, in 380, with special reference to the doctrine of the Trinity, that all people subject to his rule "should hold that faith which the divine Peter the Apostle delivered to the Romans, and which now the pontiff Damasus, and Peter, Bishop of Alexandria, follow."—*Cod. Theod.*, XVI, 1.

The Roman church was a very active missionary church. A large number of the churches throughout the whole West had been founded as missions from Rome and looked to it with a natural sense of dependence for guidance and direction as to the mother church. The conversion of the Anglo-Saxons to Catholic Christianity by missionaries sent from Rome by Pope Gregory I had results of great importance, as we shall see hereafter, for the preservation and increase of the papal power in a critical period of its history.

So many things we have been able to notice, tendencies in the church itself, Roman ideas and traditions of empire, characteristics of the Roman church and its bishops, which shaped from within, as we may say, the external constitution. But not merely these things, others also, of a different sort, worked towards the same result. Especially deserving of mention are certain historical events, happening beyond the control of the Roman bishops, or not directly sought by them, which became, however, when they had once occurred, most active influences in this development.

First to be considered is the founding of Constantinople. The first emperor who professed Christianity removed the seat of the government to the East, mainly in all probability for strategic reasons, and though at a later time emperors resided for long periods in the West, Rome ceased to be the seat of government even for them. The bishop of Rome was left with no more powerful and overshadowing presence beside him, to reduce his importance by the constant comparison. He was not so directly under the control of the emperor as he would otherwise have been, and his theological views seemed at a distance much less important than if he had been the bishop of the immediate court. As a result, the bishops of Rome were able to preserve much more independence of action than were the bishops of Constantinople,

and to maintain a consistency of theology impossible to
their rivals, subject to the demands of a court which was
continually in revolution.

In another direction the distance of the emperor had
important consequences. After the Lombard conquest
of Italy the political control of the Eastern emperor over
the city of Rome and its neighborhood became hardly
more than nominal. The exarch of Ravenna was in
name the representative of the emperor, but he could
do nothing to help Rome in its struggle to preserve its
independence of the Lombard, and the conduct of the
defence, and even the local political administration,
passed naturally into the hands of the bishop, the most
important officer in the city. In this way there was gradually added to the general ecclesiastical power which the
bishops were acquiring the virtually independent political
government of a little state.

This incipient temporal power was greatly extended
by Gregory I, who commissioned civil and military officers, made peace independently of the empire, and
claimed a position above the exarch. This little territory thus acquired was enlarged by the gifts of the Frankish kings, and grew into the States of the Church, so controlling an influence in the later policy of the papacy, and
a stone of offence in all international politics from Gregory I to the present time. That it was of immense value
to the popes, as supreme rulers of the world church
through all the medieval times, that they were not bishops
of any political realm, save of the shadowy Roman Empire,
but occupied an independent temporal position, cannot be
denied; that it has been a decided injury to the Catholic church in modern times, when all interests, both
ecclesiastical and political, are viewed from a wholly different point of view, is almost equally clear.

Another event, the sack of Rome by Alaric, in 410,
aided somewhat in the growth of this local power. The

aristocratic society of the capital city, closely bound up with the Roman past, by tradition and by the nominal positions which they still held, had remained obstinately pagan. The bishop of Rome, supported by the mass of the population, and holding an office of great power, was yet not of the highest local consideration so long as the senate and the aristocracy remained unchristian. Alaric's sack of Rome, which largely spared the Christians, scattered and ruined this pagan society and left the bishop and his clergy without social, as they had been without official, rivals.

Another event of this sort was a decision of the Council of Sardica, in the year 343. This council had been called to reconcile, if possible, the parties which had grown up in the church out of the Arian controversy; but it had failed of its object, and the Arian representatives had seceded to hold a meeting by themselves in Philippopolis. The party remaining, we might call it an *ex-parte* council, decreed a limited right of appeal from local decisions to Julius, at that time bishop of Rome. The measure was adopted as a means of self-defence to protect the orthodox bishops of the eastern European provinces from the Arian majority there, but its influence became in time much wider than was originally intended. It came to be understood to legalize all sorts of appeals to Rome, and especially when, with the decline of historical knowledge, the decrees of the Council of Sardica became confused with those of the much more influential Council of Nicæa, they seemed to give a sanction of the highest authority to the claims of the pope. Many other things also favored the growth of appeals to Rome, and a supreme judicial authority in the papacy gradually came to be recognized throughout the West, though not without some determined resistance.

In the year 445, Leo I, involved in a desperate conflict with the archbishop of Arles, obtained from the Emperor

Valentinian III an edict declaring in the most explicit terms the supremacy of the bishop of Rome over the church of the empire in both judicial and administrative matters, as a necessary means of peace and unity, and commanding the imperial officers to compel the disobedient to submit to his authority. This was apparently decisive in the struggle with Arles, but that it had any large or permanent influence in favor of the papacy does not seem likely. The empire was now falling rapidly to pieces. The imperial power was weak, and only here and there really respected. Large parts of the West were already in the hands of Arian Germans. Had it not been for the fact that the current was already setting strongly towards papal supremacy, and all influences combining to further it, this edict of Valentinian's would probably have had no appreciable effect. As it was, its effect could not have been great.

A more important cause of the advancement of the papacy was undoubtedly the dissolution of the Western Empire itself. It might seem as if the church would be involved in this dissolution, and that when the imperial authority disappeared the authority of the pope, which had grown up under its shadow, and upon the model which the empire had furnished, would fall to ruins with it. But the church was now too strong and too independent. The causes which destroyed the empire did not affect it, and it easily maintained its real authority when that of the empire had become a mere theory. Indeed the immediate effect of the destruction of the political unity and of the establishment of independent German kingdoms was to draw the surviving Roman life in the provinces into a more close dependence upon the church as the only representative of the old common life. The dissolution of the empire left the papacy the immediate and natural heir of its position and traditions.

In the period which followed the German conquest,

by far the most decisive influence was the alliance of
the papacy with the Franks; it was, indeed, one of the
most eventful coalitions ever entered into in history.
It is no abuse of terms to call this an alliance, for though
doubtless there was no definite treaty, nor even a conscious bargain, it was really a combination which the
two great powers of the future, fairly equal parties in
position and promise, formed with one another at the
outset of their common history, and which they drew
more and more close as the circumstances of their growth
made it increasingly useful. It was one of the essential
influences which preserved the papacy from the great
danger of being completely absorbed in the overshadowing Frankish power that there was behind them both
this history of mutual helpfulness and respect. The details of this alliance and its results belong elsewhere.
It should be held in mind, however, as one of the most
helpful historical influences in the formative age of the
papal monarchy.

This cannot pretend to be a complete statement of the
causes which led to the supremacy of the Roman church
and of its bishop over the Western church. No such
statement has ever yet been made, and very likely none
is possible. It is complete enough, however, to show
how all things, influences the most widely separated in
character and time, religious and political and traditional,
sentiment and law and theology, deliberate purpose and
unforeseen events, all combine to lead to this common
conclusion.

This is only another way of saying that the necessities
of the time demanded such a result, and that the monarchical church had a great work to do which could have
been done by nothing else so well. It is not difficult now
to see what this work was.

Two great dangers threatened the early church. One

was that it might be absorbed in the state, and come to
bear the same relation to it that the pagan religion had
borne, its subservient handmaid, a subordinate department of the government to be controlled and directed
to political ends. How great this danger was can be seen
in several periods of the history of the church in the Eastern Empire when such a result actually happened. But
however great this danger may have been under the empire, it became far greater on the establishment of the
German kingdoms in the West. Not merely the Arian
states, but the Catholic Carolingian state, threatened at
times the absorption of the church in the state and the
control of it for purposes foreign to its own. It is impossible to see how the church could have escaped this
danger without the compact and strong interstate organization which had been given it, directed by a single head
and according to a single plan. Such a power, extending beyond the limits of a single state, and fairly on a
level with that of the king, commanded respect for its
vigorous teaching of the necessary separation of church
and state and of the independent sphere of church activity.

The other danger to which the early church was exposed was that the barbarizing process from which the
Christian religion did suffer so greatly might complete
its work, and the spiritual truths of Christianity, so
faintly held and rarely proclaimed in their simple form,
might be entirely lost from civilization. This danger
also, like the other, became extreme with the coming in
of the Germans. Christianity had obtained such a hold
upon the Roman world that the classical paganism was
absorbed, with results which were deplorable certainly,
even if unavoidable, but which were not absolutely fatal.
But would not a new deluge of religious barbarism, foreign to classical ideas, and far less cultivated in other
directions, have failed to gain even a faint conception of

the higher truth and have destroyed completely all understanding of the religious side of the new faith, if this had not been embodied and encased in an external shell of forms and doctrines and constitution strongly enough fixed to resist the attack? The very paganizing itself which Christianity had undergone, by bringing it down nearer to the level on which the Germans stood, was a defence against further paganizing. The German conquest did undoubtedly have some further corrupting effect, but that it did not have a greater influence and actually complete the work of barbarization, as it did complete it in science and in language, is due to the profound impression which the church, with its real power, its gorgeous ceremonial, and its authoritative and infallible teaching made upon the Germans. That the church was so well organized, its forms and ritual so well settled, and its teaching so definite and uniform when the invasions fell upon it, was what saved it from destruction and made it a great reconstructive force in the new order of things.

This work of reconstruction, which the church began even while the destruction of the old world was still going on, must be regarded as a very large part of the positive work which the monarchical church had to do. It was necessary for the future that something should incorporate the Germans into the ancient civilization, and make them its continuators, and though this was to be a long and almost hopeless labor, it was absolutely essential that it should be begun at once. But everything was in ruins except the Catholic church. That was organized and in active operation. It did not fall or lose vitality when the empire fell. The overthrow of the political unity only bound the disunited provinces so much the more closely to itself. The Germans had nothing to put in its place. It therefore remained, as it had been, a living force out of the past, continuing the ancient world into the medieval. But without this strong and universal government the church would not only have run great risks of failing to impress itself upon the German barbarians, but it could never have created in them that respect for its power, and that idea of its indisputable authority which not merely kept the conqueror within bounds, but carried over into the new states and the new conditions so many of the results which antiquity had reached. In every separate kingdom, even in the Anglo-Saxon, which was held to the ancient world by no other bond, the priest of every insignificant hamlet was a member of an independent government which extended far beyond the boundaries of the kingdom, and which awakened awe and commanded obedience when it spoke through him. He was a check on the destructive passions of the barbarian lord of the village, and taught him new virtues and new ideas.

Besides the papacy there grew up in the early church another institution which demands our attention from its wide and long-continued influence—the monastic system.

Monasticism is undoubtedly of oriental origin, and originates in oriental ways of looking at life as itself an evil and something from which the holy man must escape as completely as he can, even if possible from consciousness itself.[1] When the changing conception of Christianity had introduced into the church ideas of sin and holiness, and of the evils of life not wholly unlike oriental ideas on the same subjects, the ascetic spirit, which was undoubtedly present in Christianity to some extent from the beginning, received a strong impulse and extended even into the West, where the natural tendencies were not ascetic. If the Christian life is one of observances, if freedom from sin is to be obtained by pen-

---

[1] Something of an idea of the early monasticism and of the original literature relating to it may be obtained from Kingsley's *Hermits*.

ance and by fleeing from temptations, then the holiest life will be secured by abandoning the world entirely, and either alone, in solitude, or in company with a few others like-minded, giving one's self wholly up to penances, and mortifications of the flesh, and pious offices. The more external and formal the religious life became, the stronger became the tendency towards the ascetic and monastic ideal.

This was not the only thing, however, which gave monasticism its disproportionate influence during the middle ages. There comes at times to nearly every man a longing for a life of quiet contemplation, in which, free from all cares and responsibilities and uncongenial duties, he may give himself up wholly to spiritual meditation, or to his favorite intellectual pursuits, under no compulsion, however, or uncomfortable sense of the duty of literary production. The history of the English university fellowships is full of examples of the influence of this feeling, and one thinks easily of more than one case in modern times, outside monasticism, where the opportunities of such a life have been used to some good purpose. This feeling is especially strong and frequent in student days, the time of life when the medieval boy was in the hands of the monk, and when in natural consequence monasticism received its largest reinforcements. For in the middle ages there was no other opportunity for a life of this sort. The monastery gave it as perfectly as it has ever been given, and the monastery alone.

In still another way monasticism furnished the only possible resort in a perfectly natural and permanent need. For the disappointed and despairing, for the broken-hearted, especially among women, whose hopes had been destroyed or whose interest in life seemed unable to survive the loss of friends, the cloister gave a refuge, and often a recovery to helpful interests and to gentle charities, saving a bit of the world's good force from total loss. The Protestant has not infrequently lamented the absence in his system of any natural and ready resort, in cases of this kind, and the consequent waste of energy, nor have attempts been wanting to supply the lack.

It must be noticed, also, that not the only motive of a religious sort which sustained monasticism was as selfish and unchristian as the desire to escape from all duty and all contact with the world, and from all knowledge of sin, in order to make sure of one's own safety in the world to come. The monastic life was very often conceived of as a genuine Christian ministry, of wider opportunity than the secular priesthood, and entered upon and lived in earnest Christian spirit. It must be borne in mind, also, that spiritual religion and genuine Christianity were much more common in the medieval monasteries than outside them, and that, however debased the monastic life may have become at any given time or place, there was throughout the whole period a constant succession of thorough monastic reformations which restored, for a time at least, its earlier purity and produced often a profound impression on the world outside; which passed on indeed from age to age an ideal of Christian living, never lowered and never forgotten as an ideal.

It is certain, however, that an ascetic monasticism has its strongest roots in a conception of life and duty which is essentially medieval. As modern forces began to make themselves felt in the closing centuries of the middle ages, not only did its power over society as a whole decline, but the system itself underwent no slight modification. It is clearly impossible that it should ever hold the place or exercise the influence under modern conditions which once belonged to it.

In the general work of civilization, in addition to its work in the line of religion, the influence of monasticism was by no means slight. It was a constant proclamation, in the midst of a barbarous and crude and warlike society, of the duty and the glory of another sort of life, of the virtues of peace and self-sacrifice and poverty and labor. It was a perpetual reminder that some things supremely worth having were not to be gained by strife or self-assertion or pride of place, but that passive virtues and gentle lives might be full of power. That monasticism reflected often the violent impulses and brutal methods of the time, and sank frequently to the general level of superstition around it is not to be denied. It furnished often examples of anything but gentle virtues and subdued passions. But notwithstanding all that may be said of its corruption, it did preserve and hold up to general view more perfectly than anything else, or, as it seems likely, than anything else could have done in such a time, the conception of a nobler life and the immense value of things not material.

The one distinguishing characteristic of Western monasticism, in contrast with that which generally prevailed in the East, was also of the greatest value to civilization. The Western organizing and legal genius seized upon the simple idea of solitary life and isolated communities which it had received from the East, and constructed great monastic orders, covering Europe with a network of societies bound together under a common law which minutely regulated the daily life.[1] One universal and regular duty which this "rule" placed upon the monk was the necessity of being constantly employed. Especially to be emphasized is the fact that this was work for the sake of work. The object sought was not so much what would be produced by the labor as to keep the body and mind so constantly occupied that temptations could find no access and sin would therefore be escaped. Consequently,

[1] A translation of the Rule of St. Benedict, the chief law of monastic conduct until the rise of the mendicant orders in the thirteenth century, may be found in *Select Historical Documents of the Middle Ages*, translated and edited by Ernest F. Henderson (Bohn's Library), pp. 274–314.

it was a matter of comparative indifference what the work was. The harder and more painful and unattractive to men in general it might be, so much the better for the monk. If sufficiently difficult, the element of penance was added, and it became a still more effectual means of grace. In this way the monk did a great amount of extremely useful work which no one else would have undertaken. Especially is this true of the clearing and reclaiming of land. A swamp was of no value. It was a source of pestilence. But it was just the place for a convent to settle because it made life especially hard. And so the monks carried in earth and stone, and made a foundation, and built their monastery, and then set to work to dike and drain and fill up the swamp, till they had turned it into most fertile ploughland and the pestilence ceased. In the same way the monk laboriously copied manuscript after manuscript which we know he could not understand from the errors in copying which he made. But it kept him at work and so we have the copy though the original may have perished.

The monk taught the farmer better methods of agriculture, and he preserved something of mechanical skill and of the manufacturing arts, and even added some improvements in them of his own. St. Theodulf's plough and St. Dunstan's anvil were not inappropriately adored as holy relics. The schools were in his hands. He kept alive whatever of ancient learning remained, and modern science owes to him an incalculable debt for his labors at her beginning. In childish scrawls he passed on from generation to generation the methods of the fine arts until genius finally awoke. It would be impossible to construct the history of the middle ages but for the monastic chronicles and the documents which the monks preserved. Their manuals of devotion are still in use in the churches of every name. Literature has been enriched by the works of their imagination in chivalric legend and the lives of the miracle-working saints, and the Christian church will never cease to sing the hymns which they composed. In its worst periods monasticism never sank below the surrounding level, and on the whole, until stronger forces began to work, it was a leader and a guide.

CHAPTER VII

THE FRANKS AND CHARLEMAGNE

In the account of the German conquest which was given in the fourth chapter the history of one tribe—the Franks—was entirely omitted. The results of their occupation of Gaul were so important, the empire which they founded, their alliance with the church, their legal notions and political institutions were all of such decisive influence upon the future that their history deserves a separate treatment. The ideas and practices of the Visigoths and of the Lombards had important results in the national history of the lands where they settled. It would be necessary to investigate Visigothic law in order to understand the details of Spanish institutional life. The Anglo-Saxons will doubtless exert upon the final political history of the world an influence greater than that of the Franks, if it be not already greater. But it was the Franks alone of all the German tribes who became a wide power in the general history of the middle ages. It is to them that the political inheritance of the Roman Empire passed, to them came the honor of taking up and carrying on, roughly, to be sure, and far less extensively and effectively, but nevertheless of actually carrying on the political work which Rome had been doing. They alone represent that unity which Rome had established, and so far as that unity was maintained at all as a definite fact, it is the Franks who maintained it. Its influence was undoubtedly wider than theirs, as felt through the church for example, and yet, without the

strong reinforcement which the empire of the Franks
brought to that idea of unity, it would in all probability
have disappeared as a separate political force before the
need for it had passed away.[1]

Originally a very loose confederation—it is doubtful
even if they were so much as a confederation—of small
tribes or families in the middle and lower Rhine valley,
some of them in alliance with Rome and on Roman territory, the Franks hardly attracted even a passing notice
from either statesman or historian during the time when
the great tribes of the East Germans were in motion.
It is only at the end of the fifth century that their career
really begins, and then, as so often in similar cases, it is
the genius of one man, a great leader, which creates the

[1] The great importance of the Frankish state, for the whole political
and institutional future of the Continent, has made its history an exceedingly interesting field of study, and since the middle of the nineteenth century it has been the subject of a most minute and careful scientific investigation by German and French scholars, who have examined every fact
from almost every conceivable point of view.   There has been, on the part
of the majority of German scholars, an apparently unconscious national
bias which has led them to exaggerate the German elements in this state,
perhaps not so much by way of actual exaggeration as by slighting or dis-
regarding the Roman contributions to the common whole.   This tendency
has called out in France—it would almost seem as a definite protest against
it—a most remarkable series of books, by M. Fustel de Coulanges, on the
history of the Franks to the end of the Carolingian period.   In these there
is to be found as marked, and apparently a more conscious and deliberate
exaggeration in the opposite direction, by minimizing the German and
emphasizing the Roman influence wherever possible.   While very evident
faults of process make every conclusion reached by M. Fustel subject to
question, and while a very large body of the more recent scholars of
France, beginning with M. Monod, have refused to follow his lead upon
many points, his books are still exceedingly interesting and stimulating,
and for the non-Continental student they serve to restore the balance,
somewhat seriously distorted by the extreme Germanizers, and to emphasize
that most fundamental fact that the new society was formed from a combination of both German and Roman elements.   Upon some points, as
for example the early history of the feudal system, M. Fustel, while not
differing upon any important detail from the broader-minded among the
German investigators, like Georg Waitz, has, however, by virtue of his
keen constructive insight put the process of growth in clearer light than
ever before.

nation. Rising out of an obscurity which is hardly light-
ened by the abundant mythology which afterwards collected about him, head of one of the little family groups
into which the Franks were divided, a "county king,"
Clovis—Hlodwig, the first Louis the Grand—appears as
one of the great creative spirits who give a new direction
to the currents of history. The main traits of his character and work stand out clearly enough despite the leg-
endary embellishments which have naturally been added.
Like very many others of his kind, utterly without a conscience, hesitating at no means for the accomplishment of
his purpose, he brought about, by a succession of treasons
and murders, the consolidation of the whole Frankish
stock under his personal rule. But even before this
process of consolidation was undertaken, he had begun
to extend rapidly the territory occupied by the Franks.
Syagrius, the son of a former Roman governor, had gathered into his hands the remains of the Roman power
north of the Loire and ruled a considerable territory
there which, in the general breaking up of things, had
fallen to no one else, nominally under the emperor, really
as a little independent kingdom. This power Clovis over-
came in the first great battle of his history, A. D. 486, and
brought under the Frankish dominion.

With the territory occupied by the Franks, and that
which was gradually added as a result of this victory,
Clovis possessed the larger part of northeastern Gaul.
To the south of him lay the two German kingdoms of
the Burgundians and the Visigoths. With the power
which he had gained in the north he turned against them.
The Burgundians were first attacked, and, though their
kingdom was not incorporated in that of the Franks
during Clovis's life, it was made tributary and compelled
to aid the further extension of his power. A few years
later the Visigoths were defeated and retired to Spain,
leaving the lands south of the Loire to Clovis, except a

small portion in the southeast which Theodoric, the Ostrogothic king in Italy, Clovis's more powerful contemporary, forced him to abandon.

Clovis had thus made subject to himself nearly the whole of Roman Gaul, and that, too, with a body of Franks originally very small—perhaps not more than three thousand men—and though later reinforced, still never very large; certainly the Romanized provincials were in a very large majority, especially south of the Loire. It might seem inevitable that the Teutonic institutions, represented by so small a proportion of the population, would be overwhelmed and disappear. It was in reality, however, to be the lot of the Franks, unconsciously and by the force of circumstances, to do that work for the future which Theodoric had, with clearer vision, seen to be necessary—the uniting of German and Roman into a common whole. But if this was to be done, it was vitally necessary that the Teutonic side of the new kingdom should be kept strong enough to survive the danger of Romanization to which it was exposed.

This was secured as a result of two very important points in which the Frankish conquest differed from that made by any other German people. In the first place, their conquest was not a migration. Instead of cutting themselves off completely from their original homes, and settling themselves in the midst of a much more numerous Roman population, with only scanty and accidental reinforcements of new German blood, as did the others, they retained permanently their original German land, and the parts of northeastern Gaul where the Roman population seems to have disappeared or become very small. They simply spread themselves out from their original lands, retaining these permanently as a constant source of fresh German life, a Teutonic makeweight to the Roman provinces occupied.

It was of equal importance, in the second place, that

step by step as their conquests spread over Roman lands, they extended also, in the opposite direction, into Germany and brought in peoples who had not been permanently affected by Roman influence. These German conquests Clovis began by his incorporation of the Alemanni and of the eastern Franks, and they were still further extended by his successors. The pure, or nearly pure, Roman lands of the west were kept in balance, in their influence on the new state, by the pure German lands of the east.

These facts were of great importance in more ways than one. Not merely was it essential to the formation of the civilization of the future, that German and Roman elements should both be preserved, and brought together in such a way that they should unite on equal terms in a new common whole, but also, if a new permanent civilization was to be constructed on the foundation of the Frankish kingdom, it was absolutely necessary that the invasions should cease. So long as every new attempt to revive order and settled government was liable to be defeated by a new invasion, and chaos likely to be introduced again, no steps could be taken towards the future. This danger could be removed only by the incorporation of Germany—the source of the invasions—in the new common life which was forming, and by the creation of a political and military power strong enough to be safe from outside attack.

The incorporation of Germany was not finished until the days of Charlemagne, but it was, long before that, complete enough to secure the Frankish state against such an attack as that by which it had itself overthrown the kingdoms of the Burgundians and the Alemanni. It also very early became strong enough not to fear the danger of Roman reaction before which Vandal and Ostrogoth had gone down, and on the field of Tours it was able to turn back the new Mohammedan invader who had destroyed the Visigothic state. It was this great political and military power which the Franks built up that gave them the opportunity to do the work which every other German tribe failed to accomplish. It was because they kept constantly open the sources of Teutonic life and vigor that they were able to use the opportunity to great results.

A third step of great importance, in this process of union, was also taken by Clovis. One institution, produced in the ancient world before the Germans entered it, had continued with vigorous life and wide influence, indeed, with slowly increasing power, through all the changes of this chaotic period. It was to be in the future a still greater power and to exert an influence even wider and more permanent than that of the Franks. It was also one of the most important channels through which the ancient civilization passed over into the new. This was the Roman church. It was to be the great ecclesiastical power of the coming time. It was, therefore, a most essential question whether the Franks, who were to grow on their side into the great political power of the future, should do so in alliance with this other power or in opposition to it.

The other Germans who entered the empire, except the Saxons, were Christians, but they had been converted to that form of Christianity which is known as Arianism. This was a belief like that which is now called Unitarian, which had grown up in the East at the beginning of the fourth century, and which continued to be a cause of theological strife for two or three hundred years. Whatever may be one's personal belief upon the theological point, the fact which condemns Western Arianism in the sight of history, and makes its fate deserved, is that, at a time when there was the utmost need that the shattered fragments of the empire should be held together in some way, and when disorganization was most dangerous, it stood for separation and local independence. It furnished no strong bond of unity on the religious side, as did the Catholic faith, to replace that political unity which was falling to pieces. Burgundian and Visigoth, Vandal and Ostrogoth and Lombard had no common religious organization and recognized no primacy in the bishop of Rome. They did indeed tolerate the Catholicism of their Roman subjects, and did not break off the connection of these with the Roman church, but that result would certainly have followed had they grown into strong and permanent states, still Arian in faith. The continued life of these nations would have meant not merely the political, but also the religious, disintegration of Europe. The unity of the future, in a Christian commonwealth of nations, was at stake in the triumph of the Roman church and the Frankish Empire.

This question Clovis settled, not long after the beginning of his career, by his conversion to Catholic Christianity. That he ever became a real Christian seems as unlikely as that Constantine did, and the two cases are in many ways parallel. That political considerations moved him we can only guess, but they seem obvious, and there is little doubt but that his further conquests in Gaul were aided by the fact that the Franks were of the same faith as the Roman provincials, while the Goths and Burgundians whom he attacked were Arians. That he could have had any conception of the more remote consequences of his act is impossible; but, as we have seen, these were the most important of its results. That the Frankish Empire could have been formed without this alliance is probable. It is possible, also, that a common church organization could have been created for all its parts, but it would have been impossible for such a church to have done the work—as important outside the Frankish bounds as within—which the Catholic church accomplished.

In these three ways, therefore, the work of Clovis was of creative influence. He brought together the Roman and the German upon equal terms, each preserving the sources of his strength, to form a new civilization. He founded a political power which was to unite nearly all the continent in itself, and to bring the period of the invasions to an end. He established a close alliance between the two great controlling forces of the future, the two empires which continued the unity which Rome had created, the political empire and the ecclesiastical.

It may seem from one point of view more strange that Roman institutions were preserved at all in this Frankish kingdom than that they threatened to supersede the German. The Frankish occupation of Gaul was a conquest. It seems to have been more distinctly a conquest than most of the other German migrations—a definite change of government and so presumptively of institutions.

It must be remembered, however, that government was in an incomplete stage of development among these Germans; if well advanced in some directions it was entirely wanting in others. In the simpler life and small land of their earlier history few difficult problems had presented themselves, and these had been met by simple means. Now, however, with the necessity of ruling a wide land and a large population of diverse race, of settling complicated legal questions, and of providing a larger revenue, there was a demand suddenly put upon the German state for an enlargement of its institutional life which no rapidity of development could possibly meet. The result was natural. Wherever in their earlier public life the Germans had developed institutions capable of application to the new conditions, these were continued in the new states, and became German elements in the final institutional product. An extremely important example of this is the system of public courts. Wherever the new demand was of a sort which could not be met by anything which they already possessed, it was the simplest, and easiest, indeed the only possible thing to do, to continue in operation the Roman machinery which they found existing. So the administrative system, taxation, legal and extra legal customs in the renting of lands, remained Roman. These are but single examples on either side. The number might be largely increased, and will be, in some cases of detail, as we proceed.

One peculiar idea of the Germans must also be taken account of here, as of influence in preserving Roman practices, that idea which is known, somewhat technically, as the "personality of the law." The German was supposed to preserve of right his native tribal law under whatever government he might live. Alemanni, Burgundians, and Lombards, brought into the Frankish kingdom and subject to its king, kept their old law and did not come under the Frankish. New laws concerning public affairs might be made, and be in force in all the subject lands, but in private law, in matters between man and man, the old tribal customary law was still their law. This principle was applied also to the Romans. The Roman law continued to be the law of the Roman subjects of these German states, at least for a very considerable time, and until Roman and German had melted into a new people with a new customary law. More than one of these German states, indeed, issued manuals or summaries of the Roman law for the use of their subjects, as they had done of their own German law.

Under other heads, as in the last chapter and in the chapter on feudalism, are to be seen some further preservative forces of great value which kept the Roman elements in use until they became organic parts of a new civilization. Those mentioned here will serve to show how it was that, even if the Franks entered as a conquering nation and consciously put a new government in place of the old, large portions of the Roman legal and institutional arrangements remained in use.

The immediate successors of Clovis continued his work. At one time, under the early Merovingians, the subject territory of the Frankish state almost if not quite touched the Adriatic. It was recognized by the other western states as the strongest of them all, and had diplomatic relations with the Roman Empire in the East on something like an equal footing.

But the royal Merovingian race was passionate and brutal. Its history is full of treasons and murders and crimes not to be mentioned. As a result its life was speedily exhausted, and it sank, physically and morally, with fearful rapidity, its princes dying like old men at twenty years of age, and its power passing into other hands.

The life of its royal family was, with no very great exaggeration, the life of the race. This was also violent and savage. Crimes were frequent. The first appeal was usually to brute force. Life and property were not secure, and the government seemed to have small power to enforce order.[1] Civil war raged almost without ceas-

[1] Gregory of Tours, in his *History of the Franks*, X, 27, gives us an interesting example of the way in which the Frankish government sometimes attempted to repress disorders. After telling how a private feud arose in Tournay, and how Queen Fredegonda, having tried in vain to persuade the parties to cease their quarrels and make peace, determined at last to bring them to order with arms, he says: "She invited, in fact, these three men to a great feast, and made them sit together upon one bench; and when the feast had continued a long time, and night had come, and the tables had been taken away, as the custom of the Franks is, the guests continued sitting on the benches where they had been seated. And they drank much wine, and became so drunk that their attendants got drunk also, and went to sleep in any corner of the house where they happened to be. Then men with three axes, as directed by the queen, stationed themselves behind these three men, and, while they were talking with one another, . . . they were cut down." Such a government might be called anarchy tempered with assassination.

ing. The subject nations became restless and by degrees
more and more independent. The empire of the Franks
seemed to be threatened with dissolution, and the work
which Clovis had begun, with failure.

Even in the early days of the Merovingian dynasty a
line of division through the national life had begun to
show itself, drawn probably at first by dynastic quarrels
but running ever deeper as time went on. This was the
difference between the west—called after a time Neustria
—set off into a separate kingdom in the Merovingian
family divisions, and the eastern kingdom—Austrasia. In
the west the Franks were few and rapidly becoming
Romanized, and Roman usages prevailed. The east was
thoroughly Teutonic.

There is also another difference to be noticed, fully as
important as the contrast and possible hostility of these
two incipient nationalities. Besides tending to make the
king more powerful, as was noticed in Chapter V, the conquest had led also, as a secondary result, to the formation
of a more powerful aristocracy than had existed before,
through the possession of land and office—of greater and
more permanent sources of wealth. This new nobility
began at once to attack the royal power, and to strive
for independence. In the western kingdom, as a result
of the Roman influence—the analogy and the continued
institutions of a highly centralized government—the royal
power was strong. In the east, where German ideas were
prevalent, the strength of the nobility grew more rapidly.

Out of these two sources of contention grew the continual civil strifes of this period. They seem at first
sight as meaningless for history as the battles of the stone
age. But taken together with the decay of the Merovingian house, they gave an opportunity for the family of
nobles, who were destined to restore the royal power and
to reconstruct the Frankish kingdom, to rise into a position of controlling influence.

This family had its house possessions in Austrasia. In that kingdom, in the reign of Dagobert I, the last of the strong Merovingian kings, there were two powerful nobles, intrusted with positions of great importance by the king, Pippin of Landen, and Arnulf, bishop of Metz. After the death of Dagobert, the son of Pippin made a premature attempt to seize the crown, and perished with his son, and the male line of Pippin came to an end. But the marriage of his daughter with the son of Arnulf united the possessions and power of the two families, and the son of this marriage, Pippin of Heristal, to use the names which were later employed to distinguish the Pippins, soon won a commanding position in the state, though not without severe struggles. The Merovingians still retained the crown as kings in name, but the real control of affairs passed into the hands of Pippin and of his descendants, the Mayors of the Palace.

The battle of Testry, fought in 687, is the turning-point of this part of Frankish history. In it the organized Austrasian nobles under Pippin, aided by some of the Neustrian, triumphed over the tendency towards a centralized government. It meant that those elements which were really more Teutonic were still to retain the direction of affairs in the reunited kingdom, and that Romanizing influences, which bade fair to split the Frankish nation into two parts, were to be held back for some generations yet. The western half of the land was to be brought into connection once more with the sources of Teutonic life, and under the rule of a thoroughly German family.

This battle was in form a triumph of the aristocracy over the royal power. It was as a representative of the nobles, and by their aid, that the new house, the Carolingian, had secured its power. But the nobles speedily found that they had only succeeded in putting a strong and determined master in the place of a powerless one. The point of view of the Carolingian princes was changed at once, as soon as they were in a position to rule in the name of the Merovingian king.

The task before them was by no means an easy one. Not merely had the nobles grown strong in the state, but the confusion of the last part of the Merovingian period had enabled many of them to assume a position virtually independent of all government control. These were the days of the earliest stage of feudalism, and the political disorder—one of its chief causes—allowed in some cases an almost complete feudal isolation. A considerable part of the work which Pippin of Heristal, and his son Charles, called Martel, or the Hammer, had to do was to break the power of these local "tyrants," as Einhard calls them in his "Life of Charlemagne," and so to make the royal power more real.

But also the outlying provinces, especially where these represented a nationality once independent, were in very doubtful obedience. Aquitania, Alemannia, Thuringia, and Bavaria had taken advantage of the dissensions among the Franks to resume a more or less complete independence under dukes of their own race. The empire which the early Merovingians had brought together threatened to fall to pieces. It must be reconstructed, or the Franks could have no great political future. The work of doing this was a long one. Charles Martel hardly more than began it. It continued through the reign of his son, Pippin, later misnamed the Short, and on to the beginning of the reign of Charlemagne.

Still another great task fell to the early Carolingians. The German north—Frisians and Saxons—was a ceaseless source of danger. These peoples were continually attacking the borders, striving to force their way into the south, the last wave of the invasions from Germany proper. Charles Martel and Pippin maintained a vigorous defence, but they could establish no permanent conquests. The Christian missionaries, mostly Anglo-Saxons, who attempted to convert them, met with no better success, and it proved the great labor of Charlemagne's life to incorporate them with the Roman and Christian world.

One decisive victory, gained by Charles Martel, reflected great glory on his family and helped to secure its position. The Arab invasion, which had entered Europe through Spain, in 711, had not been held back by the Pyrenees. The Duke of Aquitania was not strong enough alone to resist them, and, in 732, an army of them had reached the neighborhood of the Loire, a thousand miles north of Gibraltar. There, in the battle of Tours or Poitiers, the infantry of the Franks withstood the attacks of the Arab horse, and turned back this invasion. Still other attacks of theirs had to be met in the south, and they held some parts of Septimania and the Rhone valley for many years, but they were never again able to penetrate so far into the country, and the danger that Europe would be overrun by Mohammedanism, as Asia and Africa had been, was past, so far at least as concerns the attack from the west.

The time of Charles Martel, and of Pippin, as Mayor of the Palace, was a time of reconstruction for the Frankish state. The power of the central government was reestablished. The nobles were brought into obedience, and the elements of dissolution held in check. The subject nationalities were compelled to give up the independence which they were resuming, and to acknowledge the supremacy of the Franks once more. The church, which had suffered with the rest of the state, and almost fallen apart, was made to feel the effects of the change also. The life and morals of the clergy were reformed. The councils, its legislative machinery, were used to serve public ends, and the vast estates of land, which it had gathered into its hands, were made to contribute to the support of the army. Pippin called Boniface, the great Anglo-Saxon missionary among the Germans, to his aid in the work of reconstruction, and, although the strong Carolingian princes never gave up their direct control of the church, the result was to give the papacy a greater influence in the Frankish church than it had had before.

Now follows a series of events which opens a new and greater epoch in Frankish history.

The kingdom of the Lombards in Italy, though quiet for long intervals, was never wholly satisfied with its incomplete occupation of that country. As soon as an ambitious king ascended the throne, and had his somewhat unruly people in hand, he was very apt to begin to push for further territory. This was a constant menace to the papacy, and to the independence of the little state of which it had come to be practically the sovereign. The papal state was not strong enough to insure its own safety, though it had defended itself with great skill. Its natural protector would have been the emperor at Constantinople, still nominal sovereign of Rome and other parts of Italy. But Constantinople was far away, and the emperor had many more immediate interests which demanded his attention. Besides this, the points of dispute between the Eastern church and the Roman, upon the worship of images and other topics, which were one day to make a complete and hostile separation between them, had already begun to appear and to create ill feeling. The appeal which the popes made for protection brought them no help, and they had only one recourse left. This was to the restored Frankish kingdom, the strongest political power of the West.

Gregory II and Gregory III both appealed to Charles Martel to come to their assistance, and the latter sent to him the keys of St. Peter's tomb. But Charles did not comply. It is probable that he had still too serious work at home, and that so long as the position of the Arabs in the south was threatening, and plans of further invasion on their part not improbable, he could not afford to engage in hostilities with the Lombards.

But his son Pippin felt himself in a more secure position. There was also, on his side, a strong reason for a close alliance with the papacy. The plan which the son of the first Pippin had attempted to carry out, before the hold of his family on the state was secure enough to warrant it, could now be taken up again. The Franks had been accustomed, for more than sixty years, to see the Merovingian kings excluded from all real government, and all the duties of the royal office performed by the Carolingian princes. Almost all the nobles were now also the vassals of Pippin, and the leaders of the church would support him. To set aside the Merovingian family, and put the Carolingian on the throne, would seem far less revolutionary at this time than it had one hundred years earlier. Still a sort of religious feeling might attach itself to the old royal family, and Pippin needed all the support which he could get. Accordingly the first move towards the alliance came from him, and an embassy to Rome, sent with the consent of the Franks, laid before the pope the question whether the condition of things was a good one where he who bore the title of king was without any real power. The answer was a satisfactory one, and with the sanction of this high religious authority, the last Merovingian king disappeared in the cloister. Pippin was elected king by the nobles and people, raised on their shields after the old German fashion, and, by a new ceremony, the bishops consecrated him king in anointing him with holy oil. This took place in the year 751.

Almost immediately after this the advance of the Lombard king became so threatening that the pope determined to go in person to beseech the new king of the Franks to come to his aid. His mission was successful. Pippin went back with him to Italy, and compelled the

Lombards to abandon their conquests. Two years later another expedition was necessary, as the Lombard king was threatening Rome again. This time, in 755, Pippin bestowed on the pope a part of the exarchate of Ravenna, which he forced the Lombards to give up, and thus added territory on the Adriatic to that around Rome of which the popes had already made themselves the virtual sovereigns. The wishes of the emperor at Constantinople were not consulted in this disposition of his property, and, without any regard to his rights, the foundations of the temporal principality of the popes were securely laid.

These events were of as wide influence upon the future of the Franks as upon that of the papacy. They drew still closer that alliance with the church which had always been a characteristic of their history. They opened the way to a new conquest—that of Italy—of vital necessity in their consolidation of Europe; and, still more important, they brought them into direct contact with Rome, and so made likely the awakening of imperial ambitions in their minds, and made it natural for others to associate with them those ideas of a revival of the imperial title in the west which had already begun to stir in Italy.[1]

These events bring us to the beginning of the reign of Charles the Great—Charlemagne—in 768. A very general opinion has ranked him among the greatest political leaders of history. A less favorable judgment, however, has not been wanting, and it will, perhaps, afford us the best point of view for a brief sketch of his reign and an understanding of his place in history, if we try to ascertain upon what grounds such high rank can be assigned him.[2]

It is necessary to remember, however, in doing so that

---

[1] Bury, *Later Roman Empire*, vol. II, p. 443, n. 1.
[2] See the collection of opinions from various authors in Waitz, *Deutsche Verfassungsgeschichte*, III, pp. 333–340. His own conclusions are given, *ibid.*, pp. 327–331.

the original sources which treat of his reign give us almost no statement of his motives or plans.[1] They tell us what things he did, but give us scarcely the slightest clew to the reason why he did them, or what ultimate purpose he had in view. It is necessary to infer the leading ideas of his policy from what he did and what he left undone. Such inference is certainly proper, and may lead to sound conclusions, but it must always lack the character of proof, and will seem to some much less conclusive than to others. To myself, the theory that Charlemagne was a man of the broadest statesmanship appears to explain the facts much more perfectly than any other, though one must certainly hesitate to affirm that he was conscious to the full of all the bearings of his policy which we may seem to detect.

But such a consciousness is not necessary; indeed, it never exists. The statesman is a man who sees the needs of his own time, the immediate dangers to which society is exposed, the next step which may be taken in advance, and, seeing this work which is to be done, sees also how to do it, knows what means the conditions of the time will allow him to employ, and how to work out the needed result with the materials and tools which he must use. The ultimate historical results of his work, and even the deeper currents of the age, he cannot see. But if he truly realizes the needs and opportunities of his time, which these deepest currents have created, he does understand them, though he does not know it, and he works unconsciously in harmony with them.

Our question, then, is this: Were the things which Charlemagne did wisely adapted to meet the needs and danger of the time, and to lead the way to a better future? Did he do the things which a great statesman ought to have done if he had realized the task demanded of him?

[1] Einhard's—Eginhard's—*Life of Charlemagne* is easily accessible in various translations.

To answer this question we must first determine, as we now look back upon the age, what the things were which most of all needed to be done for the secure unfolding of civilization. This is not difficult to do. The ultimate outcome of the middle ages was to be, as was said at the beginning of our study, a new civilization based upon that of the classic nations, with the new Teutonic race as its active agent. To bring about a condition of things which would allow such a civilization to arise, three things must be accomplished in the political world. In the first place, the invasions must be brought to an end. No secure and productive civilization would be possible so long as everything was likely to be thrown back into confusion by a new settlement of barbarians who must be absorbed and civilized. In the second place, the Christian nations of Europe must be held together in a common whole, in order that the unity, which Rome had established, and which is the foundation of Christendom, might be preserved. Finally, the government of the state must be strong enough to keep order and to hold in check anarchy and the brute passions, for safety of person and property is indispensable to any advancing civilization. All these were secured in some way before modern history opened. Had it been possible to secure them permanently in the ninth century it might have saved the world some centuries of time.

We have, then, these three things which the statesman of Charlemagne's age, if he had been gifted with the power to read his own time and to see into the future, would have endeavored to accomplish—to guard his empire against future invasion, to consolidate Christian Europe, and to establish a strong central government, preserving order throughout the whole.

In taking up for examination the conquests which were made by Charlemagne, it seems impossible to believe that they were dictated by any other motive than the desire to render permanent the power which the Franks had established. That his leading motive was ambition, the passion of conquering for the sake of conquering, appears entirely irreconcilable with the facts. If Charlemagne had looked about him to ascertain from what sources new invasions might come to endanger the Frankish state, guided also by the experience of the past, so far as he would know its history at all in detail, he would have been likely to conclude that there were two and only two sources of danger, the Arabs of Spain and the Saxons of northern Germany.

As a matter of fact, there was no danger now to be feared from the Arabs. They were at strife among themselves, and in no position to undertake further conquests, as they had been in the past, and would be again in the near future. Very possibly this fact explains why Charlemagne pushed his conquests no farther than he did in that direction, but satisfied himself with a few campaigns and a little strip of territory in northeastern Spain.

The Saxons were a very different enemy. For more than a hundred years they had kept up almost constant warfare on the Frankish borders, as earlier still the Germans had along the Roman frontiers. If any new German invasion was to repeat the history of the earlier one, it was from them that it must come. Charlemagne certainly acted as if he realized this fact. They were a stubborn foe, but his determination was more stubborn still. There was apparently far less to be gained from them than from Spain. They were poor and uncivilized. Their land was a cold and hard wilderness; indeed, for purposes of mere conquest, it would seem as if he could have gone in no other direction so difficult and so little remunerative. But he made their subjugation the constant business of thirty years. He led his army into their land, compelled them to submit and to become Christians in name, and established officers and regulations for

their government. But hardly had he turned his back
when his work was all undone, Christianity thrown off,
and his officers driven out. With infinite patience he
did the work over and over again, generally with wise
measures, sometimes with unwise, as in the massacre of
Verden, but in the end he succeeded. They acknowledged his superiority, submitted to his government, and
accepted Christianity. In no very long time the teachings of the missionaries had replaced their compulsory
faith with a more genuine Christianity, and within a
few generations they looked upon him as the founder,
rather than the destroyer, of their national existence,
and reckoned him among the great apostles of the Christian religion. Their incorporation in the Roman Christian system of things was complete, and the invasions
were over forever. The Hungarians were to make devastating inroads, and the Northmen conquered England
and made some settlements on the mainland, but within
the limits of Charlemagne's empire no more new and
independent states could be founded by armies of invading barbarians.

In the way of consolidation, Charlemagne had but little
more to do than to put the finishing touches upon a process long going on and almost completed before his day.
Central and southern Germany, and the Lombard state,
and the fringe of Greek territory of which he took possession, were already marked out for Frankish occupation before his reign began, and in no direction, except
against the Saxons, were his conquests pushed farther
than to give him security from attack, as against the
Slavs and Danes, and in southern Italy, or to connect
his territories with one another and round them into a
compact whole, as in the Danube valley.

Of the importance of this part of his work for the future, and of the way in which it continued the work of
Rome, he could have had no conception. What he was

striving to do was to render this Frankish empire secure and permanent. But he did bring together, into a common political union, nearly all the peoples which were to form the great nations of the future, and those which lay outside his immediate rule seem also to have looked upon him as in some direct way their head.[1]

Finally, in no part of his work does the political genius of Charlemagne appear so evident as in the measures which he adopted to strengthen the power of the central government. It had been the great weakness of all the German governments of earlier generations that they did not make their power felt and obeyed in every locality in the state. The result had been disorder and confusion and the growth of narrowing local interests in the place of general and national ones. Charlemagne's task, as it presented itself to him, would very likely have seemed to be to secure obedience and order, but if this could have been done, if a thoroughly centralized government could have been established and made permanent, it would have meant also the union of the various subject peoples into a common nationality, and a rapidly advancing civilization.

The chief executive officer of the early Frankish state was the count—the *graf*—administering in the name of the king a subdivision of the state, the county. After the conquest this office had been very considerably developed under the Roman influence, and its duties widened, especially upon the judicial side, and it came to be theoretically an executive, military, and judicial office, representing the king and not ill adapted to bring the central government into contact with all parts of the kingdom. But it was natural to choose for the office some large landholder of the county, who would have local interests and local ambitions, and, though the Merovingian kings seem to have recognized the danger of

[1] See Einhard's *Life of Charlemagne*, chap. XVI.

this, and to some extent to have sought to avoid it, the nobles, whose interests lay in the opposite direction, were in the main successful in forcing this policy upon them. It is evident that the prerogatives of the count's office, the local exercise of sovereignty, would be of great advantage to the noble in building up a principality of his own, and they were very commonly used for this purpose, even to the extent of forcing the free landholders of the district into dependent or vassal relations to the count. This turning of the office into a local power greatly impaired its value as an instrument of the general government, and there was imperative need of reformation at this point if the state was really to control its subjects.

Charlemagne made a most vigorous effort to force the counts to be faithful to their duties as agents of his government, and to cease the abuse of their powers for private ends. He certainly did bring about a great change in these respects, but that his success was not so great as he wished is evident from the frequent denunciations in his laws of the local usurpation of power. Even if his success had been complete, the experience of the past would show that there was here a constant danger to be guarded against and that the state needed some more efficient means of overseeing the counts and of holding them strictly to their duties. The practical statesmanship of Charlemagne seems clear in the arrangement which he devised for this purpose.

Like almost every other case of the making of new institutions in history, it was the adaptation of an earlier institution to a new and wider use. Charlemagne got the suggestion for the new office from the earlier royal *missi—missi dominici*—messengers sent out by the king for special purposes, the inspection of the royal domain lands for example. This office he gradually adapted to the new purpose he had in mind until, apparently by 802, it had become a most effective instrument of government.

The details of the arrangement vary greatly at different times, but in general they seem to have been like this: The empire was divided into large districts, or circuits, containing a considerable number of counties. To each of these districts *missi* were sent annually, usually two in number, different men each year, one a high officer of the church and the other a layman of rank. On coming to their district they divided it into subdistricts according to geographical convenience, each containing a number of counties. In each of these subdivisions they held an assembly four times in their year of office—in January, April, July, and October. To this assembly must come all the counts and bishops of the subdistricts, all the subordinate officers of the counties and bishoprics, and all the vassals of the king. Representatives of the freemen of the territory were selected to report upon the conduct of affairs and to inquire into abuses, and any of the inhabitants might enter complaint before the *missi* concerning any special act of oppression. In this way the administration of the count and of the bishop were kept under close watch, and accusations of injustice or misuse of power on their part were quickly heard by the central government. The *missi* had the right themselves to hear appeals, to correct abuses, and to punish the local officers of their districts for disobedience or insubordination. They were supposed to represent the king, and to have the rights which he would have had if present in person, but especially important cases seem to have been referred directly to the king for decision. They also made a tour of inspection through the different counties and might hold courts in each of them. At the close of their year of service they drew up written reports to the king of the state of things in their circuits, and these formed the basis of instructions to the new *missi* of the following year.

Such an office was certainly very wisely adapted to

meet the difficulties of the time, to hold the local officers faithful to their public duties, and to bring the power of central government into direct contact with every locality, and make it respected and obeyed.[1] The best comment upon its purpose and usefulness is the fact that, as the power of the general government grew weaker under the successors of Charlemagne, the office gradually disappeared, leaving, if anything, only faint traces of its former existence.[2]

For the defence of the frontier—mark, the marches— the office of graf took on a new form, which developed in time into a new feudal rank—the *markgraf, marchisus,* marquis. To the markgraf was assigned a much larger territory than to the ordinary count, and he was allowed to exercise more extensive power. In this same period appeared also the *vicecomes*—the viscount—who acted as a representative of the count, in his absence, or when he held more than one county.

Under Charlemagne's government the old national assemblies with legislative rights are not to be found. Assemblies were held at regular intervals which were like them in form, but if there is anything in these assemblies which may be taken to represent the people, it had no influence upon legislation. Assemblies of the nobles, lay

[1] Under the Carolingians the office of duke, as an executive and military office over a number of counties, practically disappeared, and the title was used only exceptionally. The reason for this seems to have been, the way in which the office had been connected, in the later Merovingian times, with the aspirations for national independence among the subject peoples, Bavarians and Aquitanians, for example, where it had allowed the development of what was really a royal power. The *missi* in Charlemagne's government served the same purpose that the dukes might have done, though in a much better way.

[2] Brunner expressed the opinion in his *Entstehung der Schwurgerichte* (1872), p. 154, that the itinerant or circuit justices of England (and so naturally of the United States) descended from the *missi* of Charlemagne through the Normans. The connection with the Carolingian *missi* through the ninth and tenth centuries is somewhat difficult to prove by documentary evidence, but the probability of such a relationship is very great.

and ecclesiastic, sometimes acting together, seem to have had a consulting influence and a formal right of consent, but the practical legislative right was apparently exercised by the king, as would naturally be the case in a strong government growing out of a past of such political uncertainty.[1]

Besides the institutions of government given special shape by Charlemagne, two other facts of a different sort, but quite as important, indicate the character of his policy, and would tend to produce the same results—permanence of order and a renewal of civilization. They are his revival of schools and education and his renewing of the title of emperor of Rome in the West.

Of Charlemagne's revival of schools we know unfortunately too little to reconstruct his general plan or to determine how wide his purpose was.[2] We know there was a palace school, in which the children of the king were taught and those of the great nobles and promising children from the provinces, and where boys were trained for public employment. In this school Alcuin taught, who had been educated in England, and we know that Charlemagne sought teachers for his schools wherever else anything of learning had remained, as in northern Italy. We know also that schools were to be maintained by the monasteries and cathedral churches, which would naturally be of an intermediate grade, and we suspect, from the regulations for his own diocese of a bishop who was also employed as a royal *missus*, that there was an intention, or desire at least, of establishing free elemen-

---

[1] Perhaps no part of Charlemagne's political activity has been discussed with such varying opinions as his legislation. If to be a great lawgiver means to formulate broad principles of justice, which shall be capable of wide application to new cases, not thought of at the time, then he was not a great lawgiver. His legislation is rather a series of special laws to meet immediate cases, as they came up, and covering a very wide range of interest, but it was not creative of a permanent system of law.

[2] See Mullinger, *Schools of Charles the Great;* and West, *Alcuin and the Rise of the Christian Schools.*

tary public schools in each parish, to be taught by the parish priest. This would be a very wise and well-organized system for the times, if it really was what Charlemagne had in mind, and if it could have been carried into effect.

We know perhaps more as to the results which followed Charlemagne's revival of schools than we do as to the actual details of his educational system. The legal documents, letters, and writings of the next generation show a very decided improvement in style and accuracy, and this improvement was never lost.[1] The schools themselves, in places at least, continued to flourish even during the dissolution of his empire, as they had not before, and his efforts for education may clearly be reckoned as the first step towards the revival of learning.

Some of the original sources represent that the act of Pope Leo III, in placing a crown upon the head of Charlemagne as he was praying in St. Peter's on Christmas day of the year 800, and proclaiming him emperor of Rome, was a surprise to him and not acceptable.[2] But the plan of reviving the empire in the West must have been under discussion; there are indications that it had been thought of before the beginning of Charlemagne's reign, and the pope would hardly have ventured upon such a step unless he had known that it was in accordance with the general idea of the time. Charlemagne may have been surprised at the time chosen, and displeased with the assumption of the leading part in the drama by the pope, but there can be no reasonable doubt that he had determined upon taking the title before long. It must have seemed to every one at the time the per-

---

[1] There is a touch of the genuine spirit of the Renaissance to be seen in the case of the monk who takes advantage of a pilgrimage to Italy to copy inscriptions with exemplary accuracy. See Wattenbach, *Geschichtsquellen*, vol. I, pp. 173 and 280. (Seventh edition.)

[2] See Bryce, *Holy Roman Empire*, chap. V, where the accounts of three annalists are translated.

fectly natural thing to do.   His empire corresponded very
nearly with the western half of the Roman Empire, more
nearly than anything which had existed since.   Men had
believed all along, in a theoretical way, in the continuation
of the Roman Empire and in the overlordship of the emperor in Constantinople over the West and these theories
were still consciously held.   Just now the power in the
East was in the hands of a woman, something which the
people of the West regarded as especially unworthy and
impossible.   The time was favorable for a renewal of the
title in Rome, the man was at hand, the empire was
undeniably reconstructed in territory and in strength.
The actors in the event may not, perhaps, have thought
of themselves exactly as Romans, but they unquestionably thought of the empire as a direct and unbroken continuation of that of Augustus and Theodosius.

To Charlemagne himself, the direct gain which might
come from a revival of the empire may have been as important a consideration as the glory of the title itself.
The Roman Empire meant, above all things else, permanence and consolidation.   With no political structure of
history has the idea of eternal endurance so connected itself
as with the Roman Empire.   This feeling was not yet
entirely extinct, as is evident from the way in which this
revival was thought of at the time as entirely natural
and in no way extraordinary.   It would be a great help
to the permanence of the empire of the Franks if the
ideas and feelings which belonged to the Roman Empire
could be identified with it.   Again, the only government
of which the men of the West could know anything, under
which the diverse nationalities, which had been brought
together by the conquests of the Franks, could become
equal and organic parts of a single state, was the Roman
Empire.   Charlemagne might be recognized as their national ruler by Franks and Lombards and Saxons and
Bavarians, but the problem of his day, and of the future,

was how to unite these all together into a single whole,
a new homogeneous nationality, in which the old race
lines should have disappeared. The Roman Empire
might do this, and it alone could. That Charlemagne
consciously reasoned about the matter in this way is
hardly possible. It is altogether probable, however, that
he did believe that the taking of the title would be of
very great help to him in his struggle to consolidate
and render lasting the power which he had created.

The attempt of Charlemagne was a failure. His reign
was not long enough to allow such a unity of races, and
such a solidarity of law and government, to form themselves as had formed under Rome, and without this his
work could not be permanent. Even if his own life could
have continued through the whole ninth century, it is
very doubtful whether his genius would have been sufficient to hold in check the forces of separation and disorder. They certainly were too strong for the weaker
men who succeeded him, and his empire fell apart and
the strong government which he had established was
overpowered.

Some of the special things which he accomplished were
permanent contributions to civilization, like the conquest
of the Saxons and the revival of schools. Many of his
special political expedients disappeared with the strong
government which they had helped to sustain, as may
have been the case with the *missi*. But there was a profound and permanent influence of the empire and good
government of Charlemagne upon the general course of
history, though they themselves may not have continued.

He had created and sustained for a generation a really
powerful central government, obeyed and respected everywhere, and this fact was not forgotten in the days of
feudal confusion and anarchy which followed. Men

looked back to it, as they had earlier looked back upon
the Roman Empire, as an age when things were as they
ought to be—a kind of golden age, when most marvellous deeds were done, to be told of in poetry and romance.
The ideal of a strong king and a real government was so
deeply impressed upon the time that feudalism was never
able to destroy it, as logically it should have done, but
itself always retained the character which Charlemagne
had been the chief one to give it, of a constitutional organization for the state, exercising its powers and rights
as delegated to it, when strictly interpreted, and in the
name of a general government which theoretically must
continue to exist.

His empire also brought together for a time all the
Christian nations of the western portion of the Continent
in a real union. The unity which Rome had established
had been, for centuries past, merely theoretical. There
was no objective fact corresponding to it. The supremacy of the emperor at Constantinople over the whole empire was too shadowy to be of any real value in maintaining even the idea of unity. The church had formed
a real unity, but the political world had none. The theory itself would soon have passed out of the minds of
men if it had never taken form in fact. Charlemagne,
if we may say so, made the facts conform to the theory.
At the beginning of the period of most complete separation, when the feudal system was about to render the
existence even of state governments practically impossible, and to divide Europe into the smallest of fragments,
he recreated, for a generation or more, the Roman unity
as an actual fact, and strengthened the belief in its continued existence, as the ideal political constitution for
the world. His revival of the empire rendered possible
its second revival, on a somewhat different basis, by the
kings of Germany, and laid the foundation for that ideal
structure, the Holy Roman Empire, alongside the Holy

Roman Church—an ideal which grew more and more perfect in theory as the actual empire declined in power.

But if the empire had never been revived a second time by Otto I, and if the theory of the Holy Roman Empire had never been developed, the real unity which Charlemagne created would have been an enormous reinforcement to the influence of the church in holding the nations of the West together in a common system, and an especially decisive aid in this direction, because with its strong unity it cut the age of confusion and separation in half, and held the disintegrating forces of the time in check in their full career.

Of still further significance is the fact that Charlemagne represented, even more completely than Theodoric or any other of his predecessors had done, the union of German and Roman elements into a common whole. In Charlemagne personally and in his government they are manifestly united, not as two distinct and separate sets of things brought together consciously and with intention, and held together by an artificial arrangement, but they are mingled in a living and natural union, as if no one were conscious of any difference between them. Within a short time at least after his death, we have evidence in language, and in customary law, and in more or less clearly felt race feeling, that the same sort of a union had taken place in the mass of the people. The German had not been raised to the level of the classical civilization. The knowledge and culture lost had not been recovered, but enormous progress towards this recovery had been made when the German and the Roman had melted together into a single people, and begun to develop a new national consciousness.

The unity, which Charlemagne had formed, might be broken up, the empire might fall again into abeyance, the strong government disappear, but in such ways as have been indicated, his work was permanent.

CHAPTER VIII

AFTER CHARLEMAGNE

THE empire of Charlemagne passed at first into the hands of his son Louis and its formal unity was preserved. But Louis was by no means the equal of his father in strength and decision, and the control of affairs passed by degrees out of his hands to the bishops and the great nobles, to his sons, and even to his wife. The elements of disunion, repressed by Charlemagne, began to reappear; but unity suffered less in his reign than the efficiency of the central government, which constantly declined—the *missi* for example were rendered less effective by making the archbishop permanently one of the *missi* for his archbishopric.

On the death of Louis, his eldest son, Lothaire, became emperor, with a nominal supremacy over his two brothers, who had received subordinate kingdoms. A civil war between the brothers resulted in the treaty of Verdun, in 843, a rearrangement of territories which has probably had more influence on later times than any other ever made. By this partition Lothaire retained the title of emperor, with Italy and a long, narrow strip of land connecting Italy with the North Sea, and including the rivers Rhone and Rhine, separating in this way the subkingdoms of his two brothers, one in what is now Germany, and the other in what is now France, and bringing his territory through its whole length into direct contact with theirs. Nearly or quite all this territory assigned to Lothaire came to be connected at a later time with the empire, as held by the German king, but it was bound to Germany by only a very loose tie, and in it easily arose the semi-independent and finally independent little states of Europe, Holland and Belgium, and Switzerland and Savoy, while over other fragments of it France and Germany have been contending through nearly all later history.

On the death of the grandsons of Charlemagne their territories were still further divided, and the double process of separation and of the destruction of the central power went on without hindrance. For a moment, almost at the end of the Carolingian period, the empire was reunited under Charles the Fat, but he was entirely without power or capacity, and after a few years he was deposed (887), and the territorial unity of the empire was finally destroyed.

We call this the fall of the Carolingian empire, and it was so in one sense, but the term is unfortunate here as elsewhere in history, because it is apt to imply more than is meant. It must not be regarded as in any sense a fall or decline in civilization. It was more like a return to conditions which had prevailed under the Merovingian kings. These conditions had been dominated and controlled by three generations of remarkable princes, who had held in check successfully the worst tendencies of the time. Now, when the government passed into the hands of ordinary men, these conditions began to prevail again, but they prevailed with a difference. That the net result of the Carolingian empire had been a great gain has been made evident. The ideas of unity and order and good government had been so strengthened that a return to the situation of things in Merovingian times could never be complete, and those conditions could never be so dangerous as formerly. The great Carolingian princes had been compelled in one respect,

indeed, to recognize and continue these conditions. They
had been obliged, in order to accomplish their own purposes, to encourage and strengthen the growing feudal
institutions, as we shall see later, and to give them legal-
ity. But whatever they may have done in this direction was far more than balanced by the vigor with which
they subordinated these institutions to the state. Without their aid the feudal system would inevitably have
developed as it did, though perhaps less rapidly. But
without their strong control of the feudal powers in their
formative period the idea that these powers were exercised under the superior rights of the general government might easily have disappeared, as it actually did
here and there.

We are to regard this age, then, as continuing the
Merovingian, but with decided gains over that period.
On the surface, however, its most characteristic feature
is the decline of the powers which the three great Carolingians had built up, and our first task is to ascertain
the immediate causes of this decline, a thing not difficult
to do. It is not possible to attribute it, as we are perhaps at first tempted to do, to the weakness of the rulers.
Some of them were certainly men of inferior ability, men
who would be regarded as weak sovereigns even to-day,
when in most countries a stupid king or an insane one is
as good as any, or even better. But the most of them
seem to have been men at least of ordinary ability. It
was a time, however, when a man of ordinary ability
could not be master of the situation. A king, in order
really to govern such a turbulent society, would have
required the extraordinary genius of a Charlemagne, if
not something more, and no one had that. The family
had produced about as many generations of genius as
any in history, and it was rather because it did not continue to do this than because it sank below the level of
average men that it proved unequal to its task.

Nor can the cause be found in those partitions of territory between the members of the family which are so frequent during the period. The old Frankish notion of equal division among the heirs apparently could not be shaken off by the Carolingians, and subdivision followed subdivision to the end of the period. This, no doubt, weakened the idea of unity, and occasionally aided the deeper causes of separation, but it must not be regarded in itself as a very efficient force in that direction. Had the general conditions been more favorable, such partitions might have gone further than they did without serious consequences, and, indeed, they might have been of assistance to the kings in maintaining a real control of affairs by reducing the size of the territory to be controlled.

More serious than these, as intensifying the general conditions with which a government had to contend, were the severe attacks which were made on all the boundaries of the empire during this age. Saracens, Hungarians, and Northmen were trying to force their way in from every direction. In the Carolingian period proper the most dangerous of these attacks was that of the Northmen. Following exactly the methods of the earlier Saxons, they appeared without warning upon the coast or up the rivers with their swift boats, collected what plunder they could in a sudden raid inland, and were off before resistance could be organized. The great rivers of Gaul opened to them the heart of the country, and the distance to which they ascended them shows most clearly how little general organization there was, and how entirely each locality was thrown upon its own resources for protection. This absence of a general system of defence, this necessity which was placed upon each locality of looking out for its own protection in the face of a constantly menacing danger, is a fact of primary importance at this time. It greatly strengthened those institutions which organized the means of private and local defence, institutions which similar conditions had produced in earlier times, and which had continued their development even under Charlemagne.

With this fact—the fact that these institutions had now become very strong and grown into a great general organization, the feudal system, so strong that it was no longer possible to control its members or to prevent their exercise of royal prerogatives—we have reached the deepest and most effective cause of the fall of the Carolingian power.

The feudal system was itself an offspring of the prevailing conditions and gave expression to them. Whether or not the later Carolingians would have been able to maintain an effective government if the feudal system had not been in the way to prevent, certain it is that this system had taken its beginning in a time when from one cause or another an effective government had not been maintained, in the last days of the empire and in the Merovingian period. Since then nothing had occurred to check its development, though Charlemagne had been able to prevent any evil results from it in his own time. It had now reached a point of development which made it in itself an active factor in the state independent of the conditions which had brought it into existence. It had established itself on firm foundations. It had absorbed to some extent already, and was absorbing more and more, the functions, powers, and rights of the central government. It had produced a body of men secure in their position, able to dictate terms to the monarch at critical moments as the price of their assistance,[1] and

---

[1] The most familiar instance of this is the famous capitulary of Kiersy, obtained from Charles the Bald, in 877. This was not, as has sometimes been said, the legal recognition of a hereditary right to benefices, but it was an agreement on the part of the king to recognize such a right for the special occasion, showing, however, the existence of a strong tendency to turn offices and fiefs into hereditary possessions.

able to beat off the attacks of the Northmen where the state failed to do its duty. It had built up, in a word, little principalities everywhere which usurped for the locality the place of the state and divided the territory into small fragments tending towards complete independence.

So while the difficulty of intercommunication made it hard to maintain a real control of affairs at a distance, and while the ignorance and barbarism of the time made impossible those general ideas and common interests and feelings which are the foundation of a national government, the feudal system deprived the state of its organs of action. Its executive offices, its judicial system, its legislation, its income, and its army all passed into the hands of private individuals, and were made use of by them, theoretically, as representing the state, but in reality beyond its control. The king was practically shut up to whatever power the feudal lords might be willing to concede to him at the moment.

The origin of this system and the state of things resulting from it will be discussed in detail in the next chapter. Here it is necessary to fix in mind the fact that the Carolingian family, which had done not a little to give it definite form and position in the state, fell its victim and lost the throne because they could no longer control their own vassals.

But the declining power of the Carolingian family, and the fact that even in the small states into which their great empire had separated they could not really govern, is not the only fact of importance which this period signifies in the political history of the world. It was not an age of chaos alone. In the breaking up of the Carolingian empire the European nations as they exist to-day first took shape.

How much of real national consciousness there was in the states that separated from one another at this time it is not easy to say. There is danger that we may read into that earlier time, when it could hardly have existed, the idea of national feeling which we now have. Certainly patriotism and a feeling of race unity and of national pride do not appear as positive forces in history, whose workings can be clearly traced, till near the end of the middle ages. There is evidence, however, that there was at least some slight national consciousness at this time; that the people in one of these new states began to distinguish themselves from those in another, and, however much they might still be divided within the state, to look upon themselves as more closely related to one another than to the people of another state. The new languages had begun to form themselves—a clear proof of the melting of Romans and Germans into a common people—and these would help to form the idea of national distinctions. Common names for the people of the whole state seem to have come into use in this period. The church of each state had its own national organization, and this furnished one of the most powerful influences of the age, both in the formation of the new state governments and in the growth of a real national unity.

But whatever may be true of the formation of a national consciousness at this time—and when the most is said it must have been very faint—the modern nations did secure in this period their geographical outlines very much as they exist to-day, and separate political organizations were formed, corresponding to these territories and uniting them—however loosely—still uniting them into a single state. These political organizations have developed into the modern governments, and within the geographical limits thus secured the feeling of national unity and patriotism grew up in the course of time.

It was in Germany that the Carolingian family was first permanently abandoned for a national dynasty. Arnulf, who was the last Carolingian who really ruled in Germany, was a man of energy, and the ten years and more of his reign, from 887 to 899, was a continual struggle against the Northmen and Slavs. Against these external enemies he was successful, but he did nothing to prevent—in some cases he aided—the growth of the local feudal dominions which were as serious a danger. After him came a dozen years of minority rule, when naturally the local powers grew rapidly, and the devastating invasions of the Hungarians, which began within a year or two after the death of Arnulf, strengthened this tendency by increasing the confusion and insecurity with which the general government could not cope.

The feudal system did not reach its maturity quite so early in Germany as in France, not having grown up naturally there but being rather introduced from without. But the conditions which favored its growth were like those in France, and the results in the end were the same. The general insecurity of the times, the constant need of protection, the weakness or the distance of the central government, and perhaps the lack of any strong conception of a national unity, enabled the strong man of the locality to found a little state within the state, and to extend his power, if circumstances especially favored him, over a large territory.

The old tribal differences which still existed among the Germans, notwithstanding all the efforts of the Carolingians to obliterate them, came to the aid of these little substates—it would be more accurate perhaps to say that these differences were the foundation on which they were first built. The Carolingians had abolished the old ducal office which represented a tribal royal power, and they had endeavored to prevent any continuance of the tribal life in the arrangements which they made for local government. During the time of their decline, however, the old tribal consciousness had begun to reassert itself, and the ducal office to reappear, at first without any recognition or legal right, but as existing by force of circumstances and by common consent.

Aided by circumstances of this sort, a family having its original seat in the eastern part of the Saxon land, in a region exposed at once to the attacks of the Danes and of the Slavs, had gradually extended its power, by the skill of its leadership and the bravery of its defence, over the whole tribe of the Saxons, and finally over the Thuringians also, and created a dominion which, under the ducal name, was really a little kingdom. Another family in Franconia—the land of the east Franks—had risen in a similar way, aided by the favor of King Arnulf, to a power almost as great, but it had made good its position only after a severe struggle with dangerous rivals. In Suabia and Bavaria the tribal spirit also revived and raised local leaders to the position of practically independent dukes. The feudal system was spreading very rapidly throughout Germany at this time, and its forms greatly helped on the rise of these local dynasties; but it is important to notice, as has been suggested, that these little states into which the east Frankish kingdom threatened to separate at the moment of the extinction of the Carolingian family there, were based at the outset rather on the old tribal differences than on feudal constructions.

It was the influence of the church of Germany—a united organization, finding all its interests involved in the continuance of a united political government—combined perhaps with a deep impression which the unity created by Charlemagne had made, and very possibly also aided by an incipient national consciousness, which prevented this threatened separation from being completely realized, and formed a new national government in the place of the one which had disappeared.

On the death of the last Carolingian, an assembly somewhat national in character came together to choose

a new king. They turned naturally first to the Saxon
duke Otto, the most powerful man in Germany, but he
was now old and was not willing to undertake the burdens of the new office. By his influence Konrad, the
duke of the eastern Franks, was elected king. This election was not made in forgetfulness of the rights of the
Carolingians, whose representatives were still to be found
west of the Rhine. Their claims were kept in mind, and
it was thought indeed to be something in favor of Konrad that he was descended from a daughter of Louis the
Pious. But there seems to have been no serious movement in favor of the old house, nor any feeling that it
could adequately meet the needs and serve the interests
of the times.

Konrad was a brave and earnest man who had a high
conception of the duties and rights of his office and strove
manfully to realize that conception. But the difficulties
were too great for him to overcome. He did not have in
his own local power, and in the tribe of the Franks, which
must be his main reliance in establishing a real government, strength enough to force the other local and tribal
powers into obedience, and his reign was a failure in this
respect. It is told us that at his death he recognized
this fact, and saw that if a national government was to
be made effective it could be done only by his great rival
whose personal power was so much stronger than his
own, by the duke of the Saxons. Following his advice, the
Germans passed over the Franconian family and elected
Henry the Saxon king, and from his accession in 918, the
process of forming a national government for Germany
really begins.

Of this national government Henry hardly more than
laid the foundation, but he did this with great skill and
with a statesman's recognition of the things that were
possible in the circumstances. He brought the dukes to
a formal obedience and to a recognition of the kingship,

but he did this by diplomatic tact rather than by force of arms, and he left to them almost complete and independent local control. It was too early yet to break their power in this particular. He organised the national forces for a most successful resistance to the Hungarians, founded many fortified posts in north and east Germany which grew later into cities, led the Saxons on rapidly in the line of development begun for them by Charlemagne, opened again the struggle with the Slavs for the valley of the Elbe, and finally drew closer the alliance between the royal power which was forming and the church which could give it so great assistance.

It was by no means the least of his successes that he secured the quiet and undisputed succession of his son Otto to the throne. Otto does not seem to have had his father's diplomatic ability, but he was a man of strong determination and quick action, and he built rapidly on the foundations which his father had laid. The dukes and the semi-independent tribes seem to have recognized the fact that it was a life-and-death struggle for them, and they broke into open rebellion almost immediately after his accession. The victory over this open resistance, which Otto everywhere gained, enabled him to go further than his father had ventured. He deposed the old ducal families from their half-royal position, set in their place devoted friends of his own, and made the duke once more, if not completely, yet more nearly, an officer of the state. Finally, he put beside the duke the *Pfalzgraf*, or palatine count, to be a check on the ducal power and to administer the royal domain lands scattered through the duchy, and so not merely deprived the duke of one source of his power but also established an important means of direct connection between the central government and the locality. It was the first step, and a long one, towards a really consolidated government for the nation. If this policy could have been continued for a generation or two without interruption the work would have been done and a real state created corresponding to the language and the race. But this was not destined to be. Hardly was Otto master of things at home when he was called upon to go to Italy and right wrongs which had been committed there, and he could not resist the temptation. The dream of the empire still lived in the German mind, and Otto was perhaps more ready to go than the Capetian princes of France were to embrace similar opportunities offered to them, because his power at home was so much greater than theirs.

In Italy no one of the local powers into which the country had separated, there as everywhere else on the fall of the Carolingian empire, had been able to gain sufficient strength permanently to overcome the others, and to lay the foundation of a united government as it had been the fortune of some to do in France and in Germany. The existence of the papacy at the head of a little state in central Italy, strengthened by rights of ecclesiastical rule which extended over Europe, had further complicated the situation, and Italy had been the scene of more constant civil strife than the other countries, and with far less meaning or result. It was consequently very easy for a foreign prince, not dependent upon the country for his resources, to exact at least a formal acknowledgment of his right to govern. In a first expedition Otto compelled a recognition of his right to settle disputed points and assumed the title of King of Lombardy. In a second, in 962, he was crowned emperor of Rome.

This might seem to him, and to the men of his time, though it was not done apparently without some opposition in Germany, to be a very great extension of his power and a most glorious achievement for the German nation, but it was in reality a fatal step both for Germany and for Italy. By this step it was finally made impossible to organize a national government for Italy; and the kings of Germany, in the place of their proper task, the consolidation of their own state, were given what seemed to them a more glorious mission, the reconstruction of the Roman Empire. But to do both things, in the face of the difficulties which each presented, was a human impossibility, and naturally the interest which they thought to be the smaller—the German nation—was sacrificed to the greater. Things were allowed at critical periods to go as they would, and the promising beginning of a national unity was broken into a hundred fragments.

In the case of Italy one can hardly lament the failure of the Italian people to form a truly national government as he does that of the Germans. Had such a government been formed it would undoubtedly have saved the Italians much political misery and tyranny, and very likely it would have made them a larger and a stronger state than they are to-day. But if it had been done either by the earlier Lombard kings or by some of the local nobles at the fall of Charlemagne's empire, Italy would probably have failed of the peculiar glories of her history; the stimulating rivalries of the little municipal republics in the latter half of the middle ages would have been lacking, and the great results which seem to be in such close dependence upon these would have occurred more slowly, and very possibly in some other part of Europe.

In France the new family which was to take the place of the Carolingian formed its power in the neighborhood of Paris. From an unknown ancestor it rose into prominence very rapidly in the ninth century by the qualities which everywhere gave success in those times.[1] Its mem-

---

[1] The later tradition, referred to by Dante, *Purgatorio*, XX, 52, that the Capetians were descended from a butcher of Paris, has no historical foundation, but it illustrates in a striking way the popular recognition of the

bers were good fighters and were able to protect their dependants. Its lands rapidly increased until they touched the Loire, and it went quickly up the ladder of feudal rank until finally a duchy was formed and the head of the family became duke of the French. No other of the local powers which had formed themselves in France was as strong as this one, though it was not relatively so much stronger than the others as the Saxon power was in Germany.

When Charles the Fat was deposed, the first attempt was made to transfer the crown to the new family, and Duke Eudes, or Odo, was made king in 888. But he was recognized only by a small part of France, and a Carolingian king was set up against him. For one hundred years the royal title passed back and forth between the two houses, neither having a secure hold upon it, though during far the larger part of the century the Carolingians were the recognized kings. Finally Duke Hugh the Great added the skill of the statesman and diplomatist to the warrior skill of his ancestors, and greatly strengthened and extended the influence of his house. His son, Hugh Capet, was elected king on the death of the Carolingian Louis V, in 987, and though Charles of Lorraine, who continued the Carolingian line, offered resistance, he was able to gain no general support, and the Capetian family secured final possession of the throne.

In the election of Hugh Capet it is probable that a conscious national feeling—a realization of the distinction of race and language—was less directly a factor than in the corresponding revolution in Germany. But the conditions which had been making France different from Germany were the conditions which had undermined the power of the Carolingian family and given the Capetian

fact that men from the lowest station were founding feudal families of high rank in the ninth century as a consequence of their personal bravery and their skill as leaders.

family its position of superiority, and the substitution of the new family for the old upon the throne made it easy for the resulting differences to intensify and perpetuate themselves. France was becoming thoroughly feudal. It was the native land of the feudal system, and there that system had developed earliest and most completely. This new feudalism was especially strong towards the West. The Capetian was the most powerful of all the feudal families. The Carolingians represented an old power above feudalism. They clung closely to the East, the primitive seat of their power. The revolution in France meant the accession to power of the new and active forces which were to shape the future, in place of the old which had done their work, and one of the most important and direct results of their action, under the native dynasty thus placed in power, was by degrees the growth of a national consciousness, from the slight germ which existed at the beginning.

The real power which the first Capetians exercised as kings was, however, very slight. The whole of France was covered with feudal dominions like the duchy of France, some of them as strong, if not stronger, than their own. Normandy, Champagne, Burgundy, and Aquitaine were only the largest of a network of local principalities which occupied the whole territory and shut out the king from all direct contact with land or people.

The duchy of France was the source from which the Capetians drew their actual power, and, managed with skill, this was enough to form a solid foundation on which to build a more general authority. The national church, with its influence and its resources, was of enormous aid to them, and it was of no slight assistance to them also that they had on their side the theory of the kingship and of the prerogatives of a strong central government which had come down from the earlier Carolingian days. These were but shadowy prerogatives, and had no more

real value than the great feudal lords might be willing
to allow them, but they formed a perfectly distinct standard towards which every accession of strength by the
Capetians was an advance. The first four generations
of the new dynasty did but little more than to secure
the hold of their family upon the throne, carefully obtaining the recognition of the son in the father's lifetime;
but they lost nothing, and the way was prepared for a
steady advance of the royal power from that time on.

In the setting up of these national governments in
France and in Germany there are certain features common to both cases which are worthy of notice.

In neither does there seem to have been any strong
feeling of attachment to the Carolingian house. How
far one may be justified in reasoning from this is doubtful, but it would seem that there was in both countries
at least an unconscious judgment that the Carolingians
represented a different condition of things from the one
then present, and a desire to choose a royal house which
would more perfectly correspond to the new development.
Certainly in both countries it was a fatal weakness of
that house that it had formed no local power; that it
did not have in its hands immediate domains, a duchy
of its own which would have been strongly devoted to
it and from which it could have drawn men and resources
independent of the great feudal nobles. This was the
corner-stone of the success of the Saxon family in Germany and of the Capetians in France. If the Carolingians had been great feudal nobles as well as kings they
might possibly have held their own.

In both these states the church, though acting independently, cast its influence in the same direction. In both
cases, as the power of the Carolingians weakened and the
subdivisions of the state became practically independent,
and as there was a feeling manifested that a general government was not necessary and that the local govern-

ments were really better for the times; in other words,
when there was an immediate danger of complete disintegration the church was one of the strongest influences
in persuading men to continue the national government,
and in effecting the transfer of the state to the new families which could give some promise of re-establishing
a strong rule. And the reason in both cases also was the
same, the danger which would threaten the general organization of the church if the state should fall apart
into entirely separate fragments. In both cases, too,
when the transfer had been made, the church, both in
means and in influence, was one of the greatest resources
of the new monarchy in its struggle to consolidate the
state.

In England the various Saxon kingdoms which were
established at the time of the conquest had been united
early in the ninth century under the supremacy of Wes-
sex. At the end of that century the strong energy and
wisdom of Alfred—a genius equal to Charlemagne's within
his narrower kingdom and a character superior to his—
had laid broad and sound foundations for a national development. The judicial organization of the state was
improved; the military system was strengthened and
tested in a long, and in the main successful, war; the old
and conflicting laws were formed into a new and enlarged
body of legislation; and learning and literature were
aided and encouraged by the king's own example. But
it was a beginning without immediate results.

England lay directly in the way of the Northmen, and
their invasion of the island was a veritable settlement
like those of the earlier Teutonic invasions. Alfred's successors struggled long, but finally in vain, with the difficulties of the situation, and England was in the end annexed to the Scandinavian empire of Cnut the Great
in the first part of the eleventh century. But Northmen and Saxons were not widely separated in race or

language, and the blending of the two in a single people was not difficult. The Saxon monarchy, which was re-established in 1042, might easily have developed into the later nation, but another element still was to be added to the complex English character.

The Northmen had made one other permanent settlement besides that in England, in northern France, and had formed a little state there early in the tenth century, the duchy of Normandy, feudally dependent upon the king of France. There they had quickly lost their identity of race and language, and had developed a peculiar and interesting civilization. On the death of Edward the Confessor, the last king of England of the Saxon line, William, the duke of Normandy, asserted a right to the English crown and speedily made it good by force of arms.

With him came a new invasion of foreigners, to be absorbed by a long process into the English people, and a century later, with the accession of the Angevin kings, came another immigration of the same sort. So that even in England, though it had the advantage of the continental states, in its smaller size which rendered the task of a common government easier, a genuine national consciousness was formed only towards the close of the middle ages. But with the accession of William, in 1066, the state took on its external form, as had the German and the French states in the preceding century.

This new government presents, however, at its beginning a marked contrast to those of the other two countries; the feudal system on its political side had not grown up in England under the Saxon kings as it had on the Continent. The German elements, which were one of the sources of feudalism, had developed there into institutions which may rightly in some particulars be called feudal, but the essential features of the historical feudal system were lacking, and no powerful baronage

had been formed standing between the English people
and the state, and exercising by right or by usurpation
the royal prerogatives. The Continental political feudal
system was introduced into England by the Conqueror,
but it was not the ordinary feudalism of Europe. It was
feudalism of the type which prevailed in Normandy,
highly centralized and serving as the machinery of government under a sovereign who remained the most powerful factor in the state. Following a practice which had
been universal in the early days of feudalism, and which
had not fallen out of use in the duchy of Normandy, he
claimed the superior allegiance, enforced by an oath, of
the vassals of every lord. The lands which he granted to
his followers were scattered about, probably more from
local conditions than by intention, in such a way that
they could in few cases be consolidated into little states
within the state, and with his gifts of land he did not
grant away royal prerogatives. He retained also, as the
direct royal domains, much larger territories than he
granted to any vassal.

The results were decisive. Feudalism was gradually
introduced into England, and after a time, in the legal
theory, the feudal principles came to control all land-
holding, but there never grew up in England any such
political system as on the Continent. The king was at
the very outset the strongest power in the state, and the
period in English history which is most nearly that of
an absolute monarchy is that of her Norman and first
Angevin kings.

In Spain, as in Italy, there was nothing corresponding to a national government, but for a different reason.
The old German kingdom of the Visigoths had fallen in
the eighth century before the Saracen invasion. In the
ninth century a row of Christian states began to form
across the northern edge of the country, partly from the
refugees who had saved themselves in the mountains of

the northwest from submission to the Arabs and partly from the Frankish counties in Charlemagne's Spanish territory. By the middle of the eleventh century the kingdoms of Leon, Castile, Navarre, Aragon, and Barcelona had taken shape, and had begun the double process of pushing the Arabs farther and farther towards the south and of uniting with one another. Both these processes go on through all the remainder of medieval history, and, indeed, it is a fact which had important political consequences in modern history that the people of Spain were not united in a common national feeling even at the beginning of the sixteenth century.

We have, then, as the outcome of this period, a foundation laid for the later national development in the leading countries of Europe, each with its own peculiar features. Let us compare briefly the state of things that existed in the eleventh century with the situation in each of the three great states—England, France, and Germany —just after the opening of modern history, say in the seventeenth century, and we shall readily find the key to the inner political history of these countries during the intervening centuries.

In Germany, at the beginning of the eleventh century, the royal power, if not absolute or undisputed, was strong. The most essential steps had been taken towards consolidating the state and destroying the tendencies towards local independence, and there was every promise that the process would go on to complete success. In the seventeenth century we find the central power reduced to a mere name, with none of the characteristics whatever of a national government, and the territory occupied by the nation split up into hundreds of little states, to all intents and purposes entirely independent. In the time between these two dates something must have greatly weakened the royal power and allowed the disruptive forces, which the Saxon kings had apparently overcome, to act again and to bring about their natural results—results much more extreme indeed and more disastrous for the nation than those which were threatened at the beginning by the revival of the old tribal spirit.

In France, in the eleventh century, the royal power was hardly more than a mere theory, and the country was broken up into numerous fragments which were practically almost as independent as those of modern Germany. In the France of the seventeenth century we find, on the other hand, an almost ideal centralization. Every function of the general government and almost every one of local government is exercised by Louis XIV, and scarcely a vestige is left of any constitutional check upon his irresponsible will. The intervening history must have been one of continuous centralization. The kings must have been able to destroy completely the feudal system, to force the nobles into obedience, and to recover without exception the prerogatives which they had usurped. French history must be the history of the formation of a real national government out of a feudal chaos.

When we examine English history in the seventeenth century we find the kings engaged in a final struggle to preserve the last relics of that absolutism which the Norman kings had exercised without a check, and that century does not close until they had virtually confessed defeat, and the real management of the state had passed into the hands of a legislative assembly representing both nobles and people—an assembly strongly aristocratic in its spirit and composition, but started already, as is plainly to be seen, in the direction of a more democratic government. English domestic history during these centuries must have been very different from either French or German. In some way a virtual alliance must have been brought about between the nobles—so much weaker at the start than the king—and the representatives of a strong middle class, and together they must have carried on the work of limiting the royal power and of finding out constitutional checks upon the exercise of the king's prerogatives which should gradually transfer the real control of affairs to themselves.

The later medieval history of Germany is the history of the destruction of a promising national organization; of France, the history of the construction of a complete absolutism; of England, the history of the formation of a constitutionally limited monarchy.

The movement towards nation formation which follows the breaking up of Charlemagne's empire was only a slight and vaguely conscious beginning, but it was a beginning clearly and definitely, and of the very greatest interest. The importance of the step in advance which was taken when the nation came finally into conscious existence, as a result of the movement which begins in the ninth century, cannot be stated in words nor in any way measured. The whole of civilization was lifted at once by that step to a higher plane. As in the opening age of civilization of which history tells us anything— not by inference backward but by record—the unit was the family, and later the tribe was formed by a union of families, and later still the city state by a coalition of tribes, and all ancient history centred about the strife of city state with city state, until one such city had grown into a great empire in which all city and race lines were obliterated in one vast unity which was neither city state nor yet nation, so by the end of the middle ages another stage in this line of progress was reached, and in modern times the unit of all political and public life and the acting force in what we call "international" politics has been the nation—not the state, nor the government, but the living organism which expresses itself through the state—a higher organism than any which had existed in the classical world.[1] It may be characterized as a community of persons having a common language and race feeling, common interests, aspirations, and history, and occupying a definite territory in which city and country are indistinguishably blended, and feeling itself a fully independent and equal member of a larger system of things, once Christendom, now perhaps the whole world. One of the most profound forces of modern times made its way into history with the gradual formation of this idea, and the broadening of all thought and the stimulating of all activities which accompanied it.

[1] If we could venture to put any trust in the apparently regular and natural character of this progress, the next step logically would seem to be the formation of some kind of an international federation, or possibly even a world state. It would not be difficult to point out at least a few tendencies of the present time which seem to point in the direction of such a result— a possibility which the Anglo-Saxon race, though seemingly in the best position to realize it, does not appear to recognize, certainly not so consciously as some other races do.

CHAPTER IX

THE FEUDAL SYSTEM[1]

OUT of the fragments of the Carolingian empire the modern nations were finally to arise. But there was in the meantime, as we have seen, a considerable period, after the fall of the old government, before any real national governments, at all corresponding to the modern idea, came into existence. This is the period when the feudal system was the prevailing form of political organization.

In any detailed history of civilization it would be necessary to give much space to the feudal system, both because of the large field which it occupies in the political life of the middle ages, and also because it is one of the most influential of medieval institutions, the source of legal principles and social ideas, which are, even now, by no means obsolete.

[1] Some portions of this chapter are a more detailed statement of the facts than is ordinarily the case in this book because there is as yet in English no fully satisfactory account either of the origin or of the final character of feudalism. The author's article "Feudalism" in the eleventh edition of the *Encyclopædia Britannica* is closely parallel to this chapter and also a summary account, but it treats of several points more fully. It has not seemed best in a book of this kind to attempt any account of feudal practices in detail. It should be noticed that the word "system" is used in the phrase "feudal system" for convenience merely and with no intention of conveying the meaning "systematic." In regard to the character of completed feudalism, the contribution made by the feudal law to national systems of law was so great that a somewhat more accurate knowledge of feudal practices was preserved, and the accounts of these matters given in such books, for example, as Hallam's *Middle Ages* and Guizot's *History of Civilization in France* are more nearly in agreement with the facts, though needing modification in many ways, than what these authors have to say of the origin of the system.

The question of the origin of the feudal system is one of the most difficult in all institutional history, for one reason, because it took its rise in ages which have left us very scanty historical material, and for another, because it originated in the domain of extra-legal and private operations, and under the influence of forces which leave but slight traces of their working. Every important point in this history has been the subject of long and violent controversy, and is so still, though to a less extent. It may be said that opinion is now practically united upon the main points in the history of political feudalism, and that present differences concern minor points of detail, or the amount of emphasis which shall be placed upon certain facts.

Before entering upon the details of the origin of the feudal system, there is one general consideration which has an important bearing upon the study which should be made clear. It is necessary here, and in all institutional history, to distinguish very carefully between two sets of causes or antecedents. First, there is the general cause, or the prevailing condition of things in the society of the time, which renders a new institution necessary; and, second, there is the old institution, on which the prevailing cause seizes, and which it transforms into a new one. Both these are always present. No institution ever starts into life wholly new. Every new institution has its foundation far in the past in some earlier one. The prevailing necessity transforms it into a new institution, but the character of the new creation is as much conditioned by the character of the old as it is by the new necessity which it is made to meet. The sneer which is sometimes heard against that sort of investigation which seeks the foundations of a new institution in those which have preceded it, as merely antiquarian, is proof only of a very narrow conception of history.

The application of this consideration to the present

case becomes clear enough when the problem before us
is specifically stated. What we have to do is not to account for the rise of feudal forms in general, but to account for that peculiar feudal system, which arose in
western Europe in the middle ages. It is undoubtedly
true that institutions have existed in Japan, and in Central Africa, and in various Mohammedan states, almost
everywhere, indeed, which are justly called feudal. It is
true that under certain political conditions human nature
turns, naturally as it would seem, to forms of government which are feudal. And it is necessary to take these
political and social conditions into account in our study
of the problem more fully than has been done, perhaps,
by some merely institutional historians. They are among
the most essential causes at work. But when taken alone
they merely account for the rise of feudal forms in general. They give us no reason for the fact that in institutional details these various feudal systems differ from
one another in essential particulars. To explain this fact
we must turn to the earlier institutional foundation on
which in each case the social forces built.

By "the feudal system," when used without qualification, we always mean the system of medieval western
Europe, and in accounting for its origin we have two
sets of facts to consider—the condition of society which
gave such forms an opportunity to develop, and the earlier institutions which were transformed by these social
and economic conditions into the historical feudal system,
and which determined the form assumed by many of the
special features of that system.

By "the feudal system" again we commonly mean, as
we should, the entire organization of society from top to
bottom. In studying it, therefore, we have constantly
to remember that this organization was a two-sided one.
There had been more or less closely combined in it two
distinct groups of practices and institutions which were

in their origin independent of one another, which had
grown up to meet different needs, and which remained
to the end clearly distinguished by contemporaries and
easily distinguishable by us. Described in the most general terms, one side was the feudal organization of government, and the other was the feudal organization of
agriculture. In the case of both alike, development of
the original beginnings had been induced by the same
general condition of things in the middle and later empire, the decay of the ancient civilization, political and
economic. On one side political influences were especially
active; certain earlier legal practices were seized upon
and developed into institutions practically new in order
to furnish to the free man locally the protection which
the general government was no longer able to give. On
the other side the economic were the chief influences,
and institutions which had for their object to secure
compulsorily the necessary cultivation of the soil were
developed and added to existing institutions. The former
gave rise to what we more often mean when we speak
of feudalism, the latter to what we may call, using a
term more frequent in England than elsewhere, the manorial system. Logically, historically, and legally, there
was no necessary connection between these two sides of
feudalism. There need have been no actual connection.
Either side might become highly developed with practically no, or an imperfect, development of the other, as
did economic feudalism in the Anglo-Saxon states. In
the actual situation, however, both earlier and later, the
vast importance of agriculture as the chief source of
wealth and the chief support of life made it inevitable
that, where political feudalism was at all developed, it
should enter into a partnership with economic feudalism.
It is of great importance to remember that their union
was never more than a partnership. They never were
amalgamated into one, but the two sides remained distinct and distinguishable so long as they existed.

It does not accord with the general purpose of this book to undertake a detailed account of the rise of the manorial system or description of its final character. These things are to be sought in the special field of economic history. Here it will suffice to say that the manorial system was created by taking as a beginning the Roman system of organizing the cultivation of a great estate as a unit, managed from a common centre, the *villa*, and adding to it the practice of attaching the agricultural laborer to the soil so that he could not leave it himself or be removed from it by the landlord. This practice created the serf class, and by combining it with the great estate cultivated as a unit, the manor was created. So simple a statement, however, does not dispose of all the difficulties of this development, nor was the manorial system, even where independent of feudalism proper, quite so completely divorced from all results that may be called political, as this would seem to imply. Especially is it necessary to notice one development intimately connected with the rise of the manor which results in many cases in the transfer to the lord of the manor of a responsibility which is political, and normally the function of the state.

In the simplest terms, which nevertheless describe accurately the general process, this transfer came about in the following way: The Roman master had over his slaves the power of life and death and of all minor punishment. The state assumed no responsibility in regard to the misdemeanors and crimes of the slave. As the slave was transformed into the serf, still unfree, the master's responsibility in these matters continued the same. But as the serf had been granted certain limited rights, a definite piece of land, the temporary possession of some personal property, disputes between them over these things, which would be of the nature of civil, not criminal, cases would arise. These also fell to the lord's decision. Here is the germ of a jurisdiction and a court, which very likely in the beginning did not extend over free men. As by degrees, however, partly from economic and partly from political reasons, free men began to be included within the manorial organization, it was inevitable that disputes between them and other members of the same community should fall into the lord's court. The state in its weakness was probably not unwilling that his responsibility should also extend itself at least to some of the criminal acts of free men. It is only necessary to suppose that the manor in time became identical in extent with the territorial jurisdiction of some local public court, the town or the hundred, to see how easy it would be to take a further step and to identify, by royal grant or private usurpation, the local public court of that territory with the private court which had grown up in the manor.

This process was greatly aided by the fact that both the general government and the landlord looked upon the administration of local justice largely as a source of revenue. Fees and fines, which in those days were paid in every case, were considered no insignificant additions to public or private income. It was evidently the economic consideration which was the chief one in this transfer, but the effect was to a considerable extent political. What is really a function of local government had passed into private hands, in many cases quite independently of the other general transformation which was going on at the same time of the functions of the central government into private possession in the rise of political feudalism proper. Where this transfer took place the local court, if it was that of a small political unit like the town, was often united with the manorial court, so that the two became practically one. If it was that of a larger unit like the hundred, the public court often continued distinct though in private hands. Whether united or distinct, however, the two jurisdictions, the manorial and the local public, were in almost all cases distinguishable from one another, and seem to have been so distinguished by contemporaries. The manorial jurisdiction proper remained a feature of economic feudalism so long as that system survived, and indeed in some countries it continued long after political feudalism proper had disappeared and local jurisdiction been fully resumed by the state. In this form it came to be transferred to some of the American colonies like Maryland.

The political feudal system proper, with which we have chiefly to deal, came into existence in the eighth and ninth centuries, owing to the disorders of the time, and the inability of the central government—even of so strong a government as Charlemagne's—to do its necessary work without some such help. It is itself a crude and barbarous form of government in which the political organization is based on the tenure of land; that is, the public duties and obligations which ordinarily the citizen owes to the state, are turned into private and personal services which he owes to his lord in return for land which he has received from him. The state no longer depends upon its citizens, as citizens, for the fulfilment of public duties, but it depends upon a certain few to perform specified duties, which they owe as vassals of the king, and these in turn depend upon their vassals for services, which will enable them to meet their own obligations towards the king. The services rendered in this way were not regarded in the feudal age as an economic return for the land, and all ranks obtained their necessary income from other sources, chiefly from the economic side of feudalism, that is, the manorial organization.

There are always present in this political feudal system two elements which seem very closely united together, but which are really distinct, and to be kept apart from one another in mind if we are to understand the origin of the system. They were distinct in origin and early history and were brought together only in the middle period of feudal growth. One of these relates wholly to land and the tenure by which it is held. This land element is the "benefice" or "fief." The other is the personal relation, the bond of mutual fidelity and protection which binds together the grades in the feudal hierarchy. This personal element is the relation of lord and vassal. In the ideal feudal system these two elements are always united, the vassal always receives a fief, the fief is always held by a vassal. In practice they were sometimes separated, and in some countries such a separation was recognized by the feudal law. There are, then, these two specific questions concerning the origin of the feudal system: How did these two institutions, vassalage and the benefice, come into existence and become united; and how did public duties, for example military service, get attached to them, and become changed in this way into private services which one paid as a form of land rent?

When we come to trace the origin of these two institutions we find that we are carried back to the time of political insecurity when the Roman Empire was falling to pieces, just before and at the moment of the German invasions. Then began the conditions which called these institutions into existence, and which, continuing in the main unchanged through the whole period, transformed them into the perfected feudal system.

As the real power which the Roman emperor had at his command declined, his ability to protect the citizens and preserve order in the outlying provinces became less and less. The peace and security which Rome had formerly established could no longer be maintained, and the provinces fell a prey to various disorders. Usurping emperors, peasants in insurrection, revolted troops, bands of invading Germans, marauders of all sorts appeared everywhere, and the state could not hold them in check. But the individual must obtain protection at some price. If he owns land, he will need protection in order to cultivate it and enjoy the returns; if he has no land, he will still need protection for his life and his means of livelihood. If he cannot get it from the state he must seek it where he can find it. In such political conditions there always arises a class of men strong enough from wealth or position or abilities to give some degree of protection to weaker men. The weaker men take refuge with the stronger and increase their power, which thus grows into a little semi-detached fragment of the state, and the germ of the feudal system has come into existence.

In the later Roman Empire, under the influence of these conditions, two practices arose which we need to notice. One of them related to land, the other to persons owning no land. In the case of the first, the small landowner, long at an economic disadvantage, and now, in the midst of the crowding evils of the time, threatened with total destruction, gave up his land to some large landowner near him, whose position was strong enough to command or compel respect from vagrant enemies, and received it back from him to cultivate, no longer as owner, but as a tenant at will. As the form of tenure to be used in such cases, a peculiar kind of lease which had been known to the Roman law as the *precarium* received a great extension in practice. Under this form the owner granted the use of a piece of property to another, without rent and with no period of time specified, but with the right to call it back at will.[1] This was the kind of

---

[1] The language of the Digest both illustrates this point and suggests the way in which *benefice* came to take the place of *precarium* as the technical word. It says, XLIII, 26, 14, "Interdictum de precariis merito introductum est, quia nulla eo nomine juris civilis actio esset; magis enim ad donationes et beneficii causam, quam ad negotii contracti spectat precarii condicio." This means that a case concerning a *precarium* does not have the same standing in the courts as an ordinary business transaction, because a grant in this form is not so much a matter of business as of gift or to confer a benefit.

tenure by which the small landholder held and cultivated the land which he had been obliged to surrender to some strong man for fear of losing it entirely. He lost the ownership of it; he held it only so long as his lord might please, but his actual condition was much improved. In the growing scarcity of laborers he was not likely to be disturbed in his tenure, and he had now an armed force which could be depended on to keep off all marauders not actually armies, and he had a right to take refuge in his lord's fortress on some not distant hilltop when a more serious invasion threatened.

The other practice was adopted to meet the case of the freeman who owned no land, and it gave rise to an institution closely resembling, possibly derived from, the clientele which Cæsar describes as prevailing in Gaul at the time of his conquest, and not unlike the earlier Roman institution of patron and client. The dependant is often called a client in the language of the time, and the institution itself the *patrocinium*. In a case of this sort the poor freeman goes to the rich and strong man who can afford him protection, and explaining that he can no longer care for or support himself, begs to be taken under his protection and furnished with shelter and support. The rich man grants the petition, adds the client to his household, and expects from him, in return, such services as a freeman may perform. There seems to have been no specified services, nor peculiar duty of fidelity in this arrangement, but its obligations were probably clearly enough defined in the customary law which all understood. In this way many local magnates of the age of the invasion collected about them considerable forces, composed also partly of armed slaves and serfs, and so added greatly to their own power, and furnished the locality with some degree of security. In some instances, both in the East and in the West, we know that such private forces amounted to respectable armies and served to protect extensive territories, or even to turn the march of an invading tribe.

It is important to notice that, in the case of the freeman entering into either of these relations, the personal one or the one relating to land, there was no loss of political status or personal freedom. The dependant, under the new arrangement, remained, in either relation, exactly what he had been before, both in reference to his duties to the government and his personal rights.

It was of course true, as the history of the Roman tax system makes evident, that the rich man might be so strong in his district that he could refuse to meet his obligations towards the government, and set the local officers at defiance, and so be able to protect from the burdens of the state the poorer men who became his clients and dependants. He could also protect them from the not infrequent abuse of power by officials. These were, no doubt, reasons for the rapid extension of these practices. But if he interfered with the real rights of the government, it was an illegal usurpation, not a recognized change in the status or duties of his dependents. That such results did follow is clear enough from the attitude of the state towards these practices, which it pronounced illegal and forbade under the heaviest penalties. But it was powerless to interfere, and even the death penalty had no effect to check them. Indeed, if the state had been strong enough to stop them, it would have been strong enough to have preserved such general security that no necessity for such customs would ever have arisen.

The results, as seen at the time of the invasions, have many features in common with the later feudal system, and it is right, in the sense mentioned at the beginning of the chapter, to speak of them as feudal, but they are still far from being the historical feudal system.

In the first place, the characteristic feature of the later

feudalism was lacking. These two practices remained entirely distinct from one another. They were not yet united into a single institution. The personal relation, or clientship, did not imply at all the reception of land, and holding land by the *precarium* tenure involved no obligation of service.

In the second place, there was no common organization, either expressed or implied, as there was in the completed feudal system, between the various local powers which had been formed. They were merely private and wholly separate fragments into which the state had fallen. In other words, there was not enough connection between them, taken alone, to have preserved the state, as a state, through a period of political chaos, but they would have produced a thousand little local states wholly independent and sovereign.

In the third place, the state regarded these institutions not merely as unconstitutional and improper for itself, but also as illegal and improper for private citizens. The local potentate might actually have usurped, as we know he did, many of the functions of the state, judicial as well as military, and have excluded the state practically from his whole territory and taken its place himself, but this was a usurpation and strictly forbidden by the laws. In the later feudal system the similar practices are not merely recognized by the government as legal, but they are even, in some cases, enjoined as duties, and become, in practice at least, the very constitution of the state, so that in many cases the sovereignty exercised by the feudal baron over his territory was the only sovereignty exercised by the state.

The Franks, when they entered Gaul, found these customs prevailing there, as in all the provinces of the empire. They dealt with them, as they did with many Roman institutions which they found; they allowed them to continue in use and they adopted them themselves.

It was under the conditions which prevailed in the Frankish kingdom, and by means of the legal expedients adopted
by the Frankish kings, that these primitive beginnings
were developed into the feudal system of Europe.

The conquest was indeed a most serious crisis in the
history of feudalism. Had they been disposed to do so,
the Frankish kings would doubtless have found it easier
than the Roman emperors had done to crush out these
institutions, still in a formative condition, and to establish a centralization, if not more complete in theory, certainly more so in fact. The government which they did
found had many of the features of an absolutism incom-
patible with the continued growth of these institutions.
If they had destroyed them, and entirely prevented their
further growth, their government would have escaped its
most dangerous enemy of the future—the one to which
it was finally compelled to surrender. But the more
simple political mind of the Frank could not perceive
this danger so clearly as the Roman did, and another fact
was an even more decisive influence against any change.
The Franks themselves had institutions and practices
which were so similar to those of the Romans that it was
the most natural thing imaginable for them to adopt these,
and to regard them at once, as they had never before
been regarded, as perfectly legal, because the corresponding German institutions were.[1] The German customs
and the Roman customs ran rapidly together into a
common practice, and the German variations from the
Roman added very essential elements of their own to the
common product, so that the feudal system presents one
of the clearest cases that we have of the union of the Ger-

---

[1] Various theories have been advanced to account for this apparently
extraordinary short-sightedness on the part of the Frankish kings, both
Merovingian and Carolingian. The fact that the Germans had similar
customs, which they had always considered not merely as legal, but as
highly commendable, especially the *comitatus*, would seem to be sufficient
to account for the changed attitude of the state.

man and the Roman factors together to form new institutions.

The most striking of these German institutions was the *comitatus*, which we have briefly described in the chapter on the German invasions. The old theory that the feudal system was created by the settlement of the *comitatus* band upon the conquered soil is now abandoned,[1] but its place has been taken by a clear recognition of the very important contribution which the *comitatus* made to the final result. The institution was one corresponding very closely to the Roman client system which we have described above. It was a purely personal relationship of mutual protection, service, and support, between a chief and certain men, usually young men of the tribe, voluntarily entered into on both sides. But it had certain distinctive features of its own, which are lacking in the Roman institution, but characteristic of the later feudalism. It was not regarded by the Germans as a mere business transaction of give and take, but was looked upon as conferring especial honor on lord and man alike. It was entered upon by a special ceremonial, and sanctioned by a solemn oath, and the bond of personal fidelity established by it was considered to be of the most sacred and binding character. All these ideas

---

[1] The most important point concerning the origin of feudalism about which scholars disagree is the relation of vassalage to the early German *comitatus*. Professor Heinrich Brunner of Berlin and some who follow him maintain that the form of vassalage which united with the benefice to create the full feudal relationship was derived directly from the *comitatus*. Against this view the arguments of Fustel de Coulanges, Waitz, and Dahn seem conclusive. Especially valuable is Dahn's summary of the whole case in *Die Koenige der Germanen*, VIII, 2, 151–171, with full references. It will be found, I think, that those who derive vassalage from the *comitatus* hold that identity of practical result, identity of function, determines institutional identity. If this is true, if institutional differences are not structural differences, and organic differences, then they are of little importance and not worth the trouble it costs the historian to investigate and establish them. A good corrective of such a frame of mind can be found in studying the scientific reasons for the change in botany from the Linnæan system of classification to that which obtains to-day.

and customs passed from the *comitatus* into the feudal system.

The Roman practices in the *patrocinium*, which the Franks found in Gaul, seemed to them, therefore, very natural and proper, and they adopted them at once, interpreting them according to their own ideas. It seems evident also, as the Franks became settled upon the land and the members of the original royal *comitatus* came to have private interests and landed possessions which made it difficult for them to fulfil the duties of the old relation, or to be used for its purposes, that their place was taken by persons who had entered into a personal relation to the king, corresponding, both in motive and in form, rather to the late Roman *patrocinium* than to the German *comitatus*. So that the institution which survived in the new state was the Roman rather than the German, which must necessarily have disappeared in the decidedly changed conditions of the national life, but it was the Roman essentially modified by ideas and usages from the German.

It was some little time after the conquest, so far as the documents allow us to judge, before the Celtic word *vassus* began to be employed for the man in this personal relation. Originally applied to servants not free, it came into gradual use for the free clients, and thus acquired from the *comitatus* idea a distinctly honorable meaning.

In reference to the land relationship, which we have described, it has been conclusively shown, in opposition to earlier theories, that the Frankish kings, following native German ideas, did probably from the beginning make donations of land, which carried only a limited right of ownership, and which fell back in certain contingencies to the donor.[1] Such practices would make it easy for the Franks to understand and adopt the Roman practice

---

[1] Brunner, *Sitzungsberichte der Preussischen Akademie*, 1885, p. 1173, and in his *Forschungen*, pp. 1–39.

of the *precarium*, and it appears to have been so adopted, quite extensively, by German private landowners who found themselves in a similar position to the Roman, and to have been continued also as before, by Roman subjects of the Frankish state. But still, to all appearances, it was not adopted in any really important way by the kings, until the beginning of the Carolingian period, and the chief agent in carrying over the *precariæ*, as the word came to be written, from the Roman to the German state, seems to have been the church.

The church appears to have used this tenure very extensively under the empire, both as a means of increasing its territories—the donor retaining the use of his grant for life—and also as a convenient way of bestowing upon persons, whose support or favor it desired to secure, land which it could not alienate. It seems to have introduced a small rent-charge, as a sign of ownership, and to have fixed more exactly the limit of such grants to a specified time, commonly five years, or the lifetime of the recipient. These practices it continued in very frequent use under the Frankish kingdom.

Through the Merovingian period of Frankish history, therefore, these institutions remained in very much the same shape in which they were under the empire, except that they were not now regarded as illegal. It is in the Carolingian period that they took the next great steps in their development—the steps that were essentially necessary to the formation of the historical feudal system. They then became united as the two sides of a single institution, and they were adopted by the government as a means of securing the performance of their public duties by the subjects of the state. The simplest example of this process is the transformation of the citizen army into a feudal army, and this gives us also, in its main features, the history of the joining together of the benefice and vassalage.

Originally neither of these primitive Roman institutions had, as it would seem, any especially military character. And this is, with an insignificant modification, as true of the Merovingian as of the Roman period. In such troubled times, however, as those which brought these institutions into use, military service would certainly be one of the most frequent services needed from such dependants, and apparently some of them at least were constantly employed as an armed force, but there was, during the earlier period, no necessary connection of this military service with these relationships either of person or of land. The first beginnings of this connection were made at the opening of the Carolingian age under Charles Martel; the completion of it—the establishment of military service as the almost indispensable rule in feudalism—was hardly accomplished before the period ends.

The occasion which led to the beginning of this change was the Arabian attack on Gaul, and the necessity of forming a cavalry force to meet it.[1] Originally the Franks had fought on foot. But the Arabs were on horseback, and their sudden raids, which continued in south Gaul long after the battle of Tours, could not be properly met, and the defeated enemy properly pursued, without the use of horse. But this was putting a heavy burden of expense on the citizen, who armed and supported himself, and who was already severely oppressed by the conditions of the service. The state must aid him to bear it. This it could do only by grants of land.

The first Carolingian princes had, however, but scanty resources in this direction. The royal domains had been exhausted under the Merovingian kings. Their own house possessions, though very extensive, would not go far to-

[1] See Brunner, *Der Reiterdienst und die Anfänge des Lehnwesens*, in the *Zeitschrift der Savigny-Stiftung für Rechtsgeschichte, Germanistische Abtheilung*, vol. VIII, 1–38; also in his *Forschungen*, pp. 39–74.

wards meeting the needs of a family, gradually usurping the royal power, and so in need of means to purchase
faithful support. They lay, besides, in Austrasia, at a
distance from the country which was in especial need of
defence. There was in the case but one resource open
—the extensive lands of the church, amounting, in some
parts of the kingdom, to one-third of the territory.

It had long been the custom for the state to make use
of church lands, a bit here and there, to meet some special need; but now, in the face of this great necessity,
there was, seemingly, a more extensive confiscation, for
which Charles Martel secured an evil place in the memory of the church. It was not, however, a confiscation in
form, and his successors succeeded in making a definite
arrangement with the church, regulating and sanction-
ing, in a limited way, this use of church lands. The
precariæ furnished a convenient tenure for the purpose.
By it the ownership of the church was, in form, preserved by the payment of a small fee, while the use of
the land passed to the appointee of the king. These
grants became technically known in the church records,
during this brief transitional period, as *precariæ verbo regis*,
grants made at the royal command. As the object was
to maintain a cavalry force, the prince bestowed these
grants of land upon his vassals who were bound to him
by a personal bond of especial fidelity and service, and
who were to be enabled, by the additional income secured
them by the grant, to furnish mounted soldiers to the
army. They divided the land among their own vassals
upon the same terms. It was at this time also that the
word "benefice" came into gradual use for the land granted.

In this way the first steps were taken towards uniting
these two institutions into a single one, and towards introducing the special obligation of military service as a
condition on which the land was held. But it must not be
understood that the process was by any means completed

as yet. It was a very slow and a very gradual change, extending throughout the whole Carolingian period.

The efforts which were made by Charlemagne to reform, or rather to enforce, the military system of the kingdom, had a very important influence in the same direction. With the growth in size of the Frankish Empire, requiring campaigns at such great distances and almost constantly, their original military system of unpaid service from all the freemen, which was common to all the German tribes, had come to be a serious burden upon the Franks. Indeed, the poorer citizens, who could no longer bear it, were striving to escape from it in every possible way, and the armies threatened to disappear. This danger Charlemagne tried to overcome by a series of enactments. He allowed several of the poorer freemen to unite in arming and maintaining one of their number in the army. He directed that vassals of private individuals must perform military service as the vassals of the king did, thus trying to hold to their duty those who had sought to escape from it by such an arrangement. He also ordained that the lord should be held responsible for the equipment and appearance in the field of his vassals, or should pay the fine for their failure to appear. Finally, when these measures proved of no avail, he issued an ordinance which apparently brought a great principle of human nature to his aid by allowing the vassals to come into the field under the command of their lords instead of with the general levy of the country under the count. The natural desire of the lord for influence and consideration would make him wish to appear at the head of as large and fine a body of vassals as possible, and the expedient seems to have proved successful enough to be adopted regularly in the generations following. But the result of it was to make the army more and more completely a feudal army, though it seems certain that the freemen who re-

mained throughout the whole feudal period holders of
land and free laborers in considerable numbers outside
the feudal system, were never excused from military
duty, and were summoned occasionally to actual service.
Still the state in the main depended no longer upon citizens for its army, but upon vassals who served as a duty
growing out of their holding of land.

In this way one important duty of the citizen, that of
defending the community, was transformed from a public
obligation into a matter of private contract, and became
one of the ordinary conditions upon which lands were held.

A like transformation took place during this same time
in regard to other functions of the state—the judicial, for
example—which also passed into the hands of private
individuals and became attached to the land. Thus the
great fiefs came to possess what the French feudal law
called "justice"—*jurisdictio*—that is, full sovereignty, so
that the state was practically excluded from all contact
with any persons residing within the limits of the fief,
a result which went far beyond any development of manorial justice. The process by which this transformation
was accomplished, in respect to the other functions of the
state, is by no means so clear as it is in the case of the
military. In the instance, for example, of the judicial
power of the state, there is probably no subject connected with the origin of the feudal system which is still
the subject of so much controversy, and on which so
many varying views are still maintained, as upon the
way in which this power passed into private hands.

The process was undoubtedly largely aided by the
"immunities." These were grants of privilege to churches
or to private individuals, by virtue of which the ordinary officers of the state were forbidden all entry upon the
specified domain, and the owner took the place of the
officers in reference to the state. This did not at once
remove these estates from the control of the government.

The landowner became independent of the ordinary officers, but not of the state, whose officer he became for his own land, though often possessing, instead of the state, the entire judicial revenue, but it did undoubtedly favor the development of private jurisdiction and virtual independence, and probably in many cases fully accounts for the sovereignty of the fief. The government, which found it so difficult during this time to control its own officers and to keep the functions of the state in operation by their means, would often find it entirely impossible to prevent the great landowner who had received a grant of immunity from throwing off all dependence upon the government and setting up a state of his own.

In the case of many fiefs, however, no immunity existed, and the process must have been a different one. Our knowledge of what it actually was is so slight that almost every one of the various theories which have been advanced to explain it has some reasonable foundation, but the probability is that in the majority of cases it was, in reality, a usurpation.

The holder of the fief was locally strong. He could and did maintain some real degree of order and security. It was by virtue of this fact that his power had been developed and continued to be obeyed. In theory the state was absolute. It was supposed to control almost every detail of life. And this theory of the power of the state continued to exist and to be recognized in the days of the most complete feudalism. But actually the state could do nothing. Its real power was at the opposite extreme from its theoretical. The conditions which had favored the development of those germs of feudalism which existed under the later empire, even where their growth had been in the interval held in check, tended to reappear after the fall of the Carolingian power. The great difficulty of intercommunication rendered it impossible for the state to bring its authority into direct contact with all parts of the country. It had no strong and organized body of officers on whom it could depend. Every officer, military or administrative, was a local magnate doing his best to throw off the control of the state, and using his official position to aid him in this purpose. There was no strong feeling of unity among the people which it could call to its aid. There were no common feelings or ideas or interests which bound the dweller at the mouth of the Loire to the dweller at the mouth of the Seine. Patriotism and a common national feeling were wanting. Everything was local and personal. Even in the church was this the case in the tenth century, Europe at large hardly knowing who was pope in Rome, and the common organization almost falling to pieces, while in Rome itself the papacy sank to its lowest point of degradation, a prey to local faction and made to serve local interests. If this was true of the church, much more was it true of the state, which had no such general organization and no such basis of common feelings. The sovereign of the moment had only such an amount of power as he might derive from lands directly in his hands, that is, from his own local fief. The great advantage which the first Capetians had over their Carolingian rivals was, as we have seen, that they had a very strong local power of this sort, while the Carolingians had really none; but even this power which the first Capetians had was not enough to enable them to exercise the functions of a real government within the other large fiefs. Certainly there was no such power in the hands of the later Carolingians. These functions, which the government was powerless to exercise, fell naturally into the hands of the local magnate and were exercised by him.

Sometimes it was a real usurpation, the baron assuming and continuing offices which the state should have discharged. More often, no doubt, it was a transformation of duties which the state had once lodged in his hands, as an immunity, perhaps, or in making him its own administrative officer, duke or count, a transformation of such a sort that the baron no longer performed these functions as a representative of the state, but by virtue of his own property right, and the persons living within his domain, fulfilled these duties, no longer as obligations due to the state, but as personal duties due to their immediate lord. Among these there would usually be vassals of his whose ancestors had dwelt in the county when his ancestors were counts by the king's appointment, and really represented the government. In those days they had attended the count's court as citizens discharging a public duty. In every intervening generation the same court had been held and attended, undergoing no pronounced change at any one time. But in the end it had been entirely transformed, and in attending it now the descendants of the earlier citizens were meeting a private obligation into which they had entered as vassals of a lord.

The local public court, no doubt, in being thus transformed into a private court, by the usurpation of the baron or by the grant of the king, retained its fundamental principles unchanged. The vassals came together to form the court, as formerly the citizens had done, accompanied by such free citizens of the district as might still remain outside the vassal relations. They made the judgment of the court by common consent, as had the earlier Teutonic court, and they adopted, by general agreement, measures of the character of local legislation, as the older local assembly had done whose place they had taken. But, in relation to the public authority of the state, the transformation was a great one, and the whole point of view had been changed.[1]

[1] A local public court, particularly of the smaller territorial units, undoubtedly in some cases passed into private possession through a develop-

The geographical extent of territory, subject in this way to the lord's "justice," would depend upon a great variety of circumstances largely peculiar to each case; certainly it depended, only in the most remote way, upon any act of the nominal sovereign's. The most decisive of these circumstances would be the personal ability of the successive generations of lords, their success in preserving some considerable amount of order and security, and making their government really respected over a larger or smaller area, and their success in compelling outlying landholders of less strength to recognize their supremacy. If they were good organizers and strong fighters, especially the last, their lands were constantly enlarging, until they reached the boundaries of other territories which had been formed in the same way. If they were undecided and weak, their subjects and their rivals took speedy advantage of it. Vassals lost no opportunity to throw off their dependence and assume for themselves the rights of sovereignty, and neighboring great barons did not hesitate to entice or to force a rival's vassals to change their allegiance, and thus to enlarge their own lands at their rival's expense. When the feudal system and the feudal law became more definitely fixed, these things became less frequent, but they never entirely ceased, and the days of formative feudalism were times when the law of the survival of the fittest reigned supreme.

As the starting-point of such a feudal territory there was often, not a fief, but an estate of allodial land, that is, land which the original owner had held in fee simple and not as a benefice from some lord. There was always present in feudal times, also, a strong tendency to turn

ment of manorial jurisdiction as described above, though in such a transfer the immunity was often not without influence. A third kind of court, the feudal proper, composed of vassals primarily and acting upon feudal questions chiefly, further complicates the judicial situation. In an account which is considering general political conditions it may be disregarded.

benefices into allodial land, that is, for the vassal to throw off all semblance of dependence upon his lord, and become independent, acknowledging in many cases not even a theoretical dependence upon any one, the state itself included. Such allodial lands, of whatever origin, might be just as thoroughly feudal in their internal organization as any other, and, if large enough, always were, that is, they were subdivided among vassals, and governed and regulated according to feudal principles, but the feudal law generally recognized their independence of outside control. Examples of such lands are those which the German feudal law styled "sun fiefs," fiefs held of the sun, and, in France, those of a part of the counts and others who styled themselves "counts by the grace of God." In many cases pretensions of this sort were not made good against the growing strength of the government; in others they were, and the little states were distinctly recognized by the general government as independent sovereignties. The little kingdom of Yvetot, whose memory has been preserved in literature, is the case of a fief which became independent, and the little territory of Boisbelle-Henrichemont, in central France, maintained a recognized independence until 1766, when the last seigneur sold his state to the king.

In general, from the tenth to the beginning at least of the thirteenth century, the political aspect of western Europe was thoroughly feudal, and even in those parts of the country where allodial lands largely predominated, as, for example, in central France, the state was as weak as elsewhere, and the real government as completely local. The small allodial proprietor, not strong enough to usurp for himself the right of "justice," was subject to the "justice" of the feudal lord of the locality, and sometimes even to the payment of dues that were distinctly feudal, though he might not be forced into the position of a full vassal.

We have endeavored to present in this sketch, as fully as possible in the space at our command, the rise of the feudal system. Comparatively insignificant practices, of private and illegal origin, which had arisen in the later Roman Empire, and which were continued in the early Frankish kingdom, had been developed, under the pressure of public need, into a great political organization extending over the whole West, and virtually supplanting the national government. The public need which had made this development necessary was the need of security and protection. Men had been obliged to take refuge in the feudal castle, because the power of the state had broken down. This breakdown of the state, its failure to discharge its ordinary functions, was not so much due to a lack of personal ability on the part of the king, as to the circumstances of the time, and to the inability of the ruling race as a whole to rise above them. The difficulty of intercommunication, the breakdown of the old military and judicial organization, partly on account of this difficulty, thus depriving the state of its two hands, the lack of general ideas and common feelings and interests, seen for example in the scanty commerce of the time, the almost total absence, in a word, of all the sources from which every government must draw its life and strength, this general condition of society was the controlling force which created the feudal system. The Germans, in succeeding to the empire of Rome, had inherited a task which was as yet too great for the most of them, Merovingian and Carolingian alike. Only by a long process of experience and education were they to succeed in understanding its problems and mastering its difficulties. This is only saying in a new form what we have before said in other connections, that the coming in of the Germans must of necessity have been followed by a temporary decline of civilization. This was just as true of government and political order as of everything else, and the feudal system is merely, in politics, what the miracle lives and scholasticism are in literature and science.

These last paragraphs have, perhaps, given some idea of the condition of things in the completely feudalized state, and of the character of feudalism as a political organization.

The perfected form which the lawyers finally gave to the feudal theory as a matter of land law and of social rank is undoubtedly the source of the popular idea that the feudal system was a much more definitely arranged and systematized organization than it ever was in practice. Among us Blackstone's *Commentaries* are probably, more than any other single source, responsible for this impression, as they are for other ideas of history which are not altogether correct. He says, speaking of the introduction of feudalism as a result of the Norman conquest:

"This new polity therefore seems not to have been imposed by the conqueror, but nationally and freely adopted by the general assembly of the whole realm, in the same manner as other nations of Europe had before adopted it, upon the same principle of self-security, and, in particular, they had the recent example of the French nation before their eyes, which had gradually surrendered up all its allodial or free lands into the king's hands, who restored them to the owners as a *beneficium* or feud, to be held to them and such of their heirs as they previously nominated to the king, and thus by degrees all the allodial estates in France were converted into feuds, and the freemen became the vassals of the crown. The only difference between this change of tenure in France and that in England, was, that the former was effected gradually, by the consent of private persons; the latter was done all at once, all over England, by the common consent of the nation."

It is needless to say that no such facts as these ever occurred, either in France or in England, but the lawyers certainly did form such a theory as this of the feudal state, and from its influence came the popular notion of what sort of an organization the feudal state was.

According to this theory the king is vested with the ownership of all the soil of the kingdom. But, like the private owner of a vast estate, he cannot cultivate it all under his own immediate direction. On the other hand, he has certain great expenses to meet, and public functions to perform, by virtue of his position as the head of the state. He must provide for defence against the national enemies, he must determine and enforce the laws, provide a currency, maintain the highways, and so on. The resources to enable him to meet these obligations must be derived from the land of the kingdom which he owns. Accordingly he parcels out the kingdom into a certain number of large divisions, each of which he grants to a single man, who gives a peculiarly binding promise to assume a certain specified portion of these public obligations in return for the land which is granted him. So long as he fulfils these duties he continues to hold the lands, and his heirs after him on the same terms. If he refuses to meet his obligations, or neglects them, the king may resume his lands and grant them to some more faithful vassal. Together, these men constitute the great barons, or grand feudatories, or peers of the kingdom, and by their united services the state gets its business performed.

In the same way these great barons divide their land among vassals, whose united services enable them to meet their obligations to the king. These vassals subdivide again, by a like process of "subinfeudation," and so on down to the knight's fee, or lowest subdivision of the feudal system—a piece of land large enough to support and arm a single warrior of noble condition.

There is, undoubtedly, a general correspondence of this theory to the actual facts which prevailed from the tenth century on. Public duties were almost wholly transformed into private services. The state did depend, to a very large extent, upon the holders of land for the performance of its functions. The land of the kingdom did tend to become feudal, held by vassals upon a tenure of service, and there was a tendency in the feudal system to develop into a hierarchical organization of regulated grades, from the king down to the smallest noble.

But not one of these tendencies was completely realized in the actual feudalism of any country of Europe, and there never was anywhere such a regular organization as the theory supposes. It is perfectly easy to see, from the way in which the feudal system came into existence, its long and slow growth by private arrangements to meet local needs, that it could have no settled and uniform constitution, even for its general features, and for minor details it could have no general system of law with fixed rules which prevailed everywhere.

Its law must be purely customary law, formed by each locality for itself, its rules determined by the local customs and usages which had grown into precedents. It was not the result of general legislation, indeed it may be said that, during the feudal period proper there was scarcely such a thing as formal legislation of the modern sort. We have, therefore, no general feudal law, but we have a thousand local systems of law, having certain general features alike, but differing more or less widely from one another on matters of detail. Even such general codes as the *Assises de Jérusalem* or the *Libri Feudorum* are not merely now and then at variance with one another on important points, but they are in some respects theoretical treatises, embodying an ideal law rather than stating practices which were widely in force. The general use into which some of these codes came in the hands of the lawyers, after there began to be professional lawyers, tended to create a uniformity of practice which had not existed earlier; but this was only from the thirteenth century on, when in most countries feudalism was losing its political significance and was passing into a mere system of land law and of social rank.[1]

In the days when feudalism was at its height as a political organization, the way in which the lord's court settled a particular question, or in which private agreement regulated a particular service, was final, and the custom thus formed in the locality became the law for that locality. These decisions and regulations might, and did, differ greatly in different places. Says Beaumanoir, one of the thirteenth-century lawyers, whose *Coutumes de Beauvaisis* became one of the law books in general use: "There are not two castellanies in France which use the same law in every case."[2] Indeed, it is hardly too much to say that there was no uniformity of practice even in the most general features of the system.

There was nowhere any series of great baronies which covered the area of a kingdom.[3] The lands held by the twelve so-called peers of France by no means made up the whole of that country. Some fiefs, not ranked among these, were as large or larger, like the county of Anjou or the county of Brittany. Some of the peers held only a portion of their land of the king. The count of Cham-

---

[1] The most permanent in influence of all the feudal law books, the Lombard feudal code, or the *Libri Feudorum*, reflects in its numerous repetitions and confused character the local and customary growth of the feudal law. It was not made after the usual method of code formation, the cutting out of repetitions and superfluous passages. It is not properly a code at all, but is a collection of various local customs and of the opinions of lawyers brought together by a gradual series of accretions.

[2] Vol. I, p. 14, Ed. Beugnot; I, p. 5, Ed. Salmon.

[3] For an interesting brief statement of conflicting practices in feudalism, see the note on p. 213 of the text of Longnon's *Atlas Historique de la France*.

pagne was the king's vassal for only a fraction of his lands. His great territory was a complex, brought together into a single hand, and held of nine suzerains besides the king, of seven ecclesiastical lords, the German emperor, and the duke of Burgundy. The king granted fiefs of every size, and had vassals of every rank and title, and many subvassals of others held small fiefs directly from the king. In Germany the number of very small fiefs held immediately of the emperor was great. Suzerains also, even kings and emperors, held fiefs of their own vassals. The same homage, for the same fief, might be paid to two lords at the same time, or a fief might be held by two or more vassals. Not merely land, but all sorts of things having value—offices, tolls, and privileges —were made into fiefs, and the variations of form and character in fiefs were almost infinite. And yet portions of the land in most kingdoms remained allodial, and were never held under any actual feudal tenure.

Gradations of rank in the nobility came to be regular and definite in later times, but they were not so when feudalism was supreme, and the size or importance of the fief by no means determined its title and rank. Viscounts had counts as vassals. Some mere lordships were as large as the fiefs held by counts, and for a fief to change its title, while remaining the same itself, was of very frequent occurrence, as in the case of the county of Brittany which became a duchy.

In general, we may say that the feudal system was confusion roughly organized, and it would be impossible within these limits, even if our plan permitted, to give any satisfactory idea of its details. It is doubtful if it would be possible, within any reasonable limits, to give a detailed account of feudal usages which would not convey a wrong impression, or which would be true of more than limited regions.

Besides these differences of detail, the national feudal

systems, which took shape in the different countries of Europe, differed more or less widely from one another in many points of general constitution. The history of feudalism runs a different course in the various states, and the permanent influence which it exercised on national institutions and history is distinct for each, as will be evident when the formation of the modern nations is reached.

It is clear that a system of this sort would be a serious obstacle to the reconstruction of a strong and consolidated state. It is a fact still more familiar to us that the legal and social privileges, the shadow of a once dominant feudalism, which the state allowed to remain or was forced to tolerate, secured for it a universal popular hatred and condemnation. But these facts ought not to obscure for us the great work which fell to the share of feudalism in the general development of civilization. The preceding account should have given some indication, at least, of what this work was. The feudal castle, torn to pieces by the infuriated mob of revolted peasants, as the shelter of tyrannous privileges, was originally built by the willing and anxious labor of their ancestors as their only refuge from worse evils than the lord's oppression.

We have seen, earlier, the great danger which threatened the political unity which Rome had established in the West in consequence of the German invasions; how they threatened to break up the Western Empire into separate and unconnected fragments; and how the influence of the church and of the idea of Rome availed to keep up some general consciousness of unity, and of a common whole to which they all belonged. But these influences, however strong in maintaining an ideal union of states, could hardly be of much value within the bounds of the separate states. The same causes of separation,

however, were at work there. There were so few common bonds between them that it was as hard for the inhabitants of the different parts of Gaul to keep alive any
real feeling of national unity, as it was for them to realize
any common relationship with the men of Italy. As the
central governments of the different states succumbed
more and more to the difficulties of their situation, and
became more and more powerless to exercise any actual
control at a distance from the court, the danger was
great and real that the state would fall apart into little
fragments owning no common allegiance, and that the
advanced political organization which civilization had
reached would dissolve again into the original elements
from which it had formerly been constructed—that Gaul,
for example, would revert to the condition from which
the Romans had rescued it. From this danger Europe
was saved by the feudal system.

Feudalism is a form of political organization which
allows the state to separate into as minute fragments
as it will, virtually independent of one another and of
the state, without the total destruction of its own life
with which such an experience would seem to threaten
every general government.

When we look at the actual condition of things in a
feudal state, its anarchy and confusion, we can hardly
see how it would be possible for disintegration to go farther, or the destruction of the government of the state
to be more complete. And yet there is an enormous
difference between a society which has thrown off all
common bonds, and actually broken into fragments that
are wholly isolated, and another in which, however fragmentary in appearance, a lively and constantly recognized theory keeps in remembrance the rights and prerogatives of the central government, and asserts without
ceasing that there is a vital bond of union between all
the fragments.

It was this that feudalism did. It was an arrangement suited to crude and barbarous times, by which an advanced political organization belonging to a more orderly civilization might be carried through such times without destruction, though unsuited to them, and likely to perish if left to its own resources. There is no intention of asserting in this proposition that such a system is ideally the best way to accomplish this result, or that it could not have been done, perhaps with less time and expense, by some other expedient, but only that this is what it did do historically, and possibly further that the general history of the world shows it to be a natural method in similar cases.

The phrase of Hegel, that the feudal system was a protest of barbarism against barbarism, and that of Henri Martin, that it concealed in its bosom the weapons with which it would be itself one day smitten, are strictly accurate.[1] It kept alive the theory of the state, with the king at its head, in the possession of almost absolute rights and prerogatives.

And this was never completely reduced to the condition of a mere theory; for themselves the kings seem never to have recognized, in the worst days, the claims to independence which the great nobles advanced, and many circumstances—accident, the rivalry of one baron with another, the dying out of a line, a dispute between vassal and lord—presented opportunities for interference of which even the weakest kings availed themselves, and so added to theory something in the way of actual fact.

[1] Is this a characteristic of every phase in the political development of the race? I translate the following suggestive sentence of M. Monod's from the *Revue Historique*, vol. XLIII, p. 95: "As we can follow through the feudal epoch the development of the monarchical idea which was to destroy feudalism, and as we can follow across the monarchical epoch the development of the national idea which was to throw dynastic interests back into the second place, so we can follow across the history of the last two centuries the development of economic and industrial interests, the social idea, which is destined to overthrow the national."

When we reach the point where there was the most complete recognition by the kings of feudal law and privileges, in the thirteenth century, we are already at the time when they were seriously undermining the feudal power.[1] The work of doing this, and of recreating a central authority, was merely the process of putting into actual exercise prerogatives which feudalism had continued to recognize as existing, though not allowing in action. It was simply the successful effort to turn theories into facts.

Feudalism had hardly reached its height, and drawn all society into its forms, when conditions began to prevail which made it possible for a general government to exist for the whole state, and to make its power felt and obeyed in distant localities. The moment that these conditions came into existence, feudalism as a political system, and a substitute for a central government, began to decline. As once all things had conspired together to build it up when it was needed, so now, because its work was done, all things united to pull it down. The history of its fall is the history of the formation of the modern nations.

---

[1] Germany occupies, as will be seen later, a peculiar position in this respect, and there feudalism was not overthrown, as far as the national government is concerned, but reached its logical conclusion and destroyed the state. But this was not due to any conscious yielding to feudalism on the part of the sovereign, nor to any peculiar effort to realize in facts the feudal theory, but entirely to outside influences which prevented the kings from accomplishing what should have been their natural work, together with a survival of original tribal feeling not found elsewhere.

CHAPTER X

AT a time when the feudal system was at its height, that is, when there was great separation and local independence, and when the universal and the common had very little power, the minds of many men were strongly held by two theories, so general and comprehensive in character, that it seems impossible that they should have existed at such a time. And yet they were consciously held by some, unconsciously by almost all. These were the theories of the Holy Catholic Church, and of the Holy Roman Empire.

These theories had their foundation, as we have seen, in ideas which had grown up in pagan Rome—the ideas of the divinely ordained, eternal, and universal empire. These ideas the Christians adopted. We find traces of them in Christian writers from the first half of the third century on. They found in them an interpretation for prophecies of the Old Testament. But they modified them, also, in consequence of the new point of view from which they regarded them. For the Christian the political work of Rome was not its great work—not the ultimate end for which it had been founded. This was to be found in the establishment of Christianity. God had allowed the universal and eternal political empire of Rome to be created, that in it might be formed the universal church, the true *Civitas Dei* of St. Augustine.

There were, then, in the plan of God for history, these two final organizations, distinct in sphere, the universal political organization, and the universal religious organization. The one was realized in facts by the Roman Empire; the other by the Catholic church; and as the actual course of history favored the continuance or the revival of the empire, and the more and more definite and perfect organization of the church government, the theories which they expressed grew in definiteness and in their hold upon men. They seemed to constitute the permanent plan of God for history, and these two powers seemed to stand as the representatives of his government of the world. The pope represented God, was his vicar, his vicegerent, in his religious government of mankind, the emperor in his political.

In the case of the ecclesiastical organization the facts correspond somewhat closely to the theory. There was such an empire, extending, not throughout the whole of Christendom, but throughout the whole of orthodox Christendom, which was to the mind of that time much the same thing. The whole Western world was united under a single head in one great religious state. To the other part of the theory the facts did not correspond so well. The political empire had a direct authority only in Germany and in Italy, though it cherished wider pretensions, and though these pretensions were not without some recognition outside those countries, a recognition, however, mainly theoretical. There was, certainly, in both cases a strong enough foundation in fact to lead an ambitious man, at the head of either of these organizations, to desire, and attempt to gain, a more extended realization of the theory.

As to the relation of these two governments to one another, the dividing line between these two empires, there was no definite idea. Each laid claim to the very highest and widest rights. Neither could exercise his power in full, as he understood it, without involving the subjection of the other. Each had historical facts to appeal to, which seemed to imply the exercise of these rights in their widest extent, and the submission of the rival power to them. But neither had a clear case against the other, and neither was willing to acknowledge any inferiority.

In such a situation a conflict was inevitable. As soon as there should come to the head of either church or empire an able and energetic man, determined to push his claims, there was certain to be a great contest, if there was at the head of the opposing system, not necessarily equal ability, but only determined resistance. This gives us the elements of that fierce conflict, which plays so large a part in the middle portion of medieval history— the conflict between the papacy and the empire. It begins a short time before the first crusade, and extends through the whole period of the crusades, but with a gradually changing character, so that in its last period it is quite different, in motive and purpose, from its opening stages.

The history of the empire we have followed somewhat fully down to this point, through its revival by Charlemagne as a general empire of the West, and its second revival by Otto I as a German and Italian empire. The history of the church we have not looked at with the same fulness.

In the chapter on the early papacy we followed its history down to a point where most of the causes which were to transform it into an imperial church were already plainly at work. That period of its history closes naturally with the reign of Gregory I, at the end of the sixth century, the greatest of all the early popes. He defended the supremacy of the Roman church against the pretensions of the Greek empire and the Greek church. He became in consequence of the weakness of the Eastern emperor the virtual temporal sovereign of Rome and the surrounding territory. He held in check the advance of the Lombards, increased the actual power of the Roman church in face of the Arianism of Spain and Gaul, reformed abuses with unsparing hand, converted the Saxon kingdoms and brought England into close union with the papacy, and by the vigor of his rule and the success with which he made it respected in every quarter he greatly strengthened the position of the church.

But the future was full of danger. It was of the utmost importance in the development of the monarchical church that a reign of such vigor and success, and one which carried the organization so far forward should have come just at the time when it did—on the eve of a long period of extremely unfavorable conditions, and even of acute danger. All the prestige and increased strength which Gregory's reign had imparted were needed to preserve the centralization which had been gained, and to prevent the absorption of the church in the state. The vigorous but irregular advance of the Lombard state, which threatened the absorption of the whole Italian peninsula, was a grave danger to the papacy. Its position as a world power was as seriously threatened by the wide-spread Arianism of the German states of the west, the Lombards, the Burgundians, and the Visigoths in Gaul and Spain. From these dangers it was saved by the alliance with the Franks, which was first formed by Clovis and afterwards made still closer and more effective by the early Carolingian princes. The importance of that alliance we have already noticed, but it is hardly possible to overstate its influence on the future. If on the one side it rendered easy the formation of the Frankish empire, the political consolidation for a time of nearly the whole of Christendom, and the incorporation in it of Germany, on the other side it seems as if without it the medieval church would have been impossible and all its vast work for civilization left to be far more slowly performed by some other agency. Had the Franks become Arian instead of Catholic, the prestige and power of the pope must have declined, the causes which gradually led to the conversion of the Arian states could hardly have operated, and though the Franks might have widened their political dominions, they could have received no aid from an imperial church, and there could have been no ready channel for the influence of the Roman ideas which they reproduced.

While this alliance was begun upon the political side, and chiefly from political motives, it was drawn still more close and rendered permanent upon the ecclesiastical side by the work of a great churchman, St. Boniface, whose name must be remembered among the constructive statesmen who created the papal monarchy. Time as well as genius favored his work, for it fell in a formative period of the utmost importance, the middle of the eighth century, when the great future possible for them in the political world was just opening before the Carolingians, and when, if ever, the hold of the church upon their empire must be secured. This Boniface did. He was by birth an Anglo-Saxon, and so trained in those ideas of thorough devotion to the pope which had been characteristic of the English church since its founding under Gregory, even though the Anglo-Saxon states had allowed to the popes but little direct control of ecclesiastical affairs. In this respect his labors upon the Continent were a renewal and enlargement of Gregory's work for the consolidation of the church. Filled with the missionary zeal of his great predecessor, which had always lived in the Anglo-Saxon church, he had come from England to convert the still pagan Germans, but the force of his genius had drawn him into ever wider and more important work. After a time the organization of the Frankish church, which was in sad need of reformation, was placed in his hands by the sons of Charles Martel, and by the pope that of the German church in the newly converted lands held under the Franks.

This work was most ably done. The Frankish church

was given a more compact organization than it had ever before possessed, and the church of Germany was created. But more important still was the wider influence of this work, for in all its details he carried into practice a theory most complete, considering the time, of the supremacy of the pope as the head of the whole church and the source of all authority. As a result, just at the moment when the Frankish kings were about to become the temporal sovereigns of the pope with a political power behind them which could not be gainsaid, not merely was the national church of their people given a stronger and more independent organization as a part of the state, but it was also imbued with the idea of the high and exalted position held by the pope, almost if not quite equal to that of the king. The princes under whom he worked, and their successor, Charlemagne, still exercised a strong and direct control over the church, but that these facts had some influence in checking their arbitrary rule in ecclesiastical matters is highly probable. That they were of decided force under their weaker successors is more distinctly evident, and the suddenness with which the church springs into prominence and control as soon as the strong hand of Charlemagne is withdrawn is a most significant fact.

The consolidation of the Continent in the hands of Charlemagne was a great advantage to the growing imperial church by giving it for the moment a political foundation, but it carried with it a corresponding danger. The advance of the Lombard had threatened to absorb the papacy in the state and to reduce it to the headship of a merely national church. From this it was rescued by the advance of the Franks, but that now threatened an equally complete absorption. A man of Charlemagne's force must dictate in ecclesiastical matters as in temporal, and had his power and genius been perpetuated in his successors it is hard to see what could have saved the popes from sinking into a position like that of the patriarchs of Constantinople, and the real control of the church from passing into the hands of the emperors.

One precedent, however, of the utmost importance had been established in favor of the papacy by the crowning of Charlemagne as emperor of Rome. Whatever it may have meant to the men of 800, it was very easy to make it appear to the men of later times a bestowal of the empire by the gift of the church and a proof that the pope was the source of imperial right and power. The church never forgot a precedent of this sort, and it did effective service in the age of conflict upon which we are entering.

Whatever might have been the fate of the church had Charlemagne's genius been inherited, the fact is that his successor was as greatly characterized by subserviency to the church as his father had been by vigorous self-will, and the ninth century, when the government of the state was daily growing weaker, and the whole Frankish empire falling to pieces is marked in the history of the church by the rapid growth of the power actually exercised by the popes, and the still more rapid growth of their pretensions to power.

At a time about contemporary with Charlemagne two most remarkable forgeries made their appearance, whose origin and the purpose for which they were originally intended are uncertain, but which became of the greatest service to the papal cause. The first of these in time was the so-called Donation of Constantine, appearing probably in the third quarter of the eighth century. According to the legend, Constantine, fatally ill of the leprosy, was cured by a miracle through the agency of Pope Sylvester I, and out of gratitude built a new capital in the East and turned over by deed of gift all his imperial rights and prerogatives over the West to the pope. The document purporting to make this grant had every appearance of genuineness to the uncritical sense of the ninth century. It was not merely general but minute in its specifications, concerning even matters of dress and regulating the rights of the inferior clergy of Rome.[1] It is easy to see what advantage could be derived from it in the contest with the emperors.

The other forgery was a great collection of ecclesiastical law documents, appearing just after the middle of the ninth century and pretending to be decretals of the popes of the first three centuries and decisions of the councils in which genuine and false, authentic and unauthentic were mingled together. A collection of such documents, not forged, had been made, earlier in Spain and had come into considerable use in the church, and this new collection became confused with that, and the name of Isidore of Seville, of great authority in the church, was attached to it. It was, however, greatly enlarged in scope over its predecessors. Whatever may have been the place of its construction, probably somewhere in northern France, it seems to have had in view at least as one of its immediate objects to defend the independence of the bishop against the claims of the archbishop. In the West the only rival of the papal power had been the metropolitan jurisdictions. The temptation had been very strong for the archbishop to consolidate his power over his subordinate bishops and to create a little independent ecclesiastical dominion by resisting, as far as he could, every attempt on the part of the pope to exercise control over him. In a rivalry of this sort the bishops very naturally preferred the distant and more widely occupied authority of the pope to that of the archbishop near at hand,

---

[1] There is a translation of this deed of gift in Henderson's *Select Historical Documents of the Middle Ages*. The document itself probably intended to grant imperial rights only over Italy and its islands, but the historical interpretation was that given above.

and immediately interested in every local affair. This
seems the more likely motive which led the author of this
forgery in a series of documents belonging, in pretence, to
the earliest generations of Christian history, to exhibit the
papacy in the full possession and exercise of those rights
of government over the church, and of interference even
in minute local concerns which had been in reality only
very slowly developed, and which were still practically
claimed rather than exercised. But whatever may have
been the motive, the effect was to put into the hands of
the popes documentary evidence whose genuineness no
one was then able to dispute, to prove that the rights
which they were just then vigorously asserting had always been their prerogative, and had been recognized
and submitted to by the primitive church.

Hardly were these two documents in existence when a
succession of able men followed one another upon the
papal throne to put to use both these and the opportunity which the falling Carolingian government afforded
them. The first of them, Nicholas I, in his reign of
nearly ten years, from 858 to 867, carried through to successful issue an obstinate struggle with Lothaire II, King
of Lorraine, and compelled the archbishop of Ravenna,
and finally Hincmar of Rheims, the ablest of all the representatives of the archbishops' cause against the papacy,
to yield obedience. The next two popes, Hadrian II and
John VIII, covering fifteen years of time, were not able to
accomplish as much in the way of actual results, but they
assumed an even loftier tone and advanced the claims
of the papacy to the highest point, John VIII asserting
that the emperor owed his crown to the pope, while the
emperor of the time, Charles the Bald, seemed to acquiesce.

In the final dissolution of the Carolingian power which
followed the deposition of Charles the Fat, in 887, the
papacy shared to the full the decline of the temporal

power. The tenth century, which saw general government throughout nearly the whole of Europe almost at the point of dissolution, saw also the papacy reach its lowest point of degradation and corruption. It came to be the prize for which the factions of the city or the nobles of the vicinity fought with one another, or the gift of corrupt women to their paramours or sons. Its general European influence did not entirely disappear, but it was hardly more than that of the Italian nobles, who through the same period called themselves emperors.

This was the condition of things at the time of the descent of Otto I from Germany into Italy, in 961. His plans, and still more clearly those of his immediate successors, looked to the establishment of a real world empire, in the government of which the papacy should act as a strong and efficient ally of the emperors. The popes of their appointment accomplished at least a partial and temporary reformation, though without the support of the Roman people, and though the realization of the ideas which the Ottos appear to have cherished would have meant the practical absorption of the papacy in the empire. But the destinies were against the Saxon family. Otto II hardly more than began his reign, which promised even greater results than his father had accomplished in the centralization of Germany and the restoration of the empire, and his death, at the age of twenty-eight, was a great misfortune both for the Holy Roman Empire and for Germany.

The minority of his son, Otto III, was a time of loss in all directions. The dukes recovered something of their former position in Germany, and the hold of the empire on Italy was loosened. When Otto reached an age to rule, he revealed a most interesting personality. His mind seems to have been entirely wrapped in dreams of the widest imperial power, encouraged apparently by his favorite, Gerbert, whom he made pope as Syl-

vester II. But he was very little concerned with the
position which he should occupy as German king. He
gained, very likely as a consequence of his lack of national feeling, no strong support in any direction, and
died at the age of twenty-two, apparently on the eve of
failure.

With his death the wide imperial ideas of the Ottos
were dropped. In Italy there was a relapse into earlier
conditions. In Germany the work of restoring the royal
power was seriously taken up, and the most permanent
result of the Saxon empire seems to have been a terrible
temptation, constantly before the king in Germany, to
neglect his proper business in his own dominions, when
his task was half done, for the sake of a visionary headship of the world.

The devotion of the Ottos to imperial interests had allowed the little feudal dominions in Germany, reinforced
in some cases by a survival of tribal loyalty, to strengthen
themselves very greatly, and to take a much more independent position towards the crown. The process of destroying the central government, by splitting the country
into minute fragments that could not be controlled, which
entailed so much suffering in future ages upon the Germans, and kept them back so long from any real national
life, got so strongly under way, because of the imperial
policy of the Saxon family in Italy, that it was no longer
possible to stop it—certainly not when that policy was
inherited as well by the succeeding kings.

It is of the utmost importance to bear this fact in
mind, because it not merely involved the destruction of
the royal power, but it alone rendered possible the desperate conflict with the church, and finally the virtual
triumph of the pope. Had the emperor been supported
by a centralized Germany, had not his plans been constantly checked by the selfish interests of the local powers,
papal resistance would have been impossible, and the

growing might of the Italian cities would have been overwhelmed before it could have developed into a serious
obstacle to the imperial authority.

The aspect of Germany at the accession of Henry III,
in 1039, had changed very much from that of a hundred
years earlier. The older duchies still existed in name,
but with a relative importance very much reduced by
the rise of numerous smaller feudal dominions beside
them. Pfalzgrafen, markgrafen, and even grafen, had
been founding little "dynasties," and gradually throwing
off any dependence upon the dukes, whose territories
were being diminished in this way and their power weakened. Konrad II, the first Franconian emperor, seems
to have deliberately encouraged the rise into independence of these smaller principalities, as a means of undermining the great ones, and the policy of the Saxon emperors, of conferring independent rights of jurisdiction
on ecclesiastical princes, tended to the same result.[1]

The policy was, in the main, a successful one, or we
may say that the process of separation and local independence had not yet gone so far but that a generation
of vigorous government, when the king interested himself
chiefly in German affairs, was able to restore the royal
power. Henry III was speedily able to acquire the
strongest real control of Germany that any sovereign
had had, or that any was to have in the future for that
matter.

But he was soon called into Italy. There the condition of things for a few years past had been nearly as
bad as at any time in the tenth century. The counts of
Tusculum had almost made the papacy hereditary in

[1] The final steps in this process, when the duchies, in the old sense, disappeared, and numerous smaller principalities rose to full equality with
the power which the duchies had once held, were taken in the Hohenstaufen
period. The geography of Germany in that period, as compared with that
under the Saxon emperors, shows how far this process had gone. Compare
Maps 22 and 26 in Droysen's *Historischer Handatlas*.

their family, and by the most corrupt means. At this time there were three rival popes, each maintaining his exclusive right to rule. All of them Henry deposed, and appointed, one after another, a succession of popes almost as solely by virtue of his imperial power as if the Roman bishopric were any minor bishopric of Germany. The series of precedents in favor of the right of the emperor over the pope which had been established by the Ottos and Henry was as clear and indisputable as any precedents on the other side to which the popes could appeal.

But with the popes of Henry's appointment a new and most powerful force rose to the control of the papacy— a strong and earnest movement for reformation which had arisen outside the circle of papal influence during the darkest days of its degradation, indeed, and entirely independent of the empire. This had started from the monastery of Cluny, founded in 910, in eastern France, as a reformation of the monastic life, but it involved gradually ideas of a wider reformation throughout the whole church. Two great sins of the time, as it regarded them, were especially attacked, the marriage of priests and simony, or the purchase of ecclesiastical preferment for money, including also appointments to church offices by temporal rulers.

Neither of these principles was new in the requirement of the church, but the vigor and thoroughness of the demand were new, and both principles were carried to further consequences than ever before. It is easy to see, also, that, if they were carried out in any thoroughgoing and complete way, they would necessarily involve a most perfect centralization of the church, and this was a part of the Cluny programme. The absolute subordination of all local churches to the central head, the pope, and the entire independence of the church, both in head and members, of all control by the state, were inevitable corollaries of its position.

The earnest spirit of Henry III was not out of sympathy with the demand for a real reformation, and with the third pope of his appointment, Leo IX, in 1048, the ideas of Cluny obtained the direction of affairs. Leo was an able man, and undertook a restoration of the papal power throughout Europe with vigor and determination, though not with uniform success. He did not recognize the right of the emperor to appoint the pope, and refused to assume the place until he had been canonically chosen in Rome, but on his death his successor was again appointed by Henry.

One apparently insignificant act of Leo's had important consequences. He brought back with him to Rome the monk Hildebrand. He had been brought up in a monastery in Rome in the strictest ideas of Cluny, had been a supporter of Gregory VI, one of the three rival popes deposed by Henry, who, notwithstanding his outright purchase of the papacy, represented the new reform demand, and had gone with him into exile on his deposition. It does not appear that he exercised any decisive influence during the reign of Leo IX, but so great was his ability and such the power of his personality that by gradual steps he became the directing spirit in the papal policy, though his influence over the papacy before his own pontificate was not so great nor so constant as it is sometimes said to have been.

So long as Henry lived the balance of power was decidedly in favor of the emperor, but in 1056 happened that disastrous event, which occurred so many times at critical points of imperial history, from Arnulf to Henry VI, the premature death of the emperor. His son, Henry IV, was only six years old at his father's death, and a minority followed just in the crisis of time needed to enable the feudal princes of Germany to recover and strengthen their independence against the central government, and to give free hands to the papacy to carry out its plans for throwing off the imperial control. Never again did an emperor occupy, in respect either to Germany or the papacy, the vantage-ground on which Henry III had stood.

The minority was thus a turning-point in the history of Germany and of the church. It was also, in one sense, a turning-point in the history of the world, for the real religious reformation, which was demanded and which had been begun by Cluny, need not, of necessity, have involved the extreme centralization in the government of the church which had been connected with it and which raised the papacy to its position of European supremacy in another century. There was needed a strong and able emperor of a thoroughly reforming spirit to separate the reform which was necessary from the absolutist tendency which accompanied it. Whether Henry III could have done this we cannot be sure. His death certainly made it impossible.

The triumph of the reform movement and of its ecclesiastical theory is especially associated with the name of Hildebrand, or Gregory VII, as he called himself when pope, and was very largely, if not entirely, due to his indomitable spirit and iron will, which would yield to no persuasion or threats or actual force. He is one of the most interesting personalities of history. The sentence of his supporter, Peter Damiani, "He ruled me like a holy Satan," has been so often quoted because it describes him in a word. His acts were often those which properly belong in the kingdom of darkness, but his purposes were righteous, as he understood the right—a most interesting example of the men so numerous in every age and in every walk of life who are so thoroughly convinced of the holiness of their cause that all the means which they can use to secure its triumph seem to them equally holy.

The three chief points which the reform party attempted to gain were the independence of the church from all outside control in the election of the pope, the celibacy of the clergy, and the abolition of simony, or the purchase of ecclesiastical preferment. The foundation for the first of these was laid under Nicholas II by assigning the selection of the pope to the college of cardinals in Rome, though it was only after some considerable time that this reform was fully secured.

The second point, the celibacy of the clergy, had long been demanded by the church, but the requirement had not been strictly enforced, and in many parts of Europe married clergy were the rule. The attempt which was made to compel obedience on this point met with the most violent opposition within the church itself, but the sympathy of the people was in the main with the reformers and their cause was finally gained. The importance of this step and its value in the centralization of the church hardly needs to be stated. Not merely was the temptation to alienate the endowments of the church for the benefit of children removed from the clergy, but all their lives were made to centre in the church. They were to have nothing else to live for, nothing else to plan for. The church secured an army of occupation, thoroughly devoted to itself, in every country of Europe. There can be no doubt but that the Cluny party believed that they were accomplishing a needed moral reform in this matter, but there is also no doubt but that they realized and hoped to secure the gain which would result from it to the ecclesiastical world monarchy.

As interpreted by the reformers, the third of their demands, the suppression of simony, was as great a step in advance and as revolutionary as the first. Technically, simony was the sin of securing an ecclesiastical office by bribery, named from the incident concerning Simon Magus, recorded in the eighth chapter of the Acts of the Apostles. But at this time the desire for the complete

independence of the church had given to it a new and
wider meaning which made it include all appointment to
important offices in the church by laymen, including kings
and the emperor.

It is the plainest of historical facts that such appointment had gone on, practically undisputed, from the
earliest times.   Under both the public and the private
law of all the German states the king had such a right.
According to the private law the founder was the patron, and as such enjoyed the right of appointment.
According to the conception of the public law the bishop
was an officer of the state.   He had, in the great majority of cases, political duties to perform as important as
his ecclesiastical duties.   The lands which formed the en-
dowment of his office had always been considered as being,
more immediately even than the land of lay vassals, the
property of the state, and were treated as such when the
occasion demanded, from times before Charles Martel to
times after Gregory VII.   At this period these lands had
clearly defined feudal obligations to perform, which constituted a very considerable proportion of the resources
of the state.   It was a matter of vital importance whether
officers exercising such important functions and controlling so large a part of its area—probably everywhere as
much as one-third of the territory—should be selected
by the state or by some foreign power beyond its reach
and having its own peculiar interests to seek.

But this question of lay investiture was as vitally important for the church as for the state.   Not merely was
the bishop a great ecclesiastical as well as political officer, but manifestly also that close centralization of the
church, which was to be the result of this movement,
could not be secured if temporal princes should have the
right of determining what sort of men should occupy
places of such influence in the government of the church.
It was as necessary to the centralization and indepen-

dence of the church that it should choose these officers as that it should elect the head of all—the pope.

This was not a question for Germany alone. Every northern state had to face the same difficulty. In England during this period the same contest was carried through to the same compromise at the end. In France the contest did not rise to the same importance from accidental reasons, but the result was essentially the same. The struggle was so much more bitter and obstinate with the emperor than with any other sovereign because of the close relation of the two powers one to another, and because the whole question of their relative rights was bound up with it. It was an act of rebellion on the part of the papacy against the sovereign who had controlled it with almost absolute power for a century, and it was the rising into an equal, or even superior, place beside the emperor of what was practically a new power, a rival for his imperial position.

For this was what the movement taken as a whole really meant. It is not possible to overstate the significance of this age as the time when the possibility which lay before it of assuming the control of the whole Christian world, political as well as ecclesiastical, dawned upon the consciousness of the Roman church. The full power which so many men in the past had been laboring to secure, though only imperfectly understanding it, the position towards which through so many centuries she had been steadily though unconsciously tending, the church now began clearly to see and to realize that it was almost attained and, seeing this, to set about the last steps necessary to reach the goal with definite and vigorous purpose.

This cannot be doubted by any one who looks over the acts and the claims of the papacy during the time of Hildebrand. The feudal suzerainty which is established under Nicholas II over the Norman states of southern Italy is based distinctly on the rights conveyed by the

Donation of Constantine, which, if carried further, might be made to cover the whole West. The kings of the growing Spanish states are reminded that territory conquered from the infidel belongs of right to the pope as vassal territory. The same claim is advanced for Hungary. The fealty of England is demanded. Most imperious letters are written to the king of France. Political affairs are taken notice of in Scandinavia and in Russia. The king of Munster, in Ireland, is informed that all sovereigns are subjects of St. Peter, and that all the world owes obedience to him and to his vicar. The difference between the actual power of the papacy under Gregory VII, and again under Innocent III, when it reaches its highest point, is due to the circumstances of the time which enable the later pope to carry through his pretensions to a more successful issue, and not at all to any clearer conception of his rights by Innocent.

It was absolutely impossible that a conflict with these new claims should be avoided as soon as Henry IV arrived at an age to take the government into his own hands and attempted to exercise his imperial rights as he understood them.

The details of that conflict it is not possible to follow: the divided condition of Germany, which fatally weakened the emperor's power; the dramatic incident of Canossa; the faithful support of the imperial cause by the Rhine cities; the rebellion of Henry's son, who, when he became emperor, followed his father's policy; the death of Henry IV, powerless and under the ban of the church; the fluctuations of success, now on one side and now on the other.

The settlement which was finally reached in the Concordat of Worms, in 1122, was a compromise.[1]   The

[1] This concordat may be found, in translation, in Henderson, p. 408; in the original, in Matthews, *Select Mediæval Documents* (Boston, 1892), p. 66 —a little book which makes easily accessible the text of a considerable number of the important documents illustrating the conflict between church and empire.

church was to choose the man for the office. He was then to receive the lay investiture, as a political and feudal officer, from the king, and finally the spiritual investiture, with the ring and staff, from the church as an ecclesiastical officer and a pastor. The state secured in this way something of a control, though not so complete as it had desired, over the interests in which it was most concerned. And the church, yielding also some of its demands, secured the point most important for its protection. It was, in all probability, as fair a settlement of the dispute as could be reached, and the question practically disappeared—not absolutely, because, as opportunity offered in the following times, each of the parties tried to usurp the rights which had not been granted to it; but the question never again became of such universal importance as when it was the central issue in the conflict between the empire and the papacy. When that great strife opened again, nearly half a century later, it had shifted to other grounds and presents a wholly changed aspect.

While, however, on the special question the church did not secure all that it had claimed or hoped for— though all, perhaps, to which it had a just claim—there was far more at stake in the contest, as we have seen, than the particular point of lay investiture, and in regard to these wider interests the victory of the church was complete. The change which had taken place in the century from the papacy as it existed under Henry III was enormous. The popes had emancipated themselves from all imperial control, never again to pass under it. But they had gained much more than this. Not merely was the papacy independent, but it had come up beside the empire as a fully co-ordinate and equal sovereignty, not merely in theory but in the power actually exercised. It was also no longer satisfied with ecclesiastical rule. It had greatly enlarged its sphere, and was claiming rights throughout Europe which were manifestly political and

therefore belonging to the emperor's domain. But the
emperor was powerless to prevent this extension of papal
prerogative, and could not possibly interfere with success in cases where the pope made himself obeyed. This
papal power continued to grow through the twelfth century, greatly aided by the general spirit of the age and
by the contemporary crusades, and at its close Innocent
III exercised a more truly international sway than any
emperor had ever done.

After the interval of a single reign a new dynasty succeeded the Franconian upon the imperial throne—the
Hohenstaufen—one of the most brilliant families of history, producing a most remarkable succession of princes.
The first of this family to take up in any wide sense the
old imperial plan, and consequently to come into collision
with the papacy, was Frederick Barbarossa, whose reign
begins in 1152.

This seems to be a new age of conflict between empire and papacy. This is its surface appearance, and
this determined largely its external character. But it
needs only to look below the surface, and not very far
below, to see that this is not a contest between empire
and papacy in the old sense. That rivalry is no longer
as it was before the one leading and central issue between the parties. It has rather fallen to the position
of an incident of the main battle. The great struggle of
Frederick's life is with powers and principalities which
did not exist a hundred years earlier. The conflict is
manifestly of the old empire, a creation of earlier medieval times and fitted to their conditions, with the spirit
and conditions of a new age to which it is unfitted, with
strong forces which are everywhere transforming Europe
and which cannot be held back. The struggle is rather
on the part of the emperor to recover and to retain an
imperial position from which he is being slowly but irre-

sistibly pushed, than to prevent any rival power from establishing a similar imperial position beside him. That had now been done beyond any possibility of further dispute.

The papacy, which was itself in the end also to fall a victim, so far as its imperial power is concerned, to the forces of the new age, was for the moment their ally. And this was in truth the necessary and proper alliance for the papacy to make. For, though the new age was to prove itself bitterly hostile to certain of the papal pretensions, its immediate triumph was not so full of danger, even to these pretensions, as the triumph of the emperor would have been, and, in the end, could not be so destructive to the other side of the papal power, its ecclesiastical supremacy.

If we look first at the Germany of that day, which would seem to be necessarily the foundation of any strong imperial power, we see at once the magnitude of the change which had taken place there, and the entire revolution in the imperial policy since the days of Henry III.

The subdivision of Germany had now been carried much further than at that time. A host of small principalities had escaped from the authority of any intermediate lord, and now depended immediately upon the emperor. Their rights of independence and local government were much more clearly defined and fully recognized than then. They were no longer—though they may have retained the titles—dukes and counts, that is, officers of the empire, but they were "princes," or, in other words, sovereigns. Some of them had already begun, with great vigor and earnestness, the work of centralizing and consolidating their own territories, and of breaking the power of their own vassals, and of the small nobles within their reach, in order to prevent that process of disintegration in their own land which they had themselves accomplished in the kingdom at large.

This change in Germany, Frederick I could not reverse. It is indeed the trait which is characteristic of his policy that he no longer tried to do so. He deliberately increased the number of the smaller principalities, or raised them in titular rank, and sometimes with extraordinary concessions of local independence. He did certainly punish with severity the refusal of Henry the Lion, the head of the great rival power in Germany, that of the Guelfs, to aid him in Italy, and broke to pieces the wide dominion which he had brought together. But while this was a personal triumph for Frederick, the power of the king in Germany gained nothing permanent from it.

The real basis of Frederick's power, and the main source of the strength which he could derive from Germany, for his Italian campaigns, were the extensive family possessions of the Hohenstaufen, increased by the inheritance of the Franconian family lands, possessions which, when brought together were greater than those of any other German family with the possible exception of the Guelfs. To these resources Frederick added whatever he could at any moment gain from the German princes, won often by further concessions from the relics of the royal power.

Frederick I may be said, then, to have begun that policy which, though it was a complete abandonment of the old imperial policy, is the sole method of the emperors of all later times, the policy of depending chiefly upon the strength derived from the personal possessions of the emperor, and of using the royal rights as ready money with which to purchase, whatever could be purchased, to add to this private strength. As Frederick's reign was the apparent turning-point from the old policy to the new one, it was naturally not followed with such complete disregard of consequences as it was to be very soon after, but it was clearly enough his policy, and we may date from his time the surrender of the central government in Germany to the sovereignty and independence of the princes.

It is in Italy, however, that the most decisive and revolutionary changes, which mark the new age, are to be seen. There Frederick found opposed to him an entirely new and most determined enemy—the cities.

Favoring causes which were begun or strengthened by the crusades, then well under way, and which we shall hereafter examine more closely, had led to a rapid development of the cities in power and in the spirit of independence. They had arisen in northern Italy to occupy the place which the princes occupied in Germany, that is, they were the fragments into which the country had divided in the absence of a strong central government. Like the princes, also, they had secured rights of local self-government, but their governments were of course republican in form and not monarchical, and their actual independence was probably greater than the German princes enjoyed at this time. They had adopted also that policy of absorption in respect to the feudal nobles in their neighborhood, which the princes were beginning to follow in Germany, though in the case of the cities with more speedy and complete success. Feudalism, as a political institution, had practically disappeared from Italy by the middle of the twelfth century. Only two or three of the great fiefs still existed. The cities had almost wholly absorbed the smaller nobility, and had created larger or smaller city principalities by extending their sway over as much of the surrounding territory as possible. It was manifestly certain that the cities would offer a most obstinate resistance to any attempt to restore a direct imperial control.

But in one way the development of commerce and of the cities had placed a new weapon in the emperor's hands. It had led to a more general and thorough study of the ancient Roman law, and this law represented the emperor as absolute in all departments of government. Frederick's lawyers said to him: "Your will is the source of law according to the recognized legal maxim of the Institutes: whatever the prince has approved has the force of law."

It was with the sanction which he derived from the authority of the Justinian code that Frederick attempted to establish a royal supervision of the local governments of the cities, and to revive a number of practically obsolete rights which could be made to yield a considerable revenue. What he did has very much the appearance of an attempt to re-establish in Italy that centralized and immediate royal government which had been practically given up in Germany.

For the cities it was a matter of vital concern. Not merely was the local independence which they had secured in danger but also their continued commercial prosperity, which would depend very largely upon freedom from restraint and the power of self-direction. Therefore they made common cause with one another, the most of them at least, and drew together closely in the Lombard League—an organization which they formed for mutual defence against the emperor.

The details of the struggle we cannot follow. The battle of Legnano, in 1176, is worthy of note, in which the cities gained a complete victory over the emperor and broke his power for the moment. But it was a victory from which they did not gain so much as might have been expected. With great skill Frederick set about the recovery of his position, and he succeeded in separating the papacy from the cities, and making a separate peace with Alexander III on the basis of mutual concessions. Then followed in Germany the overthrow of Henry the Lion and the destruction of the power of the Guelfs, and after this Frederick found the cities as ready as himself to make peace.

By the treaty of Constance, which was concluded between them in 1183, the general sovereignty of the emperor was recognized, the officers elected by the cities were to be confirmed by him, certain cases might be appealed from the city courts to his representatives, and the special rights which he had claimed were commuted for an annual payment from each city large enough to afford him a considerable revenue. In reality, however, the local sovereignty and independence of the cities were recognized by the emperor, and the hope of establishing a consolidated national government in Italy, if he had cherished it, was abandoned, as it had been in Germany. Certainly both these countries had now fallen into fragments, never again to be united into a national whole until after the middle of the nineteenth century.

The emperor had now made peace with all his enemies, and the last part of his reign was only slightly troubled with opposition. He was master of large resources and possessed very great and real power. It might seem to him almost possible to establish as an actual fact the Holy Roman Empire of the theory, and there are indications that he thought such a success not beyond his reach. But although his position was a brilliant one, a really strong and imperial position, it rested upon a very different and far less secure foundation than the power of the Ottos or of Henry III. The only actual empire which was now possible would be a federal, or feudal sovereignty—the overlordship of fully independent and self-governing states. It could no longer rest upon the solid support of a great nation which would look upon it as a glorious expression of its national life.

Shortly after the Peace of Constance, however, an advantage was secured by Frederick which promised to restore, in large measure at least, all that the emperor had lost in this way, and which determined the character of the final contest between the empire and the papacy.

He obtained for his son Henry, already acknowledged as his successor, the hand of Constance, heiress of the Norman kingdom, which included Sicily and southern Italy. If this could be made, as a solid and centralized state, the basis of an imperial power, then possibly, having this advantage to begin with, all Italy could be consolidated, and the same thing could afterwards be done in Germany; certainly, from its geographical position, the Norman kingdom would be more suitable than the German for the centre of a world empire. This was a possibility full of the greatest danger to the papacy, threatening to surround its little territory with a strong imperial state, and the popes did not fail to see the danger.

Notwithstanding his short reign, Henry VI was in many respects the most interesting of the Hohenstaufen emperors, and he was probably the ablest of them all. His Sicilian kingdom he obtained only after a long resistance, but he obtained it at last, and in such a way that he was really an absolute sovereign there. Attempted movements in opposition in Germany he succeeded in overcoming. The pope was powerless against him, and he disposed of a part of the papal territory in Italy as if it were his own. Supported by so much real strength, his imperial ideas were of the highest and widest, and the actual international influence which he exercised in the last year or two of his life was greater than that of any other emperor. He had formed a definite plan for the consolidation of Germany and Sicily into a single monarchy, hereditary instead of elective, and his success seemed altogether likely when suddenly he died, in 1197, in his thirty-second year, leaving his son, Frederick, three years old.

In Germany there followed a double election, his brother Philip representing the Hohenstaufen party, and Otto, the son of Henry the Lion, the Guelf and papal party, and in the civil strife which resulted the princes rapidly recovered the ground which they had lost in the last few years.

In Rome, a few weeks after the death of Henry, Innocent III was elected pope. Under him the papal power, without a real rival and strengthened by the general trend of European affairs during the past century, rose to its highest point. He forced the strongest of European sovereigns to obey him; he disposed of the imperial title almost as openly as Henry III had of the papal; he bestowed on several princes the title of king, and established a circle of vassal kingdoms almost completely around the circumference of Europe. The imperial position as the head of Christendom, which Henry VI had for a moment appeared to occupy, he held in reality for many years. He died in 1216, just at the beginning of the reign of Frederick II.

Relieved thus at the start of a rival with whom he could hardly expect to cope, and whose successor was his inferior, Frederick II took up with earnestness and ability the plans of his father. With a more absolute control of Sicily than any earlier king, with large military strength drawn from Germany, with the prestige of a successful crusade, he seemed about to accomplish what his grandfather had failed to do, to reduce the cities of north Italy to the condition of his Norman kingdom under an immediate absolutism. For a few years following his great victory of Cortenuova, in 1237, his final success seemed certain, and the papacy seemed utterly powerless to resist him further.

But the strength of his position was more apparent than real. His resources were mainly drawn from Sicily, and though rich, Sicily showed signs of exhaustion under the strain. The support of Germany had been secured only by concessions which sanctioned in legal form by royal charter the practical independence which the princes, both ecclesiastical and lay, had secured, and made it still greater by further sacrifice of royal rights. But what he had gained by such means was utterly insecure because Germany was so divided by local and personal interests that civil strife, and almost anarchy, was certain to appear at the first favorable moment. The Italian cities were by no means so completely overcome as they seemed, nor was the papacy. France and England had no wish to see the head of the church entirely overthrown and the papal seat left vacant, as it was for two years on the death of Celestine IV in 1241.

Finally, the next pope, Innocent IV, who as bishop had been the emperor's friend, but as pope must be his enemy, succeeded in escaping to France, and at Lyons held a council of the church where Frederick was deposed from the empire. This acted as a signal for all his enemies. Civil war broke out in Germany, and an opposition king was elected there. The cities in north Italy rebelled and gathered new strength. Misfortune after misfortune befell the emperor, and, though he could not be conquered, his power was gone.

After Frederick's death, in 1250, the empire could never be restored. The great states which had composed it fell apart; within themselves they were broken to fragments and for a few years anarchy reigned almost everywhere. After some time the German kingdom and the empire reappeared in name. But the old medieval empire was no longer possible. It had been completely overthrown and destroyed, not in truth by its rival, the papacy, but by the conditions of a new age, by the forces which were turning the medieval world into the modern, and they made its reconstruction beyond the power of man.

But for the moment the papacy was left without a rival. Its victory seemed complete and its pretensions rose accordingly. It appeared about to step into the vacant place, and to be on the point of assuming the im-

perial titles and prerogatives, when it found itself confronted with a new enemy, as determined as the old one
and far stronger, an enemy whose success over its political pretensions was destined to be complete, the new
spirit of national patriotism and independence. To this
new conflict we shall come at a later point.

It is as impossible here, as elsewhere, to determine
what history would have been if the thing which did
not happen had occurred. But if it was an inherent
tendency, as it seems to have been, of either of these
two great powers to establish a universal empire over
Christendom, if this was the object for which, consciously
or unconsciously, either was striving, the one thing which
prevented such a result was the opposition of the other.
At the time when the danger was the greatest there was
no other power in Europe which could have offered suf-
ficent resistance to either of them. If there was such a
danger it was the greatest from the papacy, for the
strength which it derived from the church was far more
real and effective for such a purpose than any which the
empire could have drawn, as things were, from Germany
and Italy or from the theory of the empire. The Holy
Roman Empire may have entailed loss and suffering,
which seemed without end, upon Germans and Italians,
but if they succeeded in holding off the formation of a
theocratic absolutism over Europe until the modern nations were strong enough to protect themselves, their sacrifices secured the future of civilization and the possibility of their own national existence to-day.

CHAPTER XI

THE CRUSADES

IN following the history of the empire and the papacy in the last chapter we have passed out of the early middle ages into a new and different time. Between the date at which that chapter opened and the date at which it closed a great change had taken place. New causes had begun to work. New forces had been set in operation or old ones greatly intensified, and the face of history had been transformed. In other words, we have passed in that interval the turning-point of the middle ages.

We have seen, in the history of the first part of the middle ages, the introduction of the German element which is so important in the modern races, and we have traced the rise and some part of the history of the three great medieval creations—the Church, the Empire, and Feudalism. We have seen the German Empire of Charlemagne reinforce the Roman idea of world unity, and in the breaking up of his empire the modern nations of Europe have taken shape. They have by no means as yet obtained their final form, even in their geographical outline, far less in government, but they have found the places which they are to occupy, they have begun the process of growth which is to result in their present government, and they are easily distinguishable and have begun to a certain extent to distinguish themselves from one another in race and language. But it is still the first half of the middle ages. Some faint signs may show themselves here and there of the beginning of better

things and of a renewal of progress, somewhat greater
activity in commerce, more frequent eagerness to know,
and a better understanding of the sources of knowledge,
some improvements in writing and in art. But in all
the main features of civilization the conditions which followed the German settlements remain with little change
and only slight advance. But the crusades are not over
when we find ourselves in an age of great changes and
relatively of rapid progress.

We must now return and take up the age of transition which leads from the earlier stage to the later, and
ascertain, if we can, the impulse which imparted fresh
life to the old forces and awakened the new. This age
of transition is the age of the crusades, the pivot upon
which the middle ages turned from the darkness and
disorder of the earlier time to the greater light and order
of modern times. The age of the crusades, then, is a
great revolutionary age. Like the age of the fall of Rome,
or of the revival of learning and the Reformation, or of
the French Revolution, it is an age in which humanity
passes, through excitement and stimulus and struggle,
on into a new stage of its development, in which it puts
off the old and becomes new.

The occasion of the crusades was Mohammedanism.
At the beginning of the seventh century Arabia had been
revolutionized by the teaching of Mohammed. Putting into definite and striking form the unconscious
ideas and aspirations of his people, and adding a central
and unifying teaching, and inspiring and elevating notions from various foreign sources, he had transformed a
few scattered tribes into a great nation and sent them
forth under a blazing enthusiasm upon a career of conquest entirely unparalleled in its motive forces, and also
in its extent, unless by one or two Mongolian conquerors.
This age of conquest lasted till about 750 A. D., and was

then succeeded by an equally rapid and astonishing civilization, with which we are all somewhat familiar from the complete picture of it which has been preserved in the "Arabian Nights." It was a civilization not merely of elegance and luxury and certain forms of art, nor merely of commercial enterprise and wealth. In the valleys of the Tigris and the Euphrates the Mohammedans became acquainted with the work of the Greeks. Something in their own race nature seems to have corresponded to the especially scientific tendency of the Greek mind. They took up the Greek science with very great enthusiasm and earnestness, and added to it whatever results of a similar sort they could find among any of the other nations with whom they came in contact—mathematical suggestions from the Hindoos, for example. They did better than this, for they made additions of their own to the stock of scientific ideas which they had inherited. Their great work, however, was not in the way of new scientific discoveries. They made no great or revolutionary advance in any one of the sciences. They made new observations. They collected and recorded many facts. They discovered new processes and methods. Their own scientific work was all of that long and patient sort, of preparation and collection and gradual improvement of tools, which precedes every apparently sudden achievement of genius. They handed over the work of the Greeks much better prepared to lead to such an advance than when the Greeks left it. But their great work was to hand it over. While the world of western Christendom was passing through its darkest ages, the forgotten sciences which the Greeks had begun were cherished among the Mohammedans, and enriched from other sources, and finally given up to Christendom again when the nations of the West had become conscious of the necessity and the possibility of scientific work and ambitious to begin it. This was the most important permanent work for general civilization of the first Mohammedan age.

The first flood of the Arabian conquest had swept over the Holy Land, and the sepulchre of Christ had remained in the hands of the Saracens. But for Mohammedan as for Christian, these were sacred places, and a pilgrimage was for him a holy and pious duty even more than for his Christian neighbor. While the immediate successors of the first conquerors—the Mohammedans of the southern races—retained control of Jerusalem, the Christians were allowed free access to its shrines, not without intervals of harsh treatment under an occasional fanatical caliph, and not without some uneasiness on the part of the Saracens at the rapidly increasing numbers of the pilgrims, especially as bands of thousands began to appear, led by princes or great nobles.

With the advance of the Seljuk Turks, in the eleventh century, new conditions were introduced. They were a rough and barbarous people as compared with the Saracens whom they supplanted, and naturally of a cruel disposition. As more and more of Palestine and of its approaches passed under their control, the pilgrims began to meet with very harsh treatment. The great sufferings and the miraculous visions of Peter the Hermit are now known to have been the inventions of a later age, but if he did not suffer what he was fabled to have undergone, undoubtedly other pilgrims did suffer something of the sort. At last the worst happened, and Jerusalem fell into the hands of the Turks.

But the immediate impulse to the first crusade came from the appeal of the emperor at Constantinople for aid. The emperor at this time was Alexius Comnenus, who had struggled bravely and skilfully for more than ten years against attacks from every quarter—Seljuks on the east, the Tartar Petchenegs in the Balkans, and the ambitious Robert Guiscard on the shores of the Adriatic.

He had met with some success and had saved at least a fragment of his empire, which had been threatened with total destruction. But he was not strong enough alone to make any great headway against the Turks. If Asia Minor was to be recovered and a real restoration of the empire to be accomplished, he must have larger forces than he could furnish from his own unaided resources. In March, 1095, his ambassadors appealed to Christendom at the Council of Piacenza, held by Urban II at a moment of triumph over the emperor Henry IV, and later in the year at the Council of Clermont in France the fiery eloquence of the pope sanctioned the appeal and aroused the whole of Europe.

The response which his appeal received in the West was, indeed, far beyond the emperor's hopes, or wishes even. The number of the crusaders was so great, much above any possibility of control by him, that the fear was at once aroused in his mind lest their advance threatened his empire with a more serious danger than that from the Seljuks. All of them, he might well believe, some of them he knew already to his cost in the case of the Normans of southern Italy, were actuated chiefly by motives of self-interest and the desire of conquest. The later attitude of the emperor towards his invited allies was not without its justification.

The response of the West to the appeal of the East for help against the infidel was so universal and overwhelming, because of the combination at the moment of a variety of influences and causes tending to such a result. Of these we may easily distinguish three leading influences which were especially characteristic of the whole eleventh century—the love of military exploits and adventures, which was beginning, even in that century, to express itself in the institutions and practices of chivalry; the theocratic ideas which were at that time advancing the papacy so rapidly to its highest point of power; and an ascetic conception of life and Christian conduct which, like the last, was not only cherished in the church, but held almost as strongly and unquestioningly by the great mass of men of all ranks.

All the middle ages were characterized by a restless love of adventure, and by greater or smaller expeditions to a distance to satisfy this feeling and to gain glory and wealth. The knight-errant is so great a figure in literature because he was so frequent in the life of the time, and even more universally a part of its ideals and imaginings. The knight-errant himself may not have been common so early, but the feeling was never stronger than in the eleventh century, and especially so among the Normans, who were so prominent in the first crusade, as the Norman conquests of southern Italy and of England witness. But this cause, however strong, was not the decisive one in the crusades. Had it been, they would not have ceased when they did, for this motive did not cease with them. It never has been more active, indeed, than it is to-day, at least in the Anglo-Saxon world, as Africa, and the Arctic and Antarctic regions, and a hundred other things abundantly testify.

Nor was the influence of the church, nor the idea that it represented God's government, and that through its voice God spake and made known His will to man, the one decisive influence. That these things were so, men thoroughly believed. The growing strength and clearness of the belief that God was in the pope, which was a feature of the reform movement of the eleventh century, was one of the great forces which aided the papacy to win its triumph over the emperor, and to rise to the summit of its power over the church and over the state as well. The call of the pope roused Europe to the great crusades, partly, at least, because it was to Europe the call of God. But the crusades ceased when they did, not because the popes ceased to urge them upon Christendom, nor because the Christian world had ceased to believe in the inspiration of the pope, for both these facts continued long after the crusades had become impossible.

It is in the universal prevalence of the third one of the influences which have been mentioned—the ascetic feeling—that we must find the one decisive cause of the crusades. It was the strong hold which this feeling had upon prince as well as peasant which made the crusades possible as a great European movement.[1] It was its decline in relative power as a determining motive of life which made them no longer possible.

It is hard for us in the beginning of the twentieth century to understand how strong a controlling force this feeling was in a time when the motives and interests which shape our modern life had not come into existence, and when the nature and laws of a spiritual world were beyond the understanding even of the best. The dark terrors of the world of lost souls, which they crudely but vividly pictured to their minds as horrible physical torments, pressed upon them with a reality almost as immediate as that of the world in which they were really living. With their limited experience and scanty knowledge, and narrow range of interests, there were no sources open to them of other impressions with which to correct or balance these. The terror of an awful future hung over them constantly; and to escape from it, to secure their safety in the life to come, was one of the most pressing and immediate necessities of the present life.[2]

[1] In the Anglo-Saxon states, in the first two hundred years after their conversion, thirty kings and queens went into the cloister. Instances of the same thing are frequent in other states. The passage in Einhard's *Life of Charlemagne*, chap. II, on the cloister life of Pippin's brother, Carloman, is very instructive concerning the general feeling towards monasticism.

[2] It is not meant, of course, that this was an ever-present dread from which there was no moment of escape. Life would have been impossible if that had been the case. But in order to understand many of the most characteristic features of the first half of the middle ages it is absolutely necessary to hold in mind the fact that, relatively, as compared with later times, these feelings were a constant and absorbing reality of life.

But with the crude and physical conception of the future world, a crude and physical conception of the means of preparation for it was inevitable.

The history of monasticism, of pilgrimages, and of the whole penitential discipline of the church is full of instances to show that, in those days, there existed among the highest and most intelligent classes of the time an intensity of belief in the direct spiritual efficacy of physical penances which we hardly expect to find to-day in the most ignorant and superstitious. A pilgrimage was not an expression of reverence for a saintly life, nor an act of worship even. It was in itself a religious act, securing merit and reward for the one who performed it, balancing a certain number of his sins, and making his escape from the world of torment hereafter more certain. The more distant and more difficult the pilgrimage, the more meritorious, especially if it led to such supremely holy places as those which had been sanctified by the presence of Christ himself. For the man of the world, for the man who could not, or would not, go into monasticism, the pilgrimage was the one conspicuous act by which he could satisfy the ascetic need, and gain its rewards.

A crusade was a stupendous pilgrimage, under especially favorable and meritorious conditions, so proclaimed universally and so entered upon by the vast majority of those who took part in it. So long as asceticism as a motive influenced strongly princes, and great nobles, and the higher classes, the men who really determined events, the great crusades were possible. When other interests of a more immediate sort rose in the place of this motive, its power declined, these men could no longer be led by it in the same way, and the crusades ceased.

But this last suggestion must be carried further back and recognized as of the utmost importance in aiding us to understand the reason for the crusades as well as for

their cessation. It was an essential condition of the movement that all these motives and causes which favored the
crusades combined together in their influence upon the
men of the West at a time when no great interests had
arisen at home to demand their attention and their
energies. The time of the migration of the nations was
past; even the viking raids had ceased. The modern nations with their problems, hard to solve but pressing for
solution, had not yet come into existence. Commerce
was in its infancy, the Third Estate had hardly begun to
form itself, and the revolution which it would work was
still far off. None of these existed as yet, with the rival
interests which they were soon to present to the duty of
maintaining a Christian kingdom in the Holy Land, or
even, with the pressure of an immediate necessity, to the
duty of saving one soul by a penitential pilgrimage. All
the energy and enthusiasm of the newly formed people
had no other channel in which to flow. There was no
other great and worthy object to which to devote themselves, and they devoted themselves to this so long as
these notions and influences were not balanced by new
and opposing ones.

   That these motives were strongly at work through the
whole eleventh century, and gradually turning men's
minds towards crusades—towards armed expeditions
which should combine adventurous warfare and rich conquests from the Mohammedan world with the advantages of holy pilgrimages—can easily be seen. Single
men and small parties some time before had begun to
undertake the Christian duty of fighting the infidel wherever he was to be found, and as the century drew to a
close their numbers were constantly increasing. The little
Christian states of Spain were greatly aided in their contests with the Moors by reinforcements of this sort, and
one of these precrusades led to the founding of the kingdom of Portugal. And also from almost every state of

the West devoted knights had gone, even by the thousand, to aid the Greek emperor against the Turks before his appeal to the pope. Some of the Italian cities had combined their commercial interests and their Christian duty in attacks upon the Saracens of the western Mediterranean regions. In 1087 Pisa and Genoa, at the instigation of Pope Victor III, and under the holy banner of St. Peter, gained important successes in Tunis, and compelled the emir to recognize the overlordship of the pope. A little earlier Pope Gregory VII had conceived the plan of sending a great army against the East to re-establish there the true faith, but his contest with the Emperor Henry IV had allowed him no opportunity to carry out the plan. The overwhelming enthusiasm of the first crusade was the sudden breaking forth of a feeling which had long been growing in intensity, because now it had gained the highest possible sanction as the will of God and a favorable opportunity to express itself in action.

The crusades continued from the end of the eleventh to near the end of the thirteenth century, a period of about two hundred years. During this time eight crusades, as they are commonly reckoned, occurred, with many smaller expeditions of the same sort. Of these at least the first four, falling within the first hundred years, or barely more, are great European movements shared by many nations and thoroughly stirring the life of the West.

The first crusade was led by princes and great nobles, from Normandy, of the royal house of France, of Toulouse, of eastern Germany and southern Italy. It went overland to Constantinople, forced its way through Asia Minor, captured Antioch from the Turks after a long siege, and with greatly reduced numbers, in 1099, stormed Jerusalem, then in possession of the Fatimite caliphs of Egypt. Its conquests it formed into a loosely organized feudal state, the kingdom of Jerusalem, divided into a number of great fiefs practically independent.

The second crusade, fifty years later, was led by the Emperor Konrad III and by King Louis VII of France on the news of the fall of Edessa, the outpost of the kingdom of Jerusalem against the Turks. It attempted to follow the overland route, but failed to find a passage through Asia Minor, and the remnants of the armies made the last part of the journey by sea. In the Holy Land it attempted nothing but a perfunctory attack on Damascus.

The third, which is perhaps the best known of the crusades, was set in motion by the capture of Jerusalem by Saladin in 1187. It was led by Richard the Lionheart of England, Philip Augustus of France, and the Emperor Frederick I. The emperor followed the old overland route and died in Asia Minor. Richard and Philip made the passage wholly by sea. The difference in character of these two men, and the many causes of disagreement which existed between them, prevented any great success, and the crusade continued to be a failure after Philip returned to France, largely because of Richard's instability and lack of fixed purpose.

A decade after, under the greatest of the popes, Innocent III, the fourth crusade assembled, with high hopes, in northern Italy to be transported probably to Egypt, by the Venetians, but it never saw its destination. It was turned into a great commercial speculation, captured Constantinople, and erected there the Latin empire, another feudal state, which lasted past the middle of the thirteenth century.

The later crusades need not be noticed. They are expeditions of single nations and lack the general character of the first four. The Emperor Frederick II by treaty re-established for a brief time the kingdom of Jerusalem; and St. Louis, at his death, in 1270, closed the series of the crusades usually numbered with the true spirit and high Christian motives of the ideal crusader.

In this line of events two things are to be especially noticed as characteristic, and as of assistance in enabling us to see the connection between the events themselves and the results which followed from them.

One of them is the different part taken in these expeditions by the states of Italy as compared with the other states. The Normans of the south enter into the first crusade like the other Europeans, and in some of the later crusades the feudal parts of Italy have their share. But, even in the first crusade, some of the city states of Italy appear as furnishing ships and conveying supplies to the real crusaders, and as time goes on this comes to be a more and more important share of the movement which falls to them. Italy does not furnish warriors; it furnishes ships, transports men and supplies, not for rewards in the world to come but for cash, sells and buys, and is constantly on the watch for commercial advantages.

The other fact is the gradual change in the route by which the crusaders reached the Holy Land as the period advanced. The first went wholly overland; the second almost wholly, making only the last stage by water. Two of the three divisions of the third crusade went wholly by water, and all the later crusades, even that of Andrew of Hungary. There was a constantly increasing demand for ships and sailors, and a constantly increasing ability to meet that demand.

Before taking up in detail the results of the crusades it is important to notice one fact in the general history of the middle ages of which they are at once a sign and a further cause. They were a great common movement of all Europe, shared in alike in motive and spirit and action, and on equal terms, by all the nations of the West and by people of every rank. They are an indication, therefore, that the days of isolation and separation are passing away. In one direction, at least, common feelings and common ideals have come into existence through all the nations, and a consciousness of the common interests of the Christian world as against the Mohammedan. And these feelings were now held not merely by a person here and there, but by the great mass of men. Christendom, as a great international community which had never entirely ceased to exist since the days of Roman unity, had come to a clearer consciousness of itself.

That consciousness was now to grow constantly clearer and to embrace by degrees all sides of civilization. The crusades are themselves a great cause leading to this result. By bringing together the men of all nations, led by a common purpose and striving for a common object, they made them better acquainted with one another, created common needs and desires, and immensely stimulated intercommunication of all kinds—manifestly the necessary conditions of a community of nations. It was because these things were so generally wanting that the feudal isolation of the preceding age had been possible. When they began to exist and to increase rapidly, as they did under the influence of the crusades, the modern common life of the world had begun to form itself, and a great step had been taken out of the middle ages.

It was no slight thing, also, that the age of the crusades was an age of intense excitement which seized equally upon those who stayed and those who went. It was a time when all men were stirred by a deep enthusiasm, and the almost stationary feudal society was profoundly moved through all its ranks. It is a common observation that whatever thus awakens the emotions of men and throws society into a ferment of feeling and action is a great impelling force which sets all the wheels of progress in motion and opens a new age of achievement.

Nor is it to be overlooked that they were on the whole generous motives and noble and high ideals which moved men in the crusades. There was selfishness and baseness in plenty no doubt, but the controlling emotion with the most of the crusaders was, especially in the early crusades, a lofty and ideal enthusiasm.

In the way of the increase of actual knowledge and of a direct influence upon learning, the immediate work of the crusades was not great. The Greeks in some respects, and the Saracens in many, were far in advance of the crusaders. The Christians had many things to learn of the Mohammedans, and did in the end learn them; but it was not in the East nor in immediate connection with the crusades. Some few things were learned directly, especially in the line of geographical knowledge, but the great influence of the crusades upon learning was indirect, in creating a consciousness of ignorance and awakening a desire to know, so that the work of the crusades in this direction was to raise the level of general intelligence rather than to increase very greatly the knowledge of specific facts.

They gave to the people who took part in them the advantages of travel. They brought them into contact with new scenes and new peoples, and showed them other ways of doing things. Above all, they made them conscious of the fact that there were people in the world superior to themselves in knowledge and government and manners and all civilization, and that they had themselves many things to learn and to reform before they could really claim the high rank in the world which they had supposed they occupied. This fact is curiously illustrated in the increasing respect which the writers of the age show for the Mohammedans, and it is a most important fact in the history of civilization. The mind of the West was aroused and stimulated by contact with a higher civilization, although it had not yet discovered its best teachers nor the right road by which to reach true science. The intense intellectual eagerness of the last part of the twelfth and of the thirteenth century, though it led into the barren wastes of scholasticism, was the beginning of modern science and the first step towards the revival of learning.

We can trace the beginning of this desire to know, as we can of so many other things which we call the results of the crusades, to times before these began. Even in the tenth century can be found many indications that the mind of Europe was beginning to awake, to feel an eager desire to learn, and even to be conscious of the fact that they must turn to the Arabs for instruction. Gerbert of Rheims—Sylvester II—is a precursor in spirit of Roger Bacon and of Laurentius Valla, as Scotus Erigena—in the century before—is of his greater namesake of the thirteenth century. We should like to believe also that the heretics who were burned at Orleans in 1022, and of whom we know almost nothing, represent a faint stirring of that critical reason which makes a clearer demand in Abelard in regard to theology, and in the Waldenses in regard to practical Christianity.

But it is only in the thirteenth century that we reach the first great intellectual age since ancient history closed, one of the greatest, indeed, of all history. If the work to which it especially devoted itself, an abstract and speculative philosophy, has been left behind by the world's advance, it was nevertheless, in its day, one great step in that advance, and in the founding of the universities the century made a direct and permanent contribution to the civilization of the world.

The strongest and most decisive of the immediate influences of the crusades was that which they exerted upon commerce. They created a constant demand for the transportation of men and of supplies, built up of themselves a great carrying trade, improved the art of navigation, opened new markets, taught the use of new commodities, created new needs, made known new routes and new peoples with whom to trade, stimulated explorations, and in a hundred ways which cannot be mentioned introduced a new commercial age whose character and results must be examined in detail hereafter.

One of the most interesting direct results of the crusades in this direction was the extensive exploration of Asia in the thirteenth and fourteenth centuries by European travellers of whom Marco Polo is the most familiar example, but only one of a host of men almost equally deserving of fame. There is nothing which illustrates better than these explorations the stimulus of the crusades, the energy and the broadening of mind, and the new ideas which are characteristic of the age.

In the political sphere the age is as full of change as elsewhere. The details must be reserved for a future chapter, but the general features may be indicated here. The great fact which is everywhere characteristic of the time is the rise into power of the Third Estate and the fall of the feudal noble from the political position which he had occupied. It will be seen later that, in the main, this was due to the increase of commerce and only indirectly to the crusades, but in one or two ways they directly aided in the process. The noble, influenced only by the feelings of his class, and thrown upon his own resources for the expenses of his crusade, did not count the cost, or he hoped to gain greater possessions in the Holy Land than those he sacrificed at home. Large numbers of the old families were ruined and disappeared, and their possessions fell to anyone who was able to take advantage of the situation. Whether these lands passed into the hands of rich burghers, as they did in some cases, or not, was a matter of little importance, since the decline of the old nobility and the substitution for it of a new nobility was a great relative gain for the Third Estate as it was for the crown.

Wherever the royal power was in a position to take advantage of the changes of the time, as was notably the case in France, it gained constantly in relative strength, and by the time the crusades were over, feudalism had disappeared as a real political institution, and the forming government of the modern state had taken its place —not that the resistance of feudalism to this revolution was by any means over, but the opportunity for a complete victory was clearly before the king.

Of considerable significance also, in this direction, is the part which the lower classes of the population took in the crusades, seen most clearly perhaps in the first. This has the appearance to us of a general movement among the peasantry, and it was a sign, certainly, of discontent with their lot, a vague and ignorant feeling that improvement was possible in some way. It was an evidence also of some new confidence and self-reliance on their part, and no doubt it did in some instances improve their condition. This movement is, on the whole, however, to be regarded like the peasant wars of later times, to which it is in its real character very similar, rather as the sign of a revolution which is slowly working itself out in other ways than as in itself a real means of advance.

These results, which have been briefly stated, when taken together indicate, clearly enough perhaps, the immediate changes which the crusades produced, and also why they came to an end when they did. The changes which they represent had created a new world. The old feelings and judgments and desires which had made the crusades possible no longer existed in their relative strength. New interests had arisen which men had not known before, but which now seemed to them of such supreme and immediate importance that they could not be called away from them to revive past and forgotten interests, though popes might continue to urge the old motives. The less intelligent part of the people, and the dreamer, or the mind wholly centred in the church, might still be led by the old feelings, and might desire to continue the crusade, and actual attempts to do so might be made, but the working mind of Europe could no longer be moved. Even the popes themselves were many times influenced by the spirit of the new age and endeavored to make use of the crusading motives and passions which still lingered to accomplish their own political ends in the interests of their Italian kingdom.

One point which has been briefly referred to already needs to be distinctly emphasized in closing the account of the age. The crusades work great changes, they clearly impart a powerful impetus to advance in every direction; a far more rapid progress of civilization dates from them. But it seems to be equally clear that in no single case do they originate the change. The beginnings of the advance go further back into the comparatively unprogressive ages that precede them. The same changes would have taken place without them, though more slowly and with greater difficulty. Indeed we may say of the age of the crusades, as of every great revolutionary age in history, that it is a time, not so much of the creation of new forces, as of the breaking forth in unusual and unrestrained action of forces which have been for a long time at work beneath the surface, quietly and unobserved.

One most prominent institution of the middle ages, which deserves a fuller treatment than can be given it here, rose to its height during the crusades and in close connection with them—that of chivalry. It goes back for the origin both of its forms and of its ideals to the early Germans. Certain forms which the primitive German tribes had in common—arming the young warrior and the single combat, for instance—and certain conceptions of character and conduct which they especially emphasized—personal bravery, truth-telling, and the respect

for woman among them—were developed, under the influence of the church and of Christianity, into the later
ceremonies of chivalry, partly solemn and partly barbarous, and into the lofty but narrow ideal of conduct which
it cherished. The arrangements of the feudal system
rendered easy the prevalence of its forms, and the spirit
of the crusading age heightened its conception of character and made it seem like a universal duty, so that it
came, for two or three centuries, to occupy a large place
in the life of the time, and relatively a larger place in literature than in life.

In the fifteenth century chivalry as an external institution, a matter of forms and ceremonies, rapidly declined. The ideal of social conduct and character which
it created never passed away, on the contrary, but became a permanent influence in civilization. In English
we express very much the same ideal in certain uses of
the word gentleman, in the phrase "the true gentleman," for example, and, in most respects, no better description of that character can be made now than was
made by Chaucer, in the description of the knight, in
his prologue to the *Canterbury Tales*, at the close of the
age of chivalry.[1] The reason why this modern conception of social character insists so strongly upon certain
virtues, and omits entirely all consideration of certain
others, equally or even more essential to a really high
character, is to be found in the peculiar conditions of the
age of chivalry, its ethical limitations and its class relations.

It was, as far as it went, a Christian ideal of life and
manners—truth, loyalty, uniform and unbroken courtesy,
bravery, devotion to the service of the weak, especially
of one's own class, the sacrifice of self to others in certain cases, the seeking of the place of danger when one
is responsible for others—and such an ideal would cer-

[1] Lines 68–72.

tainly have come into civilization in some way. Historically it was through chivalry that it became a social
law. In making up a full account, however, the other
fact must be included, that the universal prevalence of
the chivalric standard may have made the proper emphasis of other virtues, which it omitted, more difficult than
it would otherwise have been.[1]

We have reached with the crusades, then, the turning-
point of the middle ages. From this time on, history
grows more diversified, and we cannot, as heretofore, follow a single line of development and include within it
the whole field. Three or four great lines of progress run
through the closing half of medieval history, lines which
are easily distinguished from one another and which are
important enough for separate treatment. They will be
taken up in the following order, which is roughly the
natural relation of their dependence one upon another.
First, the commercial development; second, the formation of the modern nations; third, the revival of learning;
fourth, the changes in the ecclesiastical world; and finally, the Reformation, the age of transition to modern
history.

While we separate these lines from one another for
convenience of study, it must be carefully remembered
that they are constantly related to one another, that they
influence one another at every step of the progress, and
that perhaps a new advance in some one of them is more
frequently dependent upon an advance in another line
than upon one in its own. The attempt will be made to
make this interdependence of the various lines of activity
as evident as possible, but it should never be lost sight
of by the reader.

---

[1] The reader of Froissart's *Chronicles*, or of Malory's *King Arthur*, needs
no citation of special cases to convince him of the coarseness and barbarism
which still remained under the superficial polish of the age of chivalry, or
of its entire disregard of some virtues.

CHAPTER XII

IF it can be said at all that there is one line of advance in civilization which is a necessary condition of progress in other directions it would seem to be economic advance. It is no doubt true that more than once in history, under peculiar circumstances, times which appear to be those of remarkable economic advancement have brought with them dangers which seemed to threaten the very existence of civilization itself, as in the last days of the Roman republic. It is also true that sometimes economic improvement has been made possible only by advance in other lines, like the establishment of a better government, as in Italy, for instance, during the reign of Theodoric the Ostrogoth.

The truth is, the various lines of progress are so interwoven, as has already been said, advance in any is so dependent on advance in all, that it is not possible to say that any one of them, either in theory or in fact, is a necessary condition of the others. But this much is true, that a country which is falling into economic decay is declining in other things as well, and that no general and permanent progress of civilization is possible unless it is based—the word seems hardly too strong to use even if it is a begging of the question—on economic improvement.

This was emphatically true of the period of medieval history which extends from the crusades to the Reformation. I hope to make evident, in the portion of this book which follows, how completely the various lines of growth which began an increasing activity from the crusades, and which led out from the middle ages into modern history, were dependent for their accelerated motion, for immense reinforcement, if not for actual beginning, upon the rapidly developing commercial activities of the time. Bad roads and no bridges; the robber baron or band of outlaws to be expected in every favorable spot; legalized feudal exactions at the borders of every little fief; no generally prevailing system of law uniform throughout the country and really enforced; a scanty and uncertain currency, making contracts difficult and payment in kind and in services almost universal; interests and desires narrowed down to the mere neighborhood; these were the conditions of the eleventh and twelfth centuries. A successful commerce meant necessarily a ceaseless war upon all these things, and the introduction of better conditions in these respects was, almost in itself, the transformation of the medieval into the modern.

The German invasions had broken up the organization of Roman commerce and destroyed large amounts of capital. They had diminished the currency in circulation, lowered the condition of the Roman artisan class and broken up their organizations, impaired the means of intercommunication, and brought in as the ruling race in every province a people on a much lower plane of economic development, with fewer wants, hardly above the stage of barter, and entirely unused to the complicated machinery of general commerce. Such a change was a severe blow to commerce. Large parts of the empire fell back into a more primitive condition, where the domain supplied almost all its own wants, very few things being bought from without and very few being sold.

But the invasions did not entirely destroy commerce. Even in the worst times there can be found many traces of what may be called interstate exchanges, of commerce between the East and the West, or between the

North and the South. The church needed, for its orna-
ments and vestments and in its services, cloths and spices
and other articles which could not be obtained in the
West. Nobles made use of numerous articles of luxury
and display in a life that was, on the whole, hard and
comfortless. Where wealth existed there was a tendency
to invest it in articles which would store great value in
small space, and which could be quickly turned into
money, or exchanged. The demand, consequently, for
the articles which commerce would supply, though it was
limited, was strong, and of a sort which insured a great
profit.

Under such circumstances the importation of the goods
needed was certain to exist. Indeed commerce never
died out. Every period of good government in any of
the new German states, as under Theodoric, even if it
lasted but for a moment, saw a revival of it. Justinian's
conquests in Italy created a natural line of intercourse
between the East and the West which continued unbroken
until the crusades. Even before his invasion, the Venetians had the reputation of making long voyages, and
notwithstanding the troublous times which followed, their
commerce was firmly established by the eighth century.
Before the eleventh, nearly all the eastern goods which
found their way into the West came through Italy, where
Venice and Amalfi were the two chief ports. Occasionally something reached southern Gaul and eastern Spain
directly, but the overland route through the Danube
valley seems to have been used only for a brief interval
or two. In the eleventh century commerce appears to
have developed rapidly for the time. The conditions
which rendered the crusades possible, that is, the beginnings of something like a real community life in Europe,
showed themselves also, and earlier than anywhere else,
in an increasing commerce, and new cities came up to
take part in it. Pisa and Genoa were able to conquer

privileges from the Mohammedan states of northern Africa. Marseilles was in a position to obtain extensive favors from the first crusaders. Inland cities, also, had begun to have extended relations, as distributing points for the goods which reached them overland from Italy, and a sea commerce of some importance had begun in the North.

The crusades, then, did not originate commerce, but they imparted to it a new and powerful impulse. They created at once a strong demand for increased means of transportation. The first crusade went overland, but the later ones partly or wholly by water. The occupation of the Holy Land by the Christians made necessary a more lively and frequent intercourse between East and West. The crusader states were able to maintain themselves only by constant new arrivals of men and supplies. The West was made acquainted with new articles of use or luxury, and desires and needs rapidly increased. Connections were formed with new peoples, as with the Mongols. New commercial routes were opened up, geographical knowledge increased, and new regions appeared in the maps.

The change in the general atmosphere of Europe which accompanied the crusades, the broadening of mind and the growth of common interests, favored increased intercommunication and exchange, and, from the first crusade on, commerce increased with great rapidity, penetrated constantly into new regions, aided the growth of manufacturing industries, multiplied the articles with which it dealt, improved greatly its own machinery—the art of navigation, currency, forms of credit, maritime law, and mercantile organization—and exerted a profound influence upon every department of human activity.

The regions embraced within the world commerce of the middle ages may be divided for convenience of examination into three divisions—the East, the North, and the states, chiefly Mediterranean, which acted as middlemen between these two extremes.

The goal at the East was India, though there was for a time some direct overland connection with China starting from the Black Sea. From the East came the articles of luxury and show, which formed the bulk of medieval commerce, and returned enormous profits—spices, incense, perfumes, precious stones, carpets, hangings, and rich cloths. The Christian merchants of Europe could not purchase these goods direct from India, but only from the Mohammedan states of western Asia, which maintained relations with the farther East. These states could sell to India but few articles in exchange—horses, linen, and manufactured metals, especially weapons—and large quantities of the precious metals had to be exported to settle the balance. These oriental goods reached the West by a variety of routes, some coming through the Black Sea, where Trebizond was an important port; others coming up the Persian Gulf and the Euphrates, and reaching Mediterranean ports like Antioch or Beyroot; others by the more southern route, through the Red Sea and Egypt. The frequency of the use and the profitableness of any one of these routes depended upon the political condition of the intermediary Mohammedan states, and varied greatly at different times. With the advance of the Turks the more northern lines were gradually rendered impossible, and this was one of the chief causes which led to the rapid decline of the commerce of Genoa in the fifteenth century, her dependence being chiefly upon the Black Sea routes. On the eve of the great discoveries of the end of the fifteenth century almost the only secure and profitable line of connection with India was through Egypt.

The Mohammedan states took of the Western merchants a much greater variety of goods than India—

food supplies, grain, oil, and honey, metals and minerals, lead, iron, steel, tin, sulphur, cloth in great variety, leather, wool, soap, furs, and slaves—Circassians being conveyed, for instance, from the Black Sea to Egypt, and even Europeans being sold without much hesitation by their Christian brethren when opportunity offered. The ships of the West, loaded with the Eastern goods which they had purchased, made the return voyage, beset with dangers from pirate attacks and unskilful navigation, and at home, at Venice or Genoa, the goods were unloaded and stored for further exchange.

From the Mediterranean ports overland routes led up into the country to important points of interior trade. In France and Germany commerce centred about the fairs, which were held at fixed seasons. In the great fairs wholesale trade was carried on, the merchants from the smaller places meeting there the importers who had the goods of the East, and so obtaining their supplies. In the fairs of the smaller places retail trading was done;[1] but a very large part of the retail trade of the interior was carried on by peddlers, who went about from village to village, carrying packs themselves or sometimes with horses.[2]

After a time the ships of the Mediterranean ventured into the Atlantic, and direct communication by water was established with the North. Venice sent regularly each year a fleet to touch at ports in England and the Netherlands, and the latter country became finally the centre of nearly all exchanges between the North and the South, so that it should fairly be reckoned as belonging in the middle region rather than in the northern.

---

[1] The markets at present held at brief intervals in the Congo State exhibit many of the characteristic features of the medieval markets or small fairs.

[2] Cutts, *Scenes and Characters of the Middle Ages*, p. 515, gives the contents of a foot-peddler's pack from the illustrations of a manuscript. It contained gloves, belts, hoods, a hat, mirrors, a dagger, a purse, a pair of slippers, hose, a musical pipe, etc.

Bruges was the chief place for this traffic, and it came to be filled with the warehouses of the different nations where their goods were stored for exchange.

The North was the great source of food supplies and of raw materials for the increasing manufactures of the middle region—grain, wool, hides, tallow, salt meat and fish, flax, hemp, timber, furs, and tin and other metals. The North developed, from the thirteenth century on, a very extensive and diversified commerce of its own, with a more compact organization through the Hanseatic League than Italian commerce had, and reaching into Russia and by degrees becoming bold enough to send its ships into the Mediterranean. Before the end of the middle ages there was also considerable manufacturing in some countries of the North.

Notwithstanding the great development of commerce and manufactures, and the multiplication of articles of use and luxury which followed, the lives of most men still continued to possess few comforts to the end of the middle ages. From the first century of the crusades many articles which we now consider among the necessities of life, chimneys, windows of glass, bedroom and table furniture, carpets, clocks, artificial lights, and other things of the sort began to make their appearance in the houses of the rich, commonly first in the cities, and were slowly adopted by the country nobles. The poorer people of the country remained in general without them, and with the insufficient diet of all classes, consisting chiefly of pork or salt meats, and the coarse grains, with very few vegetables, and the general uncleanliness of person and of surroundings, it is not strange that the average length of life was short and that frequent plagues carried off large numbers of all ranks.

By the fifteenth century commerce had lost much of its earlier simplicity. It had become greatly diversified, and had taken on many of its more modern features.

With this transformation of its character some of the problems of international exchange began to arise before the mind of the time, now capable of taking wider views than once, and men began to grope, at least in a half-conscious way, for the solution of questions which we do not seem to have settled, at least to the satisfaction of all, even yet—the relation of the supply of gold and silver to the national wealth, and the theory that national wealth may be increased and commerce developed by legislative restrictions of one sort or another upon the commerce of other people.[1]

It can hardly be supposed that the theories of international trade, which began to take shape at this time, were permanent contributions to civilization, but certainly they have profoundly affected its course ever since. Recent times have not been more intensely interested in any subject than in the question whether legislation should continue to be controlled by them or not. These theories were formed at a time when the facts upon which they were supposed to be based were very imperfectly understood. Experience in general commerce was only just beginning, and any real knowledge of the laws which operate in it, or even of its primary facts, was entirely impossible. These ideas were pure theories, almost as completely so as the speculations of any closet philosopher who ever lived. Probably there is not to be found in any other department of civilization an attempt to carry out pure theories in practice on such a scale as this. But these ideas had an apparent and temporary basis of fact in the existence of a narrow but extremely profitable trade, so situated that it could be artificially controlled—

[1] The legislation of a distinctly protective character, of which ours is the direct descendant, began in the fourteenth century, though there are unconnected cases of the same sort of legislation much earlier. The theories upon which the mercantile system was based began to be put into definite shape in the sixteenth century. See Lalor's translation of Roscher's *Political Economy*, vol. II, App. II and III, especially pp. 441 ff.

one, in other words, which could be made to operate for
a time like the exclusive possession of a gold mine—and
there was no experience at hand to show that this condition of things was temporary and exceptional. Those
theories had further an extremely plausible foundation
in the apparent self-interest of the moment, and they
obtained a hold upon the popular mind which the better
informed have found it extremely hard to loosen.[1]

For our purpose these forming theories are far less
important in themselves than as signs of the wider views
and more comprehensive grasp of mind which they certainly indicate and which was now possible, made possible in large part by the extension of commerce itself.

These expanding ideas are revealed still more clearly
in the possibility which dawned upon the minds of many
men in the fifteenth century of far wider extensions of
commerce than any which lay along the old lines—the
first faint traces of the idea of a world commerce, and
even of a conception of the world itself in anything like
its actual reality. It was only the first beginning of these
ideas, but they were held strongly enough for men to
take the risk of acting upon them, and the discoveries
of the last years of the century resulted, which not merely
opened new worlds to commerce but broadened immensely
all horizons.

The impulse to exploration and the daring spirit and
pluck of the explorer had come with the first expansion
of commerce, and as early as the thirteenth century the
then "dark continent" of Asia had been traversed by
many Europeans. The immediately active cause, how-

---

[1] The difficulty in the case is hardly more, however, than that which
every science finds in getting its own carefully formed inductions accepted
in the place of the pure theories with which the popular mind explains all
partially understood facts. That the theories in this case are apparently
closely bound up with selfish interests makes the process a more exciting
one, and gives the adversary, perhaps, an unusual advantage, but it cannot make the result different in the end.

ever, of the oceanic discoveries of the fifteenth century was the coming up of new nations eager to take part in the extremely profitable commerce in Eastern goods, at the moment when the Turkish conquests in the northern and eastern parts of the Mediterranean were narrowing down the possibilities of that commerce as it had existed, and the footing of the Venetians in Egypt made competition with them very difficult. The Portuguese were the first of these new nations to cherish this commercial ambition, and they turned their attention to finding a way to India around Africa. In the first half of the fifteenth century Prince Henry of Portugal nobly devoted his life to the encouragement of these explorations, because, as he thought, they fell naturally within the duty of princes, since they afforded no good hope of profit to tempt the merchant.

It required no little daring to sail into unknown seas in an age when men fully believed that they might meet with the adventures of Sindbad the Sailor, and worse things also, and progress was necessarily slow. One expedition advanced along the coast as far as it dared, and when it returned in safety the next one ventured a little farther. In 1434 they passed Cape Bojador; in 1441, Cape Branco; in 1445, Cape Verde; in 1462, Cape Sierra Leone; in 1471 they reached the Gold Coast; the equator was crossed in 1484, or possibly a little earlier; in 1486 Bartholomew Diaz turned the Southern Cape, henceforth the Cape of Good Hope; and finally, in 1498, Vasco da Gama reached India. This first success the king of Portugal immediately followed up by sending fleets especially fitted out for trading, and though they were bitterly opposed in India by the Arabs of Egypt, whose monopoly was threatened, they returned with loads of spices.

The revolution wrought by the opening of this new route was tremendous. Venice, though in a favored position, had been compelled to buy her goods in Egypt at a great disadvantage, as the Arabs had a practical monopoly. Heavy tolls and dues were added to the original cost, and the Portuguese were able to buy in India at only a fraction of the cost to the Venetians in Egypt. Venice was thrown into a panic. Contemporary evidence is said to show that when the news first came that spices had reached Portugal direct from India, the price of such goods fell more than fifty per cent in Venice.[1]

For the Venetians it was certainly a question of life and death. Their whole commercial existence depended upon the result. They urged the Arabs of Egypt most earnestly to oppose the Portuguese in India in every way possible; they discussed for a moment the opening of a Suez canal, and even the project of securing an overland route around the Turkish dominions in alliance with the Russians. But it was all in vain. The world's commerce had outgrown the Mediterranean. Six years before Vasco da Gama's success Columbus had reached America, and the world passed at once out of the middle ages.

Commerce had hardly more than begun its new activity before its influence began to be felt far outside its own proper field. It is entirely impossible to indicate, in anything approaching a chronological order, the various ways in which this influence was directly exerted. Even an attempt to state them in something like a logical sequence can be of value only as serving to indicate for examination the points of contact between this increasing commerce and other lines of advance during the same time.

[1] The trade continued, however, extremely profitable. The Portuguese are said to have sold their spices at the time of their supremacy at a profit of at least six hundred per cent. At the beginning of the seventeenth century the profits of a successful voyage often reached two hundred per cent. These high profits, however, had to make good many losses. The average annual dividend, declared by the Dutch East India Company, from 1605 to 1720, was 22⅞ per cent on a capital stock partly "water."

With the growth of commerce cities began to arise. Italy and Gaul had numerous great cities in Roman times, and most of these continued after the invasion undestroyed, but with their relative importance diminished, and in many cases certainly with their institutions modified. Roman Germany had a few cities, and of these at least Cologne retained a noticeable civic and commercial life through the period before the crusades. The interior and north of Germany had no cities in the Roman times, and only slight beginnings of them before the eleventh century.

With the revival of commerce these old cities wakened to a new activity and grew rapidly in size and wealth.[1] New cities sprang up where none had existed before, perhaps about a fortified post or near a monastery where a local market or fair began to be held. The privileges granted to the market attracted merchants to settle there and gradually widened into considerable rights of self-government and a local law, and, often at least, as the city formed about the market and was enabled by circumstances to take its place as an independent member of the national community, the original market rights gradually developed into the city constitution.

The natural tendency on the part of the city to strive for local independence and self-government was greatly

[1] The long-disputed question as to the continuance of Roman municipal institutions across the dark ages is one which concerns the special institutional history of municipal government rather than the history of the rise of cities in general. The causes of the general movement are those indicated above, whatever may be true as to the origin of special features in the municipal constitution. It seems pretty clearly proved that in Germany a majority of the cities reached their rights of self-government by a gradual enlargement of the market privileges which were granted them at the beginning of their history. This fact does not preclude, however, the influence of Roman institutions elsewhere, and it is highly probable that such an influence was felt in individual cases at least. While the general causes and general features of the moment are similar in all the states, it would be absurd to assume a uniformity in details which exists nowhere else in the middle ages.

aided by the fact that at the time when the movement began the feudal system was at its height as the prevailing form of political organization throughout Europe. It was itself the realization, as far as possible, of the idea of local independence, and though the feudal lord on whose territory the city had grown up might struggle to maintain his control over it, the logic of the whole situation was on the side of the city. The example which the lord had set in his effort to escape from his dependence upon his suzerain was a very plain one to follow, and the feudal system furnished forms of easy application which secured a practical independence.[1]

This was especially true of France, and though the cities of Italy exhibit more fully some other results of the movement which are extremely important in the history of civilization, the French cities reveal more clearly than those of any other country the political tendencies in the general government of the state, which the rise of the cities everywhere favored, but which were more completely realized in the kingdom of France than in any other of the large states of Europe.

In France, though opposed in spirit to the feudal system, the movement follows distinctly feudal forms, and the tendency is always towards the formation of "communes." By no means all the cities of France succeeded in reaching this result, and in organizing actual communes, probably only a small proportion of them did, but the tendency is in that direction, and those that failed stopped at some intermediate point in the process.

The commune is, strictly speaking, a corporation regarded as a feudal person, and, as such, having the obligations and the rights of a vassal in respect to its lord

[1] An interesting case is the little republic of Andorra, where feudal forms allowed the establishment of a local independence which has been preserved into our own times. See the article by Professor Bernard Moses, in the *Yale Review*, vol. II (1893), pp. 28–53.

and able to become a suzerain in its turn. The act of forming a commune within the limits of a feudal territory was an act of subinfeudation—the formation of a subfief where none had existed until then. Before the formation of the commune the town was a group of persons, brought together in ordinary cases from a great variety of sources, some of them were full freemen, or even small nobles, of the country or neighborhood, some were foreigners to the country or to the fief who had settled in the place for purposes of trade, and so were subject to various feudal dues to the lord, some of them were serfs of varying degrees of right with respect to the lord, and therefore subject to special exactions for his benefit. If regarded as a whole in this stage of its history, the town was considered a serf and was so treated in law. By the grant of a commune this group of persons was transformed into a single person and raised to the position of a vassal, subject no longer to the varying and indefinite rights of the lord over serf and foreigner as individuals, but only to the limited obligations specified in the contract of the fief between the lord and the commune. This contract was under the ordinary feudal sanctions. The officers of the commune paid homage and swore the vassal's oath to the lord, and he, in turn, swore to observe his obligations towards them.

The special obligations which the commune entered into towards the lord differed in different cases like those of other vassals, but within the limits established by these obligations in the given case the commune obtained the right to regulate its own affairs as every vassal did. This meant, of course, for the city the right of local self-government, though the growth of the general government in France did not allow the result which was reached in Italy and Germany, the establishment of a virtually independent city state.

Besides the commune proper, there was in France a

multitude of cities and towns which never became full communes, but which obtained by definite contracts more or less extensive rights of self-government and of freedom from exactions. These were the *villes de bourgeoisie*, or chartered towns. The number of these towns was much greater than that of the real communes, and their influence on the general results which followed from this movement was precisely the same. The difference was not one of principle or of character, except in the strictly legal sense, but one which concerned the completeness of the local rights secured.

It is easy from what has been said to understand the attitude of the local baron towards the commune. To grant the right to form such an organization was to cut off so much of his fief from his own immediate control. It was to diminish his rights of exaction and to reduce his power. Opposition was natural. In very many cases the commune succeeded in establishing itself only after a long and bitter conflict, and as the result of a victory which forced the lord to yield.

This was particularly true of the attitude of the ecclesiastical nobles towards the town. The seat of every bishop was in an important city. The larger abbeys also were, as a rule, in the towns, and so it happened that the towns which began to strive for local independence were more likely to be in ecclesiastical than in lay fiefs. The larger portion of the long-continued and desperate struggle between the rising cities and the older power was in fiefs held by the church.

Among the lay nobility it was more likely to be the small noble, the lord of the locality, who opposed the city than the great lord whose domain included a province. The small noble saw the town growing up in his little territory, perhaps out of nothing or next to nothing, and menacing his dominion with a serious danger, possibly even threatening to annex it entirely, and to crowd him to the wall. The inferior nobility were in many cases contending for existence, and sometimes in France, as happened so generally in Italy, they were absorbed into the town; in some cases they seem to have gone into the commune voluntarily and with good-will.

The great nobles whose territories were principalities followed no common policy. If the count or the duke was strong, and his government a really centralized one, as was the case in some instances, he seems to have favored the growth of the towns with chartered rights but not of communes, keeping the real control in his own hands. If his power was weak and divided, usurped by vassals whom he could not hold to obedience, he favored the development even of the commune as a means of weakening them. In some cases, also, the great lords seem as bitterly opposed to the cities as the great officers of the church.

The wavering policy of the French kings towards the movement, which is not in reality so inconsistent as it appears at first, is to be explained in the same way by their relation to their vassals. The early Capetians no doubt perceived the advantage which the independence of the towns would give them in weakening the power of the feudal barons, and did not hesitate to grant their aid to the efforts of the cities whenever they were able to do so. They early labored to establish the principle that the commune, once formed, belonged immediately to the king, and was in an especial degree under his protection. But the early Capetians were in a peculiar position. From the weakness of their general power they were especially dependent upon the support of the church, and this was in truth one of the chief sources of their strength. In many cases they could not break with these allies nor afford to support their enemies, though they might on other grounds have been glad to do so. We have them, therefore, following a policy which seems contradictory, aiding the communes where they could do so safely, and opposing them elsewhere, because in the latter cases there was danger of losing more than might be gained.

As the monarchy grew stronger and more independent of the support of the church, we find the kings adopting a more consistent policy, and at the beginning of the thirteenth century distinctly favoring the cities. As they grew stronger still, and something like a real centralization began to be possible, then the commune with its rights of independent local government stood, as the king looked at it, much in the same attitude towards the general government as the independent feudal baron. It represented a bit of the territory of the state in which the central power did not have free sway. Consequently, we have later kings endeavoring to break down the privileges of the communes and to gain a direct control by introducing into them royal executive and judicial officers. This process can be clearly traced before the close of the thirteenth century, and it is very speedily concluded, partly because of the isolated position of the communes and their inability to combine as the barons did, and partly because they had always recognized a more direct right of government on the part of the king, and had never become independent, as had the cities of Italy and Germany.

Towards the towns which were not communes, the *villes de bourgeoisie*, the policy of the kings was more consistent and more steadily favorable. These towns had not gained a complete self-government and were not closed against the officers of the king, but their formation was as great an aid to him as that of the communes in his efforts to build up the power of the central government by weakening the baronial power.

But in many other ways, and really in more decisive ways than by dividing their fiefs and weakening their local power, the growth of the cities, or the increase of commerce as the underlying cause, rendered it no longer possible for the feudal lords to maintain the position which they had held in the state.

One of the direct results of the growth of commerce which had this effect was that a much larger amount of money was brought into circulation, and its use was made more general. In the thirteenth century not only did gold begin to be coined, but also coins of much smaller denominations than formerly, a sure sign that commercial transactions were becoming more frequent among the lower classes, and that sales were beginning to take the place of barter. From the cities and smaller towns the money would work its way into the country and gradually come into more common use among the laborers on the farms.

This increased circulation of money struck at the very root of feudalism. The economic foundation of the feudal system was the scarcity of money and the impossibility of using it freely for purchases to supply daily needs which must be supplied in any state of society. It was scarcely possible, in such conditions, for rent and income to take any other form than that of personal services and payments of produce. Feudalism as a means of carrying on government had its foundation also in the political conditions of the time, as we have seen, but it was hardly possible for these conditions to change, to such an extent as to lead to the overthrow of the system, so long as it was difficult in all political relations as well as in agriculture, which was the main source of income, to substitute some other kind of payment for payments in services and in kind.

As soon as money came into increased general circulation the situation was changed. It became possible to substitute definite and specific contracts for the arrangements, always more or less vague, of the manorial customs, and the increased usefulness of money was a convincing argument with the lord, in very many cases at least, that the money paid in commutation of services would be of greater value to him than the services themselves, uncertain and irregular, and performed with great reluctance as they usually were. But the introduction of money payments in this way, in the place of customary services, while it left the feudal lord in title and rank and social position what he had been, deprived him of his immediate personal hold upon his subjects and undermined his political power. This was still more the case as money took the place of services on the political side, as in the payment of scutage instead of military service, which began to be important in England soon after the second crusade.

It must not be understood that this was the sole or even the chief cause of the fall of feudalism. A hundred causes worked together to that end. Nor must it be supposed that all feudal or manorial services disappeared. It was only here and there in the most favored localities that this was the case, and in some of these even, some such services have remained, in form at least, to the present time, while in some parts of Europe feudalism can scarcely be said to have declined at the end of the middle ages. Nearly everywhere it had, however, and for peasant and burgher, in their rise to independence, scarcely anything was so helpful as the increased circulation of money.

This more general use of money had also most important consequences in another direction. It made taxation possible. The extension of commerce had led to large accumulations of wealth in the cities. Here was a new resource for the state which, if it could be made to contribute to public purposes in some systematic and reliable way, would relieve the central power of its dependence upon the feudal system, and give it a new and more solid foundation on which to build, an indispensable foundation indeed. Arrangements long in use provided an easy way of introducing the cities directly into the state machinery, and of obtaining from them their consent to a levy of taxes of which they were to pay the larger portion. The cities showed evident signs of a reluctance to part with their wealth, as was natural, but there were, on the other hand, reasons of their own which prevailed with them to consent.

The accumulation of capital in the towns and the extension of commerce throughout the country created an intense demand for order and security. Nothing makes so strong a demand for these things, or tends to secure them so perfectly, as the possession of wealth. The feudal confusion, the private wars, the robber baron, so prominent a feature of declining feudalism, were the deadly foes of commerce, as the merchant was of them. His protection was to be found in the establishment of a public power able to suppress these evils and to maintain order throughout the state, and wherever such a public power was forming the capitalist class of the day came to its aid with all its resources. No doubt it was anxious to do this with as little expense to itself as possible, but it was ready to sacrifice its wealth unsparingly in its own defence when directly attacked, and it did not fail to see the advantage it would gain from providing the king with a revenue which would support a standing army and a national system of courts of justice.

Commerce and wealth came to the aid of the forming national government not merely in the fact that they created a demand for established order but also by a demand for uniformity. Commerce extended from common centres through the entire state, and bound it together in a united system with lines as living and real as those of the church organization. The interests of the merchant were alike everywhere, and it was extremely important for him to know what he had to expect in every locality. The arbitrary exactions of the uncontrolled feudal lord; the varying tolls and dues of every little fief; a hundred systems of coinage on whose purity and honesty no dependence could be placed; worse still, if possible, the local customary law differing from every other in points perhaps of the greatest importance to the merchant and enforced by an interested local court from which there might be no appeal—these things were, in the long run, more serious obstacles in the way of commerce than private wars and robber barons. The whole influence of the merchant class and of the cities was towards doing away with this local confusion of practice, and towards putting in the place of it a national control, national coinage, courts, and law.

In the matter of a national law the influence of the cities was especially strong. It was in this respect not merely a general influence, a favoring condition, which the cities created. In the cities the professional lawyer made his appearance and the study of the Roman law was begun and actively pursued. This was possible because the growth of the cities and the accumulation of wealth in them meant leisure. That leisure which had been possible in the earlier middle ages only to the ecclesiastic became possible now to men outside the church. They could devote themselves to intellectual pursuits with a certainty of support. The new study of the Roman law, which began in this way, and which the cities strongly favored, as a general and highly organized system ready made for their purpose in place of the feudal variety and confusion, gave congenial employment to this new class and gave rise to the professional lawyer. He was a layman and a *bourgeois*, but he was a man of thoroughly trained intellect, of self-respect and pride as great as the noble's, and he cherished the strongest ideas, derived from the system of law in which he had been trained, of the supremacy of a national law, and of the right of the sovereign to exact obedience everywhere. It followed that, in his efforts to recover the legislative and judicial power, and to establish a uniform law, the king had not merely the general support of the cities, but they furnished him also with a ready-made and highly perfected legal system capable of being immediately applied, and with a force of trained men earnestly devoted to its establishment and enforcement.

We have here sketched somewhat briefly the influences which commerce everywhere tended to exert, and the results which it everywhere tended to produce. These are to be found reaching their logical conclusion, in combination with other causes, only in France, and there the logical result involved the destruction of the independence of the cities. Other states of Europe show results of this movement which are peculiar to themselves, and some of them exhibit tendencies which just as truly belong to it, but which do not appear so clearly in French history because there the political result was so fully worked out in the establishment of an absolute central government.

In Italy the existence of the Holy Roman Empire, together with the policy which the popes adopted in defence of their political independence, prevented the formation of any native national government while the empire furnished the pretence of one. In consequence of this the cities, when they became strong, found themselves depending upon a shadowy state whose sovereignty they recognized in form, but which was not at hand to exercise a real and direct government. As a result, the cities in Italy found it easy to become little independent states, after the manner of the feudal principalities in Germany. Their early and rapid growth enabled them to absorb nearly all the nobles of the country, and they

intrenched themselves so strongly that when the Hohenstaufen emperors attempted to bring them under a direct control, they were able, in combination, as we have
seen, to maintain and secure their independence.

The peculiarities of their growth had made them as
independent of one another as they were of the state,
and except when brought together by some common
danger, each pursued its own interests without regard to
the others. It often happened that conflicting interests
led to the fiercest struggles between them, ending only
with the ruin of one of the rivals, as in the contest between Florence and Pisa, or between Venice and Genoa.
Many of them were able to extend their sovereignty over
the surrounding territory and smaller towns, and to bring
together a considerable state as did Milan. In nearly all
of them, towards the end of the middle ages, corruption
among the citizens or the necessities of their military
defence made it easy for unscrupulous and enterprising
men to establish tyrannies and to destroy their republican governments, as in the case of the Medici family
in Florence or the Sforza family in Milan.

The diversity of life in these Italian cities, the multi-
plicity of their interests, their rivalries with one another,
and the party struggles within their walls, stimulated a
general mental activity among their citizens, especially
in the case of the large leisure class which their great
wealth had created. And so in the cities of Italy, earlier
than anywhere else, a keen and cultivated intellectual
society formed itself, which was characterized by many
modern traits, and which prepared the way for the revival of learning.

In Germany a considerable number of cities in favored localities reached the same position of local independence as those of Italy, and for the same reason—
their immediate dependence upon a nominal national
government which had lost all power to interfere in the

management of local affairs.   There existed, then, in Germany, as in Italy, permanently independent little city states regulating their own affairs under a republican government.   Many of these continued independent into modern times, and three of them—Lübeck, Hamburg, and Bremen—are at present states of the federal empire of Germany.

Many of these cities were, however, in the end, to undergo the same fate which befell the French cities, and to be absorbed into some neighboring centralized state founded upon a feudal territory.   But these states were formed in Germany only at a relatively late date, some of the most extensive of them not until after the middle ages, and there was no one of them, at whatever time formed, large enough to include within its government the circle of commercial territory in which the cities were interested.   It happened, therefore, in Germany, that the cities which succeeded in preserving their independence were thrown upon their own resources for protection, and were obliged themselves to repress the evils which a national government would naturally have held in check, and which even a forming central power, like that of France, was able to deal with in a constantly increasing degree.   As a consequence of this there appears in Germany a political result of the commercial development which is not seen in the same form elsewhere—the city leagues.   The Italian cities united together in the Lombard League, in their struggle against the Hohenstaufen emperors, but that was a league for mutual defence against a special danger, and it did not have the permanence nor the political character of the German leagues.

The greatest of these leagues was the Hanseatic, formed during the thirteenth century and reaching its height in the fourteenth.   Its power extended over the whole north of Germany and into all the countries bordering on the

Baltic and North Seas. Almost a nation itself in its organization and resources, it dealt with states on equal terms and protected its commercial rights with great fleets. The League of the Rhine Cities, almost as powerful, and perhaps even of earlier formation, was an equally effective agent in keeping the peace and protecting commerce, within the range of its influence. So efficient an instrument in preserving order did the league prove itself to be that at the very close of the middle ages the free cities of southern Germany entered into an alliance of the sort with the princes, who had succeeded in forming states in that part of the country—the so-called Swabian League—to put down disorder, caused mostly by the despairing and desperate efforts of the small nobles to preserve their political independence.

In England the city never played so important a part in public affairs as on the Continent, and the reason for this fact is easy to be found. In England, though the feudal system was established as completely as on the Continent, as a matter of organization, the state never split into fragments—the law was always national law. The central government was always strong and had all parts of the state in hand, and the improvement of that government was an orderly and natural process of growth, in which all parts of the community shared alike, no one part needed to be uprooted and destroyed by the others. The existence of a definite machinery of free local self-government—the township or the hundred organization—furnished as ready a means by which the city could secure control of its own affairs as the forms of the feudal system gave to the commune in France. But this very fact incorporated it completely in the organization of the shire or the state, of which the township or the hundred formed a regular part, and prevented the English city from establishing a perfect independence like the Italian or German city, or even from coming so near

to it as did the communes of France. In the long struggle for English liberty the boroughs were to play an honorable part, but they did it, not as independent powers,
but as corporate elements of the state.

Translated into other terms, this increase of commerce
and development of the cities becomes the rise of the
Third Estate into a position of influence and power, beside the other two. This is a fact of the utmost importance in the general history of civilization, because this
progress once begun, though it was to be here and there
very slow, and sometimes even ended, to all appearance,
in reality never ceased, and our own time is characterized by its complete triumph and the practical absorption,
both economically and politically, of the other two estates in the third.

All the middle ages may have recognized the existence
of three classes in the population—a working class besides the clergy and the nobles—but politically and in all
practical concerns no account was taken of this third
class until it began to possess wealth. The First Estate,
the clergy, with the Second Estate, the nobles, controlled
everything, and no one outside their ranks had any voice
in affairs.

With the growth of commerce this condition of things
began to be changed. Wealth meant power. The ready
money of the merchant was as effective a weapon as the
sword of the nobles, or the spiritual arms of the church.
Very speedily, also, the men of the cities began to seize
upon one of the weapons which up to this time had been
the exclusive possession of the church, and one of the main
sources of its power—knowledge and intellectual training.
With these two weapons in its hands, wealth and knowledge, the Third Estate forced its way into influence, and
compelled the other two to recognize it as a partner with
themselves in the management of public concerns.

The formation of the Third Estate must not be regarded as the formation of the "people" in the modern
sense of that word. This distinction is very important
historically and one that should be made clear if possible.

According to our modern democratic ideas the "people" includes the whole body of inhabitants in the country. If we say, "the will of the people controls the state,"
we mean the will of the mass of the population without
distinction of classes. But such an idea would have been
impossible even to the end of the middle ages. It would
have been foreign to all its notions. Even within the
self-governing cities the governments were not democratic, and they tended, in most cases, to become more
and more aristocratic, and the distinction between "patricians" and common people was as clearly drawn as outside their walls, though based upon different grounds.

The rise of the Third Estate did not mean the formation of the "people." It was the first step towards it,
but, in the middle ages, it went no farther than to bring
up beside the other classes, who had heretofore controlled
the state, and who continued to retain their distinct existence as classes, and nearly everywhere kept a prepon-
derance of influence, another class, clearly marked within
itself as a class and clearly separated from them. Beyond
this the middle ages did not go, except in Italy, where
something almost like the "people" may be seen, in some
of the cities, though in England, also, one very decisive
step towards modern times was taken in the association
of the smaller nobles with the "commons." The government which resulted from the rise of the Third Estate
was a government of classes and separate interests, with
the characteristic weaknesses of such a government, and
unless reinforced from other sources presented no serious
obstacle to the growth of absolutism.

The Third Estate was itself divided into two well-
marked divisions—the city population and the laboring

class of the country districts. This distinction was so clearly marked that in some countries the peasants were reckoned as forming a Fourth Estate. The agricultural laborers of Europe can hardly be said to have gained political rights or any share in the government at the close of the middle ages; indeed, with insignificant exceptions, and with the exception of some of the American colonies, it was reserved for the nineteenth century to make this advance. The Third Estate, considered as having an influence on public affairs, was in reality only the burgher class. This class was, however, as a matter of fact, drawn largely from the country population, though the nucleus around which it gathered was in all cases, except in the new towns, the city population which had descended from earlier times. As commerce increased, means of employment naturally multiplied. Manufactures developed; new lines of industry and of mechanical work were opened. An easier and more advantageous life was to be had in the cities than in the country, and a current set constantly into them of the more enterprising and better situated peasants to take advantage of the more favorable conditions there, and to reinforce the Third Estate. The cities themselves encouraged this tendency, as sometimes also did the suzerain, or the sovereign of the city, by the grant of his protection to immigrants. The drift from the country had its reflex influence also upon the people remaining there, by securing them better treatment or even special privileges from lords anxious to retain the peasants on their lands.

In the case of the laboring classes of the country the end of the Roman Empire and the beginning of the middle ages had seen the slave transformed into the serf. This change consisted in giving certain limited rights to a class which had before possessed no rights whatever. A serf is a slave to whom a few but not all the rights of a freeman have been granted. He has taken the first

step towards becoming a freeman. That he is chained
to the soil is at the beginning as much of an advantage
as it is later a disadvantage, for it secures him a home,
a family, and certain limited rights of property, none of
which can be taken away from him. It was perfectly
natural that in the course of time, as the general conditions which surrounded the serf improved, the limitations
upon his right should come to be the main things noticed,
and that it should be forgotten how very little those limitations were regarded centuries before in comparison with
the rights then gained.

The change to serfdom was accomplished in the later
empire by economic causes, chiefly by the difficulty of
getting a sufficient number of agricultural laborers. The
slavery of Christian men was not entirely extinguished,
however, though forbidden. It lingered on in various
ways until the very end of the middle ages.

In the times which follow the German conquests there
is to be seen a mixture of phenomena. Exactly opposite
things seem to be happening at different dates or in different places at the same date. In some cases freemen
sink down towards the serf class, and many of those in
the higher grades of serfdom represent earlier free laborers. Sometimes, on the contrary, the lower classes
may be seen rising towards the higher, and reinforcing
from this source the same upper grades. In a general
view of the whole period we may say that the condition
of the laborer is, in most particulars, improving; or the
fact would be, perhaps, more accurately stated in this
way: that the forms of land tenure and the general economic conditions of the middle ages made it, on the whole,
easy for the serf who was somewhat more enterprising
than his class, or who found himself in a better situation,
to improve his condition and to rise towards the rank of
a freeman.

This fact explains the great variety of rights possessed

by the agricultural laborers of a given time in any one of the countries of Europe, and as well the great variety of legal conditions which can often be found upon a single estate. These various gradations of right and of tenure represent the intermediate steps or stages through which the serf is passing on his way to freedom. On the same estate there may be some, perhaps, whose condition is hardly to be distinguished from that of slaves, others who have a few more rights, others still more, and some who are almost indistinguishable from full freemen.

This second change from serf to free laborer, like the earlier one from slave to serf, was determined by economic causes, often by the same one indeed, the scarcity of laborers and the consequent willingness of the landlord to grant better conditions of tenure in order to gain new laborers or to keep his old ones. The change consisted almost everywhere in the transformation of vague and indefinite personal services into clearly expressed and definitely limited services, and these into payments of rent, sometimes in produce and then finally in many places in money. When a fixed money payment took the place of labor services the serf had become a freeman.[1] It is characteristic of the later part of the middle ages that these various forms of servile tenure coexist on the same estate, and very frequently in the case of the same man, who will be held to render in part services and in part rent payments.

In the more favored parts of Europe this process of emancipation was completed by the end of the middle ages. In Italy serfdom had disappeared as early, probably, as the end of the fourteenth century. In England

---

[1] In some places, notably in Italy, there were large numbers of emancipations by charters, which gave religious reasons for the act, or moral considerations, drawn often from the Roman law, like the natural equality of all men. If these are really exceptions to the operation of the causes mentioned in the text. they are not numerous enough to affect the movement as a whole.

the same result was reached, with some exceptions, by the beginning of the sixteenth.   Of parts of France and of Germany the same thing is true.   In some of the less favorably situated parts of the Continent serfdom or some features of serfdom lived on until the revolutionary age which opened the nineteenth century.

CHAPTER XIII

THE FORMATION OF FRANCE

WHEREVER the influences which were described in the last chapter had an opportunity to work under favorable political conditions, only one result was possible—a national consciousness began to arise and the national government began to be more directly an expression of that consciousness: governments, in other words, began to exist having reality as well as a name to be. The improvement of the intellectual conditions, which will be the subject of Chapter XV, rendered also essential service in the same direction, in the growth of general intelligence and the creation of a wider community of ideas. But the results which followed an increasing commerce had a more direct and immediate influence upon the formation of state governments than had any outcome of the intellectual advance. We have just seen in how many directions these results were a direct attack upon the older feudal conditions and institutions, and it is naturally in order now to examine the special efforts which were made by the forming governments to take advantage of these new influences, and in doing so to sketch the forms of government and constitution resulting in the various states of the time.

In two of the leading states of Europe governments which may be called really national were established—in France and England. Their history is consequently of greater interest to us and will occupy us most fully. One other country, Spain, arrived at a government which embraced the whole territory of the state, but which was not supported, as in the other two cases, by a thoroughly united national feeling. In neither Italy nor Germany was any true general government for the whole state established, for reasons which we have already seen; but in both cases some interesting political results are to be noticed and many indications that a genuine national feeling and spirit existed, though unable to express itself through political institutions. In many of the minor states which arose in portions of these two countries, governments, which were really national in everything except extent of territory, were formed.

In the case of France the great fact at the opening of its national history was feudalism. We have seen how completely that system prevailed in the France of the tenth century, and the prevalence of feudalism meant the existence of two fatal obstacles in the way of the formation of any efficient national government. It meant the geographical subdivision of the country into practically independent fragments, and it meant the subdivision of the general authority in the same way, so that the usual functions of a general government could no longer be exercised throughout the state by the nominal central power, but were exercised in fragments by local powers. We have seen also how the Capetian dynasty arose out of this feudalism itself, and though possessed in theory of very extensive powers, had in reality only so much power as it could derive from its own family resources.

These facts indicate clearly enough the twofold task which lay before the Capetian dynasty at the beginning of its history, and which it performed so faithfully and so successfully. It must reconstruct the geographical unity of France by bringing all the fragments into which its territory had been separated under its own immediate control—a task which was to be rendered doubly difficult by the fact that several of the largest of these fragments were in the possession of a foreign sovereign, the king of England. It had, in the second place, to recover the prerogatives usurped by the rulers of these fragments so that it might itself exercise them in fact as well as possess them in theory, and in doing so it must, in great measure, create the national institutions through which these functions of a central government could be exercised.

The first four Capetian kings, from Hugh Capet to Philip I, do not seem to have been altogether unconscious of the great problems which they had to solve, but their situation was such that they could do but little. The first steps were necessarily slow, and it should be considered by no means a small contribution to the final result that these kings were able to strengthen the hold of the Capetian family upon the throne of France, as they unquestionably did, to prevent any further loss of royal power, and to maintain the respect for the kingship in the turbulent society of the time. In certain localities where special conditions favored a kind of natural independence there may have been loss rather than gain, as in Flanders and Brittany, but on the whole the current was in the direction of a stronger monarchy. They continued also and confirmed the alliance with the church, which had aided so greatly the rise of their family and from which it had still so much to gain. In comparison with these more general and negative, but not therefore unimportant, results, any specific gains which these kings made were insignificant. Philip I does not rank in history as a very strong or energetic king, but he saw clearly enough what was the first necessary step to be taken, the consolidation of his own feudal state, the duchy of France, and he bequeathed that policy to his successor.

With Louis VI, the Fat, in 1108, the work was taken vigorously and successfully in hand, and the succession opens of the great sovereigns of the Capetian house—of the sovereigns who may justly be called great in the work of constructing France, if not in any wider sense. The chief effort of Louis's reign was to overthrow the small nobles who were his vassals as duke, and who had been making themselves as independent in their smaller territories as the great vassals had throughout the greater France, and some of whom had brought it to such a pass that it was almost impossible for the king to travel with freedom from one part of his domain to another. This work he practically accomplished, and he centralized the duchy to such an extent that later kings had its undivided resources to draw upon in the more severe struggle which was before them.

This struggle with the great barons Louis VI also began with vigor, though without any very marked success. In Flanders, Champagne, and Aquitaine he asserted the rights of the king and attempted to maintain them with force, and he carried on an almost continuous war with his great rival the Duke of Normandy. Earlier Capetian kings had recognized the great strength of the dukes of Normandy and the importance of having them as allies or of weakening their power as opportunity offered, but the accession of Duke William to the English throne in 1066 had greatly increased the danger from this source. The continual quarrels in the English royal family through the whole period furnished an opportunity which could be turned to advantage by the French kings, and Louis supported the son of Robert against Henry I, though in the end unsuccessfully. The position of the English in France was stronger, indeed, at the close of Louis's reign than at the beginning, by reason of the marriage of Henry's daughter Matilda with the Count of Anjou, who had been Louis's ally. The great gain of Louis's life was the centralization of the duchy and the decidedly stronger position which the king had gained throughout all central France.

In the next reign, that of Louis VII, the territory held by the English kings upon the Continent was extended so widely that it threatened the very existence of an independent France under the Capetian house. The wide fiefs which had been brought together by the dukes of Aquitaine, covering nearly a quarter of the present territory of France, fell to an heiress, Eleanor, on the death of her father, William X, the last duke. Louis VI had not neglected the opportunity and had secured the hand of Eleanor for his son Louis. But there existed between this pair, apparently, a complete incompatibility of temper. Eleanor had little respect for Louis, and her conduct was not altogether proper, at least not in the eyes of her somewhat austere husband, and on his return from the second crusade the marriage was annulled. But such a prize did not long remain unsought, and in the same year she married young Henry of Anjou, son of Matilda, who already was in possession of all the English provinces on the Continent, and soon after succeeded to the English throne. By this marriage the whole of western France was united under Henry II, considerably more than one-third its present area, and a far larger portion than was directly under the control of the Capetian king. But these lands were only loosely held together, and they were feudally subject to Louis. It is interesting to notice that Henry was not willing to lead his army in person against his suzerain when Louis had thrown himself into Toulouse to defend that city against his attack, the feudal theory proving itself so strong even in such a case. But Louis could make no headway against so large a power, though he tried to do what he could and aided the rebellious sons of Henry against their father.

His successor, Philip Augustus, made it the great object of his reign to enlarge the royal domain, that is, the part of France directly under the king's government. The domain was enlarged when, for any reason, one of

the great barons, a count or a duke, had given up his
territory to the king.   Then there was no longer standing between the rear vassals and the king a great lord
who held the territory as his own little principality, more
or less completely closed against the royal interference.
The king had taken his place, and the small nobles of
the territory were brought into immediate dependence
upon him, so that he had now possession both of the
rights of the old count or duke, and also of the more
extensive rights of the national sovereign, which might
at last be exercised.   Sometimes, also, the kings got possession of rear fiefs before the county or duchy was finally
absorbed, and in both these ways, though mainly by the
first, the new kingdom of France was forming and the
royal power of the Capetian family was extending itself
over the national territory by the disappearance of the
great barons who had been its peers at the beginning of
its history.

The long reign of Philip Augustus was a time of most
rapid progress in this geographical reconstruction of
France.   The county of Artois, the king secured by his
marriage;   the counties of Vermandois and Amiens soon
after as the result of a disputed succession.   These accessions greatly enlarged the domain towards the north-
east.   But the great problem was to recover the lands
held by the English, and at this Philip labored all his
life.   The constant quarrels in the English royal family
—of Henry II with his sons, of Richard and John, of
John and Arthur, and finally between John and the English barons—greatly aided his efforts, and Philip was always on the side opposed to the reigning king.   Before
the reign of John he had made only very slight gains,
the most important being the suzerainty of the county
of Auvergne, which Henry II had been forced, just before
his death, to transfer to Philip.   But Philip's abandonment of the third crusade, while it was still unfinished,

and his return to France to take advantage of the absence of Richard are evidences of the power of political motives over his mind, and of his superior realization of the duties of his office, as compared with the English king.

Immediately after the accession of John came the opportunity for which Philip had waited. In 1200, John deprived the heir of one of his vassals, the eldest son of Hugh, Count of La Marche, of his promised bride and married her himself. The count took arms with the support of other nobles of Poitou, and appealed for justice to John's suzerain, King Philip. Philip summoned John to appear before his feudal court and make answer. When the court met, early in 1202, John did not appear, and sentence was pronounced that he had failed to meet his feudal obligations, and had therefore forfeited all the fiefs which he held of the king of France.[1] Philip proceeded to execute the sentence immediately by force of arms. He had the feudal law clearly on his side. John further prejudiced his case by his murder of Arthur in the next year. He was hampered also by many enemies, and by treachery among his vassals, and though he may have been physically brave and mentally able, he was morally a coward, and his defence against Philip's attack was weak in the extreme. Speedily all of Normandy, Maine, Anjou, and Touraine, and parts of Poitou and Saintonge, were in Philip's possession, never to be recovered as fiefs by the English. The great victory of Bouvines, which Philip gained in 1214, over the Emperor Otto IV, and the Count of Flanders, allies of John, raised the prestige of the king to its highest point, and excited a popular enthusiasm which may almost be called national.

---

[1] The researches of M. Ch. Bémont—see two articles in the *Revue Historique*, vol. XXXII—have made it certain that the condemnation of John was the result of the appeal to the king by the nobles of Poitou, and not of the murder of Arthur, as formerly supposed. Numerous later studies of the question have not seriously shaken M. Bémont's conclusions.

The reign of Philip Augustus had multiplied the area of
the royal domain by three, had strengthened the position
of the king beyond the possibility of rivalry or even successful resistance from any single baron and had given it
the sanction of uninterrupted success.

The reign of his son, Louis VIII, lasted only three years,
but it made no break in the line of advance.   More territory was recovered from the English, including the important city of La Rochelle, and the hold of the king on
southeastern France was strengthened.

With Louis IX, St. Louis, there followed another long
reign, and another period of enormous advance, relatively
not so great in territory as under Philip Augustus, but
one which left the royal power, at its close, institutionally
much farther along on the road to absolutism.

Louis IX was only eleven years old at his father's
death, but his mother, Blanche of Castile, who assumed
the regency, was worthy to be a sovereign in the Capetian line.   The great barons, however, had now begun
to realize to what end events were carrying them, and to
see, as they had to some extent before this date, that
their only hope of resisting the policy of the crown was
to be found in concerted action.   They consequently took
advantage of Louis's minority to form combinations
among themselves to deprive the queen of the regency,
and in intent, to check the advance of the royal power
by arms.   The skill of the queen-regent, however, defeated all their plans, and a similar result attended another attempt of the sort after Louis reached his majority.   All these unsuccessful efforts in the end really aided
the royal cause.   In 1259, Louis made a treaty with Henry
III, of England, by which for certain small fiefs added
to his land in the southwest of France, Henry abandoned
all claims to Normandy, Maine, Anjou, and Poitou, and
agreed to hold Guienne as a fief from Louis.   A treaty of
the year before with the king of Aragon had made a simi-

lar division of disputed lands in the southeast. Louis
also profited by the results of the bloody extermination
of the Albigenses which had been begun in the reign of
Philip Augustus. The attempt of Raymond VII, Count
of Toulouse, to better his condition by joining one of
the coalitions of barons against the king had resulted in
his losing some of his lands to the king, and he was
obliged to renew his consent to the earlier treaty, by
which the king's brother, Alfonso, Count of Poitiers, was
to succeed to Toulouse at Raymond's death. This happened in 1249. In the year after Louis's death Alfonso
himself died without heirs, and the great county of Toulouse was joined to the crown.

To offset somewhat these great accessions of territory
under the direct control of the king, the system of appanages must be noted, begun, in a large way, by Louis
VIII to provide for his younger sons. The provinces,
however, which were separated by this arrangement from
the domain and made to depend feudally upon some
prince of the royal house, were not ceded to him in full
sovereignty, and the system did not lead to the formation of a new series of independent principalities, nor
prove as dangerous to the royal authority as might seem
probable.

Louis's son, Philip III, though without originality of
his own or strength of character, followed faithfully the
example set by his father, and was well served by officers
trained in that school. The great fiefs of Toulouse and
Champagne were added to the domain, the jurisdiction
of the royal courts enlarged, the development of a supreme court advanced, the king's authority enforced in
every way possible in the great fiefs which remained,
the independence of the communes weakened, and quietly
and without exciting open opposition the royal authority
strengthened in all directions. The growth of a strong
central government was now so well begun, in other words,

that it could go on almost of itself under a sovereign who was able to do but little to direct the process.

The regular alternation which seems curiously enough to prevail in the Capetian dynasty during most of the medieval portion of its history brings us, with the accession of Philip IV, to another strong king, and to an epoch of almost revolutionary progress. But this was almost wholly institutional. From this time on to the close of the long English war, no great accession of territory was made, though many small ones were, like the seizure of Lyons by Philip IV. France was now almost constructed geographically. The great central portion was under the direct government of the king, except so far as the appanages interfered with this. Guienne, Brittany, Burgundy, and Flanders were the only great fiefs still remaining independent, and, with the exception of Guienne, they remained so until the end of the middle ages, and the most of Flanders was never recovered. To these must be added, to complete the later French territory, Provence, which, though not a fief of France, was held by a long series of French princes and was finally absorbed by France under Louis XI.

The early deaths of the three sons of Philip the Fair, and the exclusion of their daughters from the succession by the principle which was later called the Salic law, make a natural close for the first period of Capetian history. With the immediately following accession of the house of Valois the Hundred Years' War with the English begins.

The great increase of territory directly subject to the control of the king during the period which closes with the death of Charles IV, the last of the direct line, had necessitated a corresponding development of the institutional side of the monarchy to provide the means required to exercise the real government which became more and more possible. The reign of Philip Augustus marked an epoch in this direction, as it did in the geographical extension of the royal power, and that of St. Louis was even more distinguished for institutional than for territorial growth.

The problem of administration, of making the central power effectively felt in all the details of local government throughout the domain, was the earliest which demanded solution. The older administrative agent, the *prévôt*, served very well when the domain was small, but was inadequate in the changed situation. He was wholly feudal in character, administered a very small territory, and was not well under control.

In the *bailli* Philip Augustus developed a most effective agent of the central power. Free from feudal influence, appointed by the king and entirely dependent upon him, transferred at intervals from one region to another, he was held under a strict control. In the district to which he was appointed, he directly represented the royal authority in the local enforcement of its regulations of all kinds, and in the care of its financial interests, and also in military and even judicial matters, and formed a close bond of connection between the central government and every locality. Besides the special functions of this new officer, he had the general duty of looking after all the interests of the king, and of extending his power and domain whenever opportunity offered. In this direction the services of the *baillis* to the crown were as effective as in their strictly official capacity, and not infrequently their zeal in interfering with the local nobility to the king's advantage carried them on faster and farther than the kings thought it wise to follow. In the great territories afterwards added to the domain in the south, this officer was known as the *sénéchal*, but had the same duties with some differences of detail. The supervision of the central government over all parts of the state was carried a step further by St. Louis in his more regular employment of *enquêteurs*, officers occasionally used before and corresponding in duties to the *missi* of Charlemagne. Intended to oversee the conduct of the local officers and to insure justice, they became, under the stronger government of Philip the Fair, agents of royal oppression and exaction.

Probably the most difficult task which the kings had to perform in creating the state was to establish national courts superior to the local and feudal courts in baronial hands, and, in connection with them, to enforce peace and good order—an orderly and judicial settlement of disputes instead of an appeal to force. The minute regulations with which the feudal law itself, as it began to be formed, had surrounded the practice of private war, mimicking on a small scale the provisions of international law and even more formal in character, are evidences of an attempt on the part of feudalism itself to escape from some of the worst evils of unchecked license. The Truce of God was able to aid in this direction during a time when the church was the only general power capable of enforcing the requirements of such a truce. But it was not possible for the evil to be entirely done away with, and good order to be really maintained, until the general causes, whose operation we noticed in the last chapter, had finally transformed society and created a strong demand for security. Then they could give the central government an effective support that would enable it to enforce obedience to the law. This transformation of society was by no means complete in the last half of the thirteenth century, but it had advanced so far that its influence can be distinctly seen, and the operation of the royal courts may begin to be called national.

The original court of the king, the *curia regis*, was an assembly of court officials, vassals, and magnates subject to the king, which met at short intervals, at his summons, to perform a great variety of functions—judicial, advisory, and semi-legislative—functions which were to be performed after a time, with the increasing complexity of government, by separate bodies differentiated from this original court. Under the early Capetian kings the portion of France under its actual jurisdiction was very small, and its means of enforcing any decree were very limited. In the period which follows, down to the reign of St. Louis, the wider extension of the royal power affected the court in two directions. In one there is to be seen a constantly increasing respect paid to the court on the part of the feudal lords, and a growing tendency to submit to its decrees, a tendency which, though not by any means universal as yet, was marked enough to be a sure sign of the increasing respect paid to the king. In another direction, in the court itself, there is evident the gradual formation from its members of a small body constantly present and especially devoted to the study of the law—a result which followed naturally from the increasing business of the court.

This latter fact is the first indication of the next important advance. From the reign of St. Louis the judicial business of the court was regularly in the hands of a permanent body of specially trained men, selected by the king, and this body now began to be called the *Parlement*. The lords and high clergy still attended occasionally, when especially summoned, in cases which particularly concerned their own interests, but the supreme court of the kingdom had now been separated from the earlier general body, the *curia regis*, and had begun its separate development.

Along with this evolution of the supreme court there went also a great increase of respect and of business in the case of the subordinate national courts, those held by the *prévôts* and the *baillis*. There are, also, two other facts to be noticed in the same connection, as of the utmost importance in the national centralization. One is the introduction of a system of appeals, and the other, the revived study of the Roman law.

The development of a series of royal courts might serve a good purpose in centralizing the domain, even if their action were confined to that, but would be of little use in binding all France together, if the feudal courts of the great fiefs, which were still left, remained supreme and independent. Under St. Louis and his son, the right of appeal, which had existed before in some parts of the kingdom, was definitely established for all France—the right of appeal to the royal courts, local and supreme, from all feudal courts of whatever grade, including those of the greatest and most independent lords, like the king of England in his capacity as duke of Guienne.[1]

That the establishment of this right of appeal from themselves to the king revolutionized the whole situation and involved in reality the total destruction of their political independence, the barons do not seem to have clearly perceived; but that they certainly resisted this advance of the royal power with some determination is evident from the numerous ordinances which were made in the following period against the means they were employing to maintain the independence of their courts. But their power of resistance was greatly undermined by the theory of the kingship, which had always existed in the feudal law, and which was now greatly developed under the influence of the Roman law. If the king was considered to be the supreme source of law and justice, and if the right of the baron to hold a court was only a delegated right, then there was no ground on which an appeal to the royal courts could be denied.

It was in the thirteenth century, especially in its latter

[1] The supreme feudal courts in some of the great fiefs, as in Normandy, Champagne, and Toulouse, were allowed to continue, their judges, under the new arrangement, being members of the *Parlement* of Paris sent for the purpose; but they continued not as independent courts, but as provincial *parlements*, clearly incorporated in the national judiciary system.

half, that the revived study of the Roman law began to have a decided practical influence upon the formation of the modern state and modern law. We cannot enter here into the special influence which it had in the field of law itself, less decisive in France than in Germany, but far more extensive everywhere on the Continent than in England. It is its influence upon institutions and the development of government which we must regard.

The channel through which the principles of the Roman law were brought at this time into an immediate influence upon the institutional side of the national growth, was the position obtained by the professional body of trained lawyers, now beginning to be formed. These men were soon employed as judges in the subordinate courts, and gradually made their way into the *Parlement* itself, and thus that body became more and more separated as a permanent institution exercising the judicial functions of the *curia regis* practically alone. And along another line also the same connection of the Roman law with the state was made through the influence of the lawyers in the other body which was just now forming from the *curia regis*, the Estates General.

It was by infusing its spirit into the progress which had begun, and directing it to certain ideals, rather than as a source of actual institutions that the Roman law affected the result. It was the law of a thoroughly centralized state. Its spirit was that of a complete absolutism. All its principles and maxims looked to the king as the centre and source of the whole institutional life of the state. The supreme right to judge, to administer, to legislate, and to tax was possessed by the sovereign. This was the theory of the state which the lawyers were drawing from the Roman law everywhere, even, to some extent at least, in England. As the practical management of public affairs of all sorts passed more and more into the hands of men trained in these ideas, and as the

Roman law gradually came to be regarded as the controlling law in all new cases, the actual facts were made
to conform more and more exactly to the theory. This
new influence was, thus, a tremendous reinforcement to
the primitive theory of the kingship which had come down
to the Capetians from the earlier dynasties and which had
lived through the age of feudal disintegration, a theory
which had been itself formed after the conquest very
largely on the Roman model. But it must be remembered that it was not now mere theory. The influence
exerted upon the growth of the state was far more decisive than that of any mere theory, for it was the controlling ideal of the men who were most active in shaping
the new institutions.[1] It has been said of this influence:
"It was this more than all other causes combined which
effected the transformation of the feudal medieval sovereignty into the absolute monarchies of the seventeenth
century,"[2] and one feels hardly justified in calling the
statement an exaggeration.

During the last part of this period three other institutions of great importance began their growth, though
their great development was to lie in the time of the

[1] Two points may be emphasized in connection with this discussion of
French judicial institutions, as facts of the utmost importance in accounting for the different results in France and England. One of them is this,
that a national system of law and national courts had never disappeared in
England as completely as they had in France. They did not have to be
reconstructed almost *de novo* under the influence of any theories, and it was
not true of England, as it was of France, that the chief dependence for a
common law was upon a confused and contradictory local and customary
law which was totally unfit to grow into a general national law with the
rapidity necessary to keep pace with geographical extension of the royal
power. From early in the reign of Henry II the royal courts rapidly built
up a common law which was truly national. The other fact is that France
did not have so complete a system of local self-government as England, a
system based upon different ideas from those of the Roman law, and able
to train individual men for the public service and the whole nation in the
exercise of liberty. This fact was, however, of more decisive influence in
the later stages of French history than at the point we have now reached.

[2] The New York *Nation*, vol. XL, p. 487.

English war which followed. These were the standing army, the system of national taxation, and the Estates General.

With the enlargement of the domain, and the more important and more distant wars which followed, the feudal levies and the older general levy proved themselves insufficient and less to be depended upon than in earlier times. Before the reign of Philip Augustus there are instances of the employment of paid soldiers, and their use constantly increased. With their employment, and the other increasing expenses of the state, the necessity arose for a larger income than the feudal revenues supplied. Some points connected with the origin of general taxation are not clear, but the first steps towards it seem to have been taken in the introduction, under Philip Augustus, of a money composition for military service not performed. During the English wars the method of this tax changed somewhat. The kings of that time were not always in a position to maintain all that their predecessors had gained, and the Estates General attempted to compel a recognition of their right to grant a tax before it could be legally collected, but without final success. The right of the king to impose taxes was in the end recognized. It was not until the close of the Hundred Years' War, in the middle of the fifteenth century, that these two things were definitely established, a regularly organized standing army, and an equally well organized and permanent system of taxation, imposed by the king and collected throughout the kingdom by his agents. It can be seen at once that when this point was reached the central government was independent of the feudal system. It had recovered from its vassals two of its most important functions, the loss of which in the ninth and tenth centuries had forced it to submit to the feudal regime. The failure of the Estates General to make good their claim to a right to vote the taxes had rendered the crown independent also of anything that may be called the people, and with its assumption, in addition, of the right of legislation, it became the only factor in the government. The absolute monarchy was complete in outline though not yet worked out in all details.

The institutions which we have been considering down to this point are all institutions of centralization. Their tendency was to increase very greatly the power of the king, to undermine all forms of local independence, and to bring the control of public matters of every kind more and more completely into the king's hands. Now we come to the beginning of an institution which contained within itself a possibility of most serious danger for this growing absolutism. It is the Estates General—States General—the appearance, or reappearance, of a public assembly having legislative functions.

Leaving one side the uncertain and not yet sufficiently investigated question as to the exact character in different countries of the earlier institution into which the representatives of the cities were now admitted, it is clear that in all the states of Europe there was such an institution already in existence. The king's vassals and the magnates of the realm, lay and ecclesiastical, came together at his summons—the clergy meeting sometimes, though by no means frequently, by themselves—to perform without distinguishing between them a variety of functions as occasion demanded, sometimes judicial, to decide cases that arose under the feudal law, and to determine what customs should be recognized as having the force of law, or in what way they should be changed, and to give advice in new cases. These last were acts which would correspond most nearly to legislation of anything during the feudal period, when formal legislation seems to have been wanting, except for enactments in the form of royal edicts which were occasionally issued with the consent of the assembly. Into this body, representatives of the Third Estate were now admitted, in all the leading countries of Europe, and it gradually assumed a more definite organization and clearer legislative functions. France was the last of the larger states to take this step; the Spanish states of Aragon and Castile were the first, soon after the middle of the twelfth century; Sicily followed in 1232, Germany in 1255, England in 1265, and France in 1302. Instances of the appearance of representatives of the towns in the earlier body may be found in some cases before, but the definite beginning of the new institution was at the dates given.

The special occasion which led to the creation of this new institution is itself significant of the progress which the royal authority had made. One of the most important resources of the early Capetians had been the wealth of the church. But they had drawn from this source, in the way of a general levy on the revenues of ecclesiastics, only with the consent of the pope, granted in each case for some object of which the pope approved. Now Philip the Fair felt himself strong enough to dispense with this consent, and to demand that the clergy should be subject, like other classes, to the state's rapidly forming tax system. The pope took up at once the defence of his rights, and the conflict, begun on the question of taxation, rapidly involved a great variety of points concerning the position of virtual political independence within the state, which the church asserted for itself. Upon some one or other of these points all the strong Capetian kings—Louis VI, Philip Augustus, and St. Louis—had come into collision with the papacy. Now the state was so nearly centralized that the war was waged on all these issues at once, and seemed to involve the whole relation of the church to the state.

It was most likely for its general effect, to make an imposing display of the fact that the whole nation was

behind him in this conflict, or at least that he controlled
the nation, that Philip called together the first, or the
first important, Estates General in 1302.[1]   In doing this,
he gave it a really representative character, and a definiteness of composition which made it a new institution.
The members of the first two estates, the clergy and the
nobles, were summoned personally and attended in person or by proxy.   The towns of the whole kingdom,
summoned through the *baillis*, elected representatives to
form the Third Estate.

It was the power of money which had raised the Third
Estate to a position in the community somewhere near the
other two.   It was not to obtain their consent to a tax,
however, that representatives of the Third Estate had in
this case been summoned to the Estates General.   The
immediate object was to obtain the support of all orders
for the king's general policy.   It was not very long, however, before the kings showed themselves disposed to submit the question of taxation to the sanction of the Estates, in order that the collection of it might be easier.
In doing this, the kings created an extremely dangerous
weapon against themselves, if the Estates General had
been able to use it.   It was not entirely their fault that
they were not.   The fact that this assembly was at first
only an advisory body, and had no power of independent
action, that the rights of legislation and of taxation were
practically in the hands of the king, was a most serious
obstacle to the formation of a constitutional monarchy,

---

[1] It is by no means improbable that, in taking this step, Philip was con-
sciously following the example set by Edward I of England, a year or two
before, in his contest with Boniface VIII over the feudal relationship of
Scotland.   The evidence is clear that Philip was familiar with these events
in England, and the idea is an interesting one that the suggestion of the
French Estates General may have come from the English Parliament.
Whatever may be true as to this particular occasion, however, the Estates
General would certainly have been formed before many years.   For the
argument of Edward I in 1279 that the clergy should pay taxes like the
laity, see Barker, *The Dominican Order and Convocation*, p. 65.

but not an absolutely fatal one. The French assembly still had within itself the possibilities of the English Parliament.[1] If it could have obtained a solid popular support and a leadership that would have commanded general respect, if there had been throughout France a general experience and understanding of self-government as a reserve fund upon which it could have drawn, it might, in all probability, have gained what was gained in the sister kingdom. It was the lack of these non-institutional and intangible but powerful elements of growth that was fatal.

The epoch of rapid geographical and institutional growth under the Capetian kings of the direct line was succeeded by a long period of confusion and disaster, in which the national development in both these directions almost entirely ceased. Soon after the accession of Philip VI, the first king of the House of Valois, the Hundred Years' War with England began. In its real meaning it was a struggle over the last English possessions in France. Philip VI had immediately taken up the old policy of weakening the English hold on Guienne by intrigue and by every other means at hand, and Edward III was not slow to defend himself. It was a result, however, of the more truly national character which both states had now assumed, that the war involved wider issues than in its earlier stages—the question of the supremacy of England over Scotland, and of France over Flanders, and finally for a time the dangerous possibility,

---

[1] The legal sources from which the fundamental and creative principles of Magna Carta were drawn in England existed with no important difference in France. The whole institutional situation, as the starting-point of later constitutional growth, was alike in the two countries except for the stronger monarchy, and local self-government in the English shires. These peculiarities of England, though of great importance as said above, affected the purpose, spirit, and character of the actors in events, not the institutional foundations upon which they built.

dangerous alike for England and for France, that the English king might actually make good that claim to the throne of France which had been advanced at first mainly as a war measure.

The Hundred Years' War opened with a series of disasters for the French, and of great victories for the English, against overwhelming odds, which are in themselves suggestive of the difference between the two nations. The French armies, still composed chiefly of nobles, their contempt for the foot-soldier increased by decisive victories over the Flemings recently gained, were filled with over-confidence in the face of English armies which seemed to be composed almost wholly of footmen. But the English foot-soldiers were different men from any that the French had met before. They had a sturdy self-reliance, and a feeling that they were a match for their noble enemies which were the outgrowth of their history, recent as well as ancient—of a long past which the French had once shared with them, but with which, in their military system as in other things, the French had broken more completely than the English. The result was the battles of Crécy and of Poitiers and the anarchy which followed in France.

The king was a prisoner in England; the dauphin was young and had not yet begun to display the capacity for government which he showed as king; the nearest prince of the blood, Charles of Navarre, was a selfish schemer; and a feeling had arisen that the king and the nobles had proved themselves unfit to deal with the situation. There was an opportunity for the Estates General to seize upon the control of affairs, and to begin the formation of a constitution which the leaders of the Third Estate quickly recognized.

The demands which the circumstances enabled them to make, some of which were granted them for the time being, were closely like the most important principles

which were being slowly expressed in the English constitution. They demanded the right to vote the taxes and
to control their expenditure, that the king's ministers
should be held responsible to the law, that the administration of justice should be without favor or bribery, and
that they should have the right to select certain members
of the king's council, and, also, the concession of period-
ical meetings for the Estates General, and these demands
were put somewhat after the English fashion in the form
of conditions attached to grants of money.

If these points had been permanently established in
the French constitution, it would have been the sudden
creation of a limited monarchy, the introduction in a
single decade of overpowering restraints upon the king,
with no history of steady growth behind them. The
whole history of France had been tending in the opposite direction, and in this fact was the great weakness of
such an attempt at revolution, and the main cause of its
failure. The reform party had no strong leadership, and
it had no general popular support. The career of Etienne
Marcel is extremely interesting, but it was not without
its demagogic features. The nobles lent no support to
the attempt, and the whole of French history did not
produce a leader from the middle class like Stephen Lang-
ton, or one from the nobles like Simon de Montfort.
The Paris mob also had, in the middle of the fourteenth
century, too great an influence on the course of events, and
exhibited at that early date the characteristic features
and fatal results which have appeared in almost every
century since, and which are so familiar to us in the
history of the French Revolution and of the Commune.
This attempt to form a limited monarchy, and the similar one which circumstances again allowed in 1413, met
with no final success, and the growth of the absolute
monarchy went on, delayed, but not changed in character.

With the next king, Charles V, the Wise, a strong and

skilful king again succeeded a weak one, and the royal power recovered its losses and made new progress. When he had well prepared for it, he renewed the English war, which had been closed for a time by the treaty of Brétigny, and, by wisely avoiding pitched battles, he wearied out his enemy and recovered nearly all Guienne. He enforced the right of appeal to the national courts, forbade private war, enlarged greatly the paid army, avoided meeting the Estates General, and strengthened the king's hold upon the taxing power, and made further progress in getting its collection into the hands of royal officers. The right of the king to decree a new tax not consented to by those who were to pay it does not seem to have been yet recognized; but the consent was obtained from no regular body, sometimes from assemblies approaching in character to the Estates General, sometimes from provincial estates, sometimes from cities, and when once granted the tax was collected permanently without a new grant, and was even increased by the king with no consent asked, and in this way France was gradually brought to regard the right of taxation as a prerogative of the king's.

After Charles V came the long reign of the weak and insane Charles VI, filled with confusion and with civil contests between the utterly selfish princes of the blood and their adherents, and closed with the almost fatal triumph of Henry V of England.

The son of Charles VI, Charles the Victorious, was the last king of France whose reign can be said to have been wholly in the middle ages and occupied entirely with the old problems. His place was created for him by the great popular movement to which Joan of Arc gave leadership, and which reveals to us in the clearest light the depth of the national feeling which had now come into existence in France. By this the English were expelled, to be prevented from ever returning by their own civil War of the Roses, and by the wholly changed international conditions which confronted the new monarchy of the Tudors at the close of that war. But if Charles VII did not make his own place, he knew how to occupy it when it had been made for him. The finances were brought into good condition, the army was thoroughly organized, the state made independent of the feudal levies, and the right of the king to impose taxes finally established.

The nobles did not allow these concluding steps in the progress to absolutism to be taken without protest and combinations to prevent them, but their greatest effort, under the lead of princes of the royal house, was made under the next king, Louis XI, and when he had succeeded in breaking up the League of the Public Weal the last really dangerous resistance to the royal power was overcome. Louis followed the same policy as his father, and at the close of his reign the absolute monarchy was complete in all essential particulars. A last trace of institutional check upon the legislative right of the sovereign remained, until a little later, in the power of the supreme court—the *Parlement*—to reject a royal edict in whole or in part—the rights of registration and of remonstrance—and a few other finishing touches to the structure of royal absolutism were left to be made in the sixteenth century and by Richelieu and Mazarin. But when the king had gathered into his hands the uncontrolled right to legislate, to tax,[1] and to maintain a standing army, the process of centralization was in all essentials finished, and the king was the state as really as in the case of Louis XIV.

In the reign of Louis XI, also, territorial acquisitions

[1] Philip de Comines, writing in the reign of Charles VIII, recognizes the importance of this point. He denies that the king has any right of taxation without the consent of those who pay, and says that England is the best governed of the countries of his time. See especially Bk. V, chap. XIX.

were begun again, the duchy of Burgundy was seized on the death of Charles the Bold, and the county of Provence, which lay, not in France, but in the old kingdom of Burgundy, was annexed—a partial compensation for the loss of Flanders, which now passed to the House of Hapsburg. In the next reign the last of the great fiefs acquired, Brittany, was brought in by the marriage of Charles VIII with its heiress.

But the reign of Charles VIII belongs really in modern political history. The ambition of the now completely formed French nation and of its sovereign for foreign conquests, and the attempt of Charles to establish the French in Italy, are its leading facts. Louis XI had seen the rise of the new interests and the beginning of the international combinations which were made to secure them, but he was still so occupied with the old problems that he had not been able to take a part in the game at all proportionate to the strength of France. Now the old problems were settled, so far as they need be, and the new interests were taking their place to direct the royal policy.

In some of the later reigns the relics of the feudal power were to make new efforts to recover the position in the state which they had lost, but these efforts were hopeless from the beginning, and feudalism as a political power disappeared with the English wars. As a system of social rank and of exclusive legal privileges and exemptions it remained until the French Revolution. The kings had carried on a long contest with feudalism, and had finally completely overthrown it, but they were not hostile to a nobility, and freely bestowed upon the nobles pensions and titles and high favor at court as some compensation for the political independence which had been destroyed.[1]

[1] It must be remarked, also, as having an important bearing on modern French history, that, although a national government had been established

The purpose of this sketch has been not so much to give an outline of the institutional history of France during these centuries as to make evident, if possible, how the central government was continually growing in strength and the king becoming with every generation. more and more independent of the feudal nobles and the real ruler of their lands.

It has been given so much more in detail than the history of the other states will be, not merely because of the important influence of the absolutism thus formed upon all later history, but also because it is, to a considerable extent, typical of what took place, sooner or later, almost everywhere upon the Continent, certainly in results if not always in processes.

and a national feeling created, still very great differences remained between the various provinces in law, in methods of legislation, and in taxation, as reminders of their original feudal separation. The differences between the *pays de droit coutumier* and the *pays de droit écrit*, and between the *pays d'états* and the *pays d'élection* are examples. The existence of custom-houses along interior provincial boundary lines seems especially foreign to the modern idea of a state. These differences remained, like those of feudal rank, until the Revolution.

CHAPTER XIV

ENGLAND AND THE OTHER STATES

OUR brief sketch of English history before the Norman conquest revealed two facts of the highest importance in their bearing upon the later English constitution. One was that only the slightest Roman influence had been felt by the Saxons, the other that the political feudal system of the Continent had obtained no footing in the island. Then followed the Norman conquest, in appearance the most revolutionary epoch of the medieval history of England. But it was, in truth, less revolutionary than it seems, though a real beginning point in some lines of national growth.

The Norman conquest was less revolutionary than it seems upon the surface because the institutions which it introduced were in the main from the same ultimate source as the Saxon. They were Frankish, that is Teutonic, and except for the feudal system Teutonic not seriously modified by the Roman institutions with which they had been in intimate relation. Their growth through the time which preceded 1066 had been along practically the same lines as the Saxon institutional growth. They had for various reasons developed more rapidly, so that the chief difference between the type of government which the Normans brought into England and that which they found there may be said to be that the latter was in a stage of development some generations behind the former. The practical result was that the substitution of the Norman general government for the Saxon was

332

easily made with no sense of violent change and no real revolution. This was true even of political feudalism, the most decided innovation, because the drift towards this side of feudalism, inchoate and uncombined beginnings as in commendation of land and primitive vassalage, made the sudden introduction of the completed system seem not illogical or revolutionary. The same circumstance affected also the opposite result. It was easy in some cases for the Normans to adopt a Saxon institution as part of their general arrangements instead of introducing something less satisfactory of their own. An instance of this kind is the office of sheriff for local administration, and probably also the economic feudal organization, the manorial system, at least in some features. Finally, the question as to whether a given institution is of Norman or of Saxon origin is, for our purpose, of little importance. In either case, the ultimate origin is Teutonic, and in either case the constitutional result, the value of the institution to the world at large, is the value given to it by Englishmen after the conquest.

The conquest brought into English history two new factors which had most decided influence upon the future. First, in the place of a weak king, personally weak and almost overshadowed by one or two great noble families, who threatened to bring about some of the results of continental feudalism, it put a strong king, strong by the fact of conquest, strong in character, and strong in the traditions and constitutional development of his office in Normandy. This meant absolutism in the actual conduct of the general government, but for the local institutions of England it meant very little. The body of the Saxon laws remained in force by the choice and will of the king, and influenced only slightly by feudalism. It was a century before the centralization which began with the conquest affected in any marked degree local institutions, particularly the shire courts.

In the second place, the conquest introduced the political feudal system into England; it was not, however, the feudal system of France. It was introduced by a strong king, because it furnished the only method for the organization of the general government with which he was familiar, but it was introduced in such a way that the king remained strong in comparison with his vassals, because of those characteristics of Norman feudalism which have been specified in Chapter VIII. As one consequence there was in England no great baron occupying such a position of independence as the duke of Normandy, or the duke of Aquitaine, or even the count of Anjou, occupied in France. As another consequence the feudal system never took the place of an inefficient national government and exercised locally its functions in England, and the results which the opposite fact produced in France and Germany never appeared there. Only for a brief time, under a weak and insecure king, Stephen, did the feudal lords usurp powers of the general government, coining money and freely waging private war, and give the English a short experience of conditions familiar to their neighbors on the mainland.

Another result of the introduction of the feudal system was to create a more definitely organized body of nobles than had existed before, no one of whom perhaps equalled in power the Godwin family of Edward the Confessor's time, but who were, as a body, stronger than the body of Saxon nobles. For the moment this fact had no results. The barons had first to learn a lesson foreign to their class anywhere else in the world of that time, the lesson of combination with one another and with the middle class, before they could begin to stand successfully against the superior might of the king. This is a fact of great significance in relation to the different roads taken by French and English history. The French baron was so placed that he could hope to secure independence, and naturally this was the object which he sought. This led him into opposition not merely to the government but also to others of his own order who were in some sense his rivals, and consequently combinations among the barons against the king are less common in French history, and when they occur have more of a personal and less of a public character. The English baron, however, having no hope of establishing by himself an independent principality, learned to seek the aid of others against the power of the king, and as he was successful, went on gradually, not to independence, but to an increasing popularizing of the general government of the state, the form which a reduction of the royal power necessarily took in England.

This was a lesson, however, which was only slowly learned. Not until a hundred and fifty years had elapsed from the date of the conquest was the formation of the English constitution really taken in hand. The Norman and the first Angevin kings were to all intents absolute monarchs. Such forms of a more popular government as continued locally in operation furnished no real check upon their action. Nor did the rights of the barons as against the king which the feudal law recognized. Taxation, such as there was, was practically at their will. There was no legislative assembly which survived apart from their feudal court, and there was no legislation except their own. Lawyers trained in the Roman law did not hesitate to declare, here as on the Continent, that the will of the prince was valid law. Slight signs of resistance had not been wanting, among the barons of resistance to the king's absolute power over them, among the middle class on account of oppressive extortion of money, as under Richard I. But these were isolated cases and led to no definite results. The history of organized and self-conscious opposition to the king, embodying its results in constitutional documents to which clear appeal could be made against the sovereign, and whose enforcement marked out a consistent policy from generation to generation—the history, in other words, of the formation of the constitutional, or limited monarchy, opened in the reign of King John, and recorded the results of the first victory in Magna Carta.

It was in all probability nothing more than the selfish wish of the barons to protect themselves against the abuse of power by the king, and to gain as much for themselves as they could, which influenced them in their rebellion against John. They did not have—it would not have been possible for them to have had—any such motive before them as was before the leaders of the resistance to the Stuarts in the seventeenth century, nor were they led by any hereditary influence from the spirit or practice of liberty of earlier generations. So far as spirit and wish of theirs are concerned, they would have preferred the results which were sought by the barons of France and Germany, and would have used their victory to reach such ends if circumstances had not made them impossible. As it was, they included incidentally in the guarantees demanded of the king in the statement of their own feudal rights, also principles affecting the people at large and more directly bearing upon popular liberty, or at least principles which could at a later time be so interpreted. Many of these guarantees were the formulation of old principles and practices, but the relation of Magna Carta to the future is far more important than its relation to the past. And yet, in relation to the future, it was suggestion and germ rather than a clear conception even of important institutions then beginning to form. According to the interpretation long prevalent, five fundamental principles of present Anglo-Saxon liberty were contained in Magna Carta. These were, the right to trial by jury, the principle of the habeas corpus, the illegality of taxes not consented to by the nation's rep-

resentatives, fixed places of meeting for the courts of
common pleas, and the principle, to put it in the words
of its latest and somewhat more general formulation, that
no person shall be deprived of life, liberty, or property
without due process of law.   But such an interpretation
reads into the document, upon some of these points, a
meaning derived from later history, and yet, in one sense,
not incorrectly.   In studying the Great Charter as a historical document, it is necessary to have regard to what
its provisions meant to those who drew them up.   But,
whatever this may have been, it does not exhaust the
meaning of Magna Carta as an influence in the growth of
English liberty.   It was not many generations before the
progress of events, of which it was the starting point, made
its clauses appear to contain a meaning foreign to the
minds of its contemporaries, and when this occurred, its
weighty sanction was a real force in the establishment
and protection of the institutions which, it was believed,
had been intended.   Trial by jury, in the later sense, as
a means of protecting the individual, is not in Magna
Carta.   It could not well have been there, for the jury
was then only just beginning to be formed, and had not
yet reached an importance, or indeed a use, which would
have justified its insertion in a document of this sort.
The "judgment of his peers" referred to is the judgment
of the feudal court or of the community of freemen, once
common to the popular courts of all the German states,
and from them passing to the later forms of courts everywhere.   The words used in the charter, *judicium parium*,
are not infrequent in the feudal documents of the Continent.   And yet the "judgment of his peers" came soon
to mean to every Englishman trial by jury, and Magna
Carta seemed to secure to him that right.   And justly
so, for the bearing of the practice which it did guarantee
upon liberty is identical with that of the jury system,
which took its place.   So, again, in the matter of the

consent to taxation. The practice, in its later form, is not referred to in Magna Carta, either in the matter of the consent or of the taxation. The reference is again to feudal law, to the recognized right of the vassal to give his consent to any extraordinary "aid," that is, to any aid besides the three regular ones specified in the charter, before he could legally be compelled to pay it. But here again the principle is involved, and later ideas extended Magna Carta to cover the new practice. In regard to the other three points relating to the administration of justice, the original meaning of the Great Charter is more closely in harmony with the later ideas, though put in a more special and narrower way. In general, Magna Carta holds rightly the great place which is given it in the history of civil liberty. It gave a solemn sanction and a definite statement, to which appeal could ever afterwards be made, to certain most fundamental principles of liberty, much wider in their application than its framers knew, and by establishing the principle that there is a body of law by which the king is bound and which he may be forced to keep, it gave direction towards the securing of national rights to nearly every subsequent case of insurrection against the sovereign in English history.

It is not necessary for us to follow step by step the familiar historical events which were associated with the growth of the English constitution. It will answer our purpose if we can obtain an idea of the amount of progress which had been made by the close of the middle ages in the work of transforming the monarchy of William the Conqueror into the virtual republic of to-day, and of the institutional forms in which the results had been embodied.

The English constitution at the close of the middle ages, as at the present time, comprised two distinct kinds of institutions, each essential in its way to the general result. First were institutions of a negative character, intended to protect the individual from the arbitrary displeasure of the executive. Such were the jury, the principle of the habeas corpus, and the statutory definitions of treason. The second were institutions which may be called positive in character, whose object was to give to the representatives of the nation some power to check the public actions of the king and some share in the operations of the government. Examples of these are, impeachment and the principle that the consent of the House of Commons is necessary to the validity of a statute. National consent to taxation is a matter that lies midway between the two and partakes of the nature of both. Demanded at first as a protection of the individual against the executive, and always serving that end, it became also the most effective means of increasing the share of the nation in the control of public affairs. Certainly civil liberty could not exist at all without the institutions of the first class, as a little study of contemporary Russia will make clear, nor could any great progress be made towards a republican constitution without those of the second.

As occupying a midway position between the two kinds of institutions mentioned above, the right of self-taxation is first to be considered. The most obstinate and long-continued struggle, also, of this period of English history was over this right, and Englishmen in all parts of the world have always considered it the most fundamental principle of their constitution. If the executive can provide a large enough revenue to meet his needs, independently of the nation, he is independent in everything else, and can do what he pleases. This struggle, when looked at as a whole, may have the appearance of a succession of special cases rather than of the following of a definite purpose, but the cases are as decisive in the current of historical events as the principle is in the constitution, and both sides saw what was involved clearly enough to make the contest obstinate and protracted.

At the time of Magna Carta, taxation had just entered the transition period between the feudal methods of aids and tallages, and the more regular methods of modern times. Into the history of this transition we cannot enter, the essential fact is that the principle of consent was an extension to a more general tax of the feudal principle, that the consent of the vassal must be obtained to an extraordinary aid. The feudal relation was a contract with definite specifications. Neither party to the contract had any right to enlarge those specifications to his advantage without the consent of the other, and the point was carefully guarded wherever possible in a matter of such importance in feudal days as the payment of money. When national taxation began to be possible, towards the close of the feudal age, its introduction was rendered easier by the application to it of this feudal principle; indeed that was the only natural thing to do, and such an application of it was by no means peculiar to England. As feudal taxation anywhere broadened into modern taxation, the principle of consent tended to broaden with it. That which was peculiar to England was that the early establishment of the principle made it the great weapon in the hands of the acting force of the nation to compel the sovereign to grant almost everything else.

It was the financial necessities of John's son, Henry III, which forced him to submit to the plan of government embodied by the barons in the Provisions of Oxford, in 1258. This was a plan for the conduct of affairs by committees of Parliament, which was a peculiar foreshadowing of the present English system, though not a direct ancestor of it, but which was fortunately premature; fortunately because no middle class of large political influence had at that time been formed, and government by committees of Parliament, if successfully established, would have ended in a narrow oligarchy. The attempt of the king to free himself from this control led to the famous struggle with Simon de Montfort, and to the Parliament of 1265, in which representatives from the boroughs made their appearance for the first time with the knights of the shire, who had begun to represent the counties in Parliament a few years earlier. The military victory of the king over the barons was complete, but it was followed by a formal recognition on his part of those points among their demands which did not involve an immediate limitation of the king's freedom of action.

Thirty years later there was another contest between the king, now Edward I, and the barons, certainly as factious on the part of the latter as any in the series, but involving the question of taxation, and closed by a new and full agreement by the king to observe the provisions of the Great Charter. The agreement not to tax without consent was now so explicitly made by the king, there had been so many precedents established of taxation by expressed consent that the principle may be said to be finally accepted by the close of the reign of Edward I, that only those taxes were legal which had been granted by the nation. Hereafter the sovereign might attempt to escape by some form of evasion from the limitation placed upon him, but when brought face to face with the question he necessarily admitted the principle.

Hardly had this point been gained when Parliament advanced another step, almost as important, in the historical sequence. In 1309 they voted a tax for the benefit of King Edward II, on the condition that certain abuses, which they specified, should be reformed, and the king was obliged to consent. This precedent was not followed for a generation, but the long war with France, which began about 1340, made the sovereign more dependent than ever upon the grants of Parliament and the practice of attaching conditions to votes of money began in earnest.[1] Edward III was compelled to acknowledge the illegality of various forms of taxation by which the principle of consent had been evaded, or for which, in earlier times, it had not been necessary. Under Richard II the Parliament began to ask how the money granted had been used, and to specify the purposes to which it should be applied. Henry IV, the first Lancastrian, held the throne by a Parliamentary title, and he allowed, if he did not always definitely recognize, the right of Parliament to attach conditions to votes of taxes, to require the redress of abuses before the taxes were voted, to direct the general use to be made of the money, and to require an account of it, and these points were still further secured before the end of the century. With the definite establishment of these rights the control of Parliament over taxation was complete. It was not yet complete beyond the possibility of question or evasion. It had still to pass through the Stuart period before that point was reached. But in the legal recognition of all the principles involved it was complete before the accession of the House of Tudor.

The increasing power of Parliament over taxation is only one form of its increasing power in the general gov-

[1] The French possessions of the English were of great assistance to the growth of liberty from the fact that they involved the sovereigns in affairs on the Continent which seemed to them of as great, and sometimes of greater, importance than those of their English kingdom, while the nation, and even the great barons of Norman origin, had but little interest in them. The baron was ready to refuse all aid to the king unless satisfied upon the point especially near to him, his rights at home; the king was ready to compromise on the demands of the barons if he could get their help in France. The French possessions were lost when they had ceased to be of use in domestic politics, and when the growth of international rivalries would have made a continental position of great disadvantage to the cause of the English people.

ernment of the country, and leads us directly to a consideration of the share of the nation in the control of public affairs at the beginning of modern history. The primary fact in this direction, upon which nearly all the rest was founded, was the composition of the House of Commons. This was determined by a fact which distinguishes the England of the later middle ages from all other European countries—the existence of a land owning middle class, of a class the great majority of whom would have ranked with the nobles in any continental state, and would have insisted upon their rank and privileges with especial strictness, but who, in England, found themselves more nearly allied in interests and desires with the Third Estate than with the great barons. This union was due to a variety of causes, prominent among which was the county organization, in which it had long existed. It was the county organization, also, which very possibly suggested the principle and the method of representation, the representation first of the counties by the knights of the shire, and then of the boroughs in 1265. The composition of Parliament in these respects was finally fixed by the "model Parliament" of 1295, in which the representatives of the towns appeared, constitutionally summoned now by the king, not by a revolutionary leader. The great result which followed from the union of the knights with the burgesses was that no Third Estate existed in England in the same sense as in the other countries of the time. The House of Commons could easily represent not a class but the nation, and this was increasingly the case as time went on. This union in the Commons was rendered easier and more complete by the fact, peculiar also to England, that all the members of a noble family, except the one actually holding the title, came to be in law commoners and early joined the House of Commons. The fact also that the clergy as a body withdrew from Parliament, some members of the order only attending the House of Lords in their capacity as barons, should not be overlooked. The alliance of the English nobility with the Commons in the struggle for liberty was determined not merely by the fact that the barons were so placed that they needed allies against the king, but also by the fact that the English Commons was a far more influential and powerful body than any contemporary Third Estate.

As Parliament increased its power there increased also, step by step, the weight and authority of the House of Commons. That process, which is so marked a feature of English history in modern times, by which the House of Commons has gradually drawn into its hands the whole government of the country, begins within less than a century after the model Parliament, almost immediately, in fact, after the definite separation of the lower house as a distinct body, before the middle of the fourteenth century, and it was clearly on the road to completion before the events of the Tudor and Stuart reigns interrupted the regular development for a time.

By a series of precedents, beginning in the reign of Edward III, the Commons had secured the recognition of the principle that their consent was necessary to the validity of a law, and that no changes should be made in the wording of a law after its adoption by Parliament. Beginning from the same time, they had established their right to inquire into abuses in the administration of the public business, and to hold the king's ministers to trial and punishment for their misconduct by an impeachment conducted by themselves. The great principle necessarily involved in this, that, since the king can do no wrong, all misconduct in the administration must be due to his ministers, who can be brought to account and punished without civil war or revolution, was not put into any explicit shape, as a recognized constitutional doctrine, until the latter part of the Stuart period; but the foundation for it was laid in the reign of Richard II. Finally, it was a very important precedent which was made by Parliament, though without any very definite idea of its meaning, in the deposition of Edward II, in 1327. By the deposition of Richard II, in 1399, this precedent was made stronger, and the fundamental principle, by which alone a revolution of the sort can be justified, was made more evident. For the thing which made the nation turn against Richard II was not the wrongs which Henry of Lancaster had suffered, but the king's violent disregard of their constitutional liberties. The principle that the king must govern according to the laws, as a development of the fundamental idea of Magna Carta, was already fixed in public consciousness before the War of the Roses began.

The age of the Tudors, which followed, was, however, a time of great danger for popular government. The near remembrance of a long civil war, the weakening of the old nobility, the accession of a brilliant king with popular graces and a strong will, a revolution in one department of the public life, the church, which tended to increase the royal power, all things combined to make the danger serious that England would be turned into the path which the continental states were following, and the king become absolute. Had Henry VIII really cared for such a result, it is difficult to say what the outcome would have been. But the Parliamentary title of their house to the throne, together with the long experience of the kings in being held to the law, was probably more decisive than indifference or absorption in something else in keeping the Tudors in the main faithful to the forms of law, notwithstanding their practical despotism. When another family succeeded to the throne, with less hold upon the nation, the complementary principle was made a part of the constitution, more clearly and consciously than before, though not without a strong party against it, that, if the king will not obey the law, the penalty is the loss of the throne. The sovereign has never since denied that he holds his place by the will of the people. The revolutions of the seventeenth century had for their result, indeed, but little if anything more than to render explicit, and beyond the possibility of further dispute, the points already established in principle before the accession of the Tudors. The growth of the English constitution in the two hundred years since 1688 seems rapid and large as compared with the four centuries from William I to Henry VII; but in reality, except in one point, the growth of democracy, the progress of the past two centuries has consisted in devising machinery for applying the principles gained by 1485 and finally fixed by the failure of the Stuarts to overthrow them, to more and more of the details of the government, as in the formation of the cabinet, for example, and in the control by the ministry of the nation's foreign policy.

For the protection of the individual the institution which was most nearly in its present form at the close of the middle ages was the jury, though the especially famous cases of its use against the executive were still to occur. The primitive institution, out of which the jury grew, was brought into England by the Normans, who had themselves derived it from the Franks. In its early form the jury was a body of men chosen from among those who were supposed to have a personal knowledge of the matter, to whom was submitted, under oath, the question as to the facts in any case which might arise in administrative or executive matters, the assessment of taxes, for example, or of fines, as in clause twenty of Magna Carta. This practice came into use in the king's courts, as distinguished from the county courts, for the settlement of disputes concerning the possession and ownership of lands, and was recognized in the laws under Henry II. From this time the development of the institution was rapid, more slow in criminal than in civil cases, and the jury gradually advanced from depending upon their own knowledge of the facts concerned to taking into account evidence submitted to them. The jury system secures two points which are of great value for individual liberty. The first is the right of the citizens themselves to decide the guilt or innocence of the accused, in view, if the case seems to demand it, of general considerations rather than of the special evidence.[1] This is a right of the utmost importance in the trial of political offenders, on charges either of technical violation of existing laws or of constructive or pretended offences. The second is the fact that, by the use of the jury, the judge occupies a position of impartiality in a criminal trial, as, in a sort, an umpire between the parties, and is not directly interested in ascertaining the facts, as in the French criminal practice, for instance, where the judge is almost a legalized inquisitor, and the accused is subjected to a judicial examination, which, however carefully it may be guarded, seems to the Anglo-Saxon mind a serious evil.[2] Neither

---

[1] Interesting instances of the application of this principle are to be found in recent American experience, in cases where juries have acquitted persons brought to trial for the violation of local liquor laws, against the most conclusive and notorious evidence because the laws did not have the sanction of the community.

So thoroughly established does our civil liberty seem to us, so little do we fear any encroachment upon it by the executive, that the popular consciousness has almost lost sight of the fact that the jury system is one of the most important institutions by which our liberty is secured. The advocates who arise periodically in favor of its abolition, because of the abuses to which it has lent itself in the enforcement of the laws, seem rarely to have any knowledge of its history. Indeed, it must be admitted that against what may be the danger of the future, the tyranny of a democracy, the jury is anything but a protection.

[2] In America we seem to be in some danger of destroying unconsciously this safeguard of liberty in the growing use of what is called the police "third degree." In this thoroughly un-Anglo-Saxon examination of suspected persons, not merely policemen but elected officers of the courts have sometimes taken part, and processes have been said to be used which at least border closely upon torture.

of these points was clearly fixed in the English practice at the close of the middle ages. The beginning had been made in the definite organization of the jury system, of which these were to be the necessary conclusions, but it was reserved for later times to draw them clearly. In fact, the independence of the judge, from executive interference, as well as his independence in the process of trial, was the most important specific element of Anglo-Saxon liberty not distinctly foreshadowed in medieval times.

Other rights of individual liberty, secured by 1485, cannot be better stated than in the words of Hallam, at the beginning of his *Constitutional History*. He says: "No man could be committed to prison but by a legal warrant specifying his offence; and by a usage nearly tantamount to constitutional right, he must be speedily brought to trial by means of regular sessions of gaol-delivery. The fact of guilt or innocence, on a criminal charge, was determined in a public court, and in the county where the offence was alleged to have occurred, by a jury of twelve men, from whose unanimous verdict no appeal could be made. Civil rights, so far as they depended on questions of fact, were subject to the same decision. The officers and servants of the crown, violating the personal liberty or other right of the subject, might be sued in an action for damages to be assessed by a jury, or, in some cases, were liable to criminal process; nor could they plead any warrant or command in their justification, nor even the direct order of the king."

To this should be added the fact that by a law of Edward III, in 1352, the judicial punishment of treason had been limited to certain definitely specified cases, a safeguard for the individual of as great importance against a democracy as against a monarchy. The English law has not greatly improved upon this ancient statute, but the American has gone much further in the same direction in the clause of the Constitution on the subject which marks out very strict limitations both of definition and of trial.

England was by no means a republic at the close of the fifteenth century. Much had yet to be done before that end was reached, but the work of converting it into a republic was well under way, and, as compared with any of the other states of the time, of equal size or promise, it entirely justifies the remark of Philip de Comines, cited in the last chapter,[1] or the words of Sir John Fortescue, written under Henry VI, and so often quoted: "A king of England cannot, at his pleasure, make any alterations in the laws of the land. . . . He is appointed to protect his subjects in their lives, properties, and laws; for this very end and purpose he has the delegation of power from the people, and he has no just claim to any other power but this."

With the close of the Hohenstaufen period in German history the power of the central government had almost totally disappeared, and the complete sovereignty and independence of the feudal subdivisions of the state were practically established if not legally recognized. The period of twenty years which followed, known as the Great Interregnum, during which there was only the merest shadow of a general government—the nominal sovereignty in the hands of foreigners, who, if they visited Germany at all, did so only for parade, and every local ruler laying his hands upon what he pleased that was within his reach—completed the process of dissolution, if it needed completion.

The policy which the electors definitely adopted, and continued in operation through the age which follows the Interregnum, is equivalent to an official declaration that this dissolution was complete. In electing an emperor

[1] See p. 329, *note*.

they selected, so far as possible, a candidate from a family having but scanty resources and small power of its own, and they changed from one family to another as often as circumstances would permit. Rudolf of Hapsburg, Adolf of Nassau, Henry of Luxemburg, and Lewis of Bavaria are all examples of this policy. It was manifestly the result of a united judgment on the part of the electors, almost formally expressed, that if a real national government was ever to be reconstructed, and a centralization established like that which was forming in France, it must be done by the independent family resources of the emperor. It could not be done, in their judgment, by the use of the sovereign rights and prerogatives which remained to the imperial office. The emperor's power as sovereign, in its actual condition, was not to be feared; the only source of danger to their position was the fact that his personal power might be great enough to lead him to try to recover the rights of government which had been lost. This policy the electors followed in general to the end of the middle ages, and they finally allowed the imperial succession to settle quietly in the Hapsburg family only when it had become manifest to all the world that it was nothing more than an empty title.

The policy which the emperors on their side adopted was an equally emphatic declaration of the same fact. Not a single one of them, during the whole period, made any serious attempt to reconstruct the central government, but every family, without exception, that gained possession of the imperial office, attempted to make all that it could out of the opportunities of the position to enlarge its own possessions and to increase its family power. Some met with greater and others with less success; but all—Hapsburg and Nassau, Wittelsbach and Luxemburg—were governed by the same rules of conduct. It was in effect a unanimous agreement on the part of the emperors that centralization was no

longer possible, that there was no use in trying to form a
national government of the German people, but that the
only successful use to which the imperial position could
be put was to make their own local state as large and as
strong as possible.

The two families most successful in this policy were
those of Hapsburg and of Luxemburg. Rudolf of Hapsburg, the first emperor chosen after the Interregnum, was
a count whose scanty possessions lay in western Switzerland and Alsace. He was a man of vigorous character,
but one in no way distinguished in power or possessions
from a hundred others in the Germany of that day who
remained unheard of in history. The fortunate fact that
he was able to break up the threatening Slavic kingdom, which was ruled over by Ottokar II, king of Bohemia, enabled him to bestow the south German duchies,
Austria and Styria, which had been Ottokar's, upon his
son, and to lay the foundations of the future greatness of
his house. The electors did not allow the crown to continue during the next generation in Rudolf's family, but
later other Hapsburg emperors followed, and were able
to continue his policy.

An equally fortunate chance occurred during the reign
of the first Luxemburg emperor, Henry VII, in the opportunity presented him to marry his son John to the
heiress of the Bohemian crown. John's son, the Emperor Charles IV, succeeded in gaining possession also
of Brandenburg, which the Emperor Lewis IV of Bavaria, who followed Henry VII, had tried to secure for
his family. The last emperor of the Luxemburg house,
Sigismund, abandoned Brandenburg but obtained the
kingdom of Hungary. He was the last of the male line
of his family, however, and the great possessions which
they had brought together passed with his daughter to
the Hapsburgs, so that the acquisitions made by the two
families who had most successfully followed the policy
of getting all that they could for themselves from the

imperial office were finally united in the hands of the Hapsburgs alone.

It was during the Luxemburg period that Brandenburg passed into the hands of the Hohenzollerns, who have erected modern Prussia upon it as the foundation. At the beginning of the thirteenth century the Hohenzollerns were, like the Hapsburgs, merely local counts in Switzerland, giving no promise of future greatness. Early in that century the elder line obtained the office of *Burggraf* of Nuremberg and an opportunity to grow rich, which was improved with the hereditary thriftiness of the family, and fortunate marriages and purchases increased their possessions and influence in southern Germany. Finally, in 1411, the Emperor Sigismund, in need of money and unable to establish a sound government in the troubled and disordered electorate of Brandenburg, gave it into the hands of Frederick of Nuremberg as pledge for a loan, and a few years later sold it to him outright. Around this as a beginning the later Hohenzollern electors and kings collected, piece by piece, the modern Prussia.

Many other small states were forming in the same way in Germany at this time, many that have not survived the political storms of modern history, and some that have continued to grow larger and stronger, or at least that have made good their place in the present federal empire of Germany. Within many of these states the course of history was very similar to that in France. A group of feudally independent territories was united under a single ruler, and by degrees the barriers which separated them were broken down and they were centralized in a common government, and in this process such elements of local liberty as had remained were destroyed and the government became an absolutism.[1] This process was

---

[1] The dramatic struggle of Franz von Sickingen against the princes of the Upper Rhine valley, in 1523, is an instance of the desperate attempt of the smaller independent nobles to maintain their position against the absorbing tendency of these little states.

one, however, which occurred in most cases, and the larger part of it in modern history rather than in medieval.

In Italy, as in Germany, the nation was able to form
no government.   In both cases, as we have seen, the Holy
Roman Empire was at fault.   In Italy it was a foreign
power which prevented the rise of any native state to a
sufficient strength to absorb the whole peninsula.   To
the influence of the empire must be added that of the
papacy as an equally responsible cause—as the one most
responsible in the last centuries of the middle ages, after
the empire had practically disappeared, and in modern
times.   The position of the pope, as sovereign of a little
state in central Italy, had forced him, as a matter of self-
defence, to use all possible means to prevent the rise of
any threatening power in Italy from the days of the Lombards down—down, indeed, to Victor Emmanuel.   When
such a power appeared to be forming the papacy would
strive to form combinations against it until its strength
was reduced below the danger-point, and if in the process
one of the pope's own allies gained too much strength,
new combinations were immediately set on foot against
the new danger.

No government for the nation was able to be formed,
but an immense variety of local governments arose, and
a most intricate entanglement of interstate politics.   In
the south, Naples was an absolute monarchy.   The States
of the Church were an ecclesiastical monarchy, very
loosely organized during most of the middle ages, but
brought into order and centralized by the political genius
of Julius II at the beginning of the sixteenth century.
Florence presents us an interesting case.   Originally a
republic, with a tendency towards democracy, it passed
under the power of a family of rich bankers, the Medici,
who, without holding any office and without destroying
the forms of the republic, filled all the offices with their

nominees and determined every public act exactly as does an American "boss" when his party is in power.[1] In the sixteenth century the state became an avowed monarchy under the Medici as grand dukes. Milan was a republic turned into a monarchy by military force, and Venice a republic which had become a very close oligarchy.

But if a national government was not formed, a national consciousness was, as in Germany, and it was given clear expression now and then. Its most remarkable product was Machiavelli's *Prince*, written, beyond a reasonable doubt, to show how, in the evil circumstances then existing, a national government might be created.

The rapid rise of Spain to a position of first rank among the nations was one of the most important political facts of the close of the middle ages. This was due to two causes: to the union of the two largest kingdoms of the peninsula by the marriage of Ferdinand and Isabella, and to the political skill of Ferdinand. Disunion among the various provinces, feudal anarchy, local independence, and a weak central government were the characteristics of Spain when he began to reign. Within a few years order was secured, the baronage reduced to obedience, the process of breaking down the securities of local independence and the old institutions of liberty well begun, the monarchy made practically an absolutism, if not in every respect legally so as yet, and, although the old provincial lines and provincial jealousies could not be entirely

---

[1] At the moment of writing, in 1893, the newspapers were saying that the speaker of the New York Assembly had stated publicly that "all legislation of the last session came from Tammany Hall, and was dictated by that great statesman, Richard Croker," the "boss" of New York City. See the New York *Nation*, vol. LVI, p. 304, which added: "Nothing that Croker desired to pass failed of passage, and nothing that he objected to was able to get even a hearing." This was exactly the position of the early Medici. Cases of the sort have not entirely disappeared from the United States since 1893.

obliterated, they were thrown into the background by the coming up of new and more national interests. It was chance rather than skill which added America to the resources of the Spanish monarchy, but it formed no inconsiderable element in the rapid rise of the new state. In all else, the internal consolidation, the conquest of Granada and Navarre, the footing gained in Italy, the judgment in regard to the policy of France, and the allies which were secured, the political skill of Ferdinand must be admitted, however disastrous his policy was to prove in other hands and in conditions which no genius could forecast.

Ferdinand was, of all the sovereigns of his day, the one who saw most clearly that, in political affairs, the middle ages had passed away and a new age begun. He could hardly have stated his opinion in these words, but he realized that the settlement of the domestic problems which he had so well in hand left the state at liberty to secure advantages for itself in Europe at large, and that the near rivalry of other European states for these advantages made it the part of wisdom to be beforehand with them, and to get a footing and allies wherever possible. The first links in the chain of modern international politics were forged by Ferdinand. It was the settlement of these domestic problems in all the states, or their settlement to such an extent that they were no longer the most pressing necessities of the moment, which brings the middle ages to an end politically, and leads to the beginning of that most characteristic feature of modern history—international diplomacy.

CHAPTER XV

THE RENAISSANCE

WE have now traced, as resulting from the influence imparted by the crusades, great economic and political revolutions which changed the face of history, and brought the middle ages to a close so far as their influence reached. These two revolutions were hardly more than well under way when there began another, growing largely out of the conditions which they were producing, starting partly from the same general impulse which aided them, a revolution of even greater importance than they in its influence upon the characteristic features of our own time, if it is possible to measure the relative values of such movements—that intellectual and scientific transformation of Europe which we call the Revival of Learning, or the Renaissance.

Each of these names expresses a great fact which was characteristic of the movement and which it is well to distinguish, the one from the other.

There was a revival of learning. The conditions which prevailed in the earlier middle ages, and obscured the learning which the ancients had acquired, were changing rapidly, the effects of the Teutonic invasion were passing away. Conquerors and conquered had grown into a single people, and the descendants of the original Germans had reached the point where they could comprehend the highest results of the ancient civilization. · New national languages had been formed, and literatures had begun, no longer ecclesiastical in authorship or theme but close to daily life. The stir of great events, and the contagion of new ideas in commerce and exploration and politics filled the air, and the horizon of men's minds and interests was daily growing wider. It was impossible that many generations of these economic and political changes should go by before men began to realize that there lay behind them a most significant history, and that the men of the past had many things to teach them. When men became conscious of this the revival of learning began.

But there was more than a revival of learning—more than a recovery of what the ancient world had known and the medieval forgotten. There was also a renaissance, a re-birth of emotions and of faculties long dormant, an awakening of man to a new consciousness of life and of the world in which he lives, and of the problems which life and the world present for the thinking mind to solve, and to a consciousness also of the power of the mind to deal with these problems and to investigate the secrets of nature.

This intellectual movement was, then, in the first place, a recovery of the learning and literature of the ancient world.

Classical literature had never passed into absolute eclipse even in the darkest days. The German states which took the place of the empire would have been glad to preserve and continue the Roman system of public schools, which extended through the provinces, if they had known how to do so. But they did not. They were themselves still too crude and backward to be able to take hold of the old educational system as a rescuing power, and to save it from the decline which had already begun, nor could they infuse new life and vigor into the dying classical literature. On the other hand, the old lacked all independent power of growth and did not have force enough to master the Germans and raise them rapidly to its own level. The disorderly and rapidly shifting po-

litical conditions of the fifth and sixth centuries did not
a little also to destroy the schools, and the attitude of
the church toward them, if not directly hostile, was dis-
couraging.

As a result, the state schools disappeared; a really
educated class no longer existed; the knowledge of Greek,
which had been very common throughout the West, was
entirely lost—St. Augustine, at the beginning of the fifth
century, could use it only with difficulty; and, as an immediate result of the conquest, the ability to use the
Latin language correctly also threatened to disappear.
The sixth and seventh centuries represent probably the
lowest point reached in the intellectual decline of the
middle ages, though the actual improvement upon them
which was made before the eleventh century was not very
great.

The place of the state schools was taken in the new
kingdoms by church schools. The course of study in the
Roman schools had been a narrow one, as we should
regard it, its object being chiefly to fit for public life and
oratory. The church schools were still more narrow—
not in the nominal course of study which followed the
classical—the *trivium*, grammar, rhetoric, and dialectics,
and the *quadrivium*, arithmetic, geometry, astronomy, and
music—but in the meagre contents of these studies and
in the practical object, to fit the pupils as priests to read
the service of the church, not always to understand it.

The first improvement in these schools came in the age
of Alcuin, under Charlemagne, as has already been related.
This was a revival of schools rather than of learning, but
it brought about an improvement in the writing of Latin,
and it was broad enough to have led in a short time to
a very decided advance, if the political and social condition had continued to make this possible. Mind was energetic and vigorous enough. There was no lack of ability. The ecclesiastical literature of the time, both the

imaginative and the legal, makes that evident. But if there was ability there was also the greatest ignorance. The historical mistakes are of the baldest, the science the most absurd, broad and general conceptions are wholly lacking. The literature reveals at once the great activity of mind and the narrow conditions of the age.

In the following centuries, here and there, slight improvements were made. The school of Rheims under Gerbert in the tenth century, the school of Chartres under Bernard in the twelfth century, are remarkable instances, but circumscribed, like all else of the time, in their influence. Some additions of importance were made to the stock of knowledge—some books of Euclid, some treatises of Aristotle. Impulses from without began to be received; some very slight Byzantine influence, perhaps under the Ottos of Germany; more important the influence from the Arabian civilization of south Europe, though this is extremely difficult to trace with any certainty in its beginnings; more effectual still, among new influences, the general awakening, and the gradual transformation of all external conditions which followed the crusades.

The first effect of these changes and of these new impulses was that the mind of Europe began to be aroused, began to have some dim idea of the work which it might do, and became eager to learn and to produce. But it still did not know. It did not have the materials of knowledge. The work of the ancients was still a sealed book to it, and it had no conception of the investigation of nature. In consequence it went to work with the greatest activity and earnestness on the materials which it did have, the dogmatic theology of the church, certain scanty principles of the Greek philosophy, and the truths which it could derive from reason, and out of these materials by purely speculative methods it built up widely comprehensive systems of thought, highly organized and scientific, so far as it was possible for them to be scientific, but one-sided and utterly barren for all the chief interests of modern life, and necessarily so because of the limitations of their material and of their method.[1]

This system, scholasticism, was the first movement of the age of the Renaissance, its prediction and its introduction. It originated under the influence of the causes which led to the Renaissance, but of these causes when they were just beginning to act and only faintly felt. It displayed the same characteristics of mind as the later age, but these while they were not yet emancipated from the control of other and thoroughly medieval characteristics. It gave most hopeful promise of what was to be, but the new spirit had as yet so little to build upon, and was so dwarfed and overshadowed by tradition and authority, that it could survive and display itself only as earnest and eager effort.

[1] Lord Bacon described the real nature of scholasticism in a passage which cannot be too often quoted in this connection. He says: "This kind of degenerate learning did chiefly reign among the schoolmen, who—having sharp and strong wits, and abundance of leisure, and small variety of reading, but their wits being shut up in the cells of a few authors (chiefly Aristotle their dictator), as their persons were shut up in the cells of monasteries and colleges, and knowing little history, either of nature or time—did, out of no great quantity of matter and infinite agitation of wit, spin out unto us those laborious webs of learning which are extant in their books. For the wit and mind of man, if it work upon matter, which is the contemplation of the creatures of God, worketh according to the stuff and is limited thereby; but if it work upon itself, as the spider worketh his web, then it is endless, and brings forth, indeed, cobwebs of learning, admirable for the fineness of thread and work, but of no substance or profit."—*Advancement of Learning*, IV, 5.

To hold up certain absurdities of scholasticism to ridicule, as has sometimes been done, as if they indicated the real character of the system, is to furnish good evidence of one's own narrowness of mind. Not merely did scholasticism make important contributions to one side of civilization—speculative theology and philosophy—but even its supposed absurdities had meaning. To debate the question whether an angel can pass from one point to another without passing through the intermediate space, is to debate the question whether pure being is conditioned by space. Very likely such a question cannot be answered, but if there is to be a system of speculative philosophy at all, it must consider such questions in some form, and they can hardly be called absurd.

The great age of active and creative scholasticism was the thirteenth century, one of the greatest intellectual ages of the world's history. It is impossible in a paragraph to give any conception of the intellectual stir, the mental eagerness and enthusiasm of that century, or even to catalogue its great names and their achievements. Two or three things must be noticed because they indicate in the clearest way how the results of the thirteenth century affected the later movement.

One of them is the pathetic story of Roger Bacon, a man who saw the danger of reliance upon authority, and proclaimed the methods of criticism and observation, and pointed out the way in which investigation should go, and the use which should be made of the new materials which had been gained, in a spirit almost modern and with such clearness of insight as should have led to the revival of learning as one of the immediate results of the thirteenth century. But he could get no one to hear him. The reign of authority and of deduction, the scholastic methods and the scholastic ideals, had become so firmly seated in their empire over men, under the influence of the great minds of that century, that no others seemed possible. His works passed out of the world's knowledge with no discoverable trace of influence until the Renaissance was fully under way, and then only the very slightest. The result of the century, in other words, was entirely opposed in nature and in method to a revival of real learning.

Another feature of the thirteenth century to be noticed was the founding of universities. Developed out of certain of the earlier schools, under the enthusiasm of the age for learning, by the introduction of new methods of teaching and of study, they spread rapidly throughout Europe, and seemed to promise most effective aid to intellectual advance. But in their case, as in Bacon's, scholasticism was too highly organized, its conceptions still too completely filled the whole mental horizon for the learned world to be able to turn in any other direction, and the universities fell completely under its control.[1] Even subjects of study which it would seem might lead to better things—the Roman law which, we should think, ought to have led to the study of history; and medicine, which ought to have suggested an idea of real science—became thoroughly scholastic, and held under heavy bonds to introduce nothing new.

The result, then, of the first or scholastic revival was the creation of a gigantic system of organized knowledge, in so far as there was knowledge, in which almost every conceivable idea had its place, and which exercised a most tyrannous sway over all mental activity, because it was so intimately bound up with an infallible system of theology which every mind was obliged to accept under peril of eternal penalties. Independent thinking in philosophy was heresy and a crime. When the Renaissance movement really began, with its new spirit and ideas and methods, it found the field wholly occupied by this great system, all the learned by profession were its devoted supporters, and the universities its home. The new spirit was compelled, therefore, to take its rise and to find its apostles outside the learned professions. The odds were against it, and it could restore true knowledge and scientific method only by severe struggle and a successful revolution.

The final outcome, then, of the thirteenth century was that scholasticism, however earnestly it may have desired such a result at the beginning, really introduced no revival of learning, but brought about an organization of knowledge and of education which was a decided obstacle to the revival when it came. This means, in other words,

[1] Chaucer almost makes "logic" synonymous with "university" in his description of the clerk of Oxenford, "that unto logik hadde longe i-go."— *Prologue*, l. 286.

that no revival could come until the questioning and criticising spirit which dimly showed itself in the formative age of scholasticism should awake again to a new activity and a better fate, and bring about a complete abandonment of the medieval point of view.

By the beginning of the fourteenth century the general conditions had come to be still more favorable for such an awakening than at the beginning of scholasticism. The economic and political progress of the thirteenth century had been very great, and the fourteenth century was a time of still more rapid change in these respects. An entirely new atmosphere was coming to prevail in the more advanced nations of Europe, new objects of interest, new standards of judgment, and new purposes to be realized. If these changes showed themselves first in the growth of national feelings and patriotism, in the rise of the lower orders and a higher regard for man as man, and in bolder commercial ventures and the exploration of unknown lands, it was barely first. We can trace their continuous expression and influence in thought and literature from a point almost as early.

And there needed to be added to these other changes which had already taken place only a change of the same sort in intellectual interests, showing itself as clearly in science and literature and art as in government and commerce, to complete the transformation of the medieval man into the modern. In the middle ages man as an individual had been held of very little account. He was only part of a great machine. He acted only through some corporation—the commune, the guild, the order. He had but little self-confidence, and very little consciousness of his ability single-handed to do great things or overcome great difficulties. Life was so hard and narrow that he had no sense of the joy of mere living, and no feeling for the beauty of the world around him, and, as if this world were not dark enough, the terrors of another

world beyond were very near and real. He lived with
no sense of the past behind him, and with no conception
of the possibilities of the future.

It is hardly necessary to say that the modern man,
who is a modern man, is the opposite of all this. We
are almost too completely a world of individuals. We
have a supreme self-confidence. Nearly any man of us
is ready to undertake any task with a firm confidence in
his ability to carry it through, and not very many of us
are shut out of a full enjoyment of the beauties of this
world by too keen a sense of the realities of another.
It was the work of the Renaissance to change the one
sort of man into the other; to awaken in man a consciousness of his powers and to give him confidence in himself;
to show him the beauty of the world and the joy of life;
and to make him feel his living connection with the past,
and the greatness of the future which he might create.

It needed but little of the successful work which men
were doing in those days in the fields of politics and of
commerce—the creation of states whether large or small,
and the accumulation of wealth—to arouse these feelings,
at least in their beginnings, and in a half-conscious way.
The impulse which intellectual progress received at this
point from the political and economic is clear—one of the
evident cases of the close dependence of the various lines
of advance upon one another already referred to. And
it is necessary in order to obtain any clear conception of
this age of transition to feel the intimate connection of all
these movements with one another, indeed their essential
unity as various sides of one great movement.

It was in Italy that this connection was first made
and this impulse first received. It was there that the
new commercial age had begun and had first produced
its results. Numerous large cities had been formed, possessed of great wealth and becoming very early little
independent states. Their fierce conflicts with one an-

other had thrown them upon their own resources, and called forth the greatest mental activity. Within their walls exciting and bitter party conflicts were a continuous stimulus to the individual citizen. A democratic tendency in most of them opened the hope of great successes to any man. Birth counted for next to nothing. Abilities and energy might win any place. Woman became the equal of man, and took part in public life with the same self-confidence. All the political and commercial activities of the time, with their great rewards open to any man, and their intense stimulus to individual ambition, combined to emancipate the individual, and to foster in him a belief in his own powers, and an independence of judgment and action, necessary as a preliminary to the revival of learning. The rapid development of Italy since the crusades, in the one direction, had prepared her to lead in the other, and this fact gives us the reason why the Renaissance was an Italian event.

It is in Dante that we find the first faint traces of the existence of these new forces in the intellectual world proper, and the beginning of their continuous modern action, and we may call Dante the first man of the Renaissance, though it is perhaps equally correct to call him a thoroughly medieval man. His theology and philosophy were medieval and scholastic, his hell was material enough, and the dream of his political thought was the Holy Roman Empire, a distinctly medieval idea. But along with these we catch gleams of other and different things. His theology may be medieval and his hell material, but there is an independence of judgment in special cases which is decidedly more modern, and, something far more important, there is the clearest possible conception of the fact that it is not a man's place in a great organization, but his individual character and spirit which determine his future destiny; that individual character not merely works itself out in the conduct of life, but that it will be a controlling factor in fixing one's place in any life hereafter. His political idea may be the Holy Roman Empire, but he reveals traces of the distinctly modern feeling that the state should exist for the sake of the individual, and that the individual should have some voice in the management of its affairs. The writing of his great poem in a modern language is no small evidence of independence. He has some feeling for the beauty of the world and of life, and some real sense of a living connection with the men of antiquity. These modern traits, however, though they may be found in Dante, are expressed but faintly. The great mass of his thought is medieval. It is only the slight beginnings of the current which we can detect in him.

But in the next generation, in Petrarch, we have the full tide. In him we clearly find, as controlling personal traits, all those specific features of the Renaissance which give it its distinguishing character as an intellectual revolution, and from their strong beginning in him they have never ceased among men. In the first place, he felt as no other man had done since the ancient days the beauty of nature and the pleasure of mere life, its sufficiency for itself; and he had also a sense of ability and power, and a self-confidence which led him to plan great things, and to hope for an immortality of fame in this world. In the second place, he had a most keen sense of the unity of past history, of the living bond of connection between himself and men of like sort in the ancient world. That world was for him no dead antiquity, but he lived and felt in it and with its poets and thinkers, as if they were his neighbors. His love for it amounted almost, if we may call it so, to an ecstatic enthusiasm, hardly understood by his own time, but it kindled in many others a similar feeling which has come down to us. The result is easily recognized in him as a genuine culture, the first of modern men in whom this can be found.

It led, also, in his case, to what is another characteristic feature of the Renaissance—an intense desire to get possession of all the writings which the ancient world had produced. It was of vital importance, before any new work was begun, that the modern world should know what the ancients had accomplished, and be able to begin where they had left off. This preliminary work of collection was one of the most important services rendered by the men of the revival of learning. For the writings of the classical authors Petrarch sought with the utmost eagerness wherever he had an opportunity, and though the actual number which he was able to find, of those that had not been known to some one or other in medieval days, was small, still his collection was a large one for a single man to make, and he began that active search for the classics which was to produce such great results in the next hundred years.

In another direction, also, Petrarch opened the age of the Renaissance. The great scientific advance which was made by this age over the middle ages does not consist so much in any actual discoveries or new contributions to knowledge which were made by it, as in the overthrow of authority as a final appeal, and the recovery of criticism and observation and comparison as the effective methods of work. Far more important was this restoration of the true method of science than any specific scientific work which was done in the Renaissance age proper. Here again it is with Petrarch that the modern began. He attacked more than one old tradition and belief supported by authority with the new weapons of criticism and comparison, and in one case at least, in his investigation of the genuineness of charters purporting to have been granted by Julius Cæsar and Nero to Austria, he showed himself thoroughly imbued with the spirit and master of the methods of modern science.

Finally, Petrarch first put the modern spirit into conscious opposition to the medieval. The Renaissance meant rebellion and revolution. It meant a long and bitter struggle against the whole scholastic system, and all the follies and superstitions which flourished under its protection. Petrarch opened the attack along the whole line. Physicians, lawyers, astrologers, scholastic philosophers, the universities—all were enemies of the new learning, and so his enemies. And these attacks were not in set and formal polemics alone, his letters and almost all his writings were filled with them.[1] It was the business of his life. He knew almost nothing of Plato, and yet he set him up boldly against the almost infallible Aristotle. He called the universities "nests of gloomy ignorance," and ridiculed their degrees. He says: "The youth ascends the platform mumbling nobody knows what. The elders applaud, the bells ring, the trumpets blare, the degree is conferred, and he descends a wise man who went up a fool."[2]

In the world of the new literature Petrarch obtained so great glory in his own lifetime, and exercised such a dictatorship that the ideas which he represented obtained an influence and extension which they might not otherwise have gained so rapidly. When he died, in 1374, the Renaissance was fully under way in Italy as a general movement, and, while in his own lifetime there is hardly another who is to be placed beside him in scholarship and knowledge of antiquity, there soon were many such, and before very long not a few who greatly surpassed him in these respects. But if his scholarship cannot be considered great according to modern standards, it will always remain his imperishable glory to have inaugurated the revival of learning.[3]

[1] Voigt, *Die Wiederbelebung des Classischen Alterthums*, vol. I, p. 72, third ed.

[2] Mullinger, *University of Cambridge*, vol. I, p. 382, note 2.

[3] Voigt, one of the soundest and most careful of all students of Renaissance history, says that Petrarch's name shines as a star of the first magni-

The next age immediately following Petrarch had for its great work the revival of Greek literature and knowledge, taught by Greeks from Constantinople. It continued, also, the work of collecting and carefully studying the writings of the ancients. Before the middle of the fifteenth century the material in hand, both of the Latin and of the Greek classics, was large enough and well enough understood to form the foundation of a real scholarship which still commands respect.

One generation later still, and a scholar, in the modern sense, appeared, Laurentius Valla. There are many things now perfectly familiar which he did not know; he had all the pride and insolence and hardly disguised pagan feeling and morals of the typical humanist; but in spirit and methods of work he was a genuine scholar, and his editions lie at the foundation of all later editorial work in the case of more than one classical author, and of the critical study of the New Testament as well. One piece of work which fell to him made more noise at the time than these, and in it the scholar had an opportunity to contribute directly to the political movements of his age. At the request of King Alfonso of Naples he subjected the so-called Donation of Constantine to the tests of the new criticism and showed its historical impossibility to the conviction of the world, thus depriving the papacy of one source of argument in support of its pretensions.

Valla was still living when the invention of the printing-press in the north put a new weapon into the hands of the humanists, and enabled them to bring the results of their labors to bear upon a vastly wider circle than before. The great results of this invention for civilization are to be found, not so much in the preservation as in the

tude in the literary and intellectual history of the world, and would not be less if he had never written a verse in the Tuscan language.—*Die Wiederbelebung des Classischen Alterthums*, I, p. 22.

cheapening of books, and the popularizing of the means of knowledge. If the printing-press reduced the price of books to one-fifth the former price, as it seems to have done before it had been in operation very long, it much more than multiplied by five the number of persons who could own and use them. Although the spread of printing throughout Europe was slow as compared with the rate of modern times—an invention of similar importance to-day would probably get into use in the principal places of the world within a year or two—it was rapid for the middle ages. Invented, apparently, in a shape at least to be called really printing, about 1450, it was introduced into Italy in 1465, possibly slightly earlier; into France and Switzerland in 1470, into Holland and Belgium in 1473, into Spain in 1474, and into England between 1474 and 1477. By 1500 it was in use in eighteen countries, and at least two hundred and thirty-six places had printing-presses. Venice alone had more than two hundred, and three thousand editions had been printed there.

One immediate consequence of this invention was that the results of the revival of learning, its new spirit of independence, and its methods of criticism, could no longer be confined to one country or to those who were by calling scholars. They spread rapidly throughout Europe, affected large masses of the people who knew nothing of the classics, and became vital forces in that final revolution of which Luther's work forms a part.

Down to nearly the end of the fifteenth century the humanistic movement had been confined almost wholly to Italy. The names and achievements which could be claimed by any other country were very few. But as the century drew to a close such names became more numerous out of Italy, and the movement passed to Europe at large.

Among the northern nations the Renaissance not merely aroused the same enthusiasm for antiquity and the same eager application, in various directions, of the new methods of study, but it also took on among them a far more earnest and practical character than it ever had in Italy. Investigation and learning ceased to be so entirely ends in themselves or means to secure personal glory, but were put to the service of answering practical questions and meeting popular needs. The most eminent representative of this tendency, and the greatest scholar of the Renaissance age proper, was Erasmus.

Given by the circumstances of his childhood an opportunity to devote himself to study from an early age, Erasmus, earnest and eager, and of extraordinary ability, made remarkable use of the scanty means of learning at his command in the monastery in which he was placed. A little later, at the University of Paris, in spite of poverty, and ill health, and other discouragements, his progress was still more rapid. In these early stages of his education Laurentius Valla seems to have had more influence over him than any one else, especially in training his judgment in respect to a correct style, a training which may have been the birth, perhaps, of a larger critical sense. At the age of thirty he went over to England to study Greek at Oxford, and there he came under the influence of two remarkable men, John Colet and Thomas More, and, if we may trust our scanty evidence, this influence was of great importance in the development of his character and purposes, especially the influence of Colet.[1]

Colet had gone to Italy for study while Erasmus was at Paris, and while there, apparently, an earnest religious purpose was awakened in his mind by some influence

[1] It is characteristic of Mr. Seebohm's very stimulating work in history, like that of M. Fustel de Coulanges in France, that it presents very clearly and completely the line of connection between the earlier and the later stages of a given movement. Meantime, the evidence is often slight, and while opposing evidence may be wholly wanting, one cannot escape the feeling that the conclusions are sometimes due to keenness of historic in-

under which he came, possibly by the spiritualistic philosophy of Pico della Mirandola, then but recently dead, perhaps by some other of the Platonic influences of that age, more likely by the strong outburst of religious and ethical emotion in Florence under the influence of Savonarola. We know so little of Colet's stay in Italy that we can affirm nothing about it with confidence, and it is quite as probable that the deeply earnest purpose which he displayed in his work on his return was natural to him, strengthened perhaps by Italian influences, possibly as much by a repugnance to what he saw there as by anything directly helpful.

Upon his return to England Colet began to lecture upon the New Testament, with a distinctly practical purpose. He sought, for example, to reproduce the thought of Paul as Paul held it, to gain an understanding of it by considering the circumstances in which it was written, and of those to whom it was written; in other words, to treat it as a living argument, with a definite historical purpose, and so to make clear what Paul sought to teach. This was the application of the spirit and the methods of the Renaissance to the living reconstruction of a past age. It was treating the New Testament as a historical document, not as a collection of scholastic propositions. And this was done not for purposes of mere scholarship, but in order to learn what that age had to give in the way of instruction and help, and to reproduce, for the benefit of the present, the spirit and ideas of the early Christianity.

The carrying out of such a purpose was, in the end, whether as a result of Colet's influence or not, the great

sight rather than to direct induction. This is true of important points in Mr. Seebohm's *Oxford Reformers*. I have chosen to follow its conclusions because they seem to me, on the whole, probable; but it should be remembered that there is very scanty evidence to prove what the Oxford reformers imparted to Erasmus, as well as to show what Colet gained in Italy. Lupton's *Life of John Colet* is a very sober and careful work.

work of Erasmus's life. His ambition was to put the documents of primitive Christianity, the New Testament and the early fathers, in carefully prepared editions, that is, as nearly as possible exactly as they were written, in the hands of all men, so that they could judge for themselves what the primitive Christianity was. The idea that the only true method of reaching a knowledge of Christianity was to go to the original sources of that knowledge, itself a direct result of the revival of learning, was constantly in his mind after he began his real work, and he expresses it over and over again, with varying degrees of clearness. If any one wants to know what Christianity is, he says, in effect, what Christ taught, what Paul taught, what the Christianity was of those who founded it, let him not go to the schoolmen or the theologian. He cannot be sure that they represent it truly. Let him go directly to the New Testament. There he will get it plainly and simply, so plainly that all men can see and understand exactly what it was.

His first step in this work was to publish, in 1505, an edition of Valla's *Annotations*, his criticism of the Vulgate, with a prefatory letter of his own. Then, in 1516, was published the first edition of his own New Testament, with revised Greek text, new Latin translation, and critical notes, in which he defended his variations from the Vulgate, and called attention to interesting features of the early Christianity which he thought needed present emphasis.[1] This passed through five authorized,

[1] The objections which were made by the conservatives to Erasmus's critical study of the New Testament, and the answers which he made are interesting in view of recent phases of the same conflict. They may be read in Seebohm. One monk writes him: "In very deed, my dear Erasmus, there is great harm [in pointing out discrepancies between the Greek and Latin copies]. Because, about this matter of the integrity of the Holy Scriptures many will dispute, many will doubt, if they learn that even one jot or tittle in them is false, . . . and then will come to pass what Augustine described to Jerome: 'If any error should be admitted to have crept into the Holy Scriptures, what authority would be left to them.'"—(*Oxford Re-*

and a few pirated, editions in his own lifetime, and sold in thousands of copies all over Europe. Besides his work on the New Testament he prepared editions of a very large number of the early fathers of the church.

While no doubt the special object in everything that Erasmus undertook was to do a genuine piece of scientific work, still the distinctly reformatory purpose in it all is evident. He wished to show men what the primitive Christianity was, and so to induce them to reject the abuses and corruptions which passed under its name. It will be evident, however, when we come to take up the Reformation that this reformatory purpose of his was not of the same sort as Luther's, and that he could not have followed his lead.[1]

The fact that Luther, during this time was moved also

formers, p. 316, third ed.) Dr. Eck, Luther's opponent, "objected . . . to the method of Biblical criticism which it adopted throughout. He objected to the suggestion it contained, that the Apostles quoted the Old Testament from memory, and, therefore, not always correctly. He objected to the insinuation that their Greek was colloquial, and not strictly classical." Erasmus replied "that, in his judgment, the authority of the whole Scriptures would not fall with any slip of memory on the part of an Evangelist— _e. g._, if he put 'Isaiah' by mistake for 'Jeremiah'—because no point of importance turns upon it. We do not forthwith think evil of the whole life of Peter because Augustine and Ambrose affirm that even after he had received the Holy Ghost he fell into error on some points; and so our faith is not altogether shaken in a whole book because it has some defects."—(_Ibid._, pp. 435-436.)

[1] Every reform movement produces two classes of reformers, each seeking, perhaps, the same ultimate end, but differing widely as to means. One believes that the reformation is to be successfully obtained only by remaining within the old organization and reforming from within out. The other believes that the old is too set in its ways to be reformed by conservative methods and by arguing, and that the only successful way is rebellion, or even revolution. It cannot be affirmed that it is so, without exception, but it is at least usual in history, certainly where the abuses are deeply seated and where the reform has been carried through at all, that the rebels, the radical reformers have been those to do it, whether by the success of their revolution, or, very likely as often, by its defeat. Erasmus belonged to the conservative reformers, to the reformers from within, and, leaving aside all theological differences between them, it was entirely impossible that he should follow Luther.

by the same controlling idea as Erasmus, and cherished the same wish to restore a truer Christianity, and that he came upon this thought independently, does not make the contribution of Erasmus to the final success of Luther's reform any less important. The idea of the necessity of an appeal to the original sources of knowledge was in the air, as an essential part of the Renaissance age. In relation to Christianity, it was absolutely certain that this appeal would be taken, and the results of it be made clear to the minds of common people as well as to the learned. This Luther did. But he could hardly have done his work, certainly not so well, but for Erasmus. Erasmus's work not merely helped to arouse and make general the idea of such an appeal, but it also put into Luther's hand, prepared for use, the material which he needed for his argument. Luther was the revolutionary leader, Erasmus the scholar.

In the connection established with the Reformation is to be found one of the ways in which the Renaissance movement became an important force in the other great movements of the time, and passed into the general revolution—social, political, and religious—with which modern history opened One other of its direct results brings it into close connection with our own time as opening one of the lines of our greatest advance.

The application to the natural and physical sciences of the new methods of investigation which the Renaissance had brought into use was not made so early as it had been to the sciences of historical and philological criticism. In these latter fields the work of positive advance had already begun, while the sciences of nature were still mainly engaged in collecting and recovering the facts known to the ancients, the work which Petrarch and the generation following him represent for classical scholarship. But the first great step of modern science, and one of the greatest ever taken in the importance of its results, the Copernican theory of the solar system, falls legitimately within the history of the Renaissance, though Copernicus did not publish his conclusions until 1543.

In his dedicatory epistle to Pope Paul III, Copernicus describes the almost ideally perfect scientific method which he had followed in his work. This method he may have learned in Italy, where he studied about ten years, going there in 1496, probably the year in which Colet returned to England. He notes, as the first step, his dissatisfaction with the old theory, then his search of ancient literature to see if another theory had been proposed, his reflection upon the suggestion which he found there until it assumed the form of a definite theory, the years of observation in which he tested the theory by the facts, and finally the order and harmony to which the facts observed were reduced by the theory.[1] From the great advance thus made by Copernicus the progress of astronomy has been constant and rapid, and the other sciences were not far behind.

In following down the main thread of intellectual work which runs through the age of the Renaissance, we have passed over various facts of interest in themselves, and perhaps as characteristic of it as those which have been mentioned, and of some bearing upon later times, but which can now receive but slight notice.

Of value in illustration of the perpetual conflict between the old and the new, if we could go into the details of it, would be the struggle of the new methods of study and their results for a place in the universities and for general acceptance. The universities held themselves obstinately closed to the new methods long after they had achieved brilliant results outside their walls. When admission was at last grudgingly allowed a few repre-

---

[1] See *The Yale Review*, vol. I (1892), p. 160, note 2, for a translation of this part of his letter.

sentatives of the new learning, it was accompanied with many petty slights and indignities—inaugural addresses were required to be submitted for examination before delivery, the use of the library was denied, a share in the government of the university was refused, or, as we should say, the right to attend the meetings of the faculty, or no place was given the new studies in the schedule of lecture hours. The church, so bound up with the scholastic system, came to its defence. Greek was judged a heretical tongue. No one should lecture on the New Testament, it was declared, without a previous theological examination. It was held to be heresy to say the Greek or Hebrew text reads thus, or that a knowledge of the original languages is necessary to interpret the Scripture correctly.

But all the forces that make history were with the new, and it could not be held back. The opening years of the sixteenth century resounded with the noise of its attack, now assured of victory, and led by Erasmus and Ulrich von Hutten and others of almost equal name. But hardly had the new learning obtained possession of the universities before it degenerated into a scholasticism of its own almost as barren as the old. Cicero became as great a divinity as Aristotle, and the letter far outweighed the spirit. When a new age of great scientific advance came on, in the seventeenth century, the new ideas of that time, led by Descartes and Leibnitz and Locke and Newton, had the same old battle to fight over again.[1]

Of equal interest is the marked sceptical tendency which accompanied the Renaissance, especially in Italy, and

---

[1] The scholastic tendency and habit are things extremely hard to work out of civilization, or more accurately, perhaps, extremely hard to bring into their proper place. Absorption in the process, and in the immediate and minute result, is something almost impossible to resist, because of the keen enjoyment which comes from successful investigation, but if yielded to it is a fearful bondage, and has ruined more promising intellectual beginnings than all the logical fallacies combined.

which would seem to be an almost inevitable attendant of times of intellectual progress. The unsettling of so many old beliefs, some of them apparently closely bound up with the Christian teaching, tended to unsettle all, and to produce a dispassionate and intellectual scepticism which in the Renaissance age is to be carefully distinguished from the emotional and æsthetic abandonment of Christian ethics which was also characteristic of the time. Gemistos Pletho, in the middle of the fifteenth century, stated his belief that men were about to abandon Christianity for some form of paganism, and Pomponazzi said, about 1520, that religions have their day of inevitable decline and Christianity is no exception to the general rule, and that signs could be discerned at that time of approaching dissolution in the fabric of our creed.[1] With this may be compared, perhaps, Voltaire's remark, that Christianity would not survive the nineteenth century.

A single paragraph is so utterly inadequate a space to give to the product of the Renaissance age in the fine arts, that all mention of it will be omitted except to notice one fact, which is especially important from our point of view, the fine expression which it gives to the leading thought of the Renaissance, that which is often called "the discovery of man"—the supremacy of man over nature—the power and grace and beauty of the ideal nature above and beyond mere physical beauty. And the value of this expression as a true exponent of the Renaissance age lies largely in the fact that it was unconscious.

Other characteristic products of the Renaissance age are also of great interest; its morals, or rather its want of morals, its calm and unconscious immorality, and often brutality, united with high æsthetic culture, of which we have so remarkable a photograph in the auto-

[1] Symonds, *Italian Literature*, vol. II, p. 477.

biography of Cellini, to which some would add the Prince of Machiavelli. But Machiavelli is one of the typical men of the time in more ways than one. He unites in himself at least two of its most marked tendencies, the political and the scientific, marvellous both for the ideal of a united Italian nation, which seems to be the mainspring of his thought, and for the example which he gives us of the calmness and total absence of feeling or moral judgment with which a purely scientific mind dissects a diseased organ in a living body.

The geographical explorations of the age belong partly to the history of commerce and have been considered there, but in certain aspects of them, represented best perhaps by Columbus, they are peculiarly the results of the Renaissance forces, and deserve extended notice here both as an outgrowth of the age and as an essential factor in its influence upon the future.

The belief that the earth is round had never been entirely forgotten. It was clearly and explicitly taught by the ancient scientists, and, though in the times of superstition and darkness a popular belief that the earth is flat did come to prevail, it was never held even in those days by men who had any trace of knowledge at all, or did any thinking on the more simple facts of astronomy. With the growth of a more general knowledge of antiquity, as a result of the revival of learning, the ancient views began to prevail again. In 1410 Peter d'Ailly had collected the opinions of the ancients on the subject with an occasional opinion from a medieval source, like Roger Bacon, in his book called *Imago Mundi*, a book which was much read and seems to have had a decided influence upon Columbus. Probably a still earlier and more decisive influence upon him was that exerted by the great Italian scientist of the time, Toscannelli, who wrote him, in 1474, a very interesting letter calling his attention in the clearest way to the possibilities which lay in a voyage to the west.[1] Toscannelli's ideas, however, were based, like Peter d'Ailly's, upon a study of the ancients. These views, derived from the ancient science, were confirmed in Columbus's mind by some facts of observation which he had gathered from various sources, stories of sailors, traditions, and other things of the sort, which tended to show the existence of land to the west.

These facts make it evident then, that, just as in the case of the first great step in advance in physical science, Copernicus's theory of the solar system, so also in the first great enlargement of our practical knowledge of the earth itself, the new progress takes its departure from a revived knowledge of what the ancient world had learned, and that the modern science rests upon the ancient.

But not merely in his sources of knowledge was Columbus a child of the Renaissance. He was still more clearly so in the spirit which moved and sustained him.

The thing which was especially new and original with him, and which led to his great success, was not his knowledge of the scientific facts. The whole scientific world of his time believed in these as thoroughly as he did. But it was this, that, believing in the truth of the scientific conclusion, he dared to act upon that belief; it was his strong and unwavering self-confidence and daring which carried him through to the end. In this he was entirely a modern man. But it is necessary to remember that no modern explorer of Central Africa or of the polar lands has needed to be quite so daring, or to have so obstinate a spirit of determination and pluck and willingness to meet the unexpected and overcome it. The modern man has a sort of confidence in the validity of science which was not possible for Columbus, and, a thing which is still more to the point, he has a knowledge of

[1] A translation of this letter is given in Fiske's *Discovery of America*, vol. I, p. 356, and the original in an appendix.

the probable dangers which he will have to face, such as Columbus could not have.

In Columbus the Renaissance age is seen not only to have recovered the knowledge upon which a new progress could be founded, but also it had produced the new spirit, the firm confidence of man in his own powers and in his mastery of nature, which was both to discover a new world in geography and to create a new world in ideas. Hardly any man, indeed, who lived in those days is so complete a representative of the age as Columbus. It was a mixed age, old and new mingled together in strange proportions and motley results; old superstitions and medieval ideas side by side with scientific criticism and modern beliefs. And so it was in the case of Columbus. He was a modern man with a strong faith in the results of science and a vigorous self-reliance. But he was also a medieval man, holding to the scholastic theology, believing that the prophets specifically foretold his enterprise, and apparently led to his undertaking quite as much by the desire to get the means for a new crusade to rescue the Holy Sepulchre as by scientific or commercial motives.

The effects of Columbus's expedition were not confined to science or to commerce. His was a most revolutionary discovery, and its intellectual results were as great as its practical ones. They were, perhaps, greater than those which have followed any other discovery of the sort. With them can be compared only the enlargement of mind which followed such scientific events as Newton's publications, or, in the present century, Lyell's proof of the geologic ages, or Darwin's explanation of the method of evolution.

Other events of the same sort combined to produce the same character of mind and to make it the prevailing intellectual tone of the times—the explorations of the Portuguese, the invention of printing, the discoveries of new classical material, the wide enlargement of the field of historical knowledge, and the overthrow of old beliefs in every direction. These events led not merely to a rapid broadening of thought and mental experience, but also to a hospitality towards new ideas which is characteristically modern.

The intellectual atmosphere which the Renaissance produced, and which was an essential prerequisite of the Reformation, can be compared, indeed, to nothing so well as to that of our own age. In spirit, in ambitions, and in methods, in openness of mind and in expectation of a greater future it was the same. The obstructive conservatism with which it had to contend was identical with that of to-day, and the same weapons were in use on both sides. In actual attainment and insight, of course, it was not the same. The conditions were more narrow and the tools it had to work with were far inferior. But that is a fact of relatively little importance, and if we would gain a right understanding of the age, and of its permanent contributions to history, we can do it best, perhaps, by comparing it, under its own conditions, with the spirit and work of to-day.

CHAPTER XVI

THE PAPACY IN THE NEW AGE

In the tenth chapter we followed the conflict between the church and the empire to its close in the thirteenth century. The papacy had come out of that conflict apparently victorious over its only rival. Frederick II had failed, and no new emperor had arisen to take his place with a power which could be at all dangerous to the pope's.

But at the moment of this victory a new enemy appeared in the field. The growth of commerce, and the other results which followed from the crusades, had already changed the character of the age, and the general attitude of mind toward the papacy. It had raised the general level of intelligence and created a new feeling of individual self-reliance in large portions of the population, even before the age of the revival of learning proper. The gradual organization of the modern nations, and their progress, step by step, towards definite constitutions and true national life, had been accompanied with a growth of the spirit of political independence, and the beginnings, at least, of a genuine feeling of patriotism. It was impossible for the political and intellectual world, which was forming under these influences, and which was animated by this new spirit, to submit tamely to those pretensions of universal political supervision which had been asserted by Gregory VII and by Innocent III and which the papacy still claimed in even more extreme language.

Isolated cases, due to these new influences, of a more or less determined resistance to these pretensions are scattered through the thirteenth century in the history of various states. In the case of exceptionally strong states or sovereigns, some are to be found even in the twelfth. At the beginning of the fourteenth occurred an instance of this resistance which became of universal importance, and which, in the final consequences that followed from it, united all the new forces of the time in a grand attack upon the papacy, to destroy its political power, and even to change the character of its ecclesiastical rule. This was the conflict between Philip the Fair of France and Pope Boniface VIII.

Boniface VIII was elected pope in 1294, after he had procured by his intrigues the abdication of the weak and unworldly Celestin V. He was a man of exactly opposite character—hasty and obstinate, and with the most extreme views of the rights of the papacy over all other powers in the world. Opportunities were offered him, one after another, for the actual assertion of these rights in almost every country of Europe, and if he could have carried through successfully the things which he attempted, the papal empire would have existed in reality.

England and France were, at the time, in the midst of that interminable series of wars which grew out of the attempts of the French kings to absorb in their growing state the territories of their independent vassals, of which the kings of England held so large a share. Philip IV, the Fair, was one of the ablest of the Capetian kings who were carrying on this inherited policy, and, at the same time, one of the most unscrupulous and determined. The necessities of the war compelled both him and Edward I of England to demand taxes from the clergy of their kingdoms in a more regular way than had ever been done before. It was near the time, as we know, of the completion of that economic revolution which substituted

money for cruder forms of payment in produce and services. Taxation was consequently beginning to assume
a great importance among the resources of a state. The
clergy, exempt by universal consent, in view of their
religious services to the state, from personal military service, had insisted, also, upon an exemption from taxation
unless the tax were specially sanctioned by themselves
or by the pope. But the large proportion of the landed
wealth of the country which was in their hands made the
question of their submission, like the other classes, to
the independent taxing power of the state, a very serious
one for the new governments, especially for one which
was endeavoring to attain independence of the feudal
nobles, and neither Philip nor Edward was disposed to
allow this exemption. Boniface VIII, appealed to by
some of the clergy in support of their rights, issued his
bull, "Clericis laicos," in which, in the strongest terms,
he forbade any prince or state to collect any unauthor-
ized taxes from the clergy, and commanded all prelates to
resist such extortion to the utmost.

The struggle with Philip, begun in this way, involved
before its close more than one other point concerning
the right of the pope to interfere in the internal affairs of
the state. They were the old claims of the papacy pushed
to an extreme point. The bull, "Unam Sanctam," issued
in 1302, gives expression in the fullest and plainest terms
to the theory of papal supremacy and the grounds on
which it was made to rest. It says: "When the apostles
said, 'Behold here are two swords!' . . . the Lord did
not reply that this was too much, but enough. Surely
he who denies that the temporal sword is in the power of
Peter wrongly interprets the word of the Lord when He
says: 'Put up thy sword in its scabbard.' Both swords,
the spiritual and the material, therefore, are in the power
of the church; the one, indeed, to be wielded for the
church, the other by the church; the one by the hand of

the priest, the other by the hand of kings and knights, but at the will and sufferance of the priest." . . . "For, the truth bearing witness, the spiritual power has to establish the earthly power, and to judge it if it be not good. Thus concerning the church and the ecclesiastical power is verified the prophecy of Jeremiah: 'See, I have this day set thee over the nations and over the kingdoms,' and the other things which follow. Therefore if the earthly power err it shall be judged by the spiritual power; but if the lesser spiritual power err, by the greater. But if the greatest, it can be judged by God alone, not by man, the apostle bearing witness. A spiritual man judges all things, but he himself is judged by no one. This authority, moreover, even though it is given to man and exercised through man, is not human but rather divine, being given by divine lips to Peter and founded on a rock for him and his successors through Christ himself, whom he has confessed; the Lord himself saying to Peter: 'Whatsoever thou shalt bind,' etc. Whoever, therefore, resists this power, thus ordained by God, resists the ordination of God." . . . "Indeed we declare, announce, and define, that it is altogether necessary to salvation for every human creature to be subject to the Roman pontiff."[1]

There was nothing particularly new in these pretensions. They had been maintained by the church for the last two hundred years. But they were expressed in clearer and stronger terms than ever before, and the line was drawn sharply between the old claims of the papacy and the new spirit of the nations. The significant thing about the contest was the answer which the nations made to these assertions.

Philip seems to have realized the new force which he had behind him, and he appealed directly to the nation. In 1302, as we know, he summoned the first Estates

[1] Translation of Henderson, *Hist. Docs. of the Middle Ages*, p. 435, where, also, a translation of the bull "Clericis laicos" may be found.

General of France, and submitted to them the papal demands. Each of the three Estates responded separately,
supporting the king and denying the right of the pope to
any supremacy over the state. The clergy, perhaps, took
this position somewhat reluctantly and with a divided
allegiance, but it illustrates in a striking way the strength
of public opinion in favor of the state that they did so at
all, and many of them undoubtedly supported the king
from real conviction.

The result in England was the same. It has been said
by some that on the point of taxation Edward yielded
to the pope, but this is certainly a misunderstanding of
the case. It is true that, in 1297, he effected a temporary
reconciliation with the church, but immediately afterwards
he exercised again his asserted right of taxation, and when
he finally abandoned it he yielded not to the church but
to the general opposition throughout the nation to the
exercise of an unconstitutional power, and agreed that no
orders in the state should be taxed except by their own
consent. This is a very different thing from recognizing
the claims of the bull "Clericis laicos," which he distinctly
refused to do. In 1299, when the pope asserted that
Scotland was a fief of the papacy and must not be attacked by the English, Edward showed no disposition
to yield his rights, and he had the support of the kingdom in his resistance.

One incident of this contest must not be omitted, for it
is the beginning of an idea which came in time to be of
the utmost importance. Philip made a formal appeal
from the pope, on the grounds of Boniface's heresy and
immorality of life, to a general council and a more lawful
pope. The appeal, at the moment, came to nothing, but
the idea that a council had the right to judge of the
legitimacy of a pope was destined in the next age to be
the starting-point of a most promising and hopeful attempt to reconstruct the constitution of the church.

The reign of Boniface came to an end with his death, in 1303, as the result of an assault upon his person by his enemies. He had failed in every attempt which he had made to control political affairs wherever the new national spirit had begun to be alive. It was the close of an epoch in the history of the papacy indeed. The old triumphs of the church over the state could no longer be repeated. The forces of modern politics, which reduced the papacy from the imperial position for which it had striven to a political insignificance scarcely less than that of the modern Holy Roman Empire, were already beginning to stir.

After the death of Boniface, Philip IV determined to prevent any recurrence of such a conflict in the future, by subjecting the papacy directly to his own power, and, after a brief interval, the reign of Benedict XI, he secured the election of a French prelate, Clement V, and the papacy passed for a period of seventy years under French influence. The outward sign of this was the removal of the residence of the popes, and so the practical capital of the ecclesiastical world, to Avignon, a city of Provence on the borders of France. The college of cardinals was filled with French prelates, and during a part of the time the kings of France, or the French kings of Naples, almost openly controlled the papal policy.

It is not difficult to imagine the result. International politics in the modern sense had not yet arisen, but the first faint traces were then to be seen of the conflicting interests, which were in the course of time, when the internal affairs of the states had been brought into more settled shape, to lead to modern inter-state politics. The nations were beginning to be jealous of one another and to fear encroachment. At least each government had objects which it was eagerly striving to accomplish within its own territories, which other states might aid or with which they might interfere. So long as the papacy con-

tinued to occupy the position of an umpire, above all
the states and not immediately under the influence of
any one of them, and so long as it had no manifest political
interests of its own to serve, it might retain something
of its imperial position.   The spirit of the new nations
might resent its direct interference in their local affairs,
but they were not so likely to resent, indeed they would
be often glad to avail themselves of its international
influence.   The true policy for the papacy to pursue,
after the rise of the nations, was to keep itself as
free as it could from all special politics, and to improve and strengthen in every possible way its international power.

The papacy at Avignon was, on the contrary, virtually
a complete abdication of this position.   It was almost as
sudden and final a destruction of the imperial power of
the popes as the ruin of the Hohenstaufen family had
been of the imperial position of the German kings.[1]   As
soon as the other states of Europe saw, or thought they
saw, that the popes were under the control of France,
that their undisputed ecclesiastical rights, and their
claims in other directions were being used to serve the
ends of French politics, that the popes were really the
tools of the kings of France, then the national spirit was
roused at once in opposition to papal interference, and
the popes lost even the respect and obedience of the
other states.   The place in general European affairs, as a

[1] No more is meant by this statement than is said.   It is not meant that
the papacy ceased to be a factor of importance in international politics, as
one among states, active in the formation of combinations, sought as an
ally, or interfering with success in the internal affairs of individual states.
But these things constitute an influence very different from that imperial
power, as an arbiter above states, which the medieval papacy came near to
attaining.   This distinction between an imperial position for papacy or empire, and action as a member of a virtual federation of nations, on even
terms with others, is fundamental and necessary to any understanding of
the changed conditions of modern as compared with medieval international
politics.

power above states, from which the papacy descended
when it went to Avignon it was never able to recover.
This was in reality due of course to the growth of new
powers and new conditions, a new general atmosphere,
which made it impossible to return to the old, but the
historical facts which brought these new forces to bear
upon the papal demands were the defeat of Boniface in
his conflict with Philip, and the consequent "Babylonian
captivity" at Avignon.

England, for example, was at war with France during
nearly the whole of this period, and the feeling that the
papacy was the close ally of her enemy had something
beyond question to do with the repeated and stringent
measures which were taken in the reign of Edward III,
to limit the right of the pope to interfere even in the
ecclesiastical affairs of the country, in the statute of
"provisors" against his right to make appointments to
English benefices, and of "præmunire" against appeals to
the papal courts, and in the refusal of the nation to pay
any longer the annual tribute which was the mark of the
feudal dependence of England upon the papacy, established by the homage of King John.

Still more clearly does this appear in the case of Germany. When the Avignonese popes, John XXII and
Benedict XII, asserted their right to decide a disputed
election, or to determine the right to the throne of a
regularly elected candidate, manifestly in the interest of
the political ambition of the king of France, then even
weakened and divided Germany was aroused by the spirit
of national independence and rejected with decision the
pope's dictation. The electors drew up a solemn declaration, in 1338, which in the same year received the
sanction of a numerously attended diet at Frankfort, re-
citing that the king derived his right to rule from God
alone and not from the pope, and that his regular election
carried with it the full power to exercise all the preroga-

tives of king and emperor, whatever rights of crowning
and consecration might justly belong to the pope.[1]

But other results of the captivity at Avignon threatened
the papacy with a far more serious disaster than the loss
of its political influence. Grave discontent began to
arise, and earnest criticism began to be heard within the
church itself against the papal position and policy. The
progress of events increased this feeling and gave it
stronger and more manifest grounds until, for a short
time, it threatened to overthrow even the ecclesiastical
supremacy of the pope, and to revolutionize the entire
constitution of the church.

Increasing luxury and nepotism were characteristic of
the papacy at Avignon. The wasteful extravagance of a
court, far more like that of a prodigal sovereign of the
world than of a Christian bishop, demanded an increased
income to meet its abnormally heavy expenses. The war
which the popes were carrying on in Italy was exceedingly
costly. The ordinary revenues would not suffice. They
had indeed proved insufficient in the thirteenth century,
from general financial causes which still continued to
operate, and the ingenuity of successive popes needed to
be exercised to devise new forms of taxation, or rather
new expedients by which money could be exacted from
the clergy of Europe. This necessity led to a great enlargement of the papal right of appointment to local
benefices throughout the Catholic world, a method of
extortion which was doubly offensive, not merely because
of the large sums thus exacted in annates and other fees,
but also because of its interference with the independence
and self-government of the local churches. The practice
excited no little outcry and opposition. It had a decisive influence in leading to the adoption of the statutes
against such practices in England under Edward III, and

[1] There is a translation in Henderson, p. 437, of the document adopted at
Frankfort.

elsewhere ecclesiastical bodies made strong protest and drew up formal declarations against the rights assumed by the popes.

This spirit of discontent and criticism was strengthened from another side. Earnest minds could not fail to condemn, as contrary to a genuine Christianity, the luxury and immorality which prevailed at Avignon and influenced the whole church from that centre. Wycliffe's party in England drew no little aid from the prevalence of this feeling. But an earlier rebellion in the church on this point had been attended with even more extreme views. A body within the Franciscan order, earnestly devoted to a simple and spiritual life, had adopted an idea which implied that, following the example of Christ and the apostles, "evangelical poverty" was a Christian duty demanded of all the clergy, and with this they held other equally revolutionary notions. Condemned by the popes as heretics, the more irreconcilable of them, with some others of like mind, took refuge with Lewis of Bavaria, who gathered about him in this way a small literary army, far more logical and thorough in their opposition to the papal demands than he was himself. In his service, the ablest of these writers, William of Ockham and Marsiglio of Padua, proclaimed doctrines which were revolutionary not merely of the world's ecclesiastical government of that time, but also of its political governments, and which were in many remarkable ways anticipations of ideas which have come to prevail in modern times. On the special point at issue between Lewis and the pope, they denied in the clearest terms the right of the pope to centre in himself the powers of the church, and maintained the superiority of a general council.

During the residence of the popes at Avignon, there was, therefore, a growing dissatisfaction and spirit of criticism both within and without the ranks of the clergy, a disposition to question the right of the papacy as an

absolute monarchy over the church, as well as to deny its
right to assume the direction of political affairs. With
the rise of this spirit there were heard also, a still more
significant fact, clear demands for a general council to
judge and control the pope. But as yet these signs of
coming civil war had been seen only here and there,
connected with special cases of dispute between the pope
and some particular opponent. Men's minds had been
somewhat familiarized with these new theories of church
government, as possibilities, but there was as yet no general acceptance of them, no European demand for a universal council to exercise supreme functions in the church,
and to take the papacy under its control. It was the
Great Schism, and the events connected with it, the
period in church history which followed the Babylonian
captivity at Avignon, which transformed these isolated
demands for a general council, used as a weapon in
special contests with the papacy, as a threat to be held
over the pope, into a strong demand of all Europe which
could not be resisted.

It was the condition of affairs in Italy, rather than
any sense of duty to the church universal, which moved
Gregory XI in 1377 to return from Avignon to Rome.
The absence of the popes had thrown the papal states into
anarchy and confusion. Revolution and counter-revo-
lution had followed one another in rapid succession, now
democratic in spirit and again papal—it was in this
period that the experiments of Rienzo were made—and
Gregory XI feared that his power in Italy would be entirely lost if he did not attempt its recovery in person.
But the French cardinals were not reconciled to the
change. They were not willing to leave the luxury and
quiet of Avignon and to subject themselves to the tumul-
tuous rudeness of Rome. The loud demand of the Romans
that an Italian pope should be elected, on the death of
Gregory XI in 1378, and popular tumults connected with

the election of Urban VI, gave them an opportunity to assert that the election had been forced upon them by bodily fear and was not therefore a free and legal election. On this ground they withdrew from Rome—in the end all the cardinals who had elected Urban abandoned him—and elected one of their own number pope, who took the name of Clement VII, and returned to Avignon. Urban on his side created a number of Italian cardinals, and the papacy had now two heads as well as two capitals. The nations of Europe chose sides almost solely as their political interests led them. France, of course, supported Clement; England, of course, supported Urban. Naples could not help opposing the Roman pope, nor Germany the pope who was under the influence of France. There were not merely two popes and two capitals, but the whole church was rent in twain, and the question whether there was in the church, as distinguished from the pope, a power to reorganize its government and to compel even the papacy to submit to reformation, was forced upon the attention of every man who had any interest in public affairs.

In the prevailing temper of the time, the discussion of this question showed a rapid tendency to break with the traditions and historical theories of the church. It was a time when the ties of the church universal seem to have been loosed in every direction and new and strange notions in theology and concerning practical religion made their appearance on every hand. Wild dreams and ideas that would one day bear good fruit were mingled together —Wycliffe and the Beguines, the Brethren of the Common Life and the Flagellants, and many forgotten names of the sort, good and bad. It was a favorable atmosphere for the rapid growth of revolutionary schemes for the settlement of the difficulty which the Schism forced upon the church. The whole tendency for centuries in the ecclesiastical world had been to centre the life and power of the church more and more completely in the pope. The doctrine of papal infallibility and of the pope's absolute headship of the church may not have been so explicitly stated as a necessary article of faith as now, but it was practically no less clearly held or firmly believed by the general body of churchmen. In the circumstances of the time, this historical tendency was forgotten by many. It was argued that it mattered little how many popes there were. There might be ten or twelve. Each land might have its own independent pope. It might be the will of God that the papacy should remain permanently divided.[1]

But the ideas which won the general acceptance of Europe were not so extreme as these, though really as revolutionary. A group of earnest and able men, of whom John Gerson, of the University of Paris, is the best known, began to advance ideas which, though they broke with the special form which the unity of the church had been assuming in the headship of the pope, did not break with the real spirit of that unity. They consequently furnished a more solid doctrinal foundation for the new plan of reformation than was possible for the wilder ideas of others, and commanded general approval for it. According to these theories, the church universal is superior to the pope. It may elect him if the cardinals fail to do so; it may depose one whom the cardinals have elected. The pope is an officer of the church, and, if he abuses his office, he may be treated as an enemy, as a temporal prince would be in a similar case. The highest expression of the unity and power of this church universal is a general council. This is superior to the pope, may meet legitimately without his summons, and he must obey its decisions.

[1] The first volume of Pastor's *Geschichte der Päpste*, which contains a very valuable account of this crisis in the history of the papacy from the Catholic point of view, has been translated into English.

The first attempt to carry into practice the appeal from the pope to a general council, and so to end the Schism, was in the Council of Pisa, in 1409. Long negotiations for the purpose of restoring peace to the church in some other way had failed. The attempt to get both popes to abdicate, and so make way for the election of a new pope for the whole church, had shortly before seemed about to succeed. Each of the two popes—Benedict XIII, of Avignon, and Gregory XII, of Rome—had been elected under solemn promise to resign if his opponent could be brought to do the same. But neither was willing to take the first step, and it soon became evident that the Schism could not be healed in this way. France then withdrew its support from Benedict, who took refuge in Spain. The majority of the cardinals of both popes abandoned their masters and united in a call for a general council to assemble in Pisa in 1409.

But the Council of Pisa did not command universal acceptance. Political and other considerations had retained a few states in the obedience of each of the popes. The council was itself injudicious and hasty, and did not sufficiently fortify its position against obvious objections. It deposed the two contending popes and sanctioned the election of a new one by the cardinals present, Alexander V—who died in 1410, and was succeeded by John XXIII—but it separated without providing for the real reformation of the church.

The situation was in reality made worse by this first attempt to heal the Schism than it had been before. There were now three popes, each claiming to be the sole rightful pope, and each recognized as such by some part of the church. But the council of Pisa had served the great purpose of bringing out, more clearly than ever before, the arguments on which its right to act rested, and of convincing Europe at large that, if it could be properly managed, a really universal council, as the voice of the united church, was the proper method of solving the difficulty.

In the next stage of events the emperor-elect, Sigismund, as representing, upon the political side, the unity of Christendom, took a leading part. The political situation in Italy forced John XXIII to depend upon the emperor's aid, and Sigismund was therefore able to make the representatives of the pope agree to a council which was to meet in the imperial city of Constance, and so outside of Italy, on November 1, 1414. This agreement Sigismund made haste to announce to all Europe and to invite proper persons from all states to be present. After a fruitless attempt to change the place of meeting, John was compelled to acquiesce, and a few weeks later issued a formal summons for the council.

Sanctioned in this way by the Roman emperor and by the pope whom the greater part of the church recognized, and supported by the deep and universal desire of Europe for union and reformation, the council which assembled at Constance was to all intents and purposes a universal one, and appeared to have a most encouraging prospect of success. Its membership reached five thousand. All Europe was represented from the beginning, with insignificant exceptions. Its spirit, too, was in contrast with that of the Council of Pisa. While resolutely determined to do away with the Schism, it was directed with caution and good judgment.

John XXIII failed to control the council as he had hoped to do, and was finally forced to recognize its right to depose him. This was done on May 29, 1415. On July 4th the council listened to the abdication, voluntary in form, of Gregory XII. Benedict XIII refused to abdicate, but finally his supporters all withdrew from his obedience and joined the council, and on July 26, 1417, he was formally deposed.

The church was now reunited in a way that was satisfactory to all Christendom, but it was without a head, and measures of moral reform were still to be adopted. The council was thus brought to the necessity of deciding a question upon which there was the widest difference of opinion—whether it should proceed first to the election of a pope or to a thorough reformation of the abuses in the government of the church, of which there was so general complaint. The earnest reform party, supported by the emperor, desired to make sure of the reformation before the choice of a pope. The cardinals, less interested in reformation and fearing a diminution of their influence, demanded the immediate election of a pope. They were supported by the Italian representatives and by many who really desired reform, but in whom the conservative feeling of the necessity of a head to the real constitution of the church was a stronger motive. The reform efforts of the council were greatly weakened by dissension. Various parties urged special measures of their own which were not acceptable to others. Local and national interests were opposed to one another. Political influences were also at work and agreement on details seemed impossible. Finally a compromise was adopted. Certain reform measures on which all could unite were to be first decreed by the council and then a pope was to be elected. In accordance with this agreement five such reform decrees were adopted in October, 1417, and on November 11th the cardinals, to whom the council had added thirty representatives, chosen from its membership for this purpose, elected a new pope, who took the name of Martin V.

The new pope was able to prevent any further action of importance by the council, and it dissolved on April 22, 1418, having reunited the church but not having reformed it. The most important of the general reform measures which it had adopted was one providing for the regular recurrence of such general councils, the first in five years, the second in seven, and thereafter at intervals of ten years.   Could this decree have been enforced, together with the declarations of the council adopted in its early sessions of the superiority of a general council over the pope, giving expression to ideas very generally prevalent at the time, the whole constitution of the church would have been changed and all its subsequent history would have been different.   The later absolutism of the pope would have been impossible, the papacy would have been transformed into a limited monarchy, and the supreme power would have been a representative assembly meeting at regular intervals, and having final legislative and judicial authority.   But so favorable a moment as that presented by the Council of Constance for accomplishing this result never recurred, and the failure of that council to secure the subjection of the pope was fatal to the plan.

The first two councils, provided for by the decree of the Council of Constance, met at the appointed time but were able to accomplish nothing.   The first was held at Pavia, in 1423, but was very thinly attended, and, though it manifested the same desire to limit the power of the pope, Martin V dissolved it before it had adopted any important measures.   It selected Basel as the place for the meeting of the next council, which would assemble in 1431.   At that time the threatening successes of the Hussites and the apparent impossibility of overcoming them by force seemed to make a general council especially necessary, but the attendance at its opening was small and became at no time large.   Its spirit, however, was most determined and its measures most thoroughgoing.   It gave itself a democratic organization by admitting the lower clergy to an equal vote with the higher; it reaffirmed the decrees of the Council of Constance in regard to the superiority of a council over the pope; denied his right to dissolve the council without its own consent; declared that the payment of annates and of all fees to the pope on appointment to benefices should cease; provided for local synods to carry throughout the church the idea of government by councils; attempted to change the method of electing the popes by the cardinals; and assumed the right to exercise in several points special papal prerogatives. But it did not gain general recognition for these assumptions. The pope, Eugenius IV, after a premature attempt to dissolve it, had been compelled by political considerations for some time to recognize it as a council, but finally he was able to declare it dissolved and to open another council under his own control in Italy. The Council of Basel in turn deposed the pope and elected one of its own in his place. But the more influential of the prelates gradually went over to the side of Pope Eugenius. The council degenerated rapidly, and finally disappeared, a complete failure.

One other phase of this later contest is of considerable interest. At the moment when the discord between the Council of Basel and the pope threatened a new schism in the church, France and Germany took advantage of the opportunity to declare in advance their neutrality in the coming struggle, and to signify their acceptance of such decrees of the council as would secure a good degree of independence to their national churches. The French national synod, held at Bourges, in 1438, recognized the superior authority of councils, declared that they ought to be held every ten years, enacted that reservations to the pope of ecclesiastical appointments, annates, and appeals to Rome in ordinary cases should cease, and adopted measures of moral reform. The following year very similar provisions were adopted for Germany by the Diet at Mainz. Such a result was in truth a natural consequence of the position taken by the councils and of the general current of opinion which had supported them, and if that position had been successfully established and the constitution of the church permanently modified, it would inevitably have led to the formation of locally independent and self-governing national churches. As it was, this attempt also came to nothing.[1]

This movement for national independence indicates the real significance of the crisis through which the church had passed. It had been a most serious danger to the papacy, looked at from the point of view of its historical development as an ecclesiastical power. Drawing its strength and life undoubtedly from the same sources from which the great political movement whose history we have followed had drawn, brought about in fact by the same forces as those which had constructed the new nations transferred now to the sphere of ecclesiastical government, this movement strove to work the same revolution there which had been worked in temporal governments. Unconscious of course of this relationship, unconscious also very largely of the end which would have been reached, but with a growing clearness of apprehension, this revolution threatened to transform as completely the Roman Catholic monarchy as it had transformed that other great medieval creation, the feudal system. The peculiar situation of things within the church—the Babylonian captivity and the Great Schism—gave an opportunity for the translation of the political ideas of the age into eccle-

---

[1] The French church retained some independence, more to the advantage of the king, however, than of the church. In 1682, in consequence of a quarrel between Louis XIV and the pope over the right of the king to make appointments in the church, an assembly of the French clergy adopted the Four Articles of the Gallican church. These asserted, 1, that the power of the pope is wholly spiritual and that kings cannot be deposed by him; 2, that popes are subject to the decisions of general councils; 3, that popes must govern according to the accepted laws of the church, and, especially, according to the rights of the Gallican church; and 4, that decisions of the popes in matters of faith have only a temporary force, and, to become permanently binding, must be accepted by a general council. These seem like a reaffirmation of the principles of the councils but they established no real independence.

siastical ideas. The growing importance of the representative system—of Diets and Estates General—in national governments made the appeal to a general council
in the government of the church seem a perfectly natural
recourse in time of difficulty, especially to lawyers, and
university teachers, and even to the great lay public. It
might not seem so simple and manifest an expedient to
those immediately concerned in the government of the
church and directly interested in its traditions or devoted
to them. But the strength of the reform movement was
not drawn from the world of the cardinals and great
prelates, but from the universities and the doctors, and
the non-ecclesiastical world.

This movement was, in truth, strong enough to have
succeeded, and it almost succeeded. If the Council of
Constance had continued to the end cautious and well-
managed, if there could have come to the front some
great leader, strong enough to have persuaded its members to lay aside their local differences for the general
cause, and to hold back outside political interests from
interference, and who could have defined clearly the
specific measures necessary to realize the policy which
unquestionably the majority desired, he could have succeeded in all probability in remodelling the government
of the church. It seems an almost unparalleled fact that
the crisis did not produce such a leader.

It may be objected that such a revolution would have
been too sudden to effect a permanent reform, that only
those revolutions are really successful which are the cul-
mination, however sudden in appearance, of a long prepared change. The principle is certainly correct, but the
application here is doubtful, for the line of preparation is
manifestly to be traced not in the ecclesiastical but in the
political world.

Knowing, as we do now, the events which followed on
so rapidly in the history of the church—the revolution so

much more violent and far-reaching of the sixteenth century—we cannot help asking the question: What would
have been the result had the Council of Constance succeeded where it failed? and allowing the imagination to
answer. It seems certain that one result would have
been the formation of a government for the church like
that which was taking shape at the same time in England,
a limited monarchy with a legislature gradually gaining
more and more the real control of affairs. It seems almost equally certain that with this the churches of each
nationality would have gained a large degree of local independence and the general government of the church
have assumed by degrees the character of a great federal
and constitutional state. If this had been the case, it is
hard to see why all the results which were accomplished
by the reformation of Luther might not have been attained as completely without that violent disruption of
the church, which was necessary and unavoidable as the
church was then constituted. Whether that would have
been on the whole a better result may be left without
discussion.

If this is in a way fanciful history, the results which
did follow were real enough. The theory of the papal
supremacy was too strongly established in the church to
be overthrown by an opposing theory only half-believed
in by its supporters. The logic of the papal position is
immensely strong if its starting-point be accepted, and
to the great body of the leading churchmen of the times,
whose training was wholly in speculative and theoretical
lines, it seemed in the end invincible. It would have
demanded a more united and abler commanded attack to
have destroyed it. The only result of the attempt, so
far as the church constitution is concerned, was to make
the position of the papal absolutism stronger than it had
been before, and to bring to an end forever any serious
opposition to it. The next great council, that of Trent,

which was so completely under the control of the pope
as to give ground for the sneer that the Holy Spirit by
which it was inspired came every day from Rome in a
mail-bag, was the legitimate successor of the Council of
Constance; and the dogma of papal infallibility, proclaimed by the Council of the Vatican, in 1870, was only
an official formulation of the principle established when
the movement for reformation by councils in the fifteenth
century failed.

The fact that the Council of Constance did actually
appear to depose popes and to provide during a brief
interval for the government of the church gives the
Catholic theologian of to-day who maintains the traditional position but little difficulty.   In his eyes, Gregory
XII was the only one of the three popes who had a rightful title.   The assembly at Constance was no real general
council, only a synod, until Gregory issued his bull of
convocation, and its acts passed before that date, including its declaration of the superior power of a council, are
all wanting in legislative validity.   By convoking the
council and then abdicating his office Gregory relieved
the church from great embarrassment, and first gave to the
council a legitimate position, so that it could act with
some prospect of success for the reunion of the church.
By accepting the acts of Gregory, the council formally
recognized him as the only legitimate pope, and, by inference, with him his predecessors during the Schism.[1]   Thus
the theory is perfectly preserved.   Whatever right the
council had in the premises it got not by virtue of its
existence as a general council, but indirectly, from the
concessions of the pope.

For the moral reformation of the church the age of
the councils accomplished nothing of real value.   Most
of the old abuses of which the people complained remained unchecked.   Avarice and immorality continued,

[1] Pastor, *Geschichte der Päpste*, vol. I, pp. 154–155.

unabashed, in the papal court, and before the close of the
century the papacy was to reach a depth of moral degradation equalled only in the tenth century.   A considerable proportion of the clergy throughout Europe imi-
tated the practices of Italy, and, heedless of the warnings
they were constantly receiving, continued to strengthen
the current of rebellion.

Politically the position of the papacy was greatly
changed, but it remained no less controlled, perhaps even
more controlled, by political considerations.   The day
when it could hope to carry out the plans of Gregory
VII, and Innocent III, and Boniface VIII, and to establish a monarchy, imperial in the political as it was in
the ecclesiastical world, would never return again.   But
the pope was a king as well as a bishop.   He was the
temporal sovereign of a little state in Italy.   With the
rise of international politics and the beginning of the modern conflict of state with state for European supremacy which we have already noticed, Italy was the first
battle-ground of all nations.   It was the practically un-
occupied piece of ground lying first at hand in which
each might hope to gain some great advantage over the
others.   In this struggle of armies and diplomacy the
popes had an immediate and vital interest.   They must
enter into it on the same footing and with the same
weapons as Austria or Spain, and this necessity of constantly striving to preserve the independence of their
little kingdom in the turmoil of European politics, or to
recover it when lost, has been a controlling element in
the papal policy down to the present time, a perpetually harassing and disabling necessity, judged from the
point of view of its religious position.

CHAPTER XVII

THE REFORMATION

By the beginning of the sixteenth century the middle ages had come to an end in almost every line of civilization. Politically, economically, and intellectually the new forces and the new methods had possession of the field. The old were not yet beaten at every point. On many matters of detail much fighting had yet to be done. In some places, perhaps, the old succeeded in maintaining itself, or even in recovering ground. But on the main issues, everywhere, the victory had been won —with one most important exception. The church was unchanged. It had remained unaffected by the new forces which had transformed everything else. It was still thoroughly medieval. In government, in doctrine, and in life it still placed the greatest emphasis upon those additions which the peculiar conditions of the middle ages had built upon the foundation of the primitive Christianity, and it was determined to remain unchanged.

This was not because no attempt had been made to transform it. It was entirely impossible that it should have passed through such an era of change as that which followed the crusades without coming into contact and conflict with the new forces. We have seen the attempt which was made, at the beginning of the fifteenth century, at the Council of Constance, to bring over into the sphere of ecclesiastical government the institutions and ideas which had been produced in the course of the political transformation, which was then under way, and to make over the government of the church in harmony with the new age. That attempt failed completely, and its only effect had been to strengthen the government of the church in its medievalism.

In the line of theological belief and of life we have not followed the attempts which had been made before the Reformation to bring about a change, but they had not been wanting, and they had not lacked clearness of purpose or earnestness.

In the thirteenth century, beginning perhaps a trifle earlier, in the valley of the Rhone, there had been a revolt from the church upon these points which had never been entirely subdued. It was the region of an early and a brilliant civilization, the land of the troubadours. An active intellectual life and an inquiring spirit apparently existed there in all classes,[1] and a line of connection with earlier forms of heresy probably gave direction to a revolt which would have occurred without it. Two sects must be distinguished from one another in the same general region—the Albigenses, more directly interested in questions of theology, and considered heretics by Protestants as well as Catholics, and the Waldenses, or Vaudois, chiefly concerned with religious questions and the conduct of life, and orthodox in theology according to Protestant standards. In the case of the Albigenses the church was able to make use of political assistance, and a civil war of some years' duration resulted in the extermination of the heretics, and finally in the annexation of the county of Toulouse by the crown of France. The Waldenses, in a more remote country, in the valleys of eastern Switzerland and Savoy, survived a persecution which was both severe and long continued. Through their earnest devotion to the study of the Bible in the vernacular, they exercised a considerable influence in many lands of continental Europe, though their share in

[1] Comba, *Waldenses*, p. 15.

the general pre-reformation movement has sometimes
been greatly exaggerated. They seem to have received
some new impulse themselves from the followers of Huss,
and when the Reformation finally came they acknowledged the similarity of its principles with their own, and
frequently associated themselves with Protestant organizations of a Calvinistic type.

While this more or less revolutionary movement was
under way, there occurred, within the church and in harmony with it, another like it in its emphasis of the simpler
Christian life, chiefly of the ascetic type, which should
not be overlooked. The two great mendicant orders, the
Franciscans and the Dominicans, both officially recognized
before 1225, represent a true monastic revival of the religious life, like the reformation of Cluny in the tenth century or of the Cistercians in the twelfth. Vowed to extreme poverty and devoting themselves with a genuine
enthusiasm to the service of the poorest classes and to religious ministrations, the mendicants did a great amount
of practical good. Before very long both orders became
wealthy and corrupt; both took eager part in the intellectual work of the century in the new universities; but
nothing should obscure the fact that in their early history
they stand for a real reformation and are a sign of the
religious tendencies of the time.

A hundred and fifty years after the rise of the Waldenses, in the last half of the fourteenth century, a revolt
of the same kind occurred in England. It was at the time
of England's first great literary age—the time of Chaucer
and Gower and Langland. It closely followed an age of
great military glory—the victories of Crécy and of Poitiers and almost as glorious victories over the Scotch.
The lower classes, as well as others, felt the stimulus of
such an age, and, in Wat Tyler's insurrection, demanded
the reform of old abuses and new guarantees for their
security. It is possible that even without the vigorous

leadership of Wycliffe so favorable an age would have produced a demand for a religious reformation. As it was,
the demand which was made seems almost wholly the
result of his personal influence, of his earnest spirit and
his deeply inquiring mind. In Wycliffe's work there was
an attempted reformation of theology and of religion, of
Christian doctrines and of the Christian life in about
equal proportions, and, from the peculiar situation of
things in England, it involved political ideas not necessarily connected with the others. It has been said that
Wycliffe "disowned and combated almost every distinguishing feature of the medieval and papal church, as
contrasted with the Protestant."[1] His "poor priests"
undoubtedly were messengers of good to the poorer
classes, and the fact that so large a number of manu-
scripts as one hundred and sixty-five, containing larger or
smaller parts of his translation of the Scriptures, has been
found, shows conclusively how widely the copies were
circulated and how carefully they were preserved. The
division of political parties in England during Wycliffe's
life served to protect him and his followers from serious
persecution; but after the accession of the House of Lancaster to the throne this reason no longer existed, and the
church had her way with the heretics. In 1401 the first
English statute was passed punishing wrong theological
opinions with death,[2] and, in the few years following, the
Lollards, as Wycliffe's followers were called, were apparently exterminated.

If it is doubtful whether Wycliffe's influence may not
have died out in England, certainly it was continued
upon the Continent in the last great religious rebellion
against the medieval church which preceded Luther's.

---

[1] Fisher, *Reformation*, p. 60.

[2] Down to this time there had been no heresy of importance in England.
On the influence of Wycliffe on the later religious history of England see
Poole, *Wycliffe*, p. 118, and Gairdner, *Lollardy and the Reformation in En-
gland.*

The close connection which was established between the English and Bohemian courts, and between the Universities of Prague and Oxford, as a result of the marriage of Richard II and Anne of Bohemia, brought some Bohemian students into contact with Wycliffe's teachings and led to the carrying of his writings to their fatherland. The reform movement which resulted in Bohemia, whose leader was John Huss, followed in all essential matters the ideas of Wycliffe, but it placed the strongest emphasis upon other points, such, for example, as the communion in two kinds, from which one wing of the Hussites, the Utraquists, derived its name. Huss himself did not lay so much stress, perhaps, upon the translation of the Scriptures into the language of the people, but his appeal to the Bible as the final authority in questions of belief, and his assertion of his right to judge of its meaning for himself, were clear and emphatic, and his followers were as earnest translators as Wycliffe or the Waldensians could have desired. Huss and his disciple, Jerome of Prague, were burned at the stake by the Council of Constance, in 1415, but political reasons, the unending strife between the Slav and the German in part, gave his cause so much strength in Bohemia that, after twenty years of desperate warfare the revolt was ended by a compromise, and the church gave way to the Hussites to a certain extent, in the points of practice upon which they insisted most strongly.

These three are the most prominent of the attempts at reformation which were made before Luther. They were all very limited in their influence. None of them had anything more than an indirect effect upon the larger pre-reformation movement, upon the general demand for reform, and the general preparation for Luther's work which was being made, and which showed itself so plainly when the time came. They were rather signs that such a demand was arising than causes of its gathering strength. They were the most prominent signs of this under-current, but by no means the only ones. There is abundance of evidence from the fifteenth century, in the case of individuals or small bodies of men—sometimes the taint was apparently almost national, and excited the alarm of the church,[1] or affected ecclesiastical officers of high rank— evidence of dissatisfaction with the practical Christianity of the day, or of a leaning toward theological explanations almost or quite Protestant in character. These cases, are, however, mostly independent of one another, and independent of the larger revolts which have been noticed. Nor upon Luther himself did these attempted reformations have any influence. All the positions which were afterwards taken by him, which brought him into a necessary conflict with the Roman church, he had taken before he knew anything essential of the work of his forerunners in the same line.

If these premature rebellions against the medieval church were not among the immediate influences leading to the Reformation, they were certainly of the same essential nature. Two features which are characteristic of them all are of great significance in this direction. They all asserted that the Christianity of their time differed in some important particulars from the primitive Christianity, and that a return must be made to the earlier usage. They differed somewhat from one another in the particulars selected, but all alike asserted the important principle that the original Christianity is the ultimate standard, and that the professions of every age must be judged by it, as recorded in the Scriptures. In the second place, they all demanded that the right of every individual Christian to study the Bible and to reach his own conclusions should be recognized by the church. These two principles—the appeal to the origi-

---

[1] See the discovery of evidence which indicates a wide-spread demand among the bishops of Spain for reformation on the same lines as Luther's, referred to in the London *Academy*, 1893, p. 197.

nal sources and the right of individual investigation—
were established in the intellectual world by the Renaissance, but it is of the utmost importance to bear in mind
the fact that they had both been definitely asserted, and
with a more or less clear consciousness, in the line of
religious advancement before the influence of the Renaissance began to be felt. It will be necessary to return
to this point when we reach the beginning of the Reformation proper.

But all these attempts at reformation in the church,
large and small, had failed, as had those of the early
fifteenth century to reform its government, leaving the
church as thoroughly medieval in doctrine and in practical
religion as it was in polity. It was the one power, therefore, belonging to the middle ages which still stood unaffected by the new forces and opposed to them. In other
directions the changes had been many, here nothing had
been changed. And its resisting power was very great.
Endowed with large wealth, strong in numbers in every
state, with no lack of able and thoroughly trained minds,
its interests, as it regarded them, in maintaining the old
were enormous, and its power of defending itself seemed
scarcely to be broken.

In this state of things is to be found the explanation of
the fact that the reformation of the church was so much
more revolutionary and violent than the corresponding
change in other directions. Everywhere else the same
revolution had really been wrought. In some cases there
had been an appeal to revolutionary methods in matters
of detail, but, in the main, the change had been a gradual
transformation by which the new had been, almost unconsciously, put in place of the old. But the church had
been strong enough to resist successfully any gradual
transformation or any change of details; it remained an
absolute theocracy in matters of doctrine and of practice,
so that when the change did come, it necessarily came sud-

denly and violently, and with incomplete results. The new forces had not been destroyed because they had been prevented from producing their natural results. They had been merely dammed up until they gathered an irresistible weight.

Nor was the preparation for the Reformation confined to the religious and the ecclesiastical. The discontent under the injustice and abuses in the management of the church; the demand for a moral reformation in the lives of the clergy; the feeling, less definite and conscious but still not slight, of opposition to the absolutism of the papacy; and the still less clearly formulated but deep-seated dissatisfaction with the mechanical and formal Christianity of the church, as being untrue to its original spiritual character, these feelings were very widely extended—European so far as the middle classes were concerned, Teutonic at least, in the case of the lower classes who suffered the most severely from the abuses complained of, and had the least opportunity for redress. These feelings constituted an indispensable preparation for the Reformation, but other conditions were equally necessary to its complete success.

The revolution which had been wrought in the intellectual world in the century between Huss and Luther was one of the indispensable conditions. At the death of Huss the West had only just begun the study of Greek. Since that date, the great body of classical literature had been recovered, and the sciences of philological and historical criticism thoroughly established. As a result, Luther had at his command a well-developed method and an apparatus of exegesis and research impossible to any earlier reformer, and without these his translation of the Bible, and the arguments of all the early Protestants, so largely historical in character, would have been wanting in many things. But also the world had become familiar with independent investigation, and with the proclamation of new views and the upsetting of old ones. By no means the least of the great services of Erasmus to civilization had been to hold up before all the world so conspicuous an example of the scholar following, as his inalienable right, the truth as he found it wherever it appeared to lead him, and honest in his public utterances to the results of his studies. He did not convince all the world of his right. But his was the crowning work of a century which had produced in the general public a greatly changed attitude of mind towards intellectual independence since the days of Huss. The printing-press was of itself almost enough to account for Luther's success as compared with his predecessors. Wycliffe made almost as direct and vigorous an appeal to the public at large, and "with an amazing industry he issued tract after tract in the tongue of the people"; but Luther had a great advantage in the rapid multiplication of copies and in their cheapness, and he covered Europe with the issues of his press. The discovery of America, the finding of a sea route to India and the beginning of a world-commerce, the opening of another world of experiences in the recovered knowledge of history and of literature, the great inventions, a revived rapidity of intercourse throughout Europe, and a new sense of community interests, indeed, all the results of the fifteenth century that can be mentioned had combined to create a new spirit and a new atmosphere. Luther spoke to a very different public from that which Wycliffe or Huss had addressed—a public European in extent, and one not merely familiar with the assertion of new ideas but tolerant, in a certain way, of the innovator, and expectant of great things in the future.

The political situation in Europe also, at the time of Luther, was, to all appearance at least, an essential condition of the ultimate success of the Reformation. The large possessions brought together through the fortunate

marriages of the Hapsburgs had been united with those
which the diplomatic skill of Ferdinand the Catholic had
acquired. The "civil arm," as represented by the Emperor Charles V, would seem to have been strong enough
to deal unhesitatingly with any unwelcome religious opinion which might arise. But Charles never found a moment when he could exert this strength against Protestantism, until it was too late. On the west was the rival
power of France, less in extent and apparent resources,
but not scattered like his own power, closely concen-
trated in the hands of the brilliant and ambitious Fran-
cis I. On the east was the equally dangerous Turkish
empire, still at the height of its strength, and determined
to push its conquests farther up the Danube valley.
Three times after the Diet of Worms, where Luther was
originally condemned, when Charles seemed free to use
his whole power for the extermination of heresy, following no doubt his personal inclination as well as what he
judged to be his political interests—in 1526, in 1529, and
again in 1530—was he forced, each time by some sudden turn in the affairs of Europe, some new combination
against him, sometimes with the pope among his enemies,
to grant a momentary toleration. In 1532 was concluded
the definite Peace of Nuremberg, the price of Protestant
assistance against the Turks, by which a formal agreement was made to allow matters to remain as they were
until the meeting of a general council. Under this arrangement Protestantism gained so much strength that
when, in 1547, the emperor at last found himself able to
attack its adherents, he could not entirely subdue them,
although he nearly succeeded.

Such, then, was the long and general preparation for
the Reformation—religious, intellectual, and political.
So deep was the current setting in this direction that
nothing could have held it back. Lefèvre and Zwingli
and Luther, beginning at the same time in three different

countries, and entirely independent of one another, the same work, show clearly how inevitable the movement was. We associate the beginning of the Reformation especially with the name of Luther, and correctly so. His attack was directed so squarely at the central point of the papal defences; he began it in so conspicuous a way, and upon a question of such general interest; it was connected, also, so directly with the empire; and the preparation for it extended so far down among the people to whom he immediately appealed, that it attracted at once universal attention, and became the forefront of the whole European movement. But it is as certain as any unenacted history can be that this was an irrepressible revolution. If Luther had been weak, or if he had been a coward, some other leader would have taken the command, and the Reformation would have occurred in the same age, and with the same general characteristics. It is not possible to understand this great movement if this inevitable character is not appreciated. It must be recognized as being, like the French Revolution, the bursting forth of the deeper forces of history, through the obstacles that confined them, sweeping a clear road for a new advance.

Luther did not create the Reformation. He was the popular leader who translated into the terms of common life, into direct and passionate words that came close home to men of every rank, the principles of religious, ecclesiastical, and intellectual reform, which had been proclaimed before him in more remote ways, and turned into great historic forces the influences which had been slowly engendered in the world of scholars and thinkers. He was, though independent himself, the popularizer of other men's labors.

But the Reformation, as it really occurred, was largely his work. His powerful personality impressed itself upon the whole movement. He gave it form and direction, and personal traits of his became characteristics of it, not so much, perhaps, because they were his personal traits, as because they were an expression in the individual of the tendencies of the age. Of these characteristics there are four which are noteworthy, as especially general and lasting.

In the first place, as the starting-point of all, Luther was one of those not infrequent men, usually men of great moral force and power, who are perpetually driven by a sense of personal guilt and sin, unfelt by the general run of men, and by a compelling necessity, to find in some way a counterbalancing sense of reconciliation with God. This feeling it was which led him into the monastery against so many influences to keep him out. But he did not free himself from it by this step. He speedily found the insufficiency of the best means at the disposal of the cloister, of worship and holy works, of penance, and private prayer, and spiritual meditation, to meet the need which he felt.

This was because of another characteristic of Luther's mind, as deep and impelling as his sense of sin. It would be absurd to deny that monasticism has furnished a complete and final spiritual refuge to thousands of pious souls in every age. But they have been, as a rule, of the contemplative and unquestioning kind. This Luther certainly was not. His intellectual nature was as active as his moral. The demand for a philosophical theory of the process by which reconciliation with God takes place, which should be satisfactory to his intellect, was as imperative as the demand for the reconciliation itself, and the one was not possible for him without the other.

The strong theological or philosophical bent of Luther's mind, this demand for an intellectual explanation before the soul could be at rest, is one of the vital points at the beginning of the Reformation, and one of the dominating

characteristics of Protestantism so long as the direct influence of the Reformation age lasted.   It was the union
in Luther's mind of these two elements—the keen sense
of guilt and the demand for a reasonable theory of the
means of relief—that led him to the first, and wholly unconscious step in his revolt against the prevailing church
system.   Had either existed alone he might have been
satisfied with things as they were.   But when, under the
heavy spiritual burden which he felt, he turned, with his
power of sharp analysis, to the accepted doctrine of the
efficacy of works, of acquired merit, it failed to satisfy
his reason, although he tested it in the genuine ascetic
spirit.   It seemed absurd to him that anything which he
might do should have any bearing upon the removal of
his guilt in the sight of God.   If a sense of forgiveness in
which he could rest was to be found, he must obtain from
some source an explanation of the method of salvation
which should differ from the prevailing one in placing less
emphasis upon the action of the individual and more
upon the divine agency.

Luther seems to have worked himself out from this
state of doubt and difficulty through long and heavy experience, and with the aid of slight suggestions received
from various sources, from Staupitz, the Vicar of his
Order, from the writings of St. Bernard and of Gerson,
and, perhaps, from men less known to history.   He had
been from the beginning of his life as a monk a most
earnest student of the Bible, as prescribed by the rules
of his Order, but he does not seem to have found any
satisfactory answer to his needs in the Bible until the
suggestion which served as a guide to him in his search
had reached him from some outside source or from his
own experience.   When he had obtained from such
sources the suggestion of justification by faith, of salvation as the free gift of God, of forgiveness of sins as the
direct result of the redemption made by Christ, accepted

by the immediate faith of the sinner, he found this idea
abundantly supported in the Scriptures, and easily
wrought into a logical and systematic theory under the
influence of St. Augustine and St. Paul as he interpreted
them. Luther had read St. Augustine to some extent
before he had hit upon the idea of justification by faith,
but it was from the standpoint of the later scholastic
theology, which had no sympathy with the main current
of St. Augustine's thought, and he had been blind to his
meaning. Now, however, he had found the key, and
under the influence of his new reading of St. Augustine,
the theoretical side of his belief grew rapidly into systematic form, though to a form slightly different from that
of his teacher, and he found his confidence that he had discovered the truth greatly strengthened. So thoroughly
in sympathy did he become with the ideas of the great
theologian of the West that he was able to detect the spu-
riousness of a work on penances, which had long passed
under St. Augustine's name, because it was out of harmony with his system of thought.

This result, the formation of a clearer theory of justification by faith as the confident and satisfactory answer
to the need of personal reconciliation with God which he
felt, was the first step in the Reformation, the great step
of the preparation of the leader to take command of the
movement when the crisis should arise which would demand a leader. These results Luther did not reach until
after he had been transferred to the University of Wittenberg, but they were in definite shape and part of his
university teaching before his attention had been called
in any especial way to their bearing upon the current
doctrine of indulgences.

When Luther had once reached these conclusions he
held them and defended them with the spirit and the
methods of the genuine humanist. He attacked with
vigor Aristotle and the schoolmen. He appealed to the

original Christianity and to its early documents as the only valid evidence, and he handled these documents in a critical spirit. He called in the evidence of history against the papal pretensions, and he accepted for himself without hesitation the results which his new position logically involved in opposition to the reigning theories of the church, the results, that is, of individual independence and of the right of private judgment, even so far as to a complete break with the church. Erasmus himself was scarcely more a child of the Renaissance in spirit and in methods than Luther. This is the third of the characteristics of Luther's work which were of wide and permanent influence in the larger movement. If the great principles which are seen and stated by the thinkers ever give a fresh impulse to the world, and turn the currents of history in new directions, it is because they are taken possession of by some popular leader and transformed from the abstract into the concrete, identified with some great interest of life held dear by the masses of men. This Luther did for the principle of free thought. It had been asserted long before him in the world of scholars, but Luther now associated it forever with one of the dearest interests of the race, its religious aspirations, so that in the future for every Bruno who might be found ready to die for the philosopher's freedom of thought, a thousand simple men would gladly embrace the stake for the liberty to believe in God as they understood him, against whatever authority, and the right of free thought was henceforth in theory at least counted among the most sacred rights of the individual.[1]

But it must be admitted—so far as the evidence allows

[1] It must not be understood that what is here said means that Protestantism, or any Protestant sect, with some rare and imperfect exceptions like the Independents of England, for a long time to come recognized the right of free thought for any but itself. The appeal to the right of private judgment within Protestantism was for many generations the appeal of the rebel against authority as truly as in the case of Luther. What is meant

us to judge, and it seems to be conclusive—that Luther
did not reach the theological position which necessitated
his rebellion against the church and his assertion of the
right of free thought, as a result of the influence of the
Renaissance upon him, nor by the use of the humanistic
methods of study. On the contrary, it seems that he was
led to adopt the principles of the Renaissance because
that result was involved in his determination to maintain
the theological conclusions which he had reached. It
was along the medieval road that Luther had advanced
—the study of the schoolmen, dependence upon speculation and authority, the use of the Bible as a theological
text-book—and the result which he reached was merely
the putting of one theological system in place of another.
Careful researches appear to make it certain that, even in
his student days, in the university of Erfurt, and before
his entry into the cloister, Luther did not come under the
direct influence of Humanism to any such extent as was
formerly supposed. It may have been that its results
and its spirit were in the air, and were absorbed by Luther
unconsciously; but it is far more likely that he arrived at
its fundamental position from another side, as the Waldenses and Wycliffe and Huss had done, before the Renaissance began, and found himself in harmony with the
principle of free inquiry and free opinion, because that
principle, in face of the dominant theocracy, seemed the
unavoidable corollary of his answer to the question,
which was for all the reformers, early and late, a purely
religious question: What is the means of union between
God and man revealed to us in Christianity, and what
does it require of us?

is that logically Protestantism rested upon this basis; that this principle
must be continually asserting itself in the Protestant world in the multiplication of sects all virtually appealing to it; and that, however intolerant
the individual man or sect might be in asserting the position of exclusive
truth, practically except where government interfered the right of rebellion
had to be recognized.

This fact does not make Luther's indebtedness to the Renaissance any the less. The position of opposition to old beliefs which Luther's conclusions forced him to take was one with which the world was now familiar, thanks to that movement, and the emancipated judgment and conscience of thousands in every land were ready to follow him, or, if circumstances rendered it impossible for some to follow, at least to sympathize fully with the stand he had taken and with his aims. And we have indicated the aid which he received in other ways from the results of the revival of learning. But many things in the character of the Reformation and of early Protestantism will remain difficult to understand, unless it be remembered that if Luther was a child of the Renaissance, as has been said, he was an adopted child. He was not by nature the heir of its spirit, nor of all its tendencies. He accepted its principles and its methods because they were necessary to him, not because he had been formed under their influence, and must therefore give them expression in his action. And he never adopted them completely nor in all their logical results. He asserted for himself the right of free thought. But when the same principle began to be applied against his doctrines by the numerous sects which sprang up as one of the first and natural results of the Reformation, he did not recognize their right with equal clearness. The belief which the early Protestant shared with the Catholic in the vital importance of theological opinion, made it easy for him to adopt the fundamental principle of all intolerance that freedom of thought means only the freedom of the conscience to hold the truth, and therefore as the system which he held contained the truth, no opposing doctrine could have any rights. As thoroughly characteristic of Luther as any of the three traits which have been mentioned—his spiritual sense, his philosophical tendency, and his humanistic spirit—was this fourth trait also of intellectual nar-

rowness, that is, the fact that he remained to the end of his
life, upon one side of his nature, a medieval monk.   That
this was in complete contradiction with his own fundamental position, and with the methods by which he defended himself, gave him no uneasiness.   He had not the
slightest consciousness of self-contradiction, nor had any
of the early Protestants, who were like him in this regard.
So intense was their interest in the theological theories
which seemed to them to contain the whole truth that
their eyes were closed to all else, and it was only here and
there during the first two hundred years after the Reformation that official Protestantism really escaped from
the medieval point of view and became true to itself in
its attitude towards dissenting thought.

By a medieval method Luther had reached a result
which was mainly intellectual, that is theological, in
character, and which was to bring him, in some of the
most decisive consequences of his work, into harmony
with the great intellectual movement of the end of the
middle ages.   But the strong impelling force in Luther's
development, it must be remembered, that which had
started him in this direction and which carried him on
irresistibly to the conclusions he had reached, was the
spiritual necessity of personal reconciliation with God,[1]
a religious need so deeply felt that its satisfaction involved
as matters of secondary import all the rest, rebellion
against the old church with its infallible authority, the
adoption of all the current popular demands of religious
and ecclesiastical reform, as closely related ends, and of
the principles established by the Renaissance as indis-

[1] The clearly intellectual element so prominent in the Reformation and
the identification which the reformers themselves so strenuously made of
theology, that is, a great intellectual interest, with religion should not lead
us to overlook the fact, as they have some recent writers, that the Reformation was primarily, in origin, purpose, and result, a religious movement.   It
is quite impossible to explain it fully by a study of its intellectual antecedents alone.

pensable allies. And now it must be noticed that this religious element in Luther's character was also the moving force in his next step, in the first public act of his which opened the Reformation.

Not very long after Luther had reached the results in which he rested, and after he had begun to teach them in his lectures on the Bible, Tetzel came into the neighborhood of Wittenberg preaching a peculiarly crude and debasing theory of the efficacy of indulgences for the forgiveness of sins—there can be no doubt of this, however much Tetzel may have modified the worst crudities when he came to put his words into print—and attracting much attention among the people. Luther was instantly aroused. He had already preached against the popular trust in indulgences, but now something further was demanded and the ninety-five theses were posted. In this act Luther was following a common university custom. The theses were propositions which he proposed to defend in set debate against all comers. They stated the beliefs on the subject which Luther had reached, but they also contained some things of which he was not entirely sure, and some things whose full bearing he did not see. They were stated in scholastic form, and not intended for the general circulation which they received.

It is certain that the moving purpose in this step of Luther's was religious rather than theological. The form was theological, but what he had most nearly at heart was the practical object. It was to save men from a fatal delusion, from trust in a false and destroying method of salvation, and to bring them back to the true Christian faith as he saw it that he attacked the popular ideas. All the other things which followed as later consequences of this action were unintended and unforeseen by him. In regard to some of them, if he had seen that he was likely to be led on to them, he would undoubtedly, feeling as he then did, have hesitated long before taking the first

step. He believed that he was defending the theology
of the church against ideas which had become prevalent
but which were nevertheless abuses. The seventy-first
of his theses pronounces a woe upon those who speak
against the truth of apostolic indulgences, and the seventy-
second a blessing upon those who object to the loose words
of the preachers of indulgences. But the leading motive
of his action was not his wish to put the true theology in
place of the false as a matter of science, it was his zeal
for the souls of men, lost, as he believed, through a mistaken belief.

The effect of the publication of the theses was a surprise to Luther. In two weeks, he says, they had gone
through all Germany. In four weeks, says a contemporary, they had gone through all Christendom as if the
angels themselves had been the messengers.[1] Luther
had intended to influence opinion in Wittenberg and
vicinity, scarcely at all beyond, but the effect was universal, so deep was the preparation for them which no one
had suspected. Instinctively, as it were, the public recognized the declaration of war, more clearly than the
leader himself, and instantly the hosts began to gather
and to draw up against one another. The next two years
was a period of rapid development in Luther's understanding of his real position towards the old church, and
of what he would be obliged to do if he was resolved to
maintain that position. It was because he had reached
his conclusions by the pathway of inner experience that he
was so slow to realize all that they meant, but the logic of
the events which followed the publication of the theses
was sharp and clear.

The first result was to bring Luther to see that some
points which he had stated were in reality opposed to
the accepted church theology, and not in harmony with
it, as he had thought. He was also made to realize that

[1] Koestlin, *Martin Luther*, vol. I, p. 172.

the question of the relation of the pope to the church was necessarily involved. This was the weak spot in Luther's case, and was especially selected by his opponents for attack. It had been far from his intention to raise the question, but he did not shrink from it when it was pressed upon him. It was in this direction, indeed, and not so much in any other, that further growth was necessary for him. He began believing in the infallibility of the church certainly, if not in that of the pope, and in the duty of the individual to submit his judgment to the judgment of the church. But the attacks which were made upon him during these two years forced him to other views. Step by step he was led on from his assertion to Cardinal Cajetan that the declaration of the pope was to be regarded as the voice of God only when it was in conformity with the Bible, and his statement in writing that a general council of the church might err, to the final position of complete rebellion, into which he was forced by the skill of Dr. Eck in the great debate in Leipsic, in 1519, that the church universal might be in error in some formally adopted declaration, and was so regarding Huss. Henceforth his position in regard to the old church was logically complete. He must make war upon it, and establish an independent church if he could, or he must submit and be burned as a heretic. The burning of the pope's bull, in December, 1520, was only an especially public and dramatic repetition of declarations already clearly made.

The primary meaning of the Reformation is religious. It was a religious motive from which the reformers acted, and a religious result which they sought as their supreme object. In this direction what they consciously attempted, was to return to a more simple and truer Christianity from the additions and corruptions which the middle ages had introduced. And in many and essential respects, the

Reformation did make such a return. In ceremonies and in forms of government the Protestant of any name is undoubtedly nearer to the original Christianity than the Catholic. In the matter of the abuses and oppressions of which Europe complained so bitterly just before the Reformation, not merely was a great change worked in Protestant lands, but also in the Catholic church itself. The work of Luther forced a reformation which was, in the most important particulars, thorough and complete. It is true that such a reform would have been made in the Catholic church in time without Luther, but the attack which he led forced a more speedy and perhaps a more decided change than would otherwise have taken place. In administration and in morals the Catholic church has been, since the middle of the sixteenth century, a reformed church.

In regard to the more directly religious question which the reformers had especially at heart, the question of the reconciliation of the sinner with God, it can hardly be denied that the Reformation was, also, a return to a more primitive and truer Christianity. Divested of technical statement the work of the Reformation in this respect was to emphasize the immediate personal relation between God and man, and to bring into practical consciousness far more clearly than had been done under the old system the fact that individual faith in Christ as the Saviour is the centre and source of the religious life.[1] Undoubtedly this fact had been realized by thousands of saintly men in the medieval centuries, undoubtedly, also, the religiously cultivated soul may realize it as truly in the Roman as in any church, but it is also equally certain

[1] Dr. Philip Schaff says: "Schleiermacher reduced the whole difference between Romanism and Protestantism to the formula, 'Romanism makes the relation of the individual to Christ depend on his relation to the church; Protestantism, *vice versa*, makes the relation of the individual to the church depend on his relation to Christ.'"—Pamphlet, *Luther Symposiac*, Union Seminary, 1883.

that the Protestant church keeps this fact much more
clearly and distinctly before the mass of men than does
the Catholic, and makes its full realization easier for
them. The crude abuses of the Catholic teaching which
led to the first public protest of Luther have been comparatively rare since that time. But it is a fact of easy
observation that the doctrine of that church upon this
point is often misunderstood by the more ignorant, and,
when misunderstood, lends itself as readily to-day as in
the days of Tetzel to debasing beliefs and to practices that
are essentially pagan.[1]

If, however, the main object which the reformers
sought was religious their way of looking at it was theological, was under the form of a doctrine rather than of
a principle of life. The improved doctrinal statement
seemed to them the greatest improvement made. It was
the right to hold this for which they contended. It was
the impossibility of holding it in the old church which
had forced them to withdraw from it and to form an
independent church. Indeed, the whole religious life
seemed to them so completely controlled and conditioned by the theological opinion that they were disposed to deny the possibility of its existence under any
form of doctrine different from their own, and that which
sustained alike the Protestant and the Catholic martyr
of this time in his sufferings was not merely the religious
life which was alike in both—no Protestant can doubt
this who studies the life of Sir Thomas More—but it
was his earnest conviction that the religious life of which
he was conscious was inseparably bound up with the intellectual system which he held and his supreme devotion
to that system and to his rights as he conceived them in
an age of bitter conflict of opinion.

[1] See, for example, the *Book of the Scapular* and the beliefs associated with
the wearing of that article among ignorant Catholics, undoubtedly without
the real sanction of the church.

This prevailingly theological character of early Protestantism has already been emphasized. But certain
consequences of it in modern times and to-day should be
noticed. In the first place, it made the more zealous
Protestants, and especially those who were under an
official responsibility for the safety of their faith, as intolerant of opposing, or, as they thought, dangerous, opinions
as the Catholic, and for the same reason, the supposed
vital necessity of a correct theology.[1] In most cases state
churches as rigidly organized and as devotedly supported
by the laws, took the place of the old ecclesiastical system. The roll of Protestant martyrs made by Protestant
bigotry is not a short nor an inglorious one, and new
theories in the sciences had always bitter opposition to
meet from Protestant theologians. Only slowly, and aided
largely by commercial considerations, was full toleration
established as the rule, but it has been reserved to the
present age, with a few glorious exceptions, and to a
growing understanding of the true position which theological opinion holds in religion, to bring Protestantism
to a consciousness of its own logical position, and to se-

---

[1] The following passage, quoted in Häusser's *Period of the Reformation*,
p. 520 (Am. ed.), from Hohenegg, Lutheran court theologian of Saxony during the Thirty Years' War, is an interesting example: "For it is as plain as
that the sun shines at midday, that the Calvinistic doctrine is full of frightful blasphemy, horrible error and mischief, and is diametrically opposed to
God's holy revealed word. To take up arms for the Calvinists is nothing
else than to serve under the originator of Calvinism—the Devil. We ought,
indeed, to give our lives for our brethren; but the Calvinists are not our
brethren in Christ; to support them would be to offer ourselves and our
children to Moloch. We ought to love our enemies, but the Calvinists are
not our enemies but God's."

John Cotton, in his argument with Roger Williams on persecution, represents, I suppose, fairly the position of most of the early Protestants. He
says: "I doe not thinke it lawfull to excommunicate an Heretick, much lesse
to persecute him with the civill Sword, till it may appeare, even by just
and full conviction, that he sinneth not out of conscience, but against the
very light of his own conscience."—*Narraganset Club Publications*, vol. II,
p. 61. That Cotton's position was exactly that of the Roman church Williams was not slow to point out. See *Ibid.*, vol. IV, p. 57.

cure complete religious liberty in Protestant states, though evidently not as yet with the universal extinction of the old feelings.

In the second place, the strong intellectual tendency in Protestantism pushed the sermon to the front as a more prominent portion of the church service than it had been. The Catholic was and is more a religion of worship, less a religion of individual thought and conviction. Protestantism implies more intellectual activity among the lay membership and an interest on their part in the problems of theology. When there was, in truth, such an interest in the community at large in theological discussion, often the most intense interest of the time, there could hardly be too many or too long sermons. But it is clear that a popular interest of the old kind in such discussions does not exist to-day. It would not be possible for any body of average Protestants of the present time to "beguile the weariness" of a long sea-voyage with three sermons a day, of the Puritan sort, as is recorded of the passengers of the Griffin, on their way to the Massachusetts colony in 1633. From this fact arises one of the practical problems which the Protestant churches are discussing—how to increase the interest in the sermon—and this explains also one of the elements of attraction which many, trained under the more rigid Protestant services, find in forms of service which have retained more of the element of worship, or even for the forms of the Roman church itself.

The result of the Reformation in the direction of intellectual freedom is now evident. It planted itself squarely on the principles enunciated by the Revival of Learning,[1]

[1] The protest of the German princes and cities against the action of the Diet, in 1529, from which the name Protestant comes, grounds itself on the principle that the majority has no right to bind the conscience of the minority.

It is at this point, also, that the greatest barrier still exists between the Roman and the Protestant forms of Christianity. It may be as difficult now for the Roman church to modify its official theology as it was in the but those who led the movement did not do so from choice, and their support of liberty of thought was never more than half-hearted. But they could not control the consequences of their action. The general result was an atmosphere of intellectual independence and inquiry in all Protestant countries, seen in the rapid multiplication of religious sects, which could not be checked, and in the history of philosophy, science, and the book-trade. The intellectual history of the world since the Reformation is the history of the growing prevalence of this spirit in Protestant countries and of its introduction into countries in which the Roman church prevailed, as the result of the sceptical philosophy of the eighteenth century and of the French Revolution.

There should be added to complete the statement of the influence of the Reformation the more detailed results which are often referred to but cannot be here treated at length. Such is its influence on the study of the Bible by people of all classes, a result especially marked in Anglo-Saxon countries, and not without its influence on Roman Catholic policy; its influence on public schools of the lower grades; on the fixing of the literary forms of

days of Luther, but to the most intelligent Protestants of to-day, undoubtedly, the theological difference seems a less vital difference than to the early reformers. But no intelligent Protestant can ever surrender his right to hold that theological opinion which seems to him, individually, the most reasonable. It is equally impossible for the Roman church to surrender its fundamental position that a correct theological belief is a necessity of the Christian faith, and that the church is able, under especial divine guidance, to determine which of two varying theological opinions is the only correct one, and has the right to require all men to believe this alone if they would be counted Christians. Authorities of the Roman church may say much upon their sympathy with free thought, but their definition of free thought must always remain different from that which prevails in the Protestant world. The qualification is always expressed or implied that freedom is not license, and that true freedom consists in submission to legitimate authority—terms, again, which must be interpreted from the Roman point of view. That church can never abandon its claim to determine what particular thought it is which shall be free, without abandoning the one most essential thing which distinguishes it from the Protestant.

national languages; and on the use of the printing-press
to influence public opinion.

The Reformation, as was implied at the beginning of
the chapter, completes the history of the middle ages.
The church was the institution which had tarried farthest
behind in the progress of the later centuries, and the
Reformation was the revolution by which, for a large
part of the church, the medieval was transformed into
the modern.   In matters directly religious, to escape from
the medieval was the object most earnestly sought by the
reformers.   In other respects the transformation took
place against their will and without their knowledge, but
it took place.   For a portion of the church, however, this
was not the case.   That part of it which remained faithful to Rome did, indeed, in some points share the change,
notably in the matter of moral and ecclesiastical abuses,
but in its chief theories and its distinguishing doctrines
the Roman church remained medieval.   Its theory of
continued inspiration and continued miracles; its belief
in the infallibility of the church or of the pope, as built
upon that theory; its doctrines of transubstantiation and
of supererogatory merit, are all medieval, based upon
mental conceptions and habits of thought which are foreign to the mind of to-day.

In general, also, the Reformation must not be judged,
as seems now and then to be the tendency, to be something final.   It was but one phase in a constant process,
gaining a peculiar importance because of its violent and
revolutionary character due to the fact that the process
had not been permitted to go on naturally.   If it is allow-
able to judge our own age, its great work, religiously and
intellectually, has been to carry a long step farther the
principles which the Reformation incompletely realized.

CHAPTER XVIII

SUMMARY

WE have now followed the course of European civilization from the time when the various streams which united to form it were drawing together at the close of ancient history, until all its various elements were completely united and had begun the more rapid advance which we term modern history. It is clearly a period of preparation, not in the sense, however, in which every age in history is a preparation for the following age. It was not so much, as now, a preparation in institutions, discoveries, and ideas, though there was something of this. It was rather a preparation of men. It is a period of history in which the races that have created modern civilization were brought together and united in the organic system which we call Christendom, in which the ideas and institutions which each contributed were also united into a common whole, and in which men were prepared to add to the results of distinctly medieval times, not slight in some directions, the higher products of ancient civilization which they had been unable to comprehend until near the close of the period. With this preparation completed, and this final union made, the modern spirit entered into history, and made itself master, in succession, of the various departments of civilization.

The two fundamental facts in this process of union are the Roman Empire and the Christian church. The first in the order of time was the Roman Empire. It united the ancient world into a common whole, which was in all essential respects as organic a union as modern Christendom. The two great classical civilizations—the Greek, of art and literature and science and philosophy; the Roman, of law and government and practical skill—were blended into a world civilization in which the best elements of various tribal civilizations became the property of all men. This common whole which Rome created was never afterwards destroyed. The keen sense of it, the cosmopolitan feeling which was characteristic of the best days of the empire, declined. Europe threatened at times to break into fragments, but such a result never happened. The old force which had at first maintained the union—the idea of Rome—grew weaker and disappeared, but not until a new one—the church—had arisen to take its place. Christendom is the creation of this new force upon the foundation which the Roman Empire had laid.

Into this empire, in its earliest age, before the decay had been detected which had already begun, entered Christianity, spreading slowly at first, then more rapidly and among higher classes. Before its third century was completed it had become the recognized religion of the imperial court. In the age of its more rapid expansion it absorbed not only the pagan society but also pagan ideas, and became less spiritual and more formal. Ceremonies and doctrinal beliefs multiplied. The simple organization of primitive days gave place to a complicated but strong hierarchy, over which the bishop of Rome had already begun to assert his headship and to secure, in a part of the church, its recognition. This strong organization arose, creating a real unity throughout the provinces of the West, at the moment when they were falling apart politically. When they had become wholly independent kingdoms it remained a living bond of union between them.

Before this point was reached the fatal weakness of the Roman Empire had become evident. The occupation of the world by the Romans had exhausted their strength. There had been no opportunity under the empire to root out the moral and economic evils which had begun their existence in the last days of the republic, nor to recover the losses which they continually inflicted. Beyond the frontier, in every generation, a watchful enemy made trial of the Roman strength, and at last found it insufficient. In the fifth century every province of the West was taken possession of by the Germans, and the fourth great source of the elements which were to be combined in medieval times was brought into connection with the other three. Teutonic kingdoms were founded, Ostrogothic in Italy, Visigothic in Spain, Vandal in Africa, Burgundian in the Rhone valley, Saxon in England, Frankish in Gaul, and finally, Lombard in North Italy, but in the end they were all overthrown except the Frankish and the Saxon. These were the two peoples destined in the end to be the especially active agents in the transmission of institutions and law through the middle ages.

The apparent result of the Teutonic settlement was ruinous to civilization. Disorder, ignorance, and superstition, which were already beginning, were intensified by the conquest. But the ruin was more in appearance than in reality. Even before the invasion most of the German tribes were prepared to respect many things which they found among the Romans, and almost immediately the two influences which were the chief agents in their absorption, the Christian church and the idea of Rome, began to work upon them. The process of union and recovery was slow, necessarily slow, because of the weakness of the recuperative influences, and of the roughness of the material upon which they acted. For three centuries history is filled with the shifting of peoples and the rise and fall of states, with no apparent gain of stability or security, the first requisites of progress. The first great advance which gave promise of better things was the empire of Charlemagne at the beginning of the ninth century.

The first Carolingians had restored the strength of the Frankish state, and recovered the lands conquered by the early Merovingians. On this foundation Charlemagne erected an empire rivalling in extent the Western Roman Empire. But his revival of the title of Emperor in the West was not alone justified by the extent of the territory over which he ruled. All things for which the name of Rome stood, in the minds of those who still remembered it, were represented in that day by the Frankish empire. Order and security, general legislation, a common government for many different peoples, the fostering of schools and religion, a promise of permanence for the future, all these were connected with the name of Charlemagne, and we may add the fact—of which they were less conscious—the speedy union into a single people of the two races, the conquerors and the conquered. His empire was not permanent. The causes of disorder were still too strong to be overcome, and the effort to establish governments of the old Roman or of the modern type was premature. But Charlemagne's attempt was a strong reinforcement of the better forces. It created for a moment security and a real union. It revived the influence of Rome. As men looked back upon it from a later time, it became a new golden age. From the time of Charlemagne progress was still slow, but Europe assumed a more settled character and never quite fell back into the earlier confusion.

The most prominent general feature of political civilization characteristic of modern times as compared with ancient, is the existence of independent nations, constituting a virtual federation in the place of one great empire.

The creation of these nations was the work of the last half of the middle ages, but in the breaking up of Charlemagne's empire they made their first appearance. In other words, the failure of the attempt to secure settled political order by a revival of the one great empire plan, was accompanied with an attempt to secure it by the modern system of national governments. The West Franks and the Eastern German tribes fell apart, and set up governments of their own, distinguished both from each other and from the Carolingian. England emerged from the age of tribal kingdoms, and began a national life under the lead of the West Saxons. But these promises of national organizations really able to govern were not immediately fulfilled. There were as yet, even within these narrower geographical limits, too few of the elements of a common life from which states draw their support to render these attempts successful. In England the Danish invasions threw the nation back into something like the conditions of the first age of conquest. In Germany the national government was the most promising of any until the Norman dynasty gained possession of England, but even in Germany it was weakened by strong tribal differences, which were not entirely overcome when it entered upon the long conflict with the papacy, entailed upon it by the Holy Roman Empire. In France the feudal system had its origin, and it had usurped the powers of the general government, even before the fall of the Carolingian family. The feudal king whom it set on the throne in the place of the old dynasty had only a name to reign, and the same result happened wherever in Europe the feudal system became powerful. Yet for France and for all Europe the feudal system was of the greatest service in an age when anarchy could not be entirely repressed, because it carefully preserved the form and theory of a general government, while it allowed local independence the freest hand.

The tenth and eleventh centuries were the age of extreme disintegration, when the local and the narrow prevailed universally. The papacy shared in the decline of all general power. Even the revival of the Roman Empire by the Saxon kings of Germany, which looks like a return to unity and to broader ideas, was the revival of a title and a theory, hardly of a reality. But the idea of the universal supremacy of the pope was already too thoroughly worked out to remain long in abeyance. The reform led by the monastery of Cluny revived the old theories with greater precision and a clearer consciousness. It created also Hildebrand, the practical statesman, who attempted to carry out the theories by raising the papacy above all states. Meanwhile the strength of the emperor had greatly increased under the Franconian family, and immediately the two great theoretical institutions which the medieval mind had constructed upon the Roman foundation came into conflict. It was a conflict between medieval ideas, fought with medieval weapons, and it ceased only when the medieval in every direction was be-beginning to give place to the modern. Its net result for the history of civilization was that it prevented the realization in facts of either theory—the world political empire or the world ecclesiastical empire.

At the moment when this strife was at its height the turning-point of the middle ages was reached. Europe was roused from its lethargy by a high purpose, and stimulated in the crusades to an activity which never afterwards declined. Already here and there new influences had begun to work, in commerce and in a desire for learning especially. Now all classes were stirred by the general enthusiasm. The new impulse received began to show itself in every direction. The course of civilization turned away from the dark ages towards modern times.

Commerce was the first to feel the new forces, because

the most directly touched by the crusades. Ships were multiplied; new articles of commerce brought into use; new routes opened; geographical knowledge increased; villages were transformed into cities; money came into more general use; wealth was accumulated, and with wealth power and influence in a new class, the Third Estate. In lands the most favored, serfdom disappeared, and the agricultural laborer shared to some extent in the general improvement. These results of increasing commerce acted directly upon the political development of Europe. The commercial classes demanded security and order. They stood ready to aid the state in repressing feudal violence. They demanded a uniform law, which they found in the Justinian code, and by their use of it, and by their influence in the governments which were forming, they secured its prevalence over the native law, thus strongly reinforcing the tendency to centralization naturally involved in the fall of feudalism. Finally, the Third Estate made its way into the government, as a class beside the other classes, and obtained an influence upon public affairs in the Diets and Parliaments and Estates General of the thirteenth century—an influence which it never discovered how to use.

Politically the nations appeared immediately upon the crusades. Germany and Italy were defrauded of the unity which their national life would have justified and broken into contending fractions by the visionary Roman Empire, which the Ottos had revived. In Spain the slow recovery of the peninsula from the Mohammedans made the united monarchy possible only at the end of the fifteenth century. But France and England reached contrasting results of the greatest interest. In France the predominant fact at the outset was the feudal system. The construction of a political unity answering to a national life was a process of breaking down feudal barriers and absorbing feudal principalities. In this process the only institution which represented a unity above the feudal divisions, the monarchy, naturally took the lead. Every element of power lost by feudalism was added to the king's authority. As soon as the geographical construction was fairly under way the institutional began. National administrative, legislative, and judicial systems were got into operation. A national taxation and a national army were formed. As a result of the line of development which it had been obliged to follow, the French nation came into existence with a closely centralized political life, directed by an absolute king. In England the predominant fact at the beginning was the uncontrolled power of the sovereign. The English barons were not feudal princes. They were so situated that they could not hope to become princes. In striving to increase their own power at the expense of the king they had recourse to the only things of which they could know anything—older institutions, which limited the king's action or offered protection against his anger. Their necessary alliance with the other classes in the nation gave still more of a popular character to the government and made it possible for the lower house of Parliament to be formed upon a really representative principle and to obtain increasing power in public affairs. The political life of the English nation expressed itself in a limited monarchy, with definitely formed institutions of public and private liberty. Politically modern history opens with the rise of conflicting interests between the newly formed states in attempts at expansion beyond their original boundaries—with the beginning of diplomacy and of international politics.

Intellectually the mind of Europe was wakened to an intense desire for learning before it knew where to find the materials of knowledge. The result was the formation of a great system of speculative learning, scholasticism, which seemed to its adherents so vitally important that it became a serious obstacle to the advance of real

learning. With the fourteenth century the true way
was found. Led perhaps by the reawakening of a genuine literary feeling, by an admiration for the writings
of the ancients and a sense of the unity of the past with
the present, the first humanists sought eagerly for all
the remains of classical civilization. Greek, which the
middle ages had never known, was recovered, as well
as a better knowledge of Latin. The spirit of criticism
was quickly awakened. True scientific work was begun.
Careful editions of literary and historical works were
prepared. A more accurate knowledge of the past was
gained. Old beliefs were brought to the test of facts,
and time-honored myths destroyed on all sides. The
right of investigation and of individual judgment was
established. In physical science Copernicus was provided with the material and the method which led to the
first great advance in the understanding of nature. The
invention of printing popularized the new learning and
gave it better weapons. The discovery of America, and
all the work of the century together, broadened and lib-
eralized men's minds, and opened a future full of promise. With this the middle ages closed in the intellectual
world and modern history began.

In the ecclesiastical world less progress had been made
by the beginning of the sixteenth century because the
resisting power had been greater. The nations as they
arose had successfully opposed the political interference
of the papacy in their domestic affairs. England, France,
and Germany in succession had proclaimed their independence. But the attempt, at the Council of Constance,
to reconstruct the government of the church upon the
model of the ideas and institutions which had grown up
in the political progress of the thirteenth and fourteenth
centuries had failed completely. The same result had
followed the several attempts to introduce religious or
ecclesiastical reform, either local or general, which had

been made before the beginning of the sixteenth century. At that date the modern spirit had, in the main, possession of all the world except the ecclesiastical portion of it. But if the modern spirit had been kept under in these matters it had not been destroyed, and when it found its leader in Luther the suddenness of the revolution showed how thorough had been the preparation for it. The Reformation sought as its conscious object a return to a more primitive Christianity in practice and belief, but it accomplished more than this. It created a general atmosphere of intellectual independence and freedom wherever it prevailed which, if not always perfectly realized, has been, nevertheless, one of the most essential conditions of modern progress.

With the Reformation the history of the middle ages was closed for every department of civilization. This is the same as to say that for every department of civilization the work of waiting, of preparation, was now over, and that an age of more rapid progress, basing itself upon the results of the world's first age of similar progress, now succeeded an age of relatively slow advance. The age which lay between had had its necessary work to do. To the results of ancient civilization, it had added new ideas and institutions from other sources, and, even more important, it had brought in a new race and trained it to understand and to build upon the best productions of the ancient world. The reason why the advance of the last four centuries has been so marvellous, comparatively speaking, is because the middle ages moulded into a perfect unity a living and organic world civilization, the best contributions of Greek and Roman, Christian and German.

In sum total the beginning of the sixteenth century shows these advances to have been made over the beginning of the fifth. A new race was on the field as the creative agent in history—the Teutonic—organized now in a

number of independent nations, and not in one great
empire, but forming an equally or even more close unity
in civilization than the old empire, in which the work of
each nation is immediately the common property of all.
This unity was now so thoroughly established, so much a
part of the world's daily habit of thought and action, that
the idea of the Roman Empire, upon which it had been
originally based, had entirely disappeared, and if any idea
of the special source of this unity had taken its place, it
was that of the Christian faith as its common characteristic and foundation—Christendom. The nations organized within this unity were no longer city states, but in
them all parts of the land were equally organic factors
in the composition of the nation. Their governments
presented, with local variations, two general types, one
of which, at least, was a decided advance upon any of
the ancient world. One was a closely centralized monarchy, in which the functions of government, recovered
from the smaller powers—the feudal lords—which had
usurped them in a time of political confusion, were vested
in an uncontrolled sovereign. The other was also in
form a monarchy, but it was a monarchy which allowed
full local self-government in the subdivisions of the state
without loss of efficiency, that is, it was a strong national
government, without close centralization. The functions
of the general government, exercised at first by the king,
were passing more and more under the control of the
people by means of a series of institutional checks upon
the royal power which were not known to the ancient
world. This control was exercised by representatives of
the people, under a representative system, real though
incomplete, which with the limited monarchy was the
most valuable contribution which this race had yet made
to practical politics. The liberty of the individual was
protected by institutions which were also new. In other
words, this type of government was that of a free state

well under way, its institutions of liberty already so definitely shaped as to be capable of transmission through long ages, and of adaptation to other races and other environments.

In economic civilization, as compared with the fifth century the commerce of the sixteenth was no longer confined to the Mediterranean, but the whole world was open to it, and an age of great colonies was about to begin. The slavery of Europeans had disappeared from the Christian states, and serfdom, which in the fifth century was just beginning to take the place of slavery, had also been left behind by a few of the more advanced nations. Labor had become more honorable than in ancient times. The class of free laborers had arisen, with but little influence as yet, but revealing clearly the possession of that power in its infancy, which they were to exercise in the future.

Intellectually, the world had come into possession, at the beginning of the sixteenth century, of the printing-press and a greatly extended geographical knowledge. These in themselves constituted a revolution, but in hardly any other particular was there an advance over the fifth century, though the attitude of mind towards life and all intellectual problems was a great advance upon the medieval. The active mind of the middle ages had been employed in the construction of great philosophical and theological systems, valuable for their own purposes but adding little to real knowledge. The great effort of the last age, now just successful, had been to learn what the ancients had known, to regain a more just estimate of man and of his powers, to begin the formulation of the great problems demanding to be solved, and to restore more productive methods of scientific work. The first great discovery in the field of physical science was just on the eve of announcement.

In art much which the fifth century possessed had been lost never to be recovered, but much also had been

added to the world's store—the Divine Comedy and
Chaucer, the cathedrals of Europe and the earlier works
of Renaissance art.

Religiously, the opening of the sixteenth century presented, in external appearance at least, no advance upon
the fifth. Those modifications of the primitive and spiritual Christianity which had been introduced at the
earlier date, because of the difficulty of holding true to
the higher life in a declining age, which had perhaps
enabled the Christian organization to meet the perils of
the age of conquest with greater safety, and to become a
more effective teacher of barbarous races, through which,
however, the gifted soul had always been able to see the
light—these modifications or corruptions still remained
as the popular Christianity, hardened into a vast, and indeed splendid, system of ceremonies and doctrinal beliefs.
In place of the formative constitution of the fifth century now appeared a most highly organized absolutism, a
great ecclesiastical empire, with perfected machinery of
government and a growing system of law. But if at the
opening of the sixteenth century the church was still in
appearance medieval, it was just on the verge of the revolution which was to make it more modern, and to mark
the first long step in advance towards a truer understanding of Christianity.

However long this catalogue may be of those things in
which the first years of the sixteenth century surpassed
those of the fifth, the great change was in the new race,
the new spirit, which now entered into the possession of
the results of the past. New impulses were felt by every
man, and the promise of a wider future. New forces were
opening the way in every direction. Humanity was entering upon another great era of the rapid conquest of
nature and of truth.

INDEX

Abelard, 268.
Adolf of Nassau, Emperor, 357.
Agriculture, feudal organization of, 192 *ff.*
Alaric, 29; 68; 123 *f.*
Albigenses, 268; 313; 407 *f.*
Alcuin, 160; 358.
Alexander III, Pope, 248.
Alexius Comnenus, 257 *f.*
Alfred the Great, 182.
Allodial land, 212 *f.*
Ambrose of Milan, 116.
America, discovery of, 284; 355; 379 *ff.*
Andorra, Republic of, 286, *note.*
Anglo-Saxon race, the institution-making power, 22; 37, *note;* 100, *note* 2; their laws, 33; 35; their invasion of England, 70 *f.;* elective monarchy, 96 *f.;* their self-developing common law, 99 *f.;* their future political influence, 101; 137; 192, *note;* German denial of indebtedness to, 101, *note;* and a world state, 188, *note;* and monasticism, 260, *note;* their law of treason, 348 *f.*
Arabs, the, their attack on Gaul, 139; 148; 205; their conquests, 148; 255 *ff.;* Charlemagne, 154; their work for civilization, 255 *ff.;* 359.
Arianism, 125; 140 *f.;* 227.
Aristotle, 359; 360, *note;* 368; 377; 419; his *Politics,* 20.
Army, standing, beginning of modern, 321; 329.
Arnulf, King of Germany, 172 *f.*
Ascetic motive, power in middle ages, 259; 260 *ff.*
Asceticism. See *Monasticism.*
Assizes de Jérusalem, 217 *f.*
Athaulf, King of the Visigoths, 68.
Athenians, inferior to Romans in political skill, 28, *note.*
Attila, 70; 72.

Augustine, St., 36; 53, *note;* 56, *note;* his theology, 117; his philosophy of history, 118, *note;* his *City of God,* 118, *note;* 224; his use of Greek, 358; influence on Luther, 419.
Avignon, the papacy at, 388 *ff.*

"Babylonian captivity," the, 390.
Bacon, Lord, on Scholasticism, 360, *note.*
Bacon, Roger, 268; 361; 379
Bailli, the, 315; 317; 324.
Basel, Council of, 399 *f.*
Beaumanoir, 218.
Belisarius, 73.
Benedict XIII, 396; 397.
Benedict, St., the "rule" of, 132, *note.*
"Benefice," the, 196; 197, *note;* 206; 215.
Bible, critical study of, 373, *note;* in the early reformation movements, 411; influence of the Reformation on the study of, 431. See *New Testament.*
Blackstone's *Commentaries,* description of feudalism in, 215.
Blanche of Castile, Queen of France, 312.
Boniface VIII, 324, *note;* 384 *ff.;* 405.
Boniface, St., 148 *f.;* 228.
"Boss," the American party, in Italian cities, 353 *f.* and *note.*
Bourgeoisie, villes de, 288; 290.
Bourges, Synod of, 400.
Bouvines, battle of, 311.
Britain, abandoned by the Romans, 70; occupied by the Saxons, 70 *f.*
Bruges, in medieval commerce, 280.
Brunner, H., on the circuit justices of England, 159, *note* 2; on the feudal system, 202, *note;* 203, *note;* 205, *note.*
Burgundians, the, 67; 68; 139; 141.
Byzantine civilization, influence of, on the West, 86, *note.*

447